Let Justice Roll Down

Books published by Westminster/John Knox Press
By Bruce C. Birch

What Does the Lord Require?
The Old Testament Call to Social Witness

With Larry L. Rasmussen
The Predicament of the Prosperous

Let Justice Roll Down

The Old Testament, Ethics, and Christian Life

Bruce C. Birch

Westminster/John Knox Press
Louisville, Kentucky

Book design by Ken Taylor

First edition

Published by Westminster/John Knox Press
Louisville, Kentucky

PRINTED IN THE UNITED STATES OF AMERICA
9 8 7 6 5 4 3 2 1

Library of Congress Cataloging-in-Publication Data

Birch, Bruce C.
  Let justice roll down : the Old Testament, ethics, and Christian life / Bruce C. Birch. — 1st ed.
     p.   cm.
  Includes bibliographical references and indexes.
  ISBN 0-664-24026-7

  1. Bible. O.T.—Criticism, interpretation, etc. 2. Christian ethics—History. 3. Ethics in the Bible. 4. Narration in the Bible. I. Title.
BS1199.E8B575   1991
241.5—dc20   91-11978

To Susan
who always believed
in this book

Contents

PART TWO
The Old Testament
Story as Moral Resource

Abbreviations

AB	Anchor Bible
AnBib	Analecta biblica
BASOR	*Bulletin of the American Schools of Oriental Research*
BJRL	*Bulletin of the John Rylands University Library of Manchester*
BWANT	Beiträge zur Wissenschaft vom Alten und Neuen Testament
BZAW	Beihefte zur *Zeitschrift für die alttestamentliche Wissenschaft*
CBQ	*Catholic Biblical Quarterly*
CBQMS	Catholic Biblical Quarterly—Monograph Series
EncJud	*Encyclopaedia judaica*
ErIsr	Eretz Israel
EvT	*Evangelische Theologie*
HBC	*Harper's Bible Commentary*
HBD	*Harper's Bible Dictionary*
HBT	*Horizons in Biblical Theology*
HSM	Harvard Semitic Monographs
HTR	*Harvard Theological Review*
HUCA	*Hebrew Union College Annual*

IBC	Interpretation: A Bible Commentary for Teaching and Preaching
IDB	*Interpreter's Dictionary of the Bible*
IDBSup	Supplementary volume to *Interpreter's Dictionary of the Bible*
Int	*Interpretation*
JAAR	*Journal of the American Academy of Religion*
JBL	*Journal of Biblical Literature*
JETS	*Journal of the Evangelical Theological Society*
JSOT	*Journal for the Study of the Old Testament*
JSOTSup	Journal for the Study of the Old Testament— Supplement Series
JTS	*Journal of Theological Studies*
NJBC	*The New Jerome Biblical Commentary*
OBT	Overtures to Biblical Theology
OTL	The Old Testament Library
RB	*Revue biblique*
RelSRev	*Religious Studies Review*
SBLDS	Society of Biblical Literature Dissertation Series
SBLSP	Society of Biblical Literature Seminar Papers
SBT	Studies in Biblical Theology
SJT	*Scottish Journal of Theology*
TDNT	*Theological Dictionary of the New Testament*
TToday	*Theology Today*
VT	*Vetus Testamentum*
VTSup	Vetus Testamentum, Supplements
WBC	Word Biblical Commentary
WMANT	Wissenschaftliche Monographien zum Alten und Neuen Testament
ZAW	*Zeitschrift für die alttestamentliche Wissenschaft*
ZTK	*Zeitschrift für Theologie und Kirche*

Introduction

The need for this volume can be readily illustrated by the comment of a woman wallpapering my house while I was writing. On seeing the title she remarked, "I didn't think there was anything in the Old Testament that related to Christian ethics. Christians are beyond that 'eye for an eye' stuff." She is not alone. Many Christians believe that there is little of ethical value in the Old Testament. At best some might acknowledge the importance of the Decalogue or elements of the prophetic traditions.

The situation is not much better in scholarly circles. In 1959, Robert Davidson wrote, "A Marcionite tendency may be fairly traced in much modern discussion of Christian ethics nor is this tendency confined to scholarly discussion."[1] In 1970, Brevard Childs made his oft-quoted statement, "In spite of the great interest in ethics, to our knowledge, there is no outstanding modern work written in English that even attempts to deal adequately with the biblical material as it relates to ethics."[2]

In the last two decades the situation has begun to change. A number of important works dealing with the methodological issues of relating the Bible to Christian ethics have been published,[3] as well as volumes on ethics and the New Testament.[4] The situation is still not as promising with regard to the Old Testament.

Until recently there had been no full-scale treatment of ethics and the Old Testament in English since J. M. P. Smith in 1923,[5] and only two works since then in German.[6] There have, of course, been many articles and monographs on specific subjects which bear on ethics and the Old Testament as the sources cited in this volume make clear, but little has been done to bring this work together in a more coherent whole.

Most recently, works by Walter C. Kaiser, Jr., and Christopher J. H. Wright have addressed the subject of Old Testament ethics.[7] These are important and insightful works, as my citations of them at many points will indicate, but they represent only the beginning of a long overdue discussion in the academy and the church on the place of the Old Testament as a moral resource for the life of the church. There are important differences of perspective and approach between this volume and those of Kaiser and Wright. There are differences that have to do with the nature of biblical authority and the way in which that authority operates in theology and ethics. These will become apparent in the course of the discussion below. There are also differences in the scope of Old Testament materials treated and the foci chosen. This is to be expected in dealing with a collection of traditions as vast and diverse as the Old Testament. The differences of approach add to the richness of the discussion.

This is a volume on the Old Testament and Christian ethics. It attempts to relate the testimonies and stories of Israel's faith as recorded in the Hebrew canon to the character and conduct of Christians and the Christian community in our own time. It tries to bridge from the Old Testament as ancient testimony to the need for moral resources in the modern church as it faces the ethical issues of a complex and challenging time. The task here is not to discuss those issues as such, but to select and focus elements of the Old Testament traditions that can inform and undergird the tasks of Christian ethics related to any set of specific issues.

This work assumes a necessary connection between the Old Testament and the modern church. It takes seriously the constant historical claim that both Old and New Testaments are to be considered scripture of the church. It likewise takes seriously the persistent contention that if ethics are to be in any way distinctively Christian they must be grounded biblically in some centrally significant way.

Simply put, the purpose of this volume is to make the Old Testament more readily accessible to the concerns of Christian ethics in the life of the church and to scholars in the service of the church. In the dialogue between scripture and Christian ethics this volume attempts to clarify and give fuller voice to the scripture pole of the dialogue by making the Old Testament more fully available to the Christian life as a moral resource.

Given the limited literature on our subject it is useful to make some statements about what this volume does *not* attempt to do lest false expectations be raised.

1. This is *not* a book on Old Testament ethics. Although this expression has been used somewhat loosely in the literature, I believe it is properly used for the descriptive task of discovering and analyzing the ethical systems of the ancient biblical communities. Such a work would be primarily a descriptive history of moral systems reflected in the different periods and settings discerned in the literature of the Old Testament. Such a volume would be useful, but that is not the purpose of this one. This is not to say that it will have no concern for this descriptive task. There are many points at which such information will be important and even crucial, but the concerns of this work are broader in scope than the descriptive enterprise. It is concerned with the manner in which traditions from various Old Testament periods and settings put together in their present canonical shape are claimed as the scripture of the church and are thus foundational for Christian ethics. Where these traditions are illumined by a better understanding of the ethics of the biblical communities I will draw on that understanding, but I do not believe that this is an end in itself nor do I believe that it can be carried on in isolation from the normative questions of the contemporary church.[8]

2. This book is *not* an attempt to write the ethics of the Old Testament. This phrase suggests that within the Old Testament can be discovered some single, coherent moral system. More often than not, such attempts impose a system on the biblical material rather than discover one. I agree with John Barton when he writes, "There would be little point in trying to write The Ethics of the Old Testament, but . . . the treatment of particular areas of Old Testament morality might actually be made easier by removing this ideal from the field of study."[9]

3. This book is *not* an introductory text or an attempt at the comprehensive survey of the subject. The discussion assumes some basic knowledge of Old Testament history, literature, and theology or the ready availability of texts and reference works that can supply basic information. It is no substitute for basic textbooks introducing the Old Testament, although it is hoped that it will be a useful textbook for classes beyond that

level in both Bible and ethics, or as a resource alongside basic introductory texts. Even in such uses it must be stressed that this discussion is representative rather than comprehensive. The possible topics of discussion between the Old Testament and Christian ethics are many and varied. This volume is but a contribution to a dialogue that is barely under way and makes no pretense to have exhaustively covered the field. I am painfully aware of issues and topics that could have been discussed had there been more time or space, or had I chosen a different manner of organizing my subject.

I am also aware that many of the subjects discussed deserve fuller treatment than space allows. My hope is that the discussion here will be seen as an invitation to wider discussion. To that end I have tried to cite sources for further inquiry that are both significant and accessible to the general church reader as well as to the scholar.

4. This book is *not* intended to address topical issues in the life of the church. It is not a book on what the Old Testament says about this ethical issue or that one. It is an attempt to clarify and make available the Old Testament witness that should inform the church on the entire range of moral issues that might be faced in the course of the Christian life. This volume is intended to invite the church with its agenda of ethical concerns to more serious dialogue and encounter with the Old Testament portion of its own scripture.

Following these disclaimers there are some things to be said positively about what I intend in this volume.

1. This book is consciously Christian and confessional in character. It treats the Old Testament as a portion of the canon of the scripture of the church. The perspective is that of one seeking to claim the church's biblical resources for the task of faithful life in today's world as the church. I am, of course, aware that the Hebrew canon is also scripture for the Jewish community, and my own work has been informed by scholarship from within the Jewish perspective.[10] It would, however, require separate treatment in a similar volume to discuss the issues of Bible and ethics in Jewish perspective. The appropriation of biblical resources to inform the life of contemporary faith communities requires specificity in the dialogue with the biblical texts.

2. This volume is committed to critical method but not to objectivity. It will be amply clear that my work is informed by the exegetical approaches which have been developed from

the historical-critical method. However, I no longer believe that it is possible or desirable to achieve objectivity in the exercise of this method. All interpreters bring their own perspectives and commitments with them to the text. The stance of so-called objectivity has often resulted in leaving these prior perspectives and commitments unexamined. Feminist and liberation hermeneutics have been particularly telling in their critique of traditional exegesis at this point.[11]

In this work I believe that theological and moral commitments which I bring with me will be visible in dialogue with the text. These are subject to critical reflection as much as the text itself. Among these commitments are a conscious personal location of myself in the ecumenical Christian community, although probably predominantly Protestant in character. I am concerned that the Old Testament be in dialogue with the New Testament as the other portion of Christian scripture. I am committed to values of inclusivity with regard to gender, race, class, and age, and I believe those concerns make a difference in how I hear and interact with particular biblical texts.

My colleague Denise Hopkins has called for a restoration of passion in biblical scholarship as a corrective to the dispassionate scholarly work that often remains remote from the arenas where church people are seeking biblical perspective on the challenging issues of life in the modern world.[12] My hope is that this volume might be a critically considered but passionate dialogue with the Old Testament as a resource for Christian ethics in the life of the church.

3. In large part the work reflected in this book is based on the received canonical shape of the text. Although critical exegesis will always inform my work, I will take seriously that the church receives the text of the Old Testament in the particular final form that we now have before us. For example, we are called on to encounter the creation account of Gen. 1 as the first testimony of the canon even if critical judgment finds that its final form was fixed very late in Israel's story. That critical judgment can inform our understanding, but we must still ask what it means to find this text in this location, juxtaposed to another creation account from quite a different background and period in Israel's life. At every point we will seek to use critical exegesis but always to return to the canon as it now stands before the church.

This also means refusing to impose artificial systems of harmonization onto the canon. Taking the canonical shape of the text seriously also means confronting and acknowledging un-harmonizable tensions when that is what the text presents us. The role and function of the canon will be discussed further in chapter 1.

4. This volume is interdisciplinary in character. It is in-tended as an intentional bridge to theology and ethics,[13] thus, at every point it is consciously inviting dialogue with theology and ethics in the life of the church. My hope is that it might model and encourage further dialogue between these disci-plines, not only between scholars but in the congregations and the governing bodies of the churches.

To foster this dialogue at all levels I have tried to avoid excessive technical jargon from both biblical and ethical fields of scholarship. I have tried to synthesize and make more acces-sible the insights and perspectives of modern Old Testament scholarship as a grounding for Christian ethics. My purpose has not been so much to break new ground as to see ground which has already been broken become planted and harvested for the work of the church in the world.

Chapter 1 focuses on methodological questions in making the connections between the Old Testament and Christian eth-ics. Chapter 2 discusses the special importance of Old Testa-ment narrative as a moral resource. Chapters 3–8 use the general narrative sequence of Israel's story as a framework for organizing the discussion of particular Old Testament texts and themes that inform the work of Christian ethics. Chapter 9 deals with the Old Testament literature, primarily wisdom, which does not fit into the narrative historical pattern of orga-nization used for chapters 3–8.

It goes without saying that in the writing of this volume I owe many debts of gratitude. I have been especially fortunate to have worked for twenty years at Wesley Theological Semi-nary in a community committed to interdisciplinary dialogue and especially rich in resources for the dialogue of an Old Testament scholar with the field of Christian ethics. In actual fact the entire faculty at Wesley understands that every disci-pline in the curriculum relates to the Christian moral life, and I have been enriched in this work by that atmosphere. Yet I would want to give special thanks to my colleagues in Christian ethics and the sociology of religion, both at Wesley and in the wider academy, for their openness to the inquiries of an interloper in their field of study. Even more must I thank my former colleague Larry L. Rasmussen, now at Union Theological Seminary in New York. For sixteen years we discussed together, taught together, wrote books together—all in the effort to bring our fields of Bible and Christian ethics more closely into dialogue and mutual support. I have learned much from him and am certain that this volume would never have been conceived except for our friendship and mutual work.

Portions of the manuscript were read by David Petersen, James Nash, Lucy and Kevin Hogan, and Carolyn Pressler. Their comments have been very helpful, and they are in no way responsible for any of the shortcomings of this volume. My editor, Jeffries M. Hamilton, has been especially helpful and supportive. I am grateful for the assistance of Mary Boyd and Geoff Royce in preparing the indexes. The book is dedicated lovingly to my wife, Susan, who believed this book would be written even when I doubted it. She helped me more than she can know.

Notes

1. Robert Davidson, "Some Aspects of the Old Testament Contribution to the Pattern of Christian Ethics," *SJT* 12 (1959): 374.

2. Brevard S. Childs, *Biblical Theology in Crisis* (Philadelphia: Westminster Press, 1970), p. 124.

3. My own work, coauthored with Larry L. Rasmussen, *Bible and Ethics in the Christian Life* (Minneapolis: Augsburg Publishing House, 1976; rev. and exp. ed., 1989). Since that time a vigorous discussion of the Bible's role in Christian ethics has developed, but primarily focused on questions of methodology and not on biblical content. Representative of this discussion are Thomas W. Ogletree, *The Use of the Bible in Christian Ethics* (Philadelphia: Fortress Press, 1983), and William Spohn, S.J., *What Are They Saying About Scripture and Ethics?* (Ramsey, N.J.: Paulist Press, 1983).

4. See Allen Verhey, *The Great Reversal: Ethics and the New Testament* (Grand Rapids: Wm. B. Eerdmans Publishing Co., 1984), and the extensive bibliography there. Ogletree's *Use of the Bible in Christian Ethics* also includes discussions of New Testament content as a moral resource, and has one chapter on the Old Testament.

5. J. M. P. Smith, *The Moral Life of the Hebrews* (Chicago: University of Chicago Press, 1923).

6. Johannes Hempel, *Das Ethos des Alten Testaments* (Berlin: Alfred Töpelmann, 1964), and H. van Oyen, *Die Ethik des alten Testaments* (Gütersloh: Gütersloher Verlagshaus Gerd Mohn, 1967).

7. Walter C. Kaiser, Jr., *Toward Old Testament Ethics* (Grand

Rapids: Zondervan Publishing House, 1983); Christopher J. H. Wright, *An Eye for an Eye: The Place of Old Testament Ethics Today* (Downers Grove, Ill.: Intervarsity Press, 1983).

8. Douglas Knight, "Old Testament Ethics," *Christian Century* 100 (Jan. 20, 1983): 58, has written that "biblical ethics is primarily a descriptive discipline," and that "one should first take pains to describe and understand the ethics of the ancient document and the people who produced it, before trying to appropriate moral norms and directives of the Bible for today." Although I believe the descriptive to be important, I do not agree with the implication that our concerns for the Bible and ethics should be *primarily* descriptive; nor do I believe that the descriptive and the normative come as sequentially as Knight suggests. The neat division between "What the Bible meant" and "What the Bible means" has been broken down in much of the recent discussion of biblical hermeneutics. The normative concerns we bring to the text influence the way in which we retrieve ancient testimony, and although we must seek critical awareness in this process, we cannot entirely separate description and application. My own views on these matters will be spelled out more fully in chapters 1 and 2.

9. John Barton, "Understanding Old Testament Ethics," *JSOT* 9 (October 1978): 44. He criticizes the work of Johannes Hempel and Walther Eichrodt in Old Testament ethics for imposing a system of ethics onto the Old Testament as a "rather artificial construct."

10. In an interfaith context I would refer to the Hebrew canon as the Hebrew scriptures. I do not find this term widely enough known or understood in the Christian community to make it meaningful. In fact, I have had instances when listeners, hearing me use that terminology, have assumed I was speaking of the Talmud. In addressing the church I continue to use the term "Old Testament." I hope it is clear in this work that I do not use it to mean that the Old Testament has been abrogated by the New Testament. Both are the scripture of the church.

11. See the discussion and the literature cited on these issues in Bruce C. Birch, "Biblical Hermeneutics in Recent Discussion: Old Testament," *RelSRev* 10 (Spring 1984): 1–7, reprinted in *A Guide to Contemporary Hermeneutics: Major Trends in Biblical Interpretation*, ed. Donald K. McKim (Grand Rapids: Wm. B. Eerdmans Publishing Co., 1986), pp. 3–12, and "Biblical Theology: Issues in Authority and Hermeneu-

tics," *A.M.E. Zion Quarterly Review* 99 (October 1988): 10–19.

12. This point was made in a panel discussion for the section on Theology of the Hebrew Scriptures at the Annual Meeting of the American Academy of Religion and the Society of Biblical Literature in Chicago in November 1988.

13. I increasingly feel that Christian ethics and theology are more closely related than the curriculum in our theological schools suggests. Although my focus is on dialogue with Christian ethics, this dialogue is necessarily theological in character.

PART ONE

Method and Approach

1

The Role
of the Old Testament
in Christian Ethics

Many in the life of the church are uneasy with the Old Testament. They are willing to acknowledge it as a witness to the early history of our Judeo-Christian tradition, but they are not so sure that it has any relevance to the life of the church in the modern world or to the complexities of their own individual moral struggles.[1]

There exists an important consensus among ethicists and biblical scholars that "the Bible is somehow formative and normative for Christian ethics,"[2] but the suggestion is often made or implied that it is the New Testament which is more formative and normative.[3] Indeed, apart from references to the Decalogue and the prophets, most of the Old Testament is ignored.

As early as the mid-second century C.E., Marcion attracted a wide following with views that included his argument that the Old Testament must be rejected and discarded (as well as portions of the New Testament canon). He believed that the Old Testament God of law and wrath had been displaced by a God of love and grace manifest in Jesus Christ and witnessed to by Paul.[4] His views were judged heretical and rejected by the early church. The importance of the Old Testament as scripture for the church, witnessing to the work of the same God who is incarnate in Jesus Christ, was reaffirmed.

Still, it is remarkable how tenacious Marcion's view of the Old Testament continues to be. Because of its breadth and complexity it is still easier for many in the church to relegate the Old Testament to second-class status when it comes to those biblical resources that are drawn upon for the Christian life.

Our task in this volume is to make those Old Testament resources more accessible to the church as resources for the moral life. To do so will require that we first address ourselves to some understandings of method and approach (chapters 1–2) and then turn to the content of the Old Testament witness itself (chapters 3–9).

The Use of the Bible
for Christian Ethics

How is the Bible formative and normative for Christian ethics? Since there are different models for describing the relationship of scripture to the moral life, it is important to make clear our understanding of that relationship. We can do so by focusing on three categories: community, moral agency, and biblical authority.

Community

The Bible had its origins and received its final shape as the canon of scripture in the faith community. As a resource for the Christian moral life it can be appropriated only in the context of the faith community.[5]

The Bible is always the story of a people. Further, the Bible assumes that the moral life is never just a matter of individual character and conduct, but is to be located in and held accountable by the faith community. That community in turn is called into being by the graceful activity of God, and it is through the life and witness of the community that individuals are related to God and seek to understand the implications of their faith for moral life in the world.

In both Israel and the early church individual moral life was seen in the context of a community identity. The Bible is the record of those traditions around which that community identity has been shaped. Israel and the early church became "interpretive communities."[6] R. B. Gill, writing on such communities, notes:

Fish's concept of interpretive communities allows us to see that one's experience and accounts of experience are not merely passive reactions to an objective reality but an active process of shaping experience according to the community's sense of purpose. . . . [Such communities] mediate between individuals and a meaningless world by giving them the patterned and purposive categories and slots into which they can place their experience.[7]

The Bible is both the witness to and the product of Israel and the early church as such interpretive communities. The moral dimensions of both individual and corporate experience are mediated through the community identity witnessed to in the canon of scripture.

The Bible remains the church's book.[8] The existence and the affirmation of the formative and normative role of scripture, however understood, represents the church's reality as a story-shaped community.[9] The whole range of the church's activity as a moral community is in interaction with the Bible as a primary source of the church's identity and purposive action in the world. The church acts as the shaper of moral identity, the bearer of moral tradition, the community of moral deliberation, and the agent of moral action, and the Bible plays a central role in each of these activities.[10] Thus, any understanding of the Bible as a resource for Christian ethics must be reached in dialogue, not only with the text but with the church (in all its complexity) as the community through which the text has been mediated to us.

To discuss the Old Testament and its implications for Christian ethics will involve us in dialogue with Israel, with the church, and with the text where the originating and the ongoing interpretive communities meet.

Moral Agency

The Bible assumes that we are moral agents. It is a quality of our humanness to be capable of moral responsibility.[11] Who we are and how we act as individuals and as communities is considered by the scriptures to be matters of moral accountability. Moral agency is the term we use to encompass the moral dimensions of our lives. It encompasses both character and conduct, our being and our doing.

1. The central question for Christian *character formation* is Who are we to be? It is a question with individual and corporate dimensions.

Character formation is the learning and internalizing of a way of life formative of our own moral identity. It is our moral "being," the expression of who we are. . . . Character includes our basic

moral perception—how we see and understand things—as well as
our fundamental dispositions, intentions, and motives.[12]

Our moral character is shaped by many different influences
on our lives, but if our identity is to be Christian the Bible
must be a central influence. We are nurtured in our basic
orientations and understandings as persons and communities
of faith by our exposure to the stories, the hymns, the admonitions, the preaching, the visions, and the commandments of
the Bible. We are shaped by these in our exposure through the
preaching and the liturgy of the church, through the teaching
of the church, and through our own patterns of devotional life
using the Bible. It is the whole of the biblical canon from
which these shaping resources come and we are shaped by
different materials in different ways.

2. The Bible also plays a role in our *decision making and
action*, the ethics of doing. Here the central question is What
are we to do? Biblical materials never make moral decisions for
us nor do they lay out strategies or courses of action. Simply
put, the Bible cannot be used as a prescriptive code book.
Many issues requiring moral decision were never imagined by
the biblical communities (e.g., bioethical issues), and others
appear for decision and action in such radically altered socioeconomic circumstances that faithful response may still be unclear and complex.

Nevertheless, the Bible is centrally important in the arena of
our conduct. The ethical traditions of the scripture make clear
central moral imperatives, supply images that challenge our
moral imagination, give norms and standards by which to measure moral choices in our radically different circumstances, establish the boundaries of and options within morally permissible
behavior, and may help locate the burden of proof on a given
issue. Further, the Bible makes clear that faithful life as God's
people requires embodiment of our faith in moral decisions and
actions consciously taken as the people of God. Moral passivity in
the face of ethical challenges is itself unfaithful.

3. Within the large framework of character formation and
decision making other categories are important for describing
the moral life and the Bible's role in shaping Christian moral
life. We would particularly highlight *virtue, value, obligation,*
and *vision.*

Christian ethics in emphasizing *virtue* calls upon the biblical
materials in worship, education, and corporate life to foster

qualities (kindness, courage, humility, love, righteous anger, and others) that are to mark us as Christian persons. Scripture's constant attention to the kind of persons we are to be is a central resource for the church in fostering moral virtue.

In its concern for *value* Christian ethics focuses on qualities that are to mark the social embodiment of morality. The Bible points to the importance of embodiment of faith commitment in faithful social structures and "the biblical materials themselves give rise to many values for the Christian moral life. Justice, love, equality, and peace (*shalom*) are prominent among them."[13]

Moral *obligation* has to do with the duties and responsibilities that arise out of the roles and contexts and commitments through which we live our lives (e.g., parent to child; citizen to nation; faith community to God). Scripture is filled with references to such moral obligation, and the church cannot discuss obligation in Christian ethics without drawing upon those biblical materials for insight and perspective.

Moral *vision* encompasses the whole of the moral life. Allan Bloom wrote in his recent best-seller *The Closing of the American Mind*, "Without the great revelations, epics and philosophies as part of our natural vision, there is nothing to see out there, and eventually little left inside. The Bible is not the only means to furnish a mind, but without a book of similar gravity, read with the gravity of a potential believer, it will remain unfurnished."[14] The Bible is the central source for the furnishing of the Christian moral universe, the source of our moral vision. In its drama, its characters, its themes, its struggles, its beauty, and its complexity we are supplied with much of our vision of life in the world lived in relationship to God.

> The Bible, then, addresses and promotes virtue, value, obligation, and vision in the Christian moral life. It names and helps form virtues and values, encourages and specifies obligations, and fosters and renews moral vision. Any use of Scripture in ethics which fastens on only one or two of these is an inadequate use, just as any reduction of Christian ethics to an ethics of virtue, value, duty, or vision only, is inadequate to the plural dimensions of the moral life.[15]

Biblical Authority

The nature and function of biblical authority is a subject of lively and often impassioned discussion among scholars and in

the life of the church.[16] Here we can only sketch the outlines
of our position in this wide-ranging discussion.

> We speak of the authority of Scripture as a way of referring to the
> acknowledged position of the Bible as normative for the Christian
> life. Authority is not a property inherent in the Bible itself. It is
> the recognition of the Christian community over centuries of ex-
> perience that the Scripture is a source of empowerment for its life
> in the world.[17]

The Bible points beyond itself in testimony to the power and
presence of God in the experience of the biblical communities. Thus, authority rests in the church's affirmation of the
Bible as a mediating witness to a God who was gracefully active
in the experience of the ancient community, but is still gracefully active in our own experience.

In Christian ethics our character and our conduct are
shaped by many different sources of authority in our lives—
our family, our culture, our education, our immediate context, as well as our faith. What is the position of the Bible as
authoritative alongside these other sources of authority?

It is our view that in Christian ethics the Bible is always
primary but never self-sufficient. It can never be the sole
source of authoritative influence in the shaping of Christian
character and conduct. James Gustafson has written, "An authority can be unique without being exclusive. The Bible has
such a status. . . . Thus, for Christian ethics its authority is
inescapable without being absolute."[18]

The Bible's primary and central role functions in a variety of
ways. In the life of the church it is the source of our identity
with a historic faith community. In the church's use of the
Bible for the shaping of moral agency, the Bible influences the
ability of the church to discern God's presence, activity, and
will in a world where many nonbiblical sources of authority are
also claiming our attention. With the Bible as a constant reference point the church can and must enter into active dialogue
with other sources of authoritative moral insight in our world,
forging out the models of God's new activity in continuity with
the Bible's witness to God's previous activity. Often the authority of scripture is as much in its modeling of a process as
in its mediating of a content. In attending to the discernment
of God's will by the biblical communities we become sensitized
to God's will in our own time.

Our identity as the church is obviously shaped by images, concepts, and metaphors that are part of the Bible's content and not just witness to a process. But . . . the content must be constantly tested by the process. Which stories and images continue to manifest the redeeming power of God? Some matters of content are reassessed by the church, e.g., the biblical acceptance of slavery, Paul's admonition for women to keep silent in the church. Some matters of content are reasserted, e.g., God's preferential option for the poor and the oppressed. Some matters of content remain central although our interactions with them may change, e.g., the gospel story of the life, death, and resurrection of Jesus.[19]

It has been our purpose in the preceding pages to locate the method and approach of this volume in the larger current discussion of the role of the Bible in Christian ethics. We have done so by very briefly suggesting our view of the Bible in relation to community, moral agency, and biblical authority. All these understandings will be more fully evident in the concrete discussion of Old Testament materials which will follow in chapters 3–9. We turn our attention now to some of the particularities of the Old Testament as a moral resource.

The Old Testament as Moral Resource

If we are to claim the Old Testament as a resource for Christian ethics in the modern church, we must be clear about the nature of this enterprise and the foundational understandings of the Old Testament from which we operate.

Morality in Ancient Israel

There has been a fundamental confusion in a good deal of the literature on ethics and the Old Testament between two distinctly different enterprises. The first is the effort to describe the actual morality characteristic of different groups and periods of time in ancient Israel. The second is to treat the Old Testament, in its completed form as scripture of the church, as intended to inform our own consideration of ethical matters.[20]

The study of morality in ancient Israel is a complex and multifaceted undertaking. Israel was not a monolithic community. Johannes Hempel in his important work *Das Ethos des Alten Testaments*[21] stresses the roots of morality in ancient Israel within different social groupings of pastoralists, peasants, and urban dwellers, each with differing values and codes of moral conduct. In addition, the history of Israel reflects radically different social conditions from seminomadic tribal society, to agriculturally based federation, to small monarchical nation, to defeated and exiled community.

Unfortunately, Hempel and others who have taken his approach have sought to find in this complexity a developmental history of a unified Israelite morality. Since, in the Old Testament, we never have access to the perspectives (moral or otherwise) of all groups in all periods of Israel's history, the result is a patchwork quilt put forward as the "ethics of the Old Testament." Barton has put it well:

> The Old Testament is evidence for, not coterminous with, the life and thought of ancient Israel; Old Testament writers may at times state or imply positions which were the common currency of ancient Israelites, but they may also propound novel, or controversial, or minority positions. . . . The mistake is . . . to assume that *extant* evidence is also *typical* or *complete* evidence.[22]

The focus of this volume is on the second of the two enterprises mentioned above. Although each portion of the Old Testament text may not represent a "typical" or "complete" record of ancient Israelite morality, it does represent the testimony ultimately judged by the faith community as worthy of being passed on to future generations; hence, its inclusion in the process which resulted in the Hebrew canon.

The Old Testament in its present form is the received scripture of the church, and as such, is put forward as a resource for the church in its theological and ethical understandings. Reflecting on how the Old Testament witness informs our efforts to discover who God wishes us to be and what God wishes us to do is not the same as discovering the actual moral practices of ancient Israel. It is confusion about these two tasks that creates unnecessary problems.

Of course, it is important to discover as much as possible about the sociohistorical context out of which a particular text arose, for that helps us to hear its witness more clearly. But for any given text the moral witness may be representative of a broad popular morality in Israel, or it may be a visionary moral witness branded unacceptable in its own time (e.g., Jeremiah). In either case its presence in the canon represents the judgment of the faith community that its witness is to be taken seriously by subsequent generations of the faithful in efforts toward the moral life. The value of the Old Testament as a moral resource is not dependent on a reconstruction of the actual popular morality or moralities of ancient Israel. Such a reconstruction will always be only partially possible.

Foundations for Christian Ethics in the Old Testament

It would be a mistake to try to find any one centering theme or concept for the Old Testament moral witness. Walther Eichrodt finds this center in "covenant,"[23] and Walter Kaiser finds it in "holiness."[24] Both of these themes are centrally important, but neither is capable of encompassing the diverse range of moral witness in the Old Testament. The end product systematizes the Old Testament materials in an artificial manner alien to the Old Testament itself. As we shall see, our approach is to allow for a more multifaceted witness from the Old Testament traditions, and it is our belief that this enhances the pertinence of that witness to our own multifaceted lives.

Nevertheless, there are important foundations for understanding the ethical witness of the Old Testament. These are to be found in a constant focus on the character, activity, and will of God, and in the constant framework of Israel's story as the people of God.

The Will, Activity, and Character of God. No one would be surprised that the moral resources of the Old Testament are focused in God.[25] God is the source and basis of morality in the Old Testament witness. There are a variety of ways for us to understand how this divine focus functions.

The most common way is to stress morality as obedience to God's explicitly revealed will. This is certainly a strong element of the Old Testament tradition. Consider the testimony of the psalmist:

> Good and upright is the LORD;
>   therefore he instructs sinners in the way.
> He leads the humble in what is right,
>   and teaches the humble his way.
> All the paths of the LORD are steadfast love and faithfulness,
>   for those who keep his covenant and his decrees.
>   (Ps. 25:8–10)

Stress on obedience to God's will as the central moral norm places chief emphasis on God in the role of lawgiver (particularly through the Sinai covenant) and to a lesser extent on revelatory experience of God through which the divine will is mediated (e.g., the call of Isaiah, Isa. 6). Although this is a very important dimension of Old Testament morality, it is one-sided emphasis on obedience to God's explicitly stated will that results in the caricature of the Old Testament as bogged down in legalism. Too narrow an emphasis here tends to reduce Old Testament morality to prescriptive legislation as the main focus.

The concept of Torah itself is broadened in the Old Testament. Although Torah can be translated as "law" in the sense appropriate to the law codes of the Old Testament, it also comes to be used in a much broader meaning. Torah is used of the whole of the Pentateuch with its unfolding story of God's creation and salvation. It is also used to describe a way of life and not just a set of rules.

> The best way to approach the Old Testament ethical system as "Torah" is to remember that the purpose of the Old Testament is not primarily to give information about morality . . . but to provide materials which, when pondered and absorbed into the mind, will suggest the pattern or shape of a way of life lived in the presence of God. . . . *"Torah" is a system by which to live the whole of life in the presence of God, rather than a set of detailed regulations to cover every individual situation in which a moral ruling might be called for.*[26]

It seems much more reflective of the full range of the Old Testament witness to focus on the *character and activity of God as well as the will of God.*[27] Focus on God as lawgiver is too narrow to do justice to the range of testimony on God's roles and activities in the Old Testament.

In later chapters different facets of God's character and actions will be discussed in relation to different portions of Israel's testimony to its experience of God. Creator, giver of the promise, deliverer, lawgiver/covenant maker, sovereign, judge, redeemer—these and other aspects of the divine character all have implications for the moral life lived in relation to God and in faithfulness to God's purposes in the world.

Some scholars have suggested that alongside obedience to God's will is a concern in the Old Testament for imitation of God as a basis for ethics.[28] Certainly texts such as Lev. 19:2,

"You shall be holy, for I the LORD your God am holy," would seem to suggest imitation of God as a basis of moral character and conduct. Our stress on the character of God would encompass such a divine modeling of human moral behavior, but is broader. It also includes morality which arises in *response* to the experience of the presence and activity of God. To have experienced the deliverance from bondage in Egypt may have some effects in imitating divine behavior (e.g., in providing for the freedom of slaves), but its far greater moral impact is in engendering responses of humility and praise for the gift of God's grace and in fostering reflection on what it means to live as God's delivered people in the world.

This stress on the facets of God's character also places the activity of God as revealer of the divine will (e.g., lawgiver) into a wider context that avoids the caricature of Old Testament morality as prescriptive and legalistic, while allowing a proper consideration of the important role of the law in Old Testament ethics.

A word must be added here about the suggestion of natural law in the Old Testament. Certainly there are texts which suggest the appeal to moral norms that arise outside of the explicit revelation of God. The wisdom tradition and its influence in various portions of the Hebrew canon appeals more to human reason and broadly accepted cultural patterns of "right" behavior than to revealed commandments or understandings of God's will (see chapter 9). Even God seems subject to some standards of seemingly natural law. Abraham seems to make such an appeal in bargaining with God in Gen. 18:25, "Shall not the Judge of all the earth do what is just?"

Even here the Hebrew testimony to God as Creator, a witness present also in the wisdom literature, places the patterns of moral order operative in the universe within the compass of God as the originator and sustainer of that order. Thus, when Job suggests that he has obeyed all the explicit moral imperatives God reveals the existence of a larger context of the creation for which God is responsible but within which the morality of Job and God is maintained (Job had in effect challenged the morality of God). To say with Prov. 8:22–31 that Wisdom was the first of God's creations and in some sense the tool for God's further creating makes even the wisdom we discern by the use of human reason the gift of God.

Thus, at every point in our discussion of Old Testament moral resources we will refer to the character and action of

God as a focus for understanding of the biblical witness and a guide for our discernment of God's presence, activity, and will in the moral issues of our own lives.

The Framework of Israel's Story. It is significant for our consideration of the Old Testament as a moral resource to note that we are always dealing with testimony from within the framework of Israel's story. We do not have in the Old Testament abstract, philosophical discourses on morality or codified, theoretical systems of ethics. We have materials that tell the story of Israel or witness from within that story. Several aspects of this feature need to be noted.

1. The character of this story is to be described as narrative and not as history. The Old Testament is the product of faith storytellers and not historians. There are, of course, historical materials included in the Hebrew canon (e.g., royal archival material in 1 and 2 Kings), and there are narratives that are rooted in historical experience (e.g., 1 and 2 Sam.). Even these narratives show little concern for historicity and often fail to give the historian the data needed for historical reconstruction. Other narratives (e.g., Gen. 2–3) are not rooted in historical experience except as they might reflect the context of the writer. The moral value of the Old Testament is not dependent on recovering its historical roots.

It is important to observe that even non-narrative materials are given narrative context in the Old Testament. Law codes are in the context of Sinai covenant-making and wilderness experience. Psalms are to be read against the backdrop of Israelite worship. Prophetic discourse assumes elements of Israel's previous story and speaks to specific contexts in its ongoing story. Even wisdom has its roots in the specific roles and practices of king and sage in Israel and in the canon is presented as a part of Israel's testimony and not simply as commonly held international literature.

2. The framework of Israel's story means that we are always dealing with Israel's experience of and interaction with God. The Old Testament is a faith story. Even witness to universal themes, such as creation, represent Israel's incorporation of those understandings into its own faith story. This is important for our understanding of the nature of moral resources in the Old Testament. The theological and the ethical cannot be separated in the Old Testament. Concerns for right moral conduct and character are always related to theological and reli-

gious claims that reflect Israel's relationship to God. Conversely, there is no concept of religion in Israel that does not issue in concern for right moral character and conduct. Religious and moral concerns are often intertwined.

> The Old Testament literature draws no sharp distinction between ethics and religion. In concerning itself with right conduct it does not distinguish between right *moral* conduct and right *religious* conduct. The law indiscriminately mixes commands on moral matters with commands on religious matters (as, e.g., the Decalogue does), and in the prophetic writings likewise religious offenses such as idolatry are frequently condemned . . . in the same breath as social injustices (. . . e.g., Ezek. 22). Hence, in speaking of OT ethics at all we are imposing a distinction of which no ancient Israelite would have been conscious.[29]

3. We must stress that Israel's story and witness as we now have it in the canon is visionary in character. It is what the community, in its final judgment, has passed on to us as a theological and moral witness. The vision of morality passed on in some of its parts may never have been a full social reality in Israel (e.g., the jubilee). It may be the witness of a persecuted minority (e.g., Jeremiah), or the eschatological vision which envisions a community unlike those Israel ever achieved (e.g., Isaiah's peaceable kingdom or Ezekiel's new Jerusalem). In a sense the moral vision of the Old Testament is the judgment of the ancient community of faith about the vision toward which we are to live. That living will no doubt fall short of the vision even as did Israel's, but it is nevertheless in claiming that vision that we find our identity joined with Israel as the people of God.

Hermeneutical Problems

Two particular problems which the Old Testament presents to the church in claiming its moral resources deserve brief attention.

Diversity and Unity. Biblical scholars and ethicists alike have struggled over the problem of diversity and unity in the Old Testament.[30] "We do not expect OT ethics to be totally homogeneous and consistent, especially when we consider that the OT contains material from a period covering at least a thousand years."[31] Two dangers are to be avoided in dealing with the diversity of the Old Testament.

The diverse witnesses of the Old Testament can be affirmed as enriching our perspectives on the biblical experience of God, but this should not be allowed to degenerate into a settling for pluralistic viewpoints as ends in themselves. The God of the Hebrew canon is one God, even if experienced in a multiplicity of ways and affirmed through a variety of images. The existence of these multiple witnesses in the same Hebrew canon invites us to contemplate them in relation to one another and in witness to the same God. We are not allowed with regard to theology and ethics to settle for the atomistic description of each witness as if they were not intended for dialogue with one another.

We should, however, also avoid patterns of imposed unity that obscure or diminish the dialogue between the Old Testament's diverse voices. In terms of Old Testament ethics a variety of efforts to find (impose?) such a unity in the Old Testament have been put forward. Hempel saw a form of evolutionary developmentalism from primitive to more sophisticated conceptions of morality.[32] Eichrodt followed a similar approach but based it around the development of covenant morality.[33] Neither these nor similar patterns do justice to the richness of the Old Testament witness, and the result is an artificial unity that cannot be defended.[34]

The Old Testament reflects the same variety of moral perspectives and approaches that we find in current ethical discussions within the church and the university. For example, Thomas Ogletree has, with great insight, shown the way in which different Old Testament materials reflect the moral perspectives of consequentialist, deontological, or perfectionist ethics.[35] Because these perspectives all relate to a God, understood in multiple images, and a community of faith, Israel, with a variety of experiences in relation to God they are not mutually exclusive, or standing in intolerable tension. They are part of the moral dialogue within the Hebrew canon, held in dialogue by the God who is their focus and the community of faith which is their framework. As such the Old Testament can inform the moral dialogue of the modern church when we open ourselves to its richness.

Morally Objectionable Perspectives. A long-standing impediment to the church's use of the Old Testament as a moral resource is the existence of actions, customs, and perspectives that are morally objectionable by our present standards.

The Old Testament naturally reflects the customs and practices of a time and social context very unlike ours. Israel's story recounts its participation in practices and attitudes we do not approve (e.g., polygamy, holy war). We will be discussing some of these in later chapters in an effort to understand them in their own social context. Here it is important to note that Israel's story is not intended to model normative moral behavior in all its particulars. Some stories reflect Israel's unexamined participation in widespread social practice (e.g., subordination of women); other stories are stories of Israel's sin (e.g., the excesses of nationalism); still other stories reflect Israel's incomplete understanding of God's will (e.g., the request for a king).

In the modern church there are particular moral objections to the pervasive patriarchy and acceptance of slavery, as well as to frequent expression of ethnocentrism in the Old Testament. None of these are without contrary moral witness in the Old Testament, but the presence of such objectionable perspectives must be acknowledged rather than avoided.

Although we shall deal with some of these matters in the context of particular discussions of Old Testament materials, it is appropriate to say one additional word here. Any adequate approach to the Old Testament as moral resource must seek not only to *retrieve* moral perspectives that inform our ethics but in some instances to *reclaim* the biblical text from elements that distort or limit its moral witness. Thus, for example, the Old Testament reflects, in much of its testimony, a subordinate view of women that is not in harmony with the broader vision of love, justice, and wholeness made clear throughout the Old Testament. This broader vision itself roots in God's activity and will, and the church must claim and apply that vision to issues of the subordination of women in ways that go beyond what the biblical community could have imagined.[36] It was in a similar way that the church finally claimed its moral obligation to oppose slavery even though both Old and New Testaments seem to accept its existence. Although it is through Israel that God's word and will are mediated, Israel is not the perfect embodiment of the living out of that divine moral vision.

The Role and Importance of the Canon

Recent Old Testament scholarship has seen the development of a lively new appreciation for the importance of the canon and its role in biblical theology (therefore ethics as well). This discussion has emphasized both the final form of the text[37] and the process within the community which resulted in the formation of the canon.[38] In this volume we will give critical attention to the process of development that can be traced within the text where that is helpful, but our final frame of reference will always be the final shape of the canon as it has been passed on to the church. The canon is the form preserved and fixed by the biblical community for its testimony to future generations of its experience with God. Although some scholars would regard the canon as problematic, it is our conviction that it acts as an important framework of control for the appropriation of Old Testament moral resources in the Christian life.

Canon and Community

The Hebrew canon developed in the context of the faith community of ancient Israel, and is also the possession of the modern church.

1. The Hebrew canon arose out of the actual experience of Israel over a lengthy period of time. Therefore, as we have noted previously, it is necessarily very diverse, and reflective of both Israel's faithfulness and failure as a moral community. The three sections of the Hebrew canon (Law, Prophets, Writings) developed out of the actual experience of Israel with its own tradition.

> The canon does not speak in a single voice. This is both a witness to the variety of experience with God and a corrective to warn us against absolutizing any selection of the voices through which Scripture speaks. That the biblical communities themselves can be seen judging and reinterpreting and measuring the tradition against their own experience of God can be read as a support for similar activity on our part. This will, of course, necessitate attention to every level of witness preserved within the text as well as to the final form as the ultimate shape given to the text by the biblical communities. *The canon is a record, not only of a destination but a record of the journey as well.*[39]

2. The Old Testament is a portion of the church's scripture. Therefore, its resources are mediated to us through the modern church where it is read and interpreted in dialogue with the church's experience of a living God and the challenge to live as God's people in our own time.

As we attend to the diverse moral witness of the Hebrew canon we become more attentive as the church to the diversity of ways in which God is at work in our world and challenges us to join that work. "The goal is a canon in truthful dialog with our own experience of faith, especially in terms of the particularities of our own social location for faith experience. The conversation will be as diverse as the canon itself, and to the degree that we can receive that diverse witness we will be enriched with new eyes and new ears for our own receiving of the biblical word."[40]

Framework of Control

In important ways the canon functions as a framework of control in our appropriation of Old Testament resources for the moral life.

1. When we see God revealed in ever new ways within the Old Testament itself we are reminded that the same God is still active in new and self-revealing ways in our own lives. "The Scripture points beyond itself to the reality of God. . . . Thus, the canon encourages a dialogic use of Scripture, not to discover God enshrined in the past, but to assist us in discerning God's activity and will in our own day."[41]

2. It is the existence of the canon that helps protect against several reductionistic uses of the Old Testament in moral concerns.

It helps avoid the absolutizing and outright idolatry of the biblical text itself. The text is a witness to the activity of God and should not be confused with God as an object of worship. The encounter with the Old Testament text is one of dynamic interaction seeking God's word for our lives and not one of static and mechanical application.

The existence of the canon protects against the selection of only portions of the biblical text as authoritative. Such selections of a "canon within the canon" are usually based on the predispositions of the selector, and are often used to bolster a position reached on other grounds.

The canon also guards against "critical reductionism." Exegetical method, as commonly practiced, has a tendency to critically examine the parts of a text without going on to examine how the parts function in the whole. This is true whether analyzing pericopes, chapters, books, or whole portions of the canon. Critical methods are to be valued and employed, but

not as an end in themselves—only to assist us to fuller understanding of God's word as it addresses us through the whole of
the text.   Emphasis on the importance of the canon helps
promote this holistic concern.

Hebrew Canon as Christian Canon

One final brief but important word. The Hebrew canon is
also a part of the Christian canon. For the church Old Testament is claimed as scripture alongside New Testament. Thus,
to consider the moral witness of the Old Testament as a resource for the Christian moral life requires that we not shrink
from noting and reflecting on the variety of ways in which the
Old Testament witness is related to the New Testament witness. When the trajectory of an Old Testament idea or principle leads naturally into the New Testament, we will follow it
there and note the relationships that seem apparent. It is because the early church claimed the Hebrew canon as scripture
that it has been passed on as authoritative to us in the church
today.

Because narrative is such an important framework for the
whole of the Old Testament witness, and because the moral
dimensions of narrative have been so seldom explored, we
turn in the next chapter to a discussion of the moral address
of biblical narrative.

Notes

1. Some sections of this chapter will necessarily be strongly dependent on my previous work coauthored with Larry L. Rasmussen, *Bible and Ethics in the Christian Life,* rev. and exp. ed. (Minneapolis: Augsburg Publishing House, 1989). The methodological issues of relating scripture to Christian ethics are discussed at length in that previous volume. This chapter will rely on some of those understandings but will attempt to address the methodological issues that are more particular to the Old Testament.

2. In *Bible and Ethics,* rev. and exp. ed., p. 14, Birch and Rasmussen report this as one element of a two-part consensus. The other part ("Christian ethics is not synonymous with biblical ethics," p. 11) will be discussed in relation to the Old Testament later in this chapter.

3. In my first introduction to the study of Christian ethics in seminary the widely used and admired text for the course was by Paul Lehmann, *Ethics in a Christian Context* (New York: Harper & Row, 1963). Although he briefly acknowledges the importance of the Old Testament, he entitled his section on biblical foundations "Christian Ethics and New Testament Ethics" (p. 26).

4. Marcion even rejected all of the Gospels but a pared-down Gospel of Luke since they were too influenced by Judaism.

5. The centrality of community became much clearer to Birch and Rasmussen in the revised edition of their work where they added a full initial chapter to emphasize its importance, *Bible and Ethics,* rev. and exp. ed., pp. 17–34, 194–196.

6. The phrase is from Stanley Fish, *Is There a Text in This Class? The Authority of Interpretive Communities* (Cambridge, Mass.: Harvard University Press, 1980), whose work has become a standard in communications theory.

7. R. B. Gill, "The Moral Implications of Interpretive Communities," *Christianity and Literature* 33 (1983): 55–56, 57.

8. See Phyllis A. Bird, *The Bible as the Church's Book* (Philadelphia: Westminster Press, 1982).

9. See the work of Stanley Hauerwas, esp. *A Community of Character: Toward a Constructive Christian Social Ethic* (Notre Dame, Ind.: University of Notre Dame Press, 1981), and *The Peaceable Kingdom: A Primer in Christian Ethics* (Notre Dame, Ind.: University of Notre Dame Press, 1983), for insight into the relationship of story (narrative) in the formation of moral community. See also Alasdair MacIntyre, *After Virtue: A Study in Moral Theory* (Notre Dame, Ind.: University of Notre Dame Press, 1981).

10. See Birch and Rasmussen, *Bible and Ethics,* rev. and exp. ed., pp. 120–140, for a discussion of these understandings of the church and the role of scripture in them.

11. We will address the Old Testament roots for this theme in chapter 3 when we discuss our created humanness.

12. Birch and Rasmussen, *Bible and Ethics,* rev. and exp. ed., p. 190. See also the discussion of character formation and the Bible's role in chs. 4 and 5, pp. 66–99.

13. Ibid., p. 193.

14. Allan Bloom, *The Closing of the American Mind: How Higher Education Failed Democracy and Impoverished the Souls of Today's Students* (New York: Simon & Schuster, 1987), p. 60.

15. Birch and Rasmussen, *Bible and Ethics,* rev. and exp. ed., p. 194.

16. Some of those works which seem to me especially helpful and have influenced my position are Edward Farley and Peter C. Hodgson, "Scripture and Tradition," in *Christian Theology,* ed. Peter C. Hodgson and Robert H. King (Philadelphia: Fortress Press, 1985), pp. 61–87; Darrell Jodock, *The Church's Bible: Its Contemporary Authority* (Minneapolis: Fortress Press, 1989); Sallie McFague, *Models of God: Theology for an Ecological, Nuclear Age* (Philadelphia: Fortress Press, 1987); Robert Gnuse, *The Authority of the Bible: Theories of Inspiration, Revelation and the Canon of Scripture* (Ramsey, N.J.: Paulist Press, 1985); and Mary Ann Tolbert, "Reading the Bible with Authority: Feminist Interrogation of the Canon" (unpublished

paper, Consultation on Feminist Biblical Hermeneutics, Society of Biblical Literature Annual Meeting, Anaheim, Calif., 1989).

17. Birch and Rasmussen, *Bible and Ethics,* rev. and exp. ed., p. 142.

18. James Gustafson, "Introduction," in H. Richard Niebuhr, *The Responsible Self* (New York: Harper & Row, 1963), p. 22.

19. Birch and Rasmussen, *Bible and Ethics,* rev. and exp. ed., p. 157.

20. See John Barton, "Approaches to Ethics in the Old Testament," in *Beginning Old Testament Study,* ed. John Rogerson (Philadelphia: Westminster Press, 1982), pp. 113–130, for a helpful discussion of the distinction between these two enterprises, and Robert R. Wilson, "Approaches to Old Testament Ethics," in *Canon, Theology, and Old Testament Interpretation: Essays in Honor of Brevard S. Childs,* ed. Gene M. Tucker, David L. Petersen, and Robert R. Wilson (Philadelphia: Fortress Press, 1988), pp. 62–74, for a useful survey of recent work on ethics in relation to the Old Testament with a constructive suggestion for work yet needed in this area.

21. BZAW 67 (Johannes Hempel, *Das Ethos des Alten Testaments;* Berlin: Alfred Topelmann, 1938; new ed., 1964). See also Hempel's own summary of his work in "Ethics in the Old Testament," *IDB,* ed. George A. Buttrick (Nashville: Abingdon Press, 1962), 2:153–161.

22. John Barton, "Understanding Old Testament Ethics," *JSOT* 9 (October 1978): 46, 49.

23. Walther Eichrodt, "The Effect of Piety on Conduct (Old Testament Morality)," *Theology of the Old Testament,* vol. 2, OTL (Philadelphia: Westminster Press, 1967), pp. 316–379.

24. Walter C. Kaiser, Jr., *Toward Old Testament Ethics* (Grand Rapids: Zondervan Publishing House, 1983).

25. This is by no means a new or unique emphasis on my part. Kaiser, *Toward Old Testament Ethics,* writes, "The character, will, word, and work of God supply the determining principles and crucial organizing tenets of Old Testament ethics" (p. 38; see also pp. 29–30). My disagreement with his work is not in intent at this point, but in his effort to center his discussion of God in the Old Testament entirely around God's holiness. The foundational focus on the character and activity of God was also an emphasis in earlier works. See, e.g., W. S. Bruce, *The Ethics of the Old Testament,* 2nd ed. (Edinburgh: T. & T. Clark, 1909).

26. Barton, "Approaches to Ethics in the Old Testament," p. 128.

27. Kaiser, *Toward Old Testament Ethics*, pp. 29–31, names the character of God as a central organizing tenet for Old Testament ethics. His actual use of this tenet focuses more sharply on positive moral laws and God's holiness, and represents a narrower portrait of the character of God than I would want to draw.

28. See Barton, "Understanding Old Testament Ethics," pp. 60–61; Paul D. Hanson, *The People Called: The Growth of Community in the Bible* (San Francisco: Harper & Row, 1986), pp. 30–34; Harry P. Nasuti, "Identity, Identification, and Imitation: The Narrative Hermeneutics of Biblical Law," *Journal of Law and Religion*, 4 (1986): 16–18.

29. Henry McKeating, "Old Testament Ethics," *The Westminster Dictionary of Christian Ethics*, ed. James F. Childress and John Macquarrie (Philadelphia: Westminster Press, 1986), p. 434.

30. See Paul D. Hanson, *The Diversity of Scripture*, OBT (Philadelphia: Fortress Press, 1982).

31. McKeating, "Old Testament Ethics," p. 434.

32. Hempel, *Das Ethos des Alten Testaments*.

33. Eichrodt, *Theology of the Old Testament*, vol. 2, pp. 316–379.

34. See the devastating critique of Hempel and Eichrodt by John Barton in "Understanding Old Testament Ethics," pp. 44–55.

35. Thomas W. Ogletree, *The Use of the Bible in Christian Ethics* (Philadelphia: Fortress Press, 1983), see esp. ch. 3, pp. 47–86.

36. See Letty M. Russell, ed., *Feminist Interpretation of the Bible* (Philadelphia: Westminster Press, 1985).

37. See Brevard S. Childs, *Introduction to the Old Testament as Scripture* (Philadelphia: Fortress Press, 1979), esp. pp. 76, 83.

38. See James A. Sanders, *From Sacred Story to Sacred Text* (Philadelphia: Fortress Press, 1987).

39. Birch and Rasmussen, *Bible and Ethics*, rev. and exp. ed., p. 174.

40. Ibid., p. 175.

41. Ibid., p. 180.

2

Old Testament Narrative and Moral Address

The OT is not a document of abstract reflection about matters of God and faith in the time of ancient Israel. It is the story of God's encounter with Israel and the various responses that engendered. More accurately, the OT is composed of stories about God and Israel which the community has now preserved in the canon as parts of a larger story. It is, of course, the narrative traditions that most obviously preserve the character of story, but even the non-narrative traditions must be understood in the context of Israel's story and the roles played by various subgroups within that story (priests, prophets, sages, poets, or apocalypticists).

Until recently biblical story has not been highly valued as a source for Christian ethics. This has been especially true in the use of the OT as a moral resource. Christian ethicists who have treated the OT materials at all have focused largely on texts with explicit moral content, usually of a propositional or admonitional character. The Decalogue has, of course, received a good deal of attention as a central text for any biblically based ethic.[1] The preaching of the prophets, with its heavy moral and social content, has also received a good deal of attention. Even here the message of the prophets has been used frequently as a source for important ethical principles, such as justice, without adequate attention to the sociohistorical context of the prophetic message or the significance of the place of individual prophets in Israel's story.

The OT is dominated by its storytelling traditions. With respect to God that story begins with the creation of the cosmos and extends to the dawn of God's new age at the end of time.

51

Within the sweep of that divine story major focus falls on Israel's story as a community called into being by divine initiative. It begins with the promise to the ancestors and ends (as
far as the Hebrew canon is concerned) with the persecutions
under Antiochus IV Epiphanes. Relatively little of the literature of the OT stands outside this story framework and does
not need to be understood with reference to the stories of
God and Israel. The Book of Proverbs may be an example.
Other books that do not refer explicitly to the God/Israel stories nevertheless find it necessary to tell stories that create
worlds of their own as framework to their contributions, for
example, the Book of Job and the Song of Songs.

In spite of the centrality of the narrative storytelling traditions in the OT, they have seldom been considered for their
moral address. How do these stories of the biblical communities of faith impact on our efforts as the church to live life
faithfully in our modern world? What does it mean that these
traditions have been handed on to us as more than mere ancient stories but as scriptural canon?

It is curious that attention to the moral address of OT narrative should be so lacking, since the telling of biblical stories
from generation to generation has been such a common form
of biblical influence on Christian lives. Indeed, with respect to
the OT, where general ignorance of biblical content is more
widespread than with the NT, the arresting drama and power of
OT stories (e.g., creation, crossing the sea, David and Goliath,
Daniel) have kept any knowledge of the OT alive for many.

The neglect of OT narrative has been part of a general loss
of appreciation for the narrative structure of biblical texts in
general, as the important work of Hans Frei[2] has demonstrated. Nevertheless the NT has suffered less from this neglect of its narrative features than has the OT, especially where
its use as an ethical resource is concerned. In the NT the
central theological and moral focus is on the person of Jesus
Christ. His birth, life, death, and resurrection, his story, are
the very heart of the NT witness, and the narratives that convey that story, the Gospels, cannot be avoided. Even during
the scholarly "eclipse of biblical narrative" which Frei describes, the story of Jesus remained widely known and highly
regarded among church people, while the Old Testament is
not now at all well known among church people. Especially
with respect to the use of the Bible for Christian ethics,[3] the
New Testament narrative, the story of Jesus, has remained

more central than is true for the OT. In crucial ways Jesus does model moral behavior for Christians, whether that be in the popular pietistic slogan "Let me live the whole week through, asking what would Jesus do," or in more sophisticated moral analyses such as John Howard Yoder's *Politics of Jesus*.[4] None of the OT characters model moral behavior in such a consistent and intentional way. Their stories reflect all the ambiguities and complexities of human experience and the struggle to find and live out faith relationships to God in the midst of life. Even the faith community, Israel, does not merely model for the church a moral norm for the faith community. The stories are often of Israel's faithlessness as well as its faith, and many periods are represented by narratives that reflect differing moral viewpoints on events (e.g., the rise of kingship). Unlike the gospel presentations of Jesus, the simple presentation of normative models for the moral life cannot be the function of OT narrative.

Narrative Theology and the Ethics of Story

Recent developments in contemporary ethics and theology have brought new attention to the central importance of narrative and story for the Christian faith.[5] Insights from this work must preface any effort to recover the moral address of OT narrative.

The categories of narrative and story are intertwined. As a literary structure narrative requires "the presence of a story and a storyteller."[6] A story may be defined as "an account of characters and events in a plot moving over time and space through conflict toward resolution."[7] Story is distinguished from history by deferring to the plotting vision of the narrator. Historical elements may be incorporated and even crucial to the story but the empirical presentation of events is subordinated to the movement of the plot toward resolution and the meaning thereby conveyed.

In a now-classic essay Stephen Crites articulated a fundamental insight now assumed by virtually all work on narrative and story, namely, that human experience itself is inherently narrative in form.[8] The experience of our lives flows continuously with developments, conflicts, and resolutions. We do not experience our lives as isolated points or moments. The present cannot be isolated and analyzed, for in doing so it has already become the past and is incorporated into individual or corporate stories. Alasdair MacIntyre has been especially influential in his rebuke of "modern philosophy's version of disconnected, isolated, and action-oriented individuals who live without meaning and have no place to go."[9]

> In what does the unity of an individual life consist? The answer is that its unity is the unity of narrative embodied in a single life. . . . The unity of a human life is the unity of a narrative quest.[10]

Abstract analysis of human experience may be valuable but only if it is remembered that it is abstracted from the more durational character of life. The wholeness of human experience and the meaning to be derived from it are more suitably spoken of in narrative form. "The implication of this view is that without a story that is both faithful to our ongoing experiences and actions, and examined critically for its truthfulness, we cannot be fully human."[11]

All persons find identity by learning and developing their own story, becoming conscious of its dimensions and adding to it as life goes on through adulthood. Obviously we are shaped by contact with the stories of our families and of significant individuals who influence our lives. Our own life stories also come into contact with the stories of communities and cultures. These stories have power as they have resonance with who and what we most essentially are as human beings. If we cannot see ourselves in the stories we encounter, they have little power to shape or transform us. Great stories are those that address us, draw us in as a part of larger stories beyond our own selves, act as a corrective to the distorted stories that seek to claim us, and give new meaning to our own stories. The biblical stories of the Christian faith tradition are such great stories. Their enduring power over the centuries and the rich stories of the church born out of the influence of the biblical story are ample witness to their greatness, but if we lose the ability to remember and tell those stories we also lose their power. Our lives participate in the plot of many stories. The power of biblical stories is their ability to help us see the many stories of our lives as part of larger stories which integrate our life story into stories of ultimate meaning. "Virtually all our basic convictions about the nature and meaning of our lives find their ground and intelligibility in some sort of overarching, paradigmatic story."[12] For Christians that larger story has been the biblical story. In spite of theologians' renewed interest in biblical narrative there is a significant need to recover the importance of biblical narrative, especially that of the OT, in the life of the church.

One of the most important developments in contemporary Christian ethics is a renewed emphasis on the formation of Christian character as of equal importance alongside the shaping of Christian conduct.[13] It makes a difference which stories interact with our personal story to form identity and mold character. When we cease to know or tell the biblical stories and the stories of our faith traditions growing out of the biblical stories, we are likely to be shaped, whether consciously or not, by cultural, national, ethnic, or ideological stories without the corrective of religious values. No amount of appeal to abstract principles of Christian ethics and no calls to Christian decision making and action based on those principles will be of much use if the shaping influence of our biblical faith stories is not a formative part of our identity. Is it any wonder that, ignorant of the biblical story, thousands of well-intentioned people buy the thinly disguised American nationalism story peddled by many media evangelists as a substitute for biblical faith?

Christian ethics is not just the abstract application of a decision-making process. Moral life flows from the way in which we engage the world, and this engagement is structured by our vision, the way we see the world as persons of faith. The biblical story has shaped the Christian way of seeing, not in terms of analytical discourse, but in the concreteness of time and place and people. We recognize something of our own lives and their meaning before God in the stories of those times and places and people.

> As in all good storytelling, we recognize ourselves in the depiction. Not the concept of liberation but the journey out of Egyptian bondage, not an essay on the teleological suspension of the ethical but Isaac and Abraham on Mount Moriah, not the penal substitutionary theory of the atonement but the blood of Jesus on Golgotha, not an exposition of the motif of Agapé but the open arms of the running father. Would a historical God speak to us in any other way than through history first and then in the "history-like" accounts of biblical narrative, the extraordinary in the ordinary?[14]

Biblical story captures the sin and grace, the evil and the good, the death and life that encounter us at every turn in our own lives and names them in the language of faith. It removes them from the abstract and names them in narrative terms that intersect with our own experience. None of this can happen if we remain ignorant of or remote and removed from the biblical story and its moral power. It is the purpose of this essay to address that concern with respect to the OT narrative in particular. How shall we understand the moral address of OT narrative in its multiple facets? How then do we foster a recovery of OT narrative as a moral resource in the life of the church?

The Moral Function of
Old Testament Narrative

In OT narrative we are confronted with testimony to the experience of reality in ways that address us because of the narrative quality of our lives. Because this is the testimony of a faith community, the narratives *disclose* a reality that unfolds in relationship to God, whose story the community seeks to tell as it is intertwined with the community's own story. In the encounter with God the community understands itself to have been *transformed*, and some of its stories seek to effect the same transformative power in those encountering the stories.[15] Within these two broad categories OT narrative is as multivalent as is human experience. Thus, when considering these narratives for their moral address, it should be clear that they do not lead easily to moral prescription or principle, although many would use them in that way.

Consider first that the OT contains narratives intended to disclose reality. They have the power to reveal the reality of the narrator's experience in ways that make deeper and more meaningful our own experience of reality. We encounter in these stories testimony to what is really real and enduring— about our own humanity, about the God who encounters us in the midst of our humanity, about the community called into being from that encounter, about the world where that community seeks to live faithfully, and about the purposes toward which God moves community and world. OT stories are not susceptible to neat typology or glib analysis because our lives are not like that. This becomes one of the strengths of OT narrative. We don't see there idealized reality but our own. This can, of course, be both comforting and disturbing since our lives include both comfort and disturbance. Robert Alter reminds us that OT narrative at its best "honors ambiguity, acknowledges complexity, and presupposes indeterminacy."[16]

OT stories disclose reality in different ways. Some stories actually create worlds or realities in the telling.[17] Such stories establish their own framework of reality and invite the reader or hearer into that world for the purpose of disclosing there a meaningful word. It is obvious that both of the creation narratives that open the book of Genesis are stories that disclose reality by creating worlds. Each of these narratives (Gen. 1:1–2:4a; 2:4b–25) characterizes the divine reality responsible for an ordering of the cosmos, the nature of that cosmos, the role of humanity within that cosmos, and the relationship of humanity to the Creator. But in the stories these characterizations are completely different between the two. We are not required to adjudicate the claims of each to truth. Each communicates its truth within the world it sets up. We are invited into these worlds to receive the disclosure of their truth. To the degree that these stories disclose a reality that rings true to our own experience, their truth can be incorporated into our story. We need not stay in the worlds they create or harmonize their worlds so that they are explainable in terms of our own story of reality. We can incorporate the different truths of the divine as transcendent and intimate, of humanity as created in the divine image and as related to all of creation, and of creation as good but also containing the responsibility of choice and its consequences.

There are OT narratives other than creation stories that create worlds. The narrative opening of Job creates a world absolutely essential for the context of tension (some would say irony) in which the unfolding dialogues of Job find their meaning. The Song of Songs creates a timeless world of its own for the poetry of lovers. The poetry would lose much of its power if forced into some more mundane and common reality. Its world suggests a world open to love which can be disclosed in the midst of, perhaps even in spite of, the other stories of reality out of which we live.

Most narratives that disclose reality do not in themselves seek to set up the worlds of reality out of which they operate. Most narratives are actions or plots which assume a world and seek to describe events and characters in that world. In doing so they may deepen our own experience of reality, and that deepening may be enhanced by study and reflection on the stories so that we better understand the reality they assume and can therefore be more open to disclosure within that reality. The episode of Moses encountering God out of the burning bush in Ex. 3 is a good example. This narrative is not concerned to establish a world. It assumes a world that includes both the sociopolitical realities of bondage and the religious experience of theophany on a sacred mountain. This narrative is much more concerned with the beginning of a plot line which moves through successive episodes to climax in the deliverance of the Hebrew slaves in the wondrous event of the crossing of the sea. To enter this story is, however, to find in its plot important disclosures concerning the nature of divine reality and human vocation in relation to that divine reality.

The disclosing of reality resides in both the story and the storyteller. After reading Phyllis Trible's retelling of the story of the Book of Ruth,[18] this writer wondered how he could ever have read that story and failed to see so many things. The failure was not in the story, a story of women's courage in a man's world which has been fixed in its text for centuries, but in the eyes with which the story was read and the understanding with which it was received. Hearing the story of Ruth told so many times with Boaz as hero and Ruth as rescued victim imposes another story even upon our reading of the text. It is thus well to remember that in our efforts to be open to the disclosure of reality from the narratives of the OT we must be prepared to be critical in our examination of the stories we bring with us and may well impose on the biblical story.

If OT narrative discloses reality, it can also have the power to transform us in that disclosure. If narratives can create worlds, they can also overturn them. Here the emphasis is on stories that shake us in the world of our own stories. In the encounter with some narratives, we are reoriented. The journey through our own life experience is no longer the same because of our encounter with the biblical story. Some of the intentional use of story in pedagogy and preaching in the life of the church seeks to heighten this transformative quality.

Any OT narrative is potentially transformative, but it appears possible to distinguish several different ways in which narratives exercise transformative power. Certain stories are experienced as perennially transformative. To mark this quality such stories may be referred to as salvation stories. In the OT the Exodus story (Ex. 1–15) is the most important of these. Israel understood clearly that this story was not just

descriptive of a moment in past history. Almost from the beginning this story was cut loose from its historical moorings
and treated as a story that addressed the reality of Israel's life
in every generation and did so with the transforming power to
make each generation the Exodus generation. Such events and
the stories that preserve them have been referred to as "reservoirs of meaning."[19] Each time the pattern of distress/deliver-
ance, the gift of God's life-giving grace, is experienced as
Exodus story in the experience of a new generation, then the
story itself grows in meaning and power. It is enhanced by all
of the transforming moments that flow from the story and
yet become part of the story and its power. Other OT narratives also function as salvation stories. The well-known cre-
dos (e.g., Deut. 26 and Josh. 24) and salvation history Psalms
such as 78 or 136 call to mind and celebrate those transforming stories. Perhaps the clearest example of Israel's understanding of the ability of some stories to transform
subsequent generations is Moses' reference to the story of
covenant making on Mt. Sinai when he is speaking to the
generation about to enter the promised land: "Not with our
fathers did the Lord make this covenant, but with us, who
are all of us here alive this day" (Deut. 5:3). In a similar
fashion these stories have continued to have transformative
power throughout the centuries of the church's continued
telling of them. They can continue to exercise power as paradigm stories of transforming power if they are told and reflected upon in light of our own experience.

Other OT narratives can have transforming power but do
not become central salvation stories. For example, there are
stories of transformation to new life that invite the reader or
listener to similar transformation. The story of Jacob in general, the episode of Jacob's wrestling with the night visitor
(Gen. 32:22ff.) in particular, is a story of transformation to
new life. This narrative could be dismissed as one of those
most bizarre and remote from our own experience unless we
attend carefully to the transformation taking place. Jacob is
fearfully facing encounter with his alienated brother Esau. In
wrestling with "a man" through the night, Jacob, the control-
ler, cannot seize control but instead is injured, given a new
name which points toward community, and sent limping away
from the place he calls "face of God," for he has come to see
God present in this struggle. When he meets with Esau the
following day, he is embraced and not assaulted, and Jacob

cries, "Truly to see your face is to see the face of God." To be open to the moral address of this story and its power to transform our lives is to see how often we, like Jacob, must pass through struggles and risk injury in order to be able to see the face of God in the face of our alienated brothers and sisters. It is to face God's encounter with our own controlling natures in the human struggles which refuse to be controlled.

Other stories transform by shattering our illusions, overturning our worlds. Crossan has shown this quality as a prominent feature of the parables of Jesus.[20] Although the parable form is not as common in the OT, a good example is Nathan's parable in confronting David in 2 Sam. 12. Nathan's dramatic and shattering declaration, "Thou art the man!" has continually left its ancient context to shatter illusions of those who thought their self-serving actions to be secret but who had not reckoned with God. A nonparable example of this type of illusion-shattering story is the story of Tamar in Gen. 38. In this narrative a resourceful woman seeking to be faithful to her familial obligations in the face of Judah's failure to fulfill his, executes a plan to conceive a child by Judah himself. When she is discovered to be pregnant she is charged with the capital offense of adultery and about to be burned. When Judah is confronted at the last moment with the truth that he is the father he unexpectedly declares of Tamar, "She is more righteous than I." In this story worlds are overturned for the ancient and modern community. Righteousness is on the side of one who subverted the rules, the laws. We are forced to rethink our own institutionalization and domestication of the good and to consider the risks that genuine righteousness might demand of us. In Tamar, we are invited to look for insight to those pressed to the margins of our societies as Tamar, a woman, was marginal in her patriarchal world.

The Recovery of Moral Address in Old Testament Narrative

The concern to recover the moral address of OT narrative exists only among those who regard the Bible as scripture and therefore as authoritative in some way for the community of faith. In the following suggestions for matters of concern in such a recovery, the church (or the synagogue) is assumed as the context.[21]

If the moral power of biblical stories is to be preserved and passed on, there is an urgent need to reassess the way in which biblical exegesis is taught to church leaders in the theological schools and to lay people in the life of the local church. In particular we need to become more aware of the limits of historical-critical method in biblical studies. For several generations this method has been taught by many as the sum total of the exegetical task. It was assumed that this method properly and rigorously applied could successfully recover the objective meaning of texts. Since its focus was most frequently on authorship, historicity, and the development of literary traditions, the results of historical-critical work were frequently the fragmenting of texts without a concern for their meaning as a whole. The result has been the blunting of the moral address of the biblical story by the fragmenting of the story itself. There is little moral power left in looking at the literary pieces of text and discussing their meaning in isolation from one another, but seldom was the meaning of the whole discussed.

Of equal concern is the way in which the claim to objectivity in historical-critical method places the experience of hearing or reading an OT narrative at arm's length from one's own experience. Biblical story has moral power as it intersects our own story, and in those intersections the stories become intertwined. Objective method seeks to avoid this. In 1962 Krister Stendahl argued that the task of the biblical theologian is properly limited to the "descriptive," whereas the "normative" meaning of scripture is not the province of biblical theology.[22] This represented the triumph of a view first introduced by Gabler in 1827 that descriptive theology must be sharply divided from the work of constructive theology.[23] Biblical scholars at the time of the Stendahl article largely believed they were engaged in describing the history and faith of the communities of the Bible in an objective and value-free fashion through the use of historical-critical methods. They viewed this task as detached from the claim of confessing communities that these materials were scripture and somehow authoritative for modern faith. This approach still predominates, and one still hears talk of "what a text meant" and "what a text means," as if the two were separable and one could legitimately choose to work only on the former. Brevard Childs recently wrote:

It is far from obvious that an appeal of objectivity will resolve the hermeneutical issues. Nor is it evident that the subjective presup-

positions of the interpreter can only be regarded as a negative
factor. . . . It is a false dichotomy which contrasts objective analysis with subjective presuppositions. The issue is rather the quality
and the skill with which presuppositions are brought to bear on
the biblical material. In sum, one of the major issues for developing a new biblical theology lies in rethinking the sharp distinction
which Gabler first introduced into the field when he separated
descriptive from constructive theology. The two aspects of biblical
theology belong together.[24]

Feminist[25] and third-world scholars[26] have taught us to recognize that there are no truly objective methods or interpreta-
tions. Texts address us in multiple ways because of the
multiple perspectives brought by the interpreters in their encounter with the biblical stories. Not only is this inherently
true, but this interaction of text and experience, the biblical
story with our own story, is to be valued, encouraged, taught,
and critically reflected upon. OT narrative cannot become a
resource for the moral shaping of our lives if its story is not
allowed to intersect our own story. Cultivated, false objectivity
is precisely the sort of exegesis that will not allow this to happen. It is for this reason that so many pastors will candidly
admit that the biblical study methods they were taught in seminary do not help them bridge the gap between analyzing a text
and claiming it (or being claimed by it) for preaching or teaching in the life of the church. It is indeed important to master
certain critical tools including those of the historical-critical
method, but beyond this critical task there must be encouragement and training in methods that will allow us to be encountered by the biblical story and to foster such encounter in
others.

A second area important in the recovery of the moral address of OT story is an increased awareness of the multiple
layers of storytelling that are necessarily a part of the unique
character of those OT narratives that seek to claim us as part
of scripture. The truth of these stories cannot be limited to
any one of these layers. They must all be heard and reflected
upon.

The first of these is the narrator's voice in the story itself—
the witness who gives testimony to the characters, events, and
conflicts of Israel's story and God's story. This immediate
voice in the literary structure of the narrative itself gives us
access to its vision of reality and the demand for response that
flows from it. "Events, characters, time, place, action, sur-

prise, tension, resolution, plot, narrator—they are all there in the stories of Scripture."[27] Sometimes the narrator's voice can be identified with specific times or places or interests, and the story may be heard as testimony to particular points of view (e.g., the contributions of the Deuteronomic historian). This may enhance our encounter with a given narrative or group of narratives, but it should be clear that meaning and truth in our encounter with OT stories do not depend on such determinations.

A second level present in the OT stories is the level of the community that preserved and passed on these particular stories. The OT canon itself represents the judgment of the ancient Hebrew community of faith concerning which stories deserve to be preserved and retold.[28] The canon is itself the testimony of the community on the stories judged to be true—those stories that have the power to disclose and transform the reality of our lives. We can only briefly suggest some functions of canon that bear on the moral address of OT narrative.

One of the issues with which Christian ethics must perennially struggle is the issue of self-deception. We have a tendency to tell false stories about ourselves because the truth is not always easy or simple or unambiguous. Hauerwas calls truthful stories "continually discomforting."[29] When we deceive ourselves, we choose safe stories that make no demands and expect nothing in return, that fit comfortably with the stories we have already chosen for ourselves. The OT canon is a part of the faith community's antidote to self-deception. Without the canon and its insistence that the canon's total witness is authoritative, we could comfortably select our own collection of stories in accord with our previously shaped story. The canon is the collection of stories that break through our self-deceptions and make the demands on us that come from bearing the promise of Abraham and Sarah, receiving the gift of Exodus deliverance, becoming the alternative community of covenant, and being enabled to sing the Lord's song in a strange land. We are forced to deal with stories of judgment as well as hope, folly as well as wisdom, sin as well as grace, death as well as life. We encounter the profound and the simple, the obscure and the plain. It is important not to limit the canon to our own selections in it. This would be to risk that our own self-deceptions will perpetuate themselves and shut out challenging or threatening stories. We must ask, for example, why stories like that of Tamar (Gen. 38) are almost unknown. It may be that their perspective on righteousness is threatening, even subversive. It is not only their presence in the canon but their resonance through the canon that makes their claim on us clear.

This reminds us of another function of canon. Narratives no longer stand alone but are caught up as episodes in larger stories, juxtaposed to one another in complementary or tension-making ways, or edited in new and revealing patterns. Those biblical communities who passed on the OT stories did not experience them as discrete and isolated episodes because they had experienced the interaction of those stories in their own lives and faith. The canonical shape and placement of stories is as important as the story-episodes themselves in hearing the moral address aimed at us by the biblical communities. Why does the whole Hebrew canon begin with Gen. 1, a creation story not shaped in its present form until the time of Babylonian exile? Is this portrait of God intended as necessary prelude to the more particularized story of Israel and the God of that particular people? Why is the upbeat Horatio Alger tale of Joseph interrupted by the story of Tamar in Gen. 38? Is it to remind us of the ambiguities of righteousness, lest the Joseph story seem too glib? Why is the story of the rise of kingship in Israel filled with the contradictory perspectives of judgment and grace? Can it be that tearing these apart into early and late sources does violence to the message of moral ambiguity and struggle that attend the grasping of sociopolitical power apart from trust in God? The canon is the shape of the community's corporate story encompassing the voices of particular narrators.

One final function of the canon must be briefly mentioned. For the contemporary community of faith seeking the moral address of scripture, the canon provides a common ground of moral reflection which allows our separate story-formed identities to speak to one another. Sharing the common canonical story allows us to speak across cultural, ethnic, and class barriers. As an example, would we in North American churches be nearly as challenged by liberation theology if it were only addressed in the terms of analytical theological discourse? Part of the unavoidable power of its challenge comes from its retelling of biblical stories such as the Exodus deliverance story in ways that tell us how those stories have intersected their own experience. Speech out of such intersections reaches us because even when our personal story is remote from the dispossessed we share the biblical story, and its retelling gives us vision and access to the experiences of the retellers. The canon thus provides an important framework for moral discourse.

This final point actually takes us to a third level through which OT story comes to us, alongside the voice of the narrator and the witness of the biblical community in the shape of the canon. It is the level of the tradition (or traditions) through which the OT stories come to us. By the time we hear the biblical story, it has been retold through many generations. So we never hear it without being affected by all those retellings. Preaching and teaching in the church mediate the biblical story, but not without contributing witness to some segment of the tradition which testifies to encounter with the biblical story over many preceding generations. Often these generations of witness enrich us, but sometimes they deceive us and distort the biblical story (e.g., the preaching to justify slavery prior to the Civil War). Thus our traditions are never to be confused with the biblical story itself but always are to be judged by our own faithful encounter with scripture itself. Further, both biblical story and the traditions of our retelling are to be critically reflected upon in the belief that God's story is still being lived in our own time and experience and ever new insights might still flow from our encounter with a living Word.

Notes

1. Walter Harrelson, *The Ten Commandments and Human Rights* (Philadelphia: Fortress Press, 1980), is an excellent treatment of the Decalogue as an ethical resource, and it makes use of much of the extensive literature available on the Decalogue.

2. Hans Frei, *The Eclipse of Biblical Narrative: A Study in Eighteenth and Nineteenth Century Hermeneutics* (New Haven: Yale University Press, 1974).

3. For general understandings of the dynamics involved in the use of the Bible for Christian ethics, see Bruce C. Birch and Larry L. Rasmussen, *Bible and Ethics in the Christian Life* (Minneapolis: Augsburg, 1976 [rev. and exp. ed., 1989]); and Thomas Ogletree, *The Use of the Bible in Christian Ethics* (Philadelphia: Fortress Press, 1983).

4. John Howard Yoder, *Politics of Jesus* (Grand Rapids: Wm. B. Eerdmans, 1972).

5. This article is deeply indebted to a number of key works in what has become a rather large bibliography on narrative and story. An especially helpful survey article is Gabriel Fackre, "Narrative Theology: An Overview," *Int* 37 (1983) 340–52. In ethics the works of Stanley Hauerwas have been especially helpful. See *A Community of Character* (Notre Dame, Ind.: University of Notre Dame Press, 1981); *Truthfulness and Tragedy* (Notre Dame, Ind.: University of Notre Dame Press, 1977); and *The Peaceable Kingdom* (Notre Dame, Ind.: University of Notre Dame Press, 1983). In narrative theology key works that have informed this essay are Terrence W. Tilley, *Story Theology* (Wilmington: Michael Glazier, 1985); George

Stroup, *The Promise of Narrative: Recovering the Gospel in the Church* (Atlanta: John Knox Press, 1981); Michael Goldberg, *Theology and Narrative* (Nashville: Abingdon Press, 1982). In biblical studies John Dominic Crossan, *The Dark Interval: Towards a Theology of Story* (Niles, Ill.: Argus Communications, 1975); and Robert Alter, *The Art of Biblical Narrative* (New York: Basic Books, 1981) have been especially important.

6. Robert Scholes and Robert Kellogg, *The Nature of Narrative* (London: Oxford University Press, 1966) 4.

7. Fackre, "Narrative Theology," 341.

8. Stephen Crites, "The Narrative Quality of Experience," *JAAR* 39 (1971) 291–311.

9. This particular characterization of MacIntyre's argument is from Ron Large's "Story and Ethics: The Moral Dimension of Narrative"(unpublished paper, 1986).

10. Alasdair MacIntyre, *After Virtue: A Study in Moral Theory* (Notre Dame, Ind.: University of Notre Dame Press, 1981) 203.

11. Tilley, *Story Theology*, 26.

12. Michael Goldberg, "Expository Article: Exodus 1:13–14," *Int* 37 (1983) 390.

13. See the works of Hauerwas cited in n. 5, as well as Birch and Rasmussen, *Bible and Ethics*, rev. and exp. ed., chs. 4 and 5.

14. Fackre, "Narrative Theology," 346. Fackre is himself citing Frei, *Eclipse*, 11 for the suggestion that biblical narrative is "history-like."

15. Fackre distinguishes disclosive and transformative aspects of biblical narrative ("Narrative Theology," 345), although he is in no way responsible for the descriptions of types within those broad categories as suggested here.

16. Alter, *Art of Biblical Narrative*, as characterized by Fackre in "Narrative Theology," 345.

17. Tilley (*Story Theology*, 40ff.) uses a similar category, "stories that set up worlds," although he calls such stories "myths." This is potentially confusing given the various ways in which that term has been used.

18. Phyllis Trible, "A Human Comedy," *God and the Rhetoric of Sexuality*, OBT (Philadelphia: Fortress Press, 1978).

19. The phrase is from Paul Ricoeur but is used effectively in discussing the Exodus story by J. Severino Croatto, *Exodus: A Hermeneutics of Freedom* (Maryknoll, N.Y.: Orbis Books, 1981).

20. Crossan, *Dark Interval*.

21. Many of these remarks may well apply to Jewish communities of faith but there will also be some differences. This essay will speak only out of this author's experience in dealing with these issues in the life of Christian churches.

22. Krister Stendahl, "Biblical Theology, Contemporary," *IDB* 1:418ff.

23. Johann Philip Gabler, "Oratio de iusto discrimine theologicae biblicae et dogmaticae regundisque recte utriusque finibus," *Kleine theologische Schriften* (ed. Th. A. Gabler and J. G. Gabler; Ulm, 1831) 2.179–98.

24. Brevard S. Childs, "Some Reflections on the Search for a Biblical Theology," *HBT* 4 (1982) 5–6.

25. E.g., Elisabeth Schüssler Fiorenza, "Toward a Feminist Biblical Hermeneutics: Biblical Interpretation and Liberation Theology," *The Challenge of Liberation Theology* (ed. B. Mahan and L. Dale Richesin; Maryknoll, N.Y.: Orbis Books, 1981) 108ff.

26. Juan Luis Segundo, *The Liberation of Theology* (Maryknoll, N.Y.: Orbis Books, 1976).

27. Fackre, "Narrative Theology," 346.

28. I am greatly indebted to the work of Brevard S. Childs and James A. Sanders for increasing my understanding of the canon and its importance. Representative of their work is Childs, *Introduction to the Old Testament as Scripture* (Philadelphia: Fortress Press, 1979); and Sanders, *From Sacred Story to Sacred Text* (Philadelphia: Fortress Press, 1987).

29. Hauerwas, *Truthfulness and Tragedy*, 95.

PART TWO

The Old Testament
Story
as Moral Resource

3

Creator
and Creation

The Hebrew canon opens with two narrative testimonies to God's role and work as Creator. Both are concerned with God's work in origination of the created order of things. In its present literary form, the first account (Gen. 1:1–2:4a) is generally attributed to priestly circles during or just following the Babylonian exile (i.e., late sixth or early fifth century B.C.E.), while the second (Gen. 2:4b–25) is usually attributed to the Yahwist epic and dated to the late tenth century B.C.E.[1] It is important to note that in the present arrangement of the canon we are introduced to God on the universal scale of relationship to all creation before the particularity of encountering God as the God of Israel. Thus, what we read later of Israel's story comes under the light of what we know about Israel's God as the God of all creation.

Similarly, the testimony to God as Creator, which resonates throughout the canon, is now to be read with the fully developed testimony of Gen. 1 and 2 as background even though some of these texts originated earlier in Israel's history and stress some different aspects of God's creative work. Together these texts throughout the canon (creation psalms, references in the prophets and the wisdom literature, God's speeches to Job) form the witness of Israel to its creation faith. Although major focus will be on the important opening chapters of Genesis we will draw upon that wider witness throughout the canon as well.

The God Who Creates and Blesses

The creation narratives of Gen. 1–2 are testimony to Israel's God as Creator. They are to be understood as theological proclamation and not as historical or scientific in character.[2] Even where these narratives show knowledge of the worldview of other ancient cultures they have freely altered those traditions in the light of Israel's own theological affirmations about God as Creator and the divine relationship to creation. Coming at the beginning of the canon, these narratives establish a theological and moral universe as much as a physical one, and that universe is focused on God. Thus, it is with the nature and activity of God as Creator that we must begin.

Sovereignty and Intimacy

Both of the creation accounts in Genesis deal with God as the originator of all things[3] as well as suggesting important understandings of continued relationship between God and the creation. The description of God's creative work is remarkably different in the two narratives, but we would argue that this juxtaposition of imagery functions in a complementary way that is important to biblical creation faith.

God is sovereign in creative power and intimately related in care to the creation. These qualities of sovereignty and intimacy are present to some degree in both accounts, but the central focus of the priestly account in Gen. 1 is on God's sovereignty, while the Yahwist in Gen. 2 is focused more on God's intimate relationship to creation.

1. Even the most casual reading of Gen. 1 leaves little doubt about its stress on the *absolute sovereignty of God*. God is pictured as transcendent and powerful. No other actors occupy the stage in this creation drama.[4] The language, often described as liturgical, enhances the sense of majesty and power.

The verb *bara'* "to create" is used (in Qal) only with God as the subject and never with reference to material acted upon. It is indicative of divine power to bring into being. It appears six times in the priestly creation account.

This sense of sovereignty is enhanced by the mode of creation in Gen. 1. It is by word alone. Over and again the text simply states, "God said, 'Let there be . . . ' and there was. . . . " The psalmist similarly claims, "By the word of the LORD the heavens were made, and all their host by the breath of his mouth. . . . For he spoke, and it came to be" (Ps. 33:6, 9). Since the prophetic literature stresses God's word as powerful to effect God's will in history, one must imagine Gen. 1 to be affirming that the same sovereign word of God is the power which brought all things into being. It is against this background that the Gospel of John later proclaims, "In the beginning was the Word. . . . And the Word became flesh and lived among us" (John 1:1, 14).

With its emphasis on God's sovereignty, the frame of reference in the priestly narrative is cosmic in scope. God's creation includes the very structures of the cosmos and not just the immediate environment of humanity (as in Gen. 2). To contemplate the sovereignty of God on such a scale is to be filled with awe. Such testimony summons us to praise and worship. We should not be surprised to find such testimony to God's creation common in the psalms which are handed on from Israel's worship. After one of the most elaborate and beautiful witnesses to God's creative power Ps. 104 says, "I will sing to the LORD as long as I live; I will sing praise to my God while I have being," and concludes simply "Praise the LORD!" (Ps. 104:33, 35c). Job is summoned to reorient his perspective, "Where were you when I laid the foundation of the earth?" (Job 38:4).

We should briefly note that this opening biblical portrait of God is both monotheistic and universal in character. There is no suggestion of the existence of other gods, and there is no reference to Israel or the particularity of its traditions. Whatever the course of development of Israel's monotheism,[5] the compilers of the canon have opened with the most expansive view of divine sovereignty. God is the God of all creation and the only power from whom creation derives its being. It is hard to avoid the implication that we are to read the rest of the Old Testament in the light of this proclamation.[6]

2. Alongside the portrait of God as sovereign Creator stands a witness to God as intimately involved with creation. This portrayal of the *intimacy of God* may be seen especially in the beginning of God's creative work in Gen. 2:7. Like a potter God gathers soil and fashions (*yaṣar*) a human creature (*'adam*). Then, into that creature God breathes the divine breath itself to give it life.

In the Yahwist narrative which follows in Gen. 2, God appears as involved and related to the creation. God provides for the needs of the *'adam*, engages in conversation, walks in the

garden, and provides for human freedom. Although anthro-
pomorphic in character, this portrait of God does not reduce
God to human terms. God is still the Creator and in sovereign
control, but God is engaged in relationships of care for
creation.

The contrast with the power of creation by word alone in
Gen. 1 could hardly be greater. Yet, how impoverished we
would be if we were lacking either one of these portraits of
God as Creator. If God's sovereign creative power is affirmed
throughout the canon, so too is the biblical witness to God's
intimate caring and involvement with creation. The speeches
to Job out of the whirlwind (Job 38–41) are especially noteworthy for their expression of the delight God takes in the
creation. This intimate relationship of care is also reflected in
the conclusion to the great creation hymn in Ps. 104:

> These all look to you
>   to give them their food in due season;
> when you give to them, they gather it up;
>   when you open your hand, they are filled
>   with good things.
> When you hide your face, they are dismayed;
>   when you take away their breath, they die
>   and return to their dust.
> When you send forth your spirit, they are created *(bara')*;
>   and you renew the face of the ground.
>
> (Ps. 104:27–30)

Since God's care in relationship obviously extends beyond the
moment of primordial beginnings, we are also beginning to
see that God's role as Creator extends beyond the event of
origination.

Chaos and Order

In the Hebrew tradition the antithesis of creation is not
nothingness but chaos. God is the one who creates by bringing
order out of chaos. The notion of *creatio ex nihilo* (creation out
of nothing) is not an Old Testament idea, but appears in the
tradition at a later point (2 Macc. 7:28; Rom. 4:17; Heb. 11:3).

In Gen. 1 God's creative work brings order out of and in the
midst of the watery chaos (*tehom*, Gen. 1:2).[7] This primordial
sea of chaotic waters is the ancient image through which Israel
sees the antithesis and even the threat to the order and pur-

pose which come from God's creative work. In Gen. 1 chaos is not vanquished but brought under control; the firmament separates and holds back the waters of chaos above and below (vs. 6–7). In the flood story, it is not rain but the waters of chaos that are unleashed and threaten to uncreate the world (7:11; 8:2).

The tradition of creation out of chaos was known widely in the ancient Near East, but depicted as a battle in which a hero-god defeats a personified monster of chaos (*Chaoskampf*).[8] The best-known are the epic narratives of the Babylonian Marduk defeating Tiamat, the primordial mother and personification of chaos, and that of the Canaanite Baal defeating Yamm, the god of the chaotic sea. Israel surely knew these traditions and was influenced by them. Some reflection of a battle with chaos tradition seems preserved in passages such as Ps. 89:9–11:

> You rule the raging of the sea;
>   when its waves rise, you still them.
> You crushed Rahab like a carcass;
>   you scattered your enemies with your mighty arm.
> The heavens are yours, the earth also is yours;
>   the world and all that is in it—you have founded them.

Sea monsters named Rahab, Leviathan, or Behemoth are all mentioned as somehow vanquished or controlled by Yahweh in connection with establishing and maintaining the order of creation (Job 9:13; 40:15–41:34; Ps. 74:13–14; Isa. 27:1; 51:9). However, for the most part, this battle with chaos tradition has been transformed. The chaotic waters have been depersonified and become the uncreated, impersonal primordial state onto which God as Creator imposes order. God sets bounds for the sea (Ps. 104:7–9; Prov. 8:27–29) and separates and restrains the chaotic waters (Gen. 1:6–7).

> The Old Testament contains no theogony, no myth which traces the creation to a primordial battle between divine powers, no ritual which enabled people to repeat the mythological drama and thereby ensure control over the conflicting forces of the natural world. Mythological allusions have been torn out of their ancient context of polytheism and nature religion, and have acquired a new meaning within the historical syntax of Israel's faith.[9]

It is important to note that the role of God as the source of order and the enemy of chaos is not limited to primordial times. Since chaos is not removed but controlled, God's activity in restraining chaos and sustaining order is a dimension of God's work in every generation. Whenever the order of things seems threatened and confusion or purposelessness reigns it is to trust in God's power as Creator, the source of order and meaning, that the community of faith must turn.

> For thus says the LORD,
> who created the heavens
>   (he is God!),
> who formed the earth and made it
>   (he established it;
> he did not create it a chaos,
>   he formed it to be inhabited!):
> I am the LORD, and there is no other.
> I did not speak in secret,
>   in a land of darkness;
> I did not say to the offspring of Jacob,
>   "Seek me in chaos."
> I the LORD, speak the truth,
>   I declare what is right.
>   (Isa. 45:18–19)

It is clear that God's work as Creator involves the origin and maintenance not only of the physical order but of the moral order of the world as well: "I declare what is right." It is also now clear that Creator and creation are not limited in their reference to origination at the beginning of primordial time.

Ongoing Creation

We have already had occasion to observe that God's creative activity is not limited to the beginning of all things but continues on through history as God's sustaining and renewing of the created order. Israel believed in *creatio continua*, the continuation of God's work as Creator throughout the history of the creation.

In fact, Israel first came to know God as Creator in its own story as a people, and not in abstract reflection on the beginning of all things.[10] The earliest references to God as Creator come in relation to God as the Creator of Israel. In the Song of the Sea (Ex. 15), one of Israel's earliest poetic texts, Frank Cross has argued persuasively that the poem reflects a portrait of Yahweh as Divine Warrior (v. 3) who triumphs over the chaotic sea, not in order to create the cosmos but to bring into being a people. Following Cross's argument that *qanah* is best translated as "create," v. 16b reads (author's translation), "while your people passed over, Yahweh, the people whom you created."[11] Similarly, the Song of Moses (Deut. 32) asks, "Is not Yahweh your Father, who created [*qanah*] you, who made you and established you?" (Deut. 32:6b).[12] This notion of God as Creator of Israel seems to originate in the Mosaic covenant tradition and continues to be reflected on throughout the Israelite tradition.

> "Israel has forgotten his Maker."
> (Hos. 8:14)

> Know that the LORD is God.
> It is he that made us, and we are his.
> (Ps. 100:3)

> But now thus says the LORD,
> he who created (*bara'*) you, O Jacob,
> he who formed you, O Israel.
> (Isa. 43:1; cf. 43:15; 44:2; 45:11)

Some scholars have argued that in earliest Israel Yahweh was praised as a Creator deity in the cosmic sense, similar to the Canaanite god El. This view rests upon an understanding of the name Yahweh as it is revealed to Moses in Ex. 3:14–15. They argue that the name should be translated "he causes to be what comes into existence," thus pointing to God as a cosmic Creator.[13] It is persuasive to see the name Yahweh pointing to God's role as Creator, but at least in its present context in Ex. 3 this meaning attached to God's name points not to origination of the world but the calling into being of Israel through divine deliverance.[14] Thus, God's creative work is tied in earliest tradition to God's redemptive work.

With the establishment of the Davidic monarchy began some new dimensions of reflection on God as Creator of a cosmic order which was to be reflected in the orderly rule of the earthly king. We earlier quoted Ps. 89 to show God's victory over Rahab, the chaotic waters. Just as God is victorious in the cosmic realm, so too the Davidic king will triumph over the enemies of earthly order.

> My faithfulness and steadfast love will be with him,
> and in my name his horn will be raised.

I will set his hand against the sea,
and his right hand against the floods.
(Ps. 89:24–25, author's translation)

In the royal tradition of the Davidic monarchy the cosmic
dimensions of God's role as Creator are affirmed as the foundation of just and righteous kingship (cf. Ps. 89:14). Just as the
king is to be the guarantor and champion of earthly order, so
is God the source of cosmic order in the world and the king is
God's servant and representative. This is seen especially in the
royal and enthronement psalms where God's creation of an
ordered world provides the basis for seeking after an orderly
society by the covenant community and its king. Enemies of
the just and righteous order are pictured like the mythological
dragons and floods of chaos which God has overcome to create the world (cf. Pss. 47; 74; 93–99). God's throne established
after victory over the chaotic waters is founded upon justice
and righteousness (Ps. 89:14), and the throne of the Davidic
king is to reflect this divine order in his earthly rule.

Reflection on God as the originator of all things appears in
a context where Israel already knew and celebrated God as
Creator of its own existence as a people and as guarantor of a
stable and just social order reflecting God's cosmic order. It
would not have been possible to limit God's role as Creator to
the primordial beginnings only.

As it now stands, the Hebrew canon opens with narratives
of God's creative work in beginning the life of creation itself,
but it continues to affirm God as Creator active throughout
Israel's story and witness. The God who creates a people in the
Exodus deliverance (see chapter 4) is now seen to be the same
God who created the world. The God whose king sits on the
Davidic throne (see chapter 6) is now seen to be this God in
whom all things originate. The God of our origins is still active
as Creator in our midst.

It was the prophet Deutero-Isaiah who saw most clearly the
implications of this understanding of *creatio continua*. If God
the Creator was still at work, then every moment, even exile, is
pregnant with God's creative new possibilities (see chapter 8).
One's vision is constantly empowered to new hope.

Behold, I am about to do a new thing;
now it springs forth, do you not perceive it?
(Isa. 43:19)

> From this time forward I make you hear new things,
>   hidden things that you have not known.
> They are created (*bara'*) now, not long ago;
>   before today you have never heard of them.
>   (Isa. 48:6–7)

This same sense of continuing creation empowers the hopeful eschatological visions (see chapter 8) which understand God's final work of consummation to be of one piece with the divine work at the beginning of creation. "For I am about to create new heavens and a new earth" (Isa. 65:17); "See, I am making all things new" (Rev. 21:5). And of course, it is this same sense of continuing creation that led the early Christian church to proclaim Jesus as God's new creation in their midst (John 1:1–13) and life in Christ as the experience of God's new creation. "So if anyone is in Christ, there is a new creation: everything old has passed away; see, everything has become new!" (2 Cor. 5:17).

Blessing

As the Gen. 1 creation narrative moves toward completion God pronounces blessings three times: over all living creatures (Gen. 1:22), over human beings (v. 28), and over the Sabbath (2:3). As Creator, God is the source of blessing throughout life.

Claus Westermann has shown that arising from the events of creation in Gen. 1 and extending on throughout the canon is a theology of blessing which must be considered alongside and as complementary to the theology of salvation (*Heilsgeschichte*; salvation history, God's mighty acts) which has been almost the sole focus of much Old Testament theology.[15] Its stress is on the sustaining presence of God rather than on the intervening activity of God.

> A theology of blessing (quite distinct from the salvation theology commonly taught in the church) refers to the generative power of life, fertility, and well-being that God has ordained within the normal flow and mystery of life. God's life-giving work is not extrinsic to creation as though it must always intrude. Rather, it characterizes the world. Creation is itself life-giving in the image of the God who gives all of life.[16]

It is not appropriate to trace this theology of blessing on through the Hebrew canon, although we shall have reference to it from time to time. Here we must simply note its foundations in a theology of creation. God's created order is the vehicle for blessing mediated to all of God's creatures in all generations. In this stress on God's trustworthy order (rather than God's intervening act) we find ethical warrant for systemic and structural efforts to discern and embody God's faithful order in our own societal patterns rather than focus too exclusively on crisis response to urgent moral issues. We are mandated to make the blessings of God's creation broadly and continuously available to all of God's creatures as God intended.

In many ways it is the culmination of the priestly creation narrative in the establishment of the Sabbath (Gen. 2:1–4a) that puts in proper focus the order of God's creation through which blessing is mediated.[17]

The rest of God on the seventh day returns us to a focus on God the Creator lest we imagine the creation of humanity on the sixth day to be the climactic moment of this creation drama. God has completed the divine work.

Sabbath then establishes a rhythm for our participation in God's creation. Creation is not sustained by our work but already completed and sustained in God's work. The goal of our work moves toward our own rest. The procession of our days is to be punctuated with rest when we contemplate not what our own hands have wrought but when we attune ourselves anew to God's work of creation. The Decalogue itself (see chapter 5) contains a commandment to "remember the sabbath day and keep it holy" as a memorial to God's creation (Ex. 20:8–11).

"God has built into the succession of ordinary days a movement which is a gift to the creature which has been created in his image."[18] Thus, Sabbath rest is to be available to all regardless of wealth or class, available to animals as well as humans (Ex. 20:10), reminding us of our common participation and worth as a part of God's creation. Since we live in a world of inequalities, Sabbath then becomes a reminder that this is not as God intended it.

The Character of Creation

Although the central focus of Israel's creation faith is firmly fixed upon God as Creator there are also some clear understandings about the nature of creation itself to be noted.

Benevolence

At the end of each day of creation in Gen. 1 "God saw that it was good" (Gen. 1:10, 12, 18, 21, 25). In v. 31 God looks back over all that has been made and judges it to be "very good." This refrain is so well known as a part of this account that we have almost lost sight of its radical character.

It was not everywhere evident in the ancient Near East that the created world was good. In other ancient religions the world was filled with hostile and potentially dangerous powers. Many aspects of popular religion were designed to give protection in this hostile world.

The Hebrew creation testimony which now opens the entire canon proclaims that God has created the world as benevolent. The Hebrew word *ṭob* is capable of indicating both moral and aesthetic qualities. On the one hand, it indicates the creation as beautiful, pleasing. It is something God takes delight in, and therefore, is to be regarded with delight by us—not regarded with suspicion or fear. On the other hand, there is a moral dimension. As good, the creation is declared to be in harmony with the divine intention. It is a trustworthy witness to God's creative intention, and it is God who judges it so.

> This goodness in Creation is not something which man [sic] notices in the works of God; it is not a judgement which man exercises. This sentence which runs through the chapter . . . will not disappear just because in the eyes of man there is much in the works of Creation that is not good. . . . Man, then, who is a creature, is thereby deprived of passing judgement on the whole of Creation. . . . Man is freed from swaying from positive to negative, he is freed from deciding for an ideological optimism or pessimism. . . . This sentence at the end of the Creation story . . . makes possible a full, unfettered joy in the gifts of Creation, a revelling in the limitless forces given to nature, a rejoicing with the happy, and an immersion in the fullness and abundance that belong to Creation. But the sentence likewise makes possible suffering with him who suffers, the ability to withstand catastrophes, to persevere in the midst of questions after the why, simply because the goodness of what is created can be disturbed only by the Creator himself [sic].[19]

The affirmation of creation as good stands over against all efforts to consider the material world or our own full humanity as inherently evil, or as spiritually debilitating. "For everything created by God is good, and nothing is to be rejected, provided it is received with thanksgiving" (1 Tim. 4:4).

Relationality

In creation all things are related.[20] No element of God's creation, including the human, is self-sufficient. In creation we are related to God, to others, and to the rest of nature.

In Gen. 1:29–30 the reliance of human and animal life on plants for food begins to sound this theme of interrelatedness, but it is in the Yahwist narrative of 2:4b–25 that it is most fully developed. A garden is planted to provide the 'adam with food and beauty (Gen. 2:9), but the 'adam must till and care for the garden (v. 15). God declares, "It is not good that the 'adam should be alone" (v. 18). Relationship is necessary to our being. First, relationship is established to the animals in the naming which implies responsibility (v. 19). Then, in order to find a partner[21] the human creature is separated into male and female. The 'adam "is created by God in such a way that he needs the help of a partner; hence mutual help is an essential part of human existence."[22] Human community becomes possible, and it is clear that we are created as social creatures. Not only are we created in relationship with plants, animals, and other human beings, but the constant interaction with God the Creator implies that our interrelatedness extends to God as well. God cares for our needs, comes walking and talking in the garden, and is affected by our disobedience (Gen. 3).

Much of our concept of relationship within creation has been shaped by the concept of dominion over nature, suggested in only two texts (Gen. 1:28 and Ps. 8:5–6). We will discuss this further at a later point. For now we simply suggest that the overwhelming picture of relationship to creation in the Old Testament is one of conviviality and interdependence. Psalm 104 praises God as Creator of heavens, seas, valleys, mountains, wild asses, cattle, trees, birds, goats, badgers, moon, sun, and lions; then, the psalmist adds unobtrusively, "People go out to their work" (Ps. 104:23). This hymn then concludes, "These all look to you" (v. 27).

From this perspective we understand our shared finitude with all of God's creation; we are creatures dependent on God's gift of life. In an age when science and technology are experiencing the limits to our own knowledge and abilities[23] this biblical perspective introduces an appropriate sense of humility.

> If we experience in our interdependence with nature an aware-
> ness of limits, we also experience a new sense of humanity's
> rootedness in creation. Humans do not occupy the stage of cre-
> ation alone. God is present in the totality of creation, not just in
> the drama of human history. Thus, our connection with all cre-
> ation is a source of renewal, support, and nourishment. As
> humans we are limited, but in creation we are related.[24]

Wholeness

Closely related to benevolence and relationality is God's intention that creation be whole and harmonious. There is a
Hebrew word for the vision of wholeness which arises out of
God's creation and becomes the goal of God's community and
God's purposes in history. It is *shalom*. Although it is often
translated as "peace" its basic meaning is "wholeness," and it
encompasses all those things that make for wholeness: justice,
unity, well-being, joy, health, relationship, and peace. Walter
Brueggemann begins his discussion of shalom with this apt
description, "The central vision of world history in the Bible is
that all creation is one, every creature in community with every other, living in harmony and security toward the joy and
well-being of every other creature."[25]

Although the term *shalom* does not itself appear in the creation narratives of Genesis it is clear that the shalom vision is
understood in imagery rooted in the creation tradition.

> I will make with them a covenant of peace (*shalom*) and banish
> wild animals from the land, so that they may live in the wild and
> sleep in the woods securely. I will make them and the region
> around my hill a blessing; and I will send down the showers in
> their season; they shall be showers of blessing. The trees of the
> field shall yield their fruit, and the earth shall yield its increase.
> They shall be secure on their soil. . . . They shall no more be
> plunder for the nations, nor shall the animals of the land devour
> them; they shall live in safety, and no one shall make them afraid.
> I will provide for them [plantations of shalom]. (Ezek. 34:25–29a
> [reading last phrase with LXX]; see also Lev. 26:4–6)

It should be clear in the interrelated creation we have described that the shalom God intends for the creation extends

to nonhuman creation as well as the human. An Israelite proverb proclaims, "The LORD has made everything for its purpose" (Prov. 16:4), and God cares for the wholeness of everything. Thus, when wholeness is denied to any part of creation we are all thereby diminished. For God, the human does not automatically take precedence over the nonhuman. "If you besiege a town for a long time, making war against it in order to take it, you must not destroy its trees by wielding an ax against them. Although you may take food from them, you must not cut them down. Are trees in the field human beings that they should come under siege from you?" (Deut. 20:19).[26]

The shalom vision of harmonious unity and wholeness arises out of an understanding of the order God intended in creation. "This order, however, is not that of Greek *kosmos*, harmonized by reason, but rather a divinely decreed order within which each creature fulfills the Creator's will."[27] As we shall see later, what breaks this wholeness of creation opposes the will of God as Creator.

Tied to History

In 1936 Gerhard von Rad wrote an influential essay that advanced the view that "because of the exclusive commitment of Israel's faith to historical salvation, the doctrine of creation was never able to attain to independent existence in its own right."[28] The influence of von Rad's argument led many to accept a radical subordination of Israel's creation faith to its salvation history. This frequently led further to a complete neglect of the creation traditions as only secondarily important. The result has often been a complete separation of creation and redemption traditions as if they were unrelated until Deutero-Isaiah.

Already in our discussion we have begun to see that God's work as Creator is a necessary foundation for understanding God's work as Deliverer. The Deliverer is the Creator, and the divine purposes in creation and deliverance are in harmony and mutually supportive.

It must be said unequivocally that in the Old Testament God's work of creation is related to God's work of salvation in history and not in a secondary fashion. As the canon now stands the beginning of God's calling forth of Israel in the promise to Abraham (Gen. 12:1–3) comes out of concern for the brokenness of creation by sin. Throughout Israel's story

God continues to appear as Creator. Israel itself is God's creation, and the Davidic kingship reflects God's created order over against the threat of chaos. Psalm 136 is an authentic reflection of Israel's doxology; it begins with praise of God as Creator and moves to praise of God as bringer of salvation in Exodus deliverance.

In Israel's faith the realms of nature and history do not stand separated but are joined by the activity of the same God who is Lord of creation and history.[29] This means that for Israel creation faith is never a retreat from social reality. It is in understanding God's intention for the wholeness and integrity of the created order that the community of faith orders its own activity in pursuit of God's purposes in the world. Human interest and responsibility cannot be drawn narrowly but must account for the interrelatedness of God's creation. As George Landes points out in a strong essay on this subject, "Radically to divorce creation from liberation can also mean to lose the perspective of the total arena in which the Creator-God's liberation power is at work."[30]

Distortions of Creation Theology

With this fuller understanding of the character of God's creation we can identify two distortions of Old Testament creation theology which have exerted wide influence in the church and must be repudiated.

1. The first is the distortion of hierarchical thinking.[31]

We do not mean hierarchy as a simple synonym for order, but as that form of thinking in which reality is seen as discrete orders of creation each sharply separated from the others and assigned moral worth on a hierarchy from lower to higher. Highest, of course, is God whose character is spirit; lowest are the material things of the earth itself. Humanity occupies the level just below God, and is therefore more spiritual and of greater moral value than other creatures and the rest of inanimate nature. Moral aspiration is toward God; moral degradation is toward nature. Theologies stressing the hierarchical ordering of creation have often drawn heavily on Genesis 1 and Psalm 8, but they have not read these texts within their own Hebrew context. The Old Testament certainly does not understand reality in terms of a radical separation of material and spiritual.[32]

The dangers of devaluing nature and supporting its exploitation for human ends are obvious, but this hierarchical view of creation is also at the root of other forms of injustice and oppression. By the time of Paul (1 Cor. 11:7) creation in the image of God had come to be applied to men only. (We will discuss "image of God" and "dominion" in Gen. 1 later in this chapter.) In much of Christian tradition women were said to be farther down the hierarchical scale and farther from God— more earthy, less spiritual. Slavery was justified by arguing that dark-skinned races were of a lower order and farther from God. Persecution of Jews was considered punishment for the racial sin of deicide which had placed them lower on the scale and far from God. In the medieval law codes, to kill a Jew was punishable by the same penalty as for poaching the king's deer. Put simply, this false hierarchical understanding of creation is one of the foundation stones of racism, sexism, anti-Semitism, and exploitation of nature. It could not be further from the Hebrew understanding of creation as interrelated and characterized by shalom.

2. We must also warn against the danger of overromanticizing the relationship of humanity to nature. In a commendable effort to avoid hierarchical patterns some scholars have stressed the oneness of all creation to the point that we lose sight of the unique roles of the various parts of God's creation. This is especially dangerous when we fail to acknowledge the special capacities and responsibilities of human beings in the created order. We will discuss this further in the following section, but here we simply note that the human capacity for decision making and exercise of power is unique.

Theologically we must take seriously the human capacity for sin. "Humans can sin, nature cannot, but both must suffer the consequences."[33] While biblical creation faith stresses the interrelatedness and wholeness of creation, it also stresses the special commission of responsibility given to men and women in the midst of creation, and the misuse of that responsibility. We must move now to a fuller discussion of the special role of the human in God's creation.

The Human Role in Creation

Both of the creation stories in the opening chapters of Genesis give a special place and responsibility in creation to God's human creatures, and stress that this role is given to both women and men. However, each uses different images and emphases, and their contributions to a biblical understanding of the meaning of our humanness must be discussed separately but complementarily. Few biblical texts are more important for grasping the biblical understanding of humanity as moral being than Gen. 1–3.

Image of God and Stewardship

1. Human creatures are given a special place in God's creation. Unlike the orders created earlier, God voices special intentions and purposes in the creation of humanity (Gen. 1:26). In the actual act of creation the special verb *bara'* is used three times for human creation (v. 27), and it is only to these human creatures that God speaks directly (vs. 28–30). This special place is highlighted in Ps. 8:5 (Heb. 2:7), "Yet you have made them a little lower than God, and crowned them with glory and honor." It is important to note that special role does not mean special valuing by God. Humanity and all the rest of creation are simply pronounced "good" in the eyes of God.

2. "So God created humankind (*'adam*) in his image, in the image of God he created them; male and female he created them" (Gen. 1:27). The term "image" (*selem*) is further qualified in v. 26 by the term "likeness" (*demut*), which is also used in 5:1 to describe God's human creation. The basic meanings of these terms have to do with representations or models. This terminology cannot be read to indicate some aspect of the divine within humanity (soul, spirit, rationality, will, etc.). It is the whole of our being that is somehow like God, and this quality is passed on through procreation as Gen. 5:1–3 makes very clear in the birth of Seth (cf. also 9:6). "*'adam* [is] God's own special representative, not simply by designation (command), but by design (nature or constitution)—i.e., as a representation of God."[34]

Outside of the primeval history in Genesis the theme of creation in the image of God is not mentioned in the Old Testament although it becomes enormously important in subsequent Jewish and Christian interpretation.[35] The real meaning of creation in the image of God is to be found in ancient Near Eastern parallels outside the Old Testament where the phrase is associated with royal ideology.[36] It was von Rad who fully developed the view that "image of God" pointed more to human purpose than being—more to teleology than ontology.

Just as powerful earthly kings, to indicate their claim to dominion, erect an image of themselves in the provinces of their empire where they do not personally appear, so man is placed upon earth in God's image as God's sovereign emblem. He is really only God's representative, summoned to maintain and enforce God's claim to dominion over the earth. The decisive thing about man's similarity to God, therefore, is his function in the non-human world.[37]

In this connection it is important to note that God's resolve to create in the divine image is coupled with a commissioning to have dominion (Gen. 1:26, 28). We will return to this commission at a later point.

Unlike the images of earthly kings, the image of the sovereign Creator is not to be a fixed image. Walter Brueggemann has noted the connection of this imaging of God in human creation with the prohibition of divine images in the Decalogue.

There is one way in which God is imaged in the world and only one: humanness! This is the only . . . part of creation which discloses to us something about the reality of God. . . . God is not imaged in anything fixed but in the freedom of human persons to be faithful and gracious. The contrast between *fixed images* which are prohibited and *human image* which is affirmed represents a striking proclamation about God and about humanness.[38]

3. Humanity is created with sexuality as a part of creation's goodness. The phrase "male and female he created them" (Gen. 1:27b) uses the biological terms for male and female (*zakar, neqebah*) and not the social terms man/husband, woman/wife (*'iš, 'iššah*). Both are created together; both participate in the image of God; both are commissioned together to function in the creation. There is nothing in this witness to suggest less than absolute equality in creation for men and women.[39] Since the pronoun shifts to the plural at this point ("them") the text also suggests that our unity in God's image includes community in our sexuality.[40]

Sexuality is not, however, a part of the identity of God. Nothing in the text syntactically allows the presence of sexual differentiation in God's human creation to be read as a duality in the nature of God. "Unlike God, but like the other creatures, *'adam* is characterized by sexual differentiation. . . . *'adam* is created like (i.e., resembling) God, but as creature, and hence male and female. . . . The second statement adds to the first; it does not explicate it."[41]

4. It is clear that the creation of humankind is not an end in itself but for the sake of commissioning to special purpose in the creation. Creation in the image of God and as male and female is in preparation for the discharge of mission within the created order, and to empower them in this mission God blesses them (Gen. 1:28).

Creation as male and female empowers humankind to fulfill the commission to populate the earth, "Be fruitful and multiply, and fill the earth" (Gen. 1:28). Procreation is a part of the divine intention for humanity. The specific command has to do with the beginning of human community in the world. It does not get used in the Old Testament to limit the purposes of sexuality only to the procreative (cf. the Song of Songs which celebrates the joy of human sexual relationship for its own sake).

The command to have dominion *(radah)* actualizes the divine intention already stated in Gen. 1:26, where the link between creation in the image of God and the charge to dominion is even clearer. It is as representative (image) of God that we are given capacity for power in the world. This is not the granting of an absolute human prerogative to do with the earth what we will. If the term "dominion" has royal connotations of rule, it is as representatives of divine rule that we exercise authority. We are not absolute monarchs in the world but trustees or stewards acting in behalf of God's sovereignty as Creator. Thus, the implied moral norm is a measuring of human actions by reference to their faithfulness in reflecting God's will and ultimate rule. The implication is that some measure of knowing this is built into the nature of the creation, suggesting a notion of natural law lying behind whatever specific Israelite moral traditions are put forth later in the canon.

It has become common to charge the Judeo-Christian tradition in its image of dominion over the earth with central responsibility in the modern ecological crisis.[42] To the extent that the history of interpretation has wrested this commission to dominion out of its context in relation to the image of God this criticism is justified. However, it is not an authentic reading of this text nor does it recognize a long tradition of Christian stewardship with respect to the earth which stands alongside of and critical of any perspective that allows the exploitation of the creation for narrow human purposes.[43]

Free Will and Responsibility

1. The Yahwist narrative in Gen. 2:4b–25 also gives a special place to humankind in God's creation. In fact, the narrative begins with human creation and builds the rest of creation around that creature. The result is a web of interrelated creation but with humanity at the center. Even the mode of human creation emphasizes a unique intimacy between Yahweh and the *'adam*—fashioned from dust and animated with the divine breath (Gen. 2:7).

2. In the Yahwist account the gifts of God's care bring with them responsibility. Plants are made to grow in the garden for beauty and food (acknowledging aesthetic as well as biological needs, Gen. 2:9), but the *'adam* must till and protect the garden (v. 15). The animals, created in a first divine response to the human need for companionship, are brought to the *'adam* for naming (vs. 18–20). This is an act of authority but one that implies responsibility of the namer for the welfare of that which is named (as a parent with a child). With respect to what we call nature it is clear that humanity is given a vocation to act with authority in behalf of the care of creation, God's gift.

3. Creation in the garden also includes sexuality. Initially God creates a creature named only with the generic term for all humankind, *ha'adam* (the text includes the definite article). In her important work on this account Phyllis Trible translates this as "the earth creature" to make visible the relationship to the soil (*ha'adamah*) from which the human was created.[44] She further argues that this includes within it the possibilities of male and female (she has moved away from the term "androgynous") which become actualized only when a portion of the *'adam* is taken and from it is fashioned woman (Gen. 2:21–24). Only at this point are the specific terms "man" (*'iš*) and "woman" (*'iššah*) introduced (v. 23). There are some ambiguities: the poem in v. 23 states that woman was taken out of man; the term *'adam* continues to be used but now in a sense clearly indicating an individual man, and later as a proper name for the man. This has led some scholars to reject Trible's interpretation.[45] Regardless of the ambiguity here several points are clearly in Trible's favor. God does not begin a new creature by taking up dust. It is a portion of the initial creature which is taken. This seems clearly to imply differentiation within the initial creation regardless of argument over the initial gender of that human creature. Further, the response of

the man when confronted with the woman is to sing of the same substance from which both came, "This at last is bone of my bones and flesh of my flesh" (v. 23). The text further comments that in committed sexual relationship they reexperience that oneness of flesh (v. 24).

In Gen. 1 sexuality seemed clearly related to procreation and the biological designations of male and female were used. In the Yahwist account the emphasis is on sexuality as what makes personal and social relationship possible—the basis of community. Procreation may be implied in the formation of a marital union suggested in Gen. 2:24, but the initial impetus for introduction of sexuality into creation was to find a partner or a companion (*'ezer*) for the *'adam*. In "the Yahwistic account of creation . . . the primary meaning of sexuality is seen in psycho-social, rather than biological, terms. Companionship, the sharing of work, mutual attraction and commitment in a bond superseding all other human bonds and attractions—these are the ends for which *'adam* was created male and female and these are the signs of the intended partnership. . . . The intended partnership implies a partnership of equals, characterized by mutuality of attraction, support and commitment."[46]

Genesis 2:25 says simply that the man and the woman "were both naked, and were not ashamed." Relationship, including the sexual dimension, is not yet clouded by shame—or fear, or guilt, or any of those other qualities which we know as the signs of broken relationship. We were created for relationships of openness and wholeness, and our sexuality is a part of that intended creation.

4. In the midst of the garden God planted the tree of the knowledge of good and evil (Gen. 2:9)[47] and commanded that its fruit not be eaten, with death as the penalty (vs. 16–17). In this manner, the Yahwist introduces the important affirmation that God has created humanity with free will. God takes the risk of allowing a choice to be made for obedience or disobedience. No time is spent in Gen. 2 giving any clue to the character of the "tree of the knowledge of good and evil."[48] What is important here is the capacity to choose and the responsibility to accept the consequences of that choice. Within the larger story of human purpose within creation is established a marker of human limitation, and because God has explicitly commanded it, the choice is one of moral choice—obedience to God or disobedience. The implication is that God the Cre-

ator has given us the expansiveness of created human capacities for life and relationship, but also has given us boundaries of duty within our humanness, and the freedom to make choices about those boundaries. It is this freedom which makes genuine relationship possible, to God and to others. Without this freedom, our interrelatedness would be no more than the biological connectedness of ecosystems. With this freedom, the morality of choices is dictated by what we can know of God's will.

Creation as Broken and Redeemed

Both the priestly and the Yahwist traditions know that creation did not stay as God intended but has been disturbed and broken by human sin. Each has a different way of treating this disruption in God's creation and the two perspectives have now been combined in the present shape of Gen. 1–11.[49]

The Yahwist narrative of creation is followed immediately by the story of disobedience to God's command which breaks the harmony of creation (Gen. 3). In the major episodes of the Yahwist primeval history sin, now unleashed in the world, continues to escalate. The priestly tradition notes the spread of violence (Gen. 6:11–13) as a prelude to the flood story when God nearly "uncreates" the world, only to renew and guarantee the creation in Gen. 9. Both traditions speak not only of the sin which disrupts creation but of God's grace which enables life to go on in spite of sin.

Sin and Brokenness

1. The first testimony to the nature of sin which we encounter in the Hebrew Bible is not the story of failure to fulfill the possibilities for which we were created. Genesis 3 is the story of an overreaching of our own human limitations to try for the prerogatives of God ("You will be like God," Gen. 3:5). The nature of sin here is that of pride and arrogance, and since God had made specific command that this boundary be observed, it is disobedience as well. The temptation which the serpent, one of God's creatures (v. 1), voices is to "be like God, knowing good and evil" (v. 5).[50] This should not be confused with a desire to have moral discernment. To know (*yada'*) in Hebrew is not limited to the cognitive sphere. Its meaning is close to that of experiencing or participating in

that which is known. Good and evil encompass all possibilities of benefit and detriment. The temptation is to experience all possibilities, as does God, without regard to limits.

The priestly tradition is less concerned to indicate the nature of sin than to focus on its consequences. In Gen. 6:11–13 it is simply reported that the world has become "corrupt" and "filled with violence." The role of the trustee, responsible for the care of creation, has been abandoned to activity which does violence to the ordered creation God intended. One must assume that among the most repugnant elements of this violence is the taking of human life. In the renewal of creation after the flood God finds it necessary to promulgate an absolute law against the taking of human life because it does violence to the image of God in which humans are created (Gen. 9:5–6).[51]

It is clear that in both priestly and Yahwistic traditions sin relates to the failure to uphold and honor the roles and boundaries given to humanity in God's creation. Perhaps in the Yahwist this might be described as an attempt to pridefully reach beyond the human, while in the priestly tradition it is a collapse into the subhuman, a state of violence that falls far short of what those created in the image of God are to be. Within this framework of moral hubris and moral collapse further understandings of the nature of sin will be developed at later points in the canon.

2. In Gen. 3 the consequences of sin are immediate. What the man and the woman immediately know (experience) is their own nakedness (Gen. 3:7). In quick succession they are so ashamed that they attempt to clothe themselves, they are so afraid at the sound of God in the garden that they hide themselves, and they are so unwilling to accept responsibility for this disobedient act that they try to blame another (vs. 7–13). Shame, fear, and guilt enter the human story as signs of the brokenness wrought by our own disobedience. The harmonious wholeness of God's creation is now disrupted and broken. In the curses pronounced by God (vs. 14–19) we may hear the ancient community's recognition that some of the world's realities are not in harmony with their understanding of what God's creation intended. Men should not have to struggle with the soil from which they are formed. Women should not experience pain in the process of giving new life. Perhaps most interesting in the light of modern moral issues relating to the roles of men and women is the recognition of the husband's

rule over the wife as an evidence of broken creation. "The sign of this disturbed relationship is this, that while the woman's relationship to the man is characterized by desire, the man's relationship to the woman is characterized by rule. The companion of chapter 2 has become a master."[52]

It should also be noted that the tradition of Gen. 3 knows only of the equal responsibility of the man and the woman before God. Each has acted in disobedience and must suffer the consequences of that act. This stands in absolute contradiction to the tradition of the woman as responsible for sin while the man was innocent (cf. 1 Tim. 2:13–15).

As a consequence of sin in the priestly tradition, the world was almost uncreated by God. It is the waters of chaos (Gen. 7:11; 8:2) which crash in upon the earth. In the priestly conception of creation chaos is always controlled by the continuing creative power of God, establishing the order of the world over against chaos. In the covenant with Noah, God promises never again to threaten that order, but the implication is that whenever we refuse or disrupt the order of God's creation we run the risk of chaos as a consequence. From minute to massive issues, humanity continues to know the reality of chaos as a threat to God's creation, and the capacity of our sin to make the experience of chaos and the disruption of God's order a reality in our lives. It is in relation to the threat of nuclear war in our time that we have had to realize that God's promise not to uncreate the world carries no guarantee that in our sinfulness we might not do so.

3. For the Yahwist, disobedience in the garden is but the first episode in an escalation of sin which tragically unfolds throughout the primeval history.[53] In the tragedy of Cain and Abel (Gen. 4:1–16) sin moves from personal disobedience to take the life of a brother. In the flood story (chs. 6–8) wickedness has become so universalized that "every inclination of the thoughts of [human] hearts was only evil continually." In the episode on the Tower of Babel (11:1–9) the arrogant desire to "make a name for ourselves" launches an assault on the heavens themselves with a tower to give humankind heavenly access.

Each of these manifestations of sin meets with divine judgment: the banishment of Cain, the flood nearly undoing creation, the scattering and confusion of languages. The picture is of a growing gap between God and humanity, and an ongoing reality of creation as disturbed and broken from what God intended.

The combining of the Yahwist pattern of escalation with the priestly pattern of creation, uncreation, re-creation results in a primeval history that preserves the escalating pattern of human sin, but gives the flood episode special emphasis within the pattern. Here it becomes clear that whatever the consequences of sin God will not revoke the creation. Re-creation (note the wind blowing again over the waters in Gen. 8:1 as in 1:2) does not restore the original creation untouched by human sin. Sin continues to be a reality (8:21; 9:2–7), but God's ongoing creation will be reliable.

4. It must briefly be made clear that nonhuman creation is a participant in the brokenness that results from sin. When sin breaks the shalom God intended for creation it is not just a human matter. With the apostle Paul we must understand that in the brokenness of sin "the whole creation has been groaning in labor pains until now" (Rom. 8:22). In the Genesis narratives the man and the woman are separated from the harmonious garden (Gen. 3:24), the harmony with the soil is broken ("cursed is the ground because of you," vs. 17–18), the ground cries out with Abel's blood (4:10), and it is the whole of creation almost destroyed in the flood. Throughout the Hebrew biblical tradition sin is treated as something that disturbs the whole of God's created order and not just the relationship between God and humanity. "Therefore the land mourns, and all who live in it languish; together with the wild animals and the birds of the air, even the fish of the sea are perishing" (Hos. 4:3).

Grace and Redemption

Fortunately the primeval history which opens the canon speaks not only of the reality of sin and its consequences but also of the reality of God's grace making redemption possible even in the midst of sin.

God is, of course, acting in the role of judge, exacting the consequences of sin. Yet, alongside the role of judge continually appears God, the caregiver. God lovingly clothes the man and the woman (Gen. 3:21); God places a mark to protect Cain (4:15); God not only saves Noah but guarantees the natural order and enters covenant around that promise (8:20–9:17).

Finally, and dramatically, the narrative shifts in Gen. 12:1–3 out of the realm of universals common to the primeval history to begin the story of Abraham and Sarah and the people who are descended from them—Israel. The testimony to God's creation and the tragedy of broken creation are important in their own right, but they also stand connected to the story of a particular people, beginning with Abraham and Sarah, who understand themselves as called into being to play a part in God's redemptive purposes for a broken creation. The discussion of this next movement in the drama is the subject of the next chapter. God the Creator is also to be revealed as God the Redeemer, and the story of Israel is to be understood as a part of God's redemptive work.

Just as creation participates in the consequences of sin, so too is creation a beneficiary of God's redemption. Redemption does not have only to do with God's relationship to the human. "Unless we see human life lived in a vacuum, redemption must involve the rest of nature as well because redemption is precisely God's effort to restore the whole network of relationships that have been broken by sin."[54]

New creation is a common way of picturing the redeemed world toward which God is working. Creation faith and salvation history come together in portraits that show a renewed nature rejoicing in the salvation of God's people.

> For you shall go out in joy,
>   and be led back in peace (_shalom_);
> the mountains and the hills before you
>   shall burst into song,
>   and all the trees of the field shall clap their hands.
> Instead of the thorn shall come up the cypress;
>   instead of the brier shall come up the myrtle.
>   (Isa. 55:12–13)

The final fulfillment of God's purposes in history is often pictured in new creation terms, such as the vision of the peaceable kingdom in Isa. 11:6–9. It is not, therefore, surprising that the early church chose to speak of Jesus Christ and new life in Christ as the experience of new creation. In Christ as new creation, "the creation itself will be set free from its bondage" (Rom. 8:21).

It is not accidental that the Old Testament opens with the expansive witness to God as Creator and all things as God's creatures. Nor is it unintentional that we should be reminded by the narrative that the reality of a world broken by sin is not the world God intended. We are reminded that God as Creator still sustains that creation, but we are given our first glimpses of a God who also chooses to be active within creation for the sake of redeeming it. This is the necessary prelude if we are to place in proper perspective the calling forth of a people to play a part in God's redemptive drama.

Notes

1. The most recent and thorough commentary on this material is Claus Westermann, *Genesis 1–11: A Commentary*, trans. John J. Scullion (Minneapolis: Augsburg Publishing House, 1984). The commentary by Gerhard von Rad, *Genesis, A Commentary*, rev. ed., trans. John H. Marks, OTL (Philadelphia: Westminster Press, 1973), has become a classic and is still valuable for its theological acumen.

2. Confusion over this continues to make for controversy. "Scientific creationism" is but the latest attempt to substitute the theological proclamations of Genesis for scientific information. The confusion is clear in these words of Henry M. Morris, one of the leading proponents of this view: "The Biblical record, accepted in its natural and literal sense, gives the only scientific and satisfying account of the origin of all things. . . . The creation account is clear, definite, sequential and matter-of-fact, giving every appearance of straight-forward historical narrative." *The Remarkable Birth of Planet Earth* (San Diego: Creation-Life Publishers, 1972), pp. vii, 84. The scientific community has also had those who wish to reduce the biblical testimony to the status of science, albeit outmoded and false science. Sociobiologist E. O. Wilson writes, "The final decisive edge enjoyed by scientific naturalism will come from its capacity to explain traditional religion, its chief competitor, as a wholly material phenomenon." *On Human Nature* (Cambridge, Mass.: Harvard University Press, 1978), p. 192. An excellent discussion of these issues can be found in Conrad Hyers, *The Meaning of Creation: Genesis and Modern Science* (Atlanta: John Knox Press, 1984).

3. In his address to the American Theological Society in 1971 George Hendry took the theological and biblical community to task for ignoring the discussion of creation as origination in favor of stressing only the themes of creation as it relates to redemption or to our creaturely dependence, "The Eclipse of Creation," *TToday* 28 (1972): 406–425.

4. The plural in Gen. 1:26 "Let us make . . ." is probably to be understood as a reference to the heavenly court or the divine assembly. Although known at the time of the priestly writer, even this is reduced to distant background in the narrative's focus on the activity of God. See Patrick D. Miller, Jr., *Genesis 1–11: Studies in Structure and Theme*, JSOTSup 8 (Sheffield: University of Sheffield, 1978), for a thorough discussion of this text.

5. See the helpful discussion in David L. Petersen, "Israel and Monotheism: The Unfinished Agenda," in *Canon, Theology, and Old Testament Interpretation: Essays in Honor of Brevard S. Childs*, ed. Gene M. Tucker, David L. Petersen, and Robert R. Wilson (Philadelphia: Fortress Press, 1988), pp. 92ff.

6. In this regard it is interesting to note that the strongest expressions of overt monotheism come in Deutero-Isaiah which has perhaps the most powerful testimonies to God's role as Creator outside of the opening chapters of Genesis. "I am the LORD, and there is no other. I form light and create darkness, I make weal and create woe; I the LORD do all these things" (Isa. 45:6b–7).

7. There has been considerable debate over the proper translation of Gen. 1:1–2. Some commentators and modern translations (e.g., NEB) have translated v. 1 as a dependent temporal clause ("When God made . . ."). Other commentators and translations (e.g., NRSV, NIV) have continued to translate v. 1 as an independent clause. I believe that the weight of argument is on the side of viewing v. 1 as a preface to the entire account, thus, an independent clause. It is not, however, a description of divine creative activity prior to the action of v. 2 where an uncreated watery chaos is the presupposition. To view v. 1, not as a preface, but as a prior creation out of nothing would force us to think of the chaos itself as divinely created, a notion totally out of harmony with Old Testament understandings. See Walther Eichrodt, "In the Beginning: A Contribution to the Interpretation of the First Word of the Bible," in *Israel's Prophetic Heritage: Essays in Honor of James Muilenburg*, ed. Bernhard W. Anderson and

Walter Harrelson (New York: Harper & Row, 1962), pp. 1–10, reprinted in *Creation in the Old Testament*, ed. Bernhard W. Anderson (Philadelphia: Fortress Press, 1984), pp. 65–73. See also Bernhard W. Anderson, "Creation in the Bible," *Cry of the Environment: Rebuilding the Christian Creation Tradition* (Santa Fe, N.Mex.: Bear and Co., 1984), pp. 30–31.

8. Hermann Gunkel first called attention to the influence of the *Chaoskampf* traditions of the ancient Near East on the Old Testament in his classic work *Schöpfung und Chaos in Urzeit und Endzeit* (Göttingen: Vandenhoeck & Ruprecht, 1895), a portion of which is translated into English by C. A. Muenchow and appears as "The Influence of Babylonian Mythology Upon the Biblical Creation Story," in Anderson, ed., *Creation in the Old Testament*, pp. 25–52. The most thorough recent treatment of this theme is Bernhard W. Anderson, *Creation Versus Chaos: The Reinterpretation of Mythical Symbolism in the Bible* (New York: Association Press, 1967).

9. Anderson, "Creation in the Bible," p. 22.

10. An excellent survey of the stages in the development of Israel's creation faith can be found in Bernhard W. Anderson, "Mythopoeic and Theological Dimensions of Biblical Creation Faith," in idem, ed., *Creation in the Old Testament*, pp. 1–24.

11. Frank M. Cross, "The Song of the Sea and Canaanite Myth," *Canaanite Myth and Hebrew Epic: Essays in the History of the Religion of Israel* (Cambridge, Mass.: Harvard University Press, 1973), pp. 112–144.

12. See Dennis J. McCarthy, "Creation Motifs in Ancient Hebrew Poetry," *CBQ* 29 (1967): 393–406, reprinted in Anderson, ed., *Creation in the Old Testament*, pp. 74–89.

13. This view was first advanced by W. F. Albright and has been carried forward with additional comparative evidence from Ugarit by Cross, *Canaanite Myth and Hebrew Epic*, pp. 60–75.

14. This is a persuasive argument against the influential argument of Gerhard von Rad in 1936 that Old Testament faith was focused almost entirely on redemption and that creation faith entered Israel secondarily and late, probably through wisdom influence. He argued that it had little standing of its own within the Hebrew tradition. The English translation of his essay "The Theological Problem of the Old Testament Doctrine of Creation" appeared in *The Problem of the Hexateuch and Other Essays*, trans. E. W. T. Dicken (New York: McGraw-Hill Book Co., 1966), pp. 131–143, and is reprinted in Ander-

son, ed., *Creation in the Old Testament*, pp. 53–64. We shall discuss von Rad's influential hypothesis further at a later point in the chapter.

15. Claus Westermann, *Blessing in the Bible and the Life of the Church* (Philadelphia: Fortress Press, 1978). See also the helpful discussion of this theology of blessing in Walter Brueggemann, *Genesis*, IBC (Atlanta: John Knox Press, 1982), pp. 36–38. Other scholars have also detected this duality in the Old Testament witness. Samuel Terrien, *The Elusive Presence* (New York: Harper & Row, 1978), has labeled these complementary emphases the ethical and the aesthetic. These correspond in large part to Westermann's salvation and blessing theologies. We must simply object to the use of "ethical" to describe only the one option. There are moral implications for any understanding of God and the divine relationship to the world.

16. Brueggemann, *Genesis*, p. 37.

17. Ibid., pp. 35–36.

18. Claus Westermann, *Creation* (Philadelphia: Fortress Press, 1974), p. 65.

19. Ibid., pp. 61–62.

20. See my earlier treatment, with Larry L. Rasmussen, of a relational theology of creation in *The Predicament of the Prosperous* (Philadelphia: Westminster Press, 1978), pp. 118–125.

21. The Hebrew word *'ezer* carries no connotation of subordination and should not be translated as "helper" or "helpmate," which in English frequently implies a subordinate.

22. Westermann, *Genesis 1–11: A Commentary*, p. 227.

23. In their report to a global conference on the environment, biologist René Dubos and economist Barbara Ward, *Only One World* (West Drayton, Middlesex: Penguin Books, 1972), p. 85, write, "There is something clarifying and irresistible in plain scientific fact. The astonishing thing about our deepened understanding of reality over the last four or five decades is the degree to which it confirms and reinforces so many of the older moral insights of humanity. The philosophers told us we were one, part of a greater unity that transcends our local drives and needs. They told us that all living things are held together in a most intricate web of interdependence. . . . What we now learn is that these are factual descriptions of the way in which our universe actually works." A portion of a famous poem by Francis Thompson (1859–1907), "The Mistress of Vision," has a relevance to ancient witness and modern testimony:

All things by immortal power
  Near or far
  Hiddenly
To each other linked are,
That thou canst not stir a flower
Without troubling of a star.

24. Birch and Rasmussen, *Predicament of the Prosperous*, p. 121.

25. Walter Brueggemann, *Living Toward a Vision: Biblical Reflections on Shalom* (Philadelphia: United Church Press, 1976), p. 15. See also the discussion of shalom in Birch and Rasmussen, *Predicament of the Prosperous*, pp. 146–159.

26. Some would wish to speak here of the "rights of nature." The language of "rights" presupposes some modern legal and philosophical concepts that should not be introduced into the biblical view. We prefer to understand the biblical concept in terms of divine, and therefore human, valuing of nature. This would, of course, have a bearing on modern legal discussions for those who are influenced by biblical values. There are some interesting modern discussions of "rights for nature." See Christopher D. Stone, "Should Trees Have Standing?—Toward Legal Rights for Natural Objects," *Southern California Law Review* 45 (1972): 450–501.

27. Anderson, "Creation in the Bible," p. 31.

28. Gerhard von Rad, "The Theological Problem of the Old Testament Doctrine of Creation," in Anderson, ed., *Creation in the Old Testament*, p. 63 (original publication in German, 1936). See also the sharp rejoinder to von Rad by H. H. Schmid, "Creation, Righteousness and Salvation: Creation Theology as the Broad Horizon of Biblical Theology," in Anderson, ed., *Creation in the Old Testament*, pp. 102ff. (original publication in German, 1973). Von Rad himself revised his opinion somewhat in a 1964 essay: "The greater part of what the Old Testament has to say about what we call Nature has simply never been considered. We are nowadays in serious danger of looking at the theological problems of the Old Testament far too much from the one-sided standpoint of an historically conditioned theology." This appears in English in "Some Aspects of the Old Testament World View," *Problem of the Hexateuch and Other Essays*, p. 144.

29. An especially important and detailed discussion of the relationship between creation and history in the Old Testa-

ment is found in Rolf Knierim, "Cosmos and History in Israel's Theology," *HBT* 3 (1981): 59–124.

30. George M. Landes, "Creation and Liberation," *Union Seminary Quarterly Review* 33 (1978): 85, reprinted in Anderson, ed., *Creation in the Old Testament*, pp. 135–151.

31. Two books that highlight the effects of hierarchical thinking on contemporary justice issues are Rosemary Radford Ruether, *New Woman, New Earth: Sexist Ideologies and Human Liberation* (New York: Seabury Press, 1975), and Elizabeth Dodson-Gray, *Green Paradise Lost* (Wellesley, Mass.: Roundtable Press, 1981).

32. Birch and Rasmussen, *Predicament of the Prosperous*, p. 114.

33. Ibid., p. 117.

34. Phyllis A. Bird, " 'Male and Female He Created Them': Gen. 1:27b in the Context of the Priestly Account of Creation," *HTR* 74 (1981): 138. This important article is also an excellent guide to the voluminous scholarly literature on Gen. 1:26–30.

35. See Paul Jewett, *Man as Male and Female* (Grand Rapids: Wm. B. Eerdmans Publishing Co., 1975).

36. See Bird, "Male and Female," 140–143.

37. Von Rad, *Genesis*, p. 60.

38. Brueggemann, *Genesis*, p. 32.

39. See Brevard S. Childs, "Male and Female as a Theological Problem," *Old Testament Theology in a Canonical Context* (Philadelphia: Fortress Press, 1985), p. 189, and Bird, "Male and Female," p. 159.

40. See Brueggemann, *Genesis*, p. 34.

41. Bird, "Male and Female," pp. 148–150. See also Brueggemann, *Genesis*, p. 33. Contra Phyllis Trible, *God and the Rhetoric of Sexuality*, OBT (Philadelphia: Fortress Press, 1978), pp. 16–21.

42. The classic essay in this regard is Lynn White, Jr., "The Historical Roots of Our Ecological Crisis," *Science* 155 (1967): 1203–1207.

43. See the strong response to White in Bernhard Anderson, "Human Dominion Over Nature," in *Biblical Studies in Contemporary Thought*, ed. Miriam Ward (Somerville, Mass.: Greeno, Hadden & Co., 1975).

44. Trible, *God and the Rhetoric of Sexuality*, pp. 72–143. Trible's chapter on this Yahwist account is centrally important for my discussion at many different points.

45. E.g., Childs, *Old Testament Theology in a Canonical Context*, pp. 189–191.

46. Bird, "Male and Female," p. 158.

47. Mention is also made of a tree of life, but it does not figure in the prohibition of Gen. 2:17 or the story of disobedience in ch. 3. It may reflect some motifs known elsewhere in the ancient Near East (cf. Westermann, *Genesis 1–11*), but in its present form the text uses the tree of life only in 3:22 as a vehicle for suggesting that due to sin, humans were denied unending life.

48. See Malcolm Clark, "A Legal Background of the Yahwist's Use of 'Good and Evil' in Gen. 2–3," *JBL* 88 (1969): 266–278.

49. Several ways of understanding the structural pattern of the primeval history have been proposed. David Clines summarizes three of these in *The Theme of the Pentateuch,* JSOTSup 10 (Sheffield: University of Sheffield, 1978), pp. 61–79. It has been the proposals of von Rad, *Genesis,* and Westermann, *Genesis 1–11,* that have been most influential. See also Gerhard von Rad, *Old Testament Theology*, vol. 1 (New York: Harper & Row, 1962), pp. 136–161. Von Rad has stressed the Yahwist pattern of sin and grace leading up to and preparing us for the story of Israel as the vehicle of God's redemption. Westermann has argued that this subordinates the independent value and witness of the primeval history to the story of Israel's election. His treatment gives greater integrity to the primeval history as finally shaped by the priestly tradition, and values it apart from its connection to the Israelite salvation history. Brevard Childs, *Introduction to the Old Testament as Scripture* (Philadelphia: Fortress Press, 1979), pp. 154–155, has rightly criticized both of these positions as too limited and argued for combining their viewpoints as complementary.

50. See von Rad, *Genesis,* pp. 88ff., for an insightful treatment of these themes.

51. See Bernhard Anderson, "Creation and the Noachic Covenant," in *Cry of the Environment*, pp. 45–61, for a much fuller treatment of the important flood episode than we can take up in this volume.

52. Bird, "Male and Female," p. 158.

53. Von Rad's treatment of this pattern is still a masterpiece of insight. See n. 49.

54. Birch and Rasmussen, *Predicament of the Prosperous,* p. 122.

4
From Promise
to Deliverance

With the movement from the primeval history (Gen. 1–11) to the call of Abraham in Gen. 12 we move from testimony about all of humanity and all of creation to begin the story of a particular community. This community is itself God's creation—Israel, God's people.

In chapter 1 we noted the special importance of community as the context for Christian ethics. It is important as we consider the narratives of promise in Genesis and of deliverance in Exodus to understand that these traditions are testimony by the Israelite community of faith to its own basic foundational identity. Here are the beginnings, the roots, of our own identity as the church. We are a continuation of that ancient community, called into being by the actions of a creator God who was not willing to let broken creation be the final word. To understand more fully the basic testimony of the Genesis and Exodus narratives (and their echoes throughout the canon) is to gain insight into our own character as a moral community.

It is the Exodus event, narrated in Ex. 1–15 and climaxed in the moment of deliverance out of bondage in Egypt through the sea (Ex. 14–15), that is the central experience. This is the birth story of Israelite community, therefore, it is our birth story as well. Such foundational events alter and influence the community's memory and its subsequent experience.[1] Thus, as we will see, the narrative accounts of Ex. 1–15 are shaped by the testimony of the community of faith to the growing meaning of the Exodus experience throughout subsequent generations. Likewise Israel's memory of its own earliest traditions is shaped by the experience of God's deliverance in the Exodus event. From the beginning of Abraham's story through the story of Joseph we are aware of the birth moment of Exodus. The stories of Israel's earliest ancestors and their religious experiences now are arranged in the canon as preparation for the Exodus moment. Mere memory has become promise.[2]

> In a mythical worldview, the event [Exodus] can be explained as fate, but in a theological conception of the world . . . this anticipation is expressed in the language of the Promise. The Promise is not historically prior to the event, just as the Word-account was not contemporary to it. Rather, it follows the event and becomes a new form of "radicalization" in its meaning. . . . The more significance the Exodus event accumulates, the more it appears as having been laid out beforehand in God's plans.[3]

The Promise of Community

In Gen. 12:1–3 God issues both a summons and a promise to Abram.

> Go from your country and your kindred and your father's house to the land that I will show you. I will make of you a great nation, and I will bless you, and make your name great, so that you will be a blessing . . . and in you all the families of the earth shall be blessed.

From this first statement of the promise unfolds a rich drama of Israel's early ancestors and their journey toward the fulfillment of God's promise and the establishment of Israelite community.[4]

The God of the Promise

It is generally agreed that the stories of Gen. 12–50, although they are now shaped by a complex oral and literary history, reflect the roots of Israelite faith in remembered traditions of relationship to a patron deity whose presence and care had already been made known to Israel's ancestors prior to the Exodus experience.[5] Those stories are now told in Genesis from the confessional perspective of a community who know that the God of their deliverance is the very God of their fathers and mothers (cf. Ex. 3:6). The God of their saving was already known to them as the God of blessing in the stories of their ancestral families.

Creation and Promise. The promise, given to Abram in Gen.
12 and reiterated in a variety of forms throughout the stories
of the patriarchs and matriarchs, is given by the same God
who created all things. It is clear in the present structure of
Genesis that we are to understand God's action of promise in
relation to God's desire to bring wholeness to a broken creation ("in you all the families of the earth shall be blessed,"
Gen. 12:3). Thus, the movement into particularity (the beginning of Israel's story) is to be read within the frame of God's
universal purposes (the beginning and well-being of all things).
Our story is not the limit of God's story; ours is but a part of
God's larger story.

Once again, as first in creation, God has taken the initiative.
It is God's grace and not Abraham's merit that is primary in
this summons toward community. The movement of promise
to the stories of Jacob, a self-serving conniver, makes this even
clearer. The Creator now reveals a divine willingness to become involved with the particularities of human history for the
sake of the blessing intended in creation. The Creator will
become also the Redeemer.[6]

Promise and Blessing. The stories of the patriarchs and matriarchs are dominated by the understanding of God as the
source of blessing, an element already observed in the creation narratives (see chapter 3). The stories of Gen. 12–50 are
stories of families and the experience of God in the midst of
family crises and triumphs.

> The meaning of this talk about blessing is that one can relate
> one's whole life, in its course from day to day and year to year, to
> God; one receives from God's hand one's whole life, especially in
> its daily unobtrusiveness. . . . The flow of ordinary daily events
> usually takes place within the family. . . . Therefore the patriar-
> chal narratives . . . have something essential to say about man in
> relation to God and as a creature with all his needs and capabili-
> ties, in growing and maturing, in the increase and decline of his
> powers, in the course of everyday life and in the arc of existence
> from birth till death within the radius of a small circle of people
> which determines the course of the day and of life.[7]

In its earliest form the theme of God's promise was an expression of trust in God's blessing. God promises fertility of
womb and soil, territory for livelihood, reconciliation among
family members.[8] In the present form of the Genesis text,

God's promises point beyond the family life of the ancient ancestors to the Exodus experience and the birth of an entire people (e.g., Gen. 12:1–3; 15:13–16; 17:1–21; 50:24). To the experience of God in the rhythms of family life and its crises is added an experience of God in the course of redemptive history. The God of blessing is inextricably linked to the God of saving in Israel's story.[9] God's promise to the mothers and fathers of Israel points beyond their own immediate stories to the fulfillment of divine purposes which begins with the Exodus experience. This larger theological perspective now shapes the book of Genesis and creates a constant awareness that we have begun to read the story of Israel and God's purposes for that community of faith.[10] This awareness of identity and interrelatedness between the God of our dailiness and the God of creation and history is a special feature of the Genesis stories often overlooked and sorely needed in the modern church.

The Nature of the Promise

Before the promise is articulated to Abram, there is a summons: "Go from your country and your kindred and your father's house" (Gen. 12:1). The promise is coupled with a call to give up those things that make for security by the standards of the ancient world—nation, family, inheritance—to live only by the security of God's promise. That promise has several important elements.

Land. The promise of land does, of course, become identified in the biblical story with the particular piece of geography occupied by Israel as a tribal league and as a nation in later times. "I am the LORD who brought you from Ur of the Chaldeans, to give you this land to possess" (Gen. 15:7). But land also has a much broader role and meaning in the biblical story. As Walter Brueggemann has shown,[11] land has to do both with specific, physical place in the world and with the sense of well-being, security, and freedom which results from the ability to live in harmony with the soil and its gifts, and in peace with one's neighbors. This promise may apply to more than one piece of geography.

In Gen. 12:1 Abram and Sarai are asked to become landless, without place, in trust that God has a place for them. It is important to note that the "land that I will show you" is not named initially. The promise of land has less to do with a specific piece of territory than with trust that the resources necessary for secure physical life and a place in the world that provides those resources come as the gift of God.[12] In fact, it is often in the experiences of being without land that Israel's most creative understandings of God as the true guarantor of our place in the world come to expression.[13] In the exile experience of wrenching dispossession from the land, the exiles are called by the prophet back to this tradition of promise to the ancestors (see chapter 8). "Look to the rock from which you were hewn, and to the quarry from which you were dug. Look to Abraham your father and to Sarah who bore you; for he was but one when I called him, but I blessed him and made him many" (Isa. 51:1–2).

The biblical promise of land is the assurance for those who choose to live as people of God's promise that there will always be a place in the world and the resources to sustain life there.

Progeny. This is the promise of descendants: "I will make of you a great [numerous] nation" (Gen. 12:2); "Look toward heaven and count the stars, if you are able to count them. . . . So shall your descendants be" (15:5). In the immediate context of the story this becomes the promise of a son to Abraham and Sarah, even though they are aged by the time of its fulfillment. Beyond this immediate context is the promise of a people, a community of God's people. It is the promise of a future. It is the assurance to Abraham and all since Abraham that our relationship to God in the divine promise is not exhausted in the momentary course of our own lives but is part of a larger plan of God to bring forth a continuous community of witness in the world. It is not only Israel in the Old Testament story who traces its descent to Abraham, but it is also the church that understands itself as the seed of Abraham (Gal. 3:7; Heb. 11:11–12). In the modern world with its need for harmony in the human family it is well to remember that Jews and Muslims also trace their descent to Abraham, and thus, are with Christians a part of that future which God promises to Abraham.

Blessing. Those who receive and live out of God's promise are not only assured of a place and a future but are given a mission: "In you all the families of the earth shall be blessed" (Gen. 12:3). This theme of divine purpose for God's people is seen, especially in the Yahwist tradition in Genesis (18:18;

22:18; 26:4; 28:14), as central for Israel's self-understanding,[14] and is later used by Peter as a text for his Pentecost sermon (Acts 3:25) and by Paul, who describes it as "the gospel beforehand" (Gal. 3:8).

The calling forth of a particular community of God's people will not be for the narrow purposes of its own blessing, but as God's way of mediating blessing to all peoples. If God is to be experienced in relation to the particularity of Israel's history, it will be for the sake of the universal purposes seen already in God's creation and blessing of the world. This theme, standing at the very beginning of Israel's story, serves as a constant corrective to the exclusivist tendencies which tempt later generations of the faith community. We have been summoned into a role in God's history of redemption; it is not our history that encompasses God.

The Response of Sojourning. God's promise is offered as an unconditional act of God's grace, but the mothers and fathers of the Genesis story (and subsequent generations of the community) must choose whether to trust and live out of that promise or not. Thus, these stories of Gen. 12–50 speak not only of God's faithful promise but of the faith and faithlessness of those to whom it comes.

> The promise is God's power and will to create a new future sharply discontinuous with the past and the present. The promise is God's resolve to form a new community wrought only by miracle and reliant only on God's faithfulness. *Faith* as response is the capacity to embrace that announced future with such passion that the present can be relinquished for the sake of that future.[15]

The life-style of trust and faith in God's promise is described as sojourning.[16] The sojourner (*ger*) is a resident alien; he lives in a place dependent on the hospitality of its inhabitants without full membership and rights in the community. In Genesis the role of sojourner is freely chosen as a part of the journey toward God's promise (Gen. 17:8; 20:1; 23:4). In the text of these stories of the promise the references to sojourning imply a being on the way to somewhere. The promise is not yet fulfilled but a journey toward it is under way. The King James Version sometimes translates this word as "pilgrimage" (Gen. 47:9; Ex. 6:4). The sojourner/pilgrim cannot yet be at home until the journey of God's promise is completed in God's own time.

One moral implication of the sojourner image is that ultimate loyalty among the people of God's promise rests in God and not in the cultures, societies, and institutions of any one setting. One participates in those settings but is not captured by them. It is the revealing and discernment of God's will which serves as the moral norm by which life is lived in various settings where one "sojourns."

Stories of the Promise

Ancestor Stories as Moral Tales. The stories of Abraham, Sarah, Hagar, Isaac, Rebekah, Jacob, Esau, Rachel, and Leah have not often been considered sources of moral insight. Space limitations do not permit us a consideration of individual episodes, but a brief word of encouragement is in order to explore the richness of these stories as moral tales which address central issues of human life in every generation.[17]

These stories are the testimony of the biblical community to life lived under promise and in anticipation of fulfillment. At one level the stories ask, How are we to know that God's promise is reliable? In episode after episode the promise is brought under threat—the failure to have a child, the removal from the land due to famine, the danger to the matriarch, the near sacrifice of Isaac, the death threat to a brother—many of the threats occurring more than once in the course of the Genesis narrative. Each time God's promise finds a way into the future. God's purposes will not be thwarted. The promise is reliable.

At another level the stories are concerned with the human vessels through which God's promise is worked. Abraham "believed the LORD; and he reckoned it to him as righteousness" (Gen. 15:6). Abraham models faithfulness and trust in response to God's promise. Even to God's command to sacrifice his beloved Isaac he responds in obedience (ch. 22).[18] God's promise, however, does not depend for its efficacy on such faithfulness. Sarah laughs skeptically at the news she is to bear a child (18:9–15). Jacob, with the help of his mother, Rebekah, contrives to grasp his own future rather than receive it as God's gift (ch. 27). In numerous ways the stories make clear that God's promise is reliable even if the human vessels through which God works are not. The promise summons us to faithful response, but it will move forward even when we are unwilling and unfaithful.

The stories are also continually about the God who has given the promise. Does this God work mechanically and aloof from our human concerns? The remarkable story of Abraham's bargaining with God over the fate of Sodom and Gomorrah (Gen. 18:22–33) suggests a God who is open and affected by our moral concerns, and is not simply the source of an external and impersonal cosmic morality.[19] If in crises our trust in God's promise is tested, can we be sure that God will provide? The story of the near-sacrifice of Isaac (22:1–19) powerfully witnesses to God not simply as the source of our trials and testing, but as the one who provides the hopeful and creative alternatives in the midst of those crises. If we are unfaithful will God abandon us? The story of Jacob's struggle with the night visitor (32:22–32; 33:10) suggests that, even for a manipulator such as Jacob, God is present in human struggles ("A *man* wrestled with him") in which we might be wounded but through which we see the face of God and hear our name anew. It is sometimes through such struggles that we are transformed and enabled to see the face of God in the face of an alienated brother (33:10).[20] These examples only briefly suggest the richness of these narratives in Genesis as moral tales of life under the promise.

From Security to Bondage. The story of Joseph with which Genesis ends (chs. 37; 39–50) deserves special comment. Taken by itself the Joseph story is based on two concerns: "to describe reconciliation in a broken family despite the lack of merit among any of its members and to depict the characteristics of an ideal administrator."[21] At least portions of this story have been shaped by the concerns of wisdom theology (see chapter 9) to provide a model for seeking wisdom and righteousness over folly and wickedness.[22] In its present context the Joseph story serves a larger purpose in connecting the stories of the promise to the stories of deliverance. It does so, not simply as a matter of geography (How did they end up in Egypt?), but also by preparing us theologically for understanding the experience of bondage which must precede the drama of deliverance.

The Joseph story is about the hiddenness of God.[23] God does not speak or act in an overt manner in this story. Unlike the previous stories of the ancestors the focus is totally on human agency and behavior. It is through the resourcefulness and integrity of Joseph that he endures and succeeds and not through the intervention of God. Joseph does not even pray to God although he uses God's name occasionally. Still, the narrative recognizes that it is God who is operative behind it all, and in the end Joseph voices this recognition, "Even though you intended to do harm to me, God intended it for good" (Gen. 50:20). In the larger context of the Pentateuch we move from stories of God very actively involved with and acknowledged by the early fathers and mothers to a God glimpsed at work behind human events and only briefly acknowledged by Joseph, to over four hundred years of the total hiddenness of God as Israel's ancestors are reduced to slavery in Egypt. No stories of God at work escape to us from this period. The book of Exodus opens with the unspoken question, "Has God forgotten or withdrawn the promise?" In this way the progressive hiddenness of God theologically prepares us for and parallels the descent into bondage.

The Joseph story also bridges to Egypt by giving us a glimpse of the dangers of security apart from trust in God and the roots of oppression which can come from the most well-meaning efforts.[24] The Joseph story has a dark side generally lost in the widespread emphasis by church and society (e.g., the popular musical *Joseph and His Amazing Technicolor Dreamcoat*) on the Joseph story as an "against all the odds boy makes good" story.

In Gen. 47:1–12 Joseph brings his father, Jacob, his brothers and their families to Egypt. Significantly in v. 4 the verbs shift from "sojourn" (*gur*) to "dwell, settle" (*yašab*). As Brueggemann has rightly seen,[25] this, and not the settlement in Canaan, is the first experience of possessing the land and experiencing the temptations to self-sufficiency and pride that come with it. "Joseph settled his father and his brothers, and granted them a holding in the land of Egypt, in the best part of the land" (47:11). From sojourners whose sole security was reliance on God's promise, Israel's ancestors now become dwellers reliant for security on their own landholdings and the powerful position of Joseph.

That this is not to be regarded as true security may be seen in the final portion of the chapter (Gen. 47:13–26). The famine foreseen in the pharaoh's dream comes upon Egypt and the surrounding lands. Joseph as chief administrator receives first the money of those needing food. When money is exhausted he takes their cattle in exchange for food. When there are no more cattle the people come to Joseph, " 'Shall we die before your eyes, both we and our land? Buy us and our land in exchange for food. We with our land will become slaves to Pharaoh. . . . ' So Joseph bought all the land of Egypt for Pharaoh . . . and the land became Pharaoh's. As for the people, he made slaves of them from one end of Egypt to the other. Only the land of the priests he did not buy" (47:19–22). Both land and people are made the possession of centralized power in the pharaoh. The structures of hierarchical authority which recognizes no autonomy of people or resources is put in place by Joseph in his effort to provide security from famine. The result, as the story well knows, is to surrender freedom for security in a manner that ultimately places the very life of the community in jeopardy. It is easy to support authoritarian guarantees of security when one believes it operates to one's own benefit, but the same structures can be turned to other than benevolent purpose and then there is no recourse available. Thus, no more ominous line appears in all of the Bible than Ex. 1:8: "Now a new king arose over Egypt, who did not know Joseph." The Hebrew ancestors are now to be numbered among those who are enslaved as the possessions of pharaoh. To that context of oppression we must now turn as the setting for God's deliverance.

The Birth of Israelite Community

The basic narrative of the Exodus experience is found in Ex. 1–15.[26] It begins with a description of the terrible conditions of oppression under which the Hebrews endured and the birth of Moses, the future agent of God's deliverance. It then proceeds to detail the call of Moses, the struggle with pharaoh, and the final climactic events at the crossing of the sea. This material has undergone a complex literary history,[27] and in its present form represents the synthesized testimony of many generations of Israel to the centrality of this salvation experience as the moment of their birth as a people. The concerns of history and the precise nature of the event itself are therefore obscured.[28] It is the theological affirmations about the character of God, the nature of God's saving work, and the understanding of the community as the recipient of God's salvation that occupy central concern in these narratives.

The witness to the Exodus experience is not limited to Ex. 1–15. Throughout the canon, in every portion except the wisdom literature, is found the continued testimony to the meaning and importance of the Exodus event as the focus of Israel's understanding of itself in relation to God. Thus, we shall draw not only upon the book of Exodus but on the trajectory of the Exodus tradition throughout the canon.

Oppression as Context

It is significant that the story of Israel's birth (and therefore of our birth as a community of faith) begins not in a moment of nationalistic triumph but in a context of slavery and oppression. It was the custom of pharaohs to use prisoners and slaves as forced labor on massive building projects, and the Hebrews are said to have worked in the treasure cities of Pithom and Rameses (Ex. 1:11). The text grippingly depicts the fear of the oppressor toward the oppressed, even to the point of genocidal policy because the Hebrew numbers had grown so great (vs. 8–22). The beginning of community for Israel is an experience that nearly extinguishes hope of any alternative. When Moses speaks to the people in 6:9 the text says "but they would not listen to Moses, because of their broken spirit and their cruel slavery."[29] This portrait of numbing oppression sets not only the social context but the theological context for the events of Exodus. It is not in Israel's own resources that power can be found to oppose the oppressive power of the empire (pharaoh), but it is in the power of God. Therein lies hope in all human situations that seem by human terms to lie beyond redemption.

Even in the midst of oppression there are signs of hope and possibility glimpsed in the story. The seemingly invincible power of pharaoh is thwarted in his genocidal policy by the courage, spirit, and resourcefulness of five women. The Hebrew midwives Shiphrah and Puah defy and mislead the pharaoh, and they contrive to let the male children live (Ex. 1:8–22).[30] Moses' mother and sister save Moses' life by setting him adrift, and he is taken in by the pharaoh's own daughter. His sister then arranges that Moses' own mother should nurse and raise him in pharaoh's own court (2:1–10).

Also important, and often overlooked, is the significance of the Hebrews' own outcry.[31] "The Israelites groaned under their slavery, and cried out. Out of slavery their cry for help rose up to God" (Ex. 2:23b; see also 3:7, 9; 6:5). The verb "cry out" (*za'aq*) implies not only misery but complaint (sometimes

in a legal context). The outcry is acknowledgment that things
are not right and the Hebrew slaves are not resigned to
things as they are. The outcry is the first sign of openness to
the new and hopeful expectation that oppression is not the
last word. "Bringing hurt to public expression is an important first step in the dismantling criticism that permits a new
reality."[32] We must carefully note that the text does not indicate that they cried out *to God*; we are not dealing with
prayer. This already points to a significant element in our
discussion of God's character—the divine responsiveness to
human pain as opposed to divine responsiveness to proper
religious ritual.

We must also recognize the role of the ancient ancestral
traditions we have already discussed as a source of openness to
a different view of things than the social and religious reality
of Egypt. That this memory is still alive in the Hebrew slaves of
our story can be seen in the identification of Yahweh with the
traditions of the ancestors in Ex. 3:6, 15; 6:3 as a basis of
appeal to the people.

> These slaves were conscious of being distinct from the others by
> virtue of a religious tradition that had been kept alive among
> them, a tradition of a God who had related to their ancestors in
> the intimacy of a covenant of promise. This memory was the
> source of the conviction that their present slave status was not the
> inevitable result of divine decree, but an evil their God would one
> day redress.[33]

The God of Deliverance

We have discussed Ex. 1–15 as Israel's birth story; these chapters also introduce us to Moses and his vocation as the agent of
deliverance. Overshadowing Israel or Moses as the focus of this
narrative is the self-revealing activity of God, the Deliverer.
Above all else these chapters are about the identity of God. From
this story can be seen basic aspects of the character of God which
remain constant throughout the biblical story and on through
the centuries of the Judeo-Christian tradition. It is important
that in stressing the uniqueness of the story we not miss the
features of God revealed there which can be generalized for
much of the rest of the biblical witness.[34]

The Freedom of God. The Exodus events represent a decisive revealing of a God of radical freedom. God's deliverance

is not compelled or made necessary; it is unrelated to any special merit on Israel's part (cf. esp. Deut. 7:8). The Exodus experience is an initiative of God's grace, a divine action freely taken for the sake of establishing relationship and community.[35] We have already seen witness to God's free and graceful initiative in the creation of the world and the promise given to the ancestors. This is the most decisive experience of God's freedom and initiative because it is in Exodus that community is established in Israel.[36] Through that lens Israel can then see God's freedom at work before and after the Exodus moment.

In the Exodus narrative the freedom of God is seen particularly in contrast to the gods of Egypt. There the gods are identified with the powerful, the wealthy, and the elite. The pharaoh is himself considered a god. If one sought evidence of divine presence and care in Egypt, one looked to the power centers. In later periods of Israel's history similar identification of the gods with the power structures was found in Canaanite and Mesopotamian culture and religion. The manifestation of divine power in behalf of Hebrew slaves is first and foremost an act of sovereign freedom that represents a searing critique of the state-controlled and manipulated gods of the ancient empires.

> In place of the gods of Egypt, creatures of the imperial consciousness, Moses discloses Yahweh the sovereign one who acts in his lordly freedom, is extrapolated from no social reality, and is captive to no social perception but acts from his own person toward his own purposes. . . . The participants in the Exodus found themselves . . . involved in the intentional formation of a *new social community* to match the vision of *God's freedom.*[37]

There has been renewed and gratifying attention to the importance of this theme of divine freedom in Old Testament theology in recent years, but the tendency has been to treat the freedom of God far too narrowly. Walter Brueggemann, Walther Zimmerli, and others following their lead have discussed God's freedom primarily in terms of the issue of divine presence.[38] God's freedom is seen in polar tension with God's accessibility. The tendency has been to treat accessibility in negative terms stressing human attempts to *control* access to God. This limits the definition of divine freedom to a kind of sovereign aloofness, but God's freedom is broadly related to *all* of God's initiatives of grace.[39] It is in the Exodus experience that we see a divine freedom that is primarily focused on God's free choice to liberate an enslaved people. Yet even in the Exodus story one way of expressing that divine freedom is to evidence divine accessibility—to the unspecified outcry of the people, to Moses and Aaron in their struggle with the pharaoh, and later in Exodus, in the cultic provision of tabernacle and ark in the people's midst. "I will be with you," God says to Moses (Ex. 3:12).[40] Throughout the Old Testament one of the evidences of God's freedom is God's freely given accessibility—in time of trouble, in the cultus, in theophany—but on God's terms. When Israel attempts to make God accessible on its own terms then God's freedom is compromised. The golden calf incident in Ex. 32–34 can be read in this way as can all forms of idolatry, but divinely given accessibility is an expression of divine freedom along with other manifestations of God's grace. The problem with the freedom-accessibility polarity is twofold. On the one hand, it limits the notion of God's freedom to the matter of presence alone when the Old Testament witnesses to God's freedom in a wide range of divine initiatives. On the other hand, it treats accessibility primarily in the negative terms of human attempts to sinfully control God's presence when the Old Testament speaks often of God's free gift of access in many forms. Both God's freedom and God's accessibility are to be affirmed. Their true polar opposites are the domestication (manipulation, control) of God and the hiddenness of God. About these we shall have more to say at a later point (see chapters 6 and 8).

The radical freedom of God made manifest in the Exodus can be seen throughout the Old and New Testaments. Ours is a God who will not be controlled or made subservient to other centers of authority. "I will be gracious to whom I will be gracious," God says to Moses in Ex. 33:19. What is often mistaken in the church for a troublesome expression of divine arbitrariness is really an expression of divine freedom and a corrective to the tendency of religious institutions to define in their own terms who are deserving of God's mercy.[41] The authorities objected to many with whom Jesus associated because they had forgotten the freedom of God to extend mercy to any whom God wills.[42] A radically free God will not be limited to any narrow notion of divine activity, and may be found in surprising ways and places, for example, in the actions of the pagan, Persian ruler Cyrus (Isa. 45:1ff.) or in the unexpected appearance to Job in the whirlwind (Job 38:1ff.). It is to the expression of divine freedom in Ex. 33:19 and in the encounter with pharaoh that Paul returns in reminding the early church that their salvation is by freely given grace and not by their own meritorious works (Rom. 9:14–18).

The Vulnerability of God. God is not only free but has chosen to use that freedom to enter into relationship. Freedom alone could result in the picture of an aloof, uncaring God. But the Exodus story is of a God who freely chooses to respond to human need.

"I have observed [Heb. "seen"] the misery of my people who are in Egypt; I have heard their cry on account of their taskmasters. Indeed, I know their sufferings, and I have come down to deliver them" (Ex. 3:7–8a). In this important statement from God to Moses on the sacred mountain God reveals the divine self as responsive to human need and suffering. Our God "sees" and "hears" our pain. In the face of such suffering God will not remain passive. God becomes active to "deliver" the Hebrews from bondage. Of all the self-revealing statements in this important verse the most remarkable is "I know their sufferings" (cf. also 2:25). The Hebrew verb "to know" (*yada'*) is not limited in meaning to cognitive knowing. Its meaning is much broader than the English verb. It indicates an experiencing of and entering into that which is known. It establishes ongoing relationship. It indicates God's suffering with or participation in Israel's suffering.[43] This is a remarkable testimony about Israel's God in an ancient world much more prone to stress the power of God.

In God's response to the pain of human suffering we see a God whose freedom has been used to become vulnerable to human experience. This vulnerability of God is what James Wharton has called God's freedom for Israel alongside God's freedom from Israel.[44] This is not our customary way of thinking about God. We are much more likely to acknowledge and celebrate God's power than God's vulnerability.

From the beginning point of the Exodus witness there is a continuous testimony in the Hebrew canon to Israel's God not only as one who is sovereign and powerful but as one who has chosen to become vulnerable to human experience. We will see more of this at a later point, especially in the Psalms and the prophets where this theme is expressed by the language of God's anguish, mourning, compassion, and participating presence (see chapters 7 and 8).[45] This theme for Christians, of course, finds its full culmination in Jesus' crucifixion, the fullest expression of divine participation in human suffering. Even here the church often chooses to celebrate resurrection as if its necessary prelude were not the cross and God's suffering there.

The Love of God. Although the term does not appear in the Exodus narratives, God's deliverance of Israel from bondage in Egypt is associated in later tradition with the love of God. This may be seen especially in Deuteronomy and Hosea.[46]

It was not because you were more numerous than any other people that the LORD set his heart on you and chose you— for you were the fewest of all peoples. It was because the LORD loved you and kept the oath that he swore to your ancestors, that the LORD has brought you out with a mighty hand, and redeemed you from the house of slavery. (Deut. 7:7–8)

When Israel was a child, I loved him,
and out of Egypt I called my son. . . .
Yet it was I who taught Ephraim to walk,
I took them up in my arms;
but they did not know that I healed them.
I led them with cords of human kindness,
with bands of love.

(Hos. 11:1, 3–4a)

In many ways divine love in these passages seems to encompass both the qualities of divine freedom and vulnerability that we have discussed. God's deliverance is out of free initiative toward Israel, and the element of participation in Israel's experience is obvious. We suggest, then, that the love of God functions to personalize in relational terms the qualities of God's freedom and vulnerability so prominent in the Exodus traditions. God's deliverance in the Exodus experience establishes relationship with Israel, and that relationship is already characterized from God's side as love.

The Divine Name. It is in the context of the Exodus drama that God reveals the divine name, Yahweh, to Moses and through Moses to Israel (Ex. 3:13–17). We have already seen the connection of this name to creation themes (see chapter 3). The play on words relates the divine name Yahweh to the verb "to be." God is one who "causes things to be," and it is

Israel as a people that is about to be brought into being by God's action.[47] For Israel to call upon the name of Yahweh is to be reminded forever of their own origin as a people in God's gracious and wondrous deliverance.

Terence Fretheim has reminded us that the giving of the divine name is itself an act of intimacy that establishes relationship. To give one's name to another is in a very real sense to become vulnerable to that other in the ancient world.

> Naming entails a certain kind of relationship. Giving the name opens up the possibility of, indeed admits a desire for, a certain intimacy in relationship. . . . Naming entails vulnerability. In giving the name, God becomes available to the world and is at the disposal of those who can name the name. This is a self-giving act of no little risk, for it means not only that God's name can be honored, but also that it can be misused and abused. . . . When God's name is given, this means life, distinctiveness, concreteness, intimacy, accessibility, communication, historicality, identification and vulnerability. One can easily see how speaking the name of God became for Israel a speaking of God's self (see Pss. 20:1; 54:1; 124:8). . . . Thus, "to put the name upon" the people (Num. 6:27) meant that they were God's people in the most intimate sense of that phrase; they were now known as the people of God's name, the people among whom God was truly present, and vulnerably so.[48]

Throughout the Old Testament, God's name is revered and honored as a sign of the intimate relationship established from the Exodus onward between God and people.[49] This was important enough that one of the Ten Commandments was intended to protect the use of the divine name (Ex. 20:7; Deut. 5:11).

God's Partiality to the Dispossessed. God's identification with Hebrew slaves in Egypt reveals a fundamental partiality of God toward the dispossessed. Exodus is but the beginning of a long list of canonical witnesses to God's special care for the poor, the hungry, the oppressed, the exploited, the suffering.[50] Text after text echoes the theme of Ps. 12:5, " 'Because the poor are despoiled, because the needy groan, I will now rise up,' says the LORD; 'I will place them in the safety for which they long.' " God not only cares for the dispossessed but is active in their behalf; "I have come down to deliver them" (Ex. 3:8).

This fundamental predilection in the divine character is the basis for hope on the part of all those who are in need, trouble, or pain. The Song of Hannah, reflected later in Mary's Magnificat (Luke 1:46–55), shows this well:

> My heart exults in the LORD;
>   my strength is exalted in my God. . . .
> There is no Holy One like the LORD,
>   no one besides you;
>   there is no Rock like our God. . . .
> The bows of the mighty are broken,
>   but the feeble gird on strength.
> Those who were full have hired themselves out for bread,
>   but those who were hungry are fat with spoil. . . .
> The LORD makes poor and makes rich;
>   he brings low, he also exalts.
> He raises up the poor from the dust;
>   he lifts the needy from the ash heap.
>
>   (1 Sam. 2:1–2, 4–5a, 7–8a)

In the Christian tradition this aspect of God's character becomes incarnate in Jesus Christ who announces and conducts his entire ministry in keeping with the divine partiality to the dispossessed (e.g., Luke 4:18–19, where Jesus is reading from Isa. 61 to describe his own ministry, and Matt. 25:31–46).

The divine partiality to those in need also forms the basis for a community that shows such partiality in its individual and corporate life.

> For its life as a free people, this community was indebted to the God who chose to take the side of slaves against the "divine" Pharaoh. So long as this primal experience was preserved in memory, it would have a decisive impact on the development of communal values and social structures.[51]

We will discuss the structures of such a community more fully in the next chapter. Let us simply note here the strong suggestion in texts like Isa. 58:5–7, 10 that divine action already models what is expected of us in terms of moral behavior.

> Is such the fast that I choose,
>   a day to humble oneself?
> Is it to bow down the head like a bulrush,
>   and to lie in sackcloth and ashes?

> Will you call this a fast,
>   and a day acceptable to the LORD?
> Is not this the fast that I choose:
>   to loose the bonds of injustice,
>   to undo the thongs of the yoke,
> to let the oppressed go free,
>   and to break every yoke?
> Is it not to share your bread with the hungry,
>   and bring the homeless poor into your house;
> when you see the naked, to cover them,
>   and not to hide yourself from your own kin? . . .
> If you offer your food to the hungry
>   and satisfy the needs of the afflicted,
> then your light shall rise in the darkness
>   and your gloom be like the noonday.

God's Opposition to Evil. Almost as a corollary to God's partiality to the dispossessed is God's implacable opposition to evil in the world—all of those forces that make for dispossession: injustice, oppression, economic exploitation, personal greed, and manipulation of others. In the Old Testament canon we will see this opposition expressed very fully in the preaching of the prophets as God's messengers (the subject of chapter 7), but the roots of this understanding of God lie in the story of God's opposition to the power of the pharaoh for the sake of Israel's freedom. It is persuasive to imagine that the particular pharaoh of the Exodus is not named because the tradition has come to see him not as a single historical person but as the personification of earthly oppressive power, cloaked in its own claims to divinity, yet brought low by the power of Israel's God, our God, whose power is exercised in behalf of "the least of these." In the texts cited above (Ps. 12:5; 1 Sam. 2:1ff.; Isa. 58:5ff.) God's care for the dispossessed is coupled with God's active opposition to that which makes for dispossession.

In the Exodus narrative the confrontation between Moses or Aaron and pharaoh, the plagues, and the Passover (Ex. 5:1–12:51) are the episodes in a dramatic struggle between divine power and the greatest imaginable earthly power. This struggle is undertaken in behalf of those who are powerless to oppose pharaonic power when used to oppress. And God is victorious.

The language is often battle language, and this is sometimes offensive to modern sensibilities. In opposition to evil in the world God appears as a warrior.[52] In the Exodus story the Hebrew slaves are powerless to stand against the military might of the pharaoh. "Do not be afraid, stand firm, and see the deliverance that the LORD will accomplish for you today. . . . The LORD will fight for you, and you have only to keep still" (Ex. 14:13–14). When the victory is miraculously won, Israel can only understand it as God's victory. Exodus 15 celebrates that victory in song by singing of God as a victorious warrior whose earthly victory over pharaoh mirrors the victory of the creator God over the forces of chaos. This same connection between God as Creator and as victorious Deliverer is made in Isa. 51:9–10:

> Awake, awake, put on strength,
>   O arm of the LORD!
> Awake, as in days of old,
>   the generations of long ago!
> Was it not you who cut Rahab in pieces,
>   who pierced the dragon?
> Was it not you who dried up the sea,
>   the waters of the great deep;
> who made the depths of the sea a way
>   for the redeemed to cross over?

The collapse of oppressive power in the Exodus story is painful and violent. Because the oppressor is deaf to any appeal that requires relinquishment of oppressive power, his power is opposed by the greater power of God in the name of freedom and justice. "I know . . . that the king of Egypt will not let you go unless compelled by a mighty hand" (Ex. 3:19). "When Pharaoh does not listen to you, I will lay my hand upon Egypt" (Ex. 7:4). In dealing with the difficult issue of violence here, we must remember that the situation of oppression is already violent (in this case genocidal) by reason of the oppressor. The destruction of the pharaoh at the hand of God represents the oppressor's choice of a violent arena in which to seek resolution of an intolerable human situation.[53]

What of God's "hardening" of pharaoh's heart?[54] The text is of a divided mind. While wanting to protect the sovereignty of God and see the divine hand behind all events, it is still clear that the tradition understands the pharaoh as a tyrant whose own intransigence has sealed his fate, and the fate of many of his innocent subjects. It is clearly also important to preserve the notion of human free will and responsibility (see chapter 3). Thus, the text preserves statements of pharaoh's own "hardening" and vindictiveness alongside statements of God at work even behind the actions of the tyrant (cf. Ex. 5:5–9; 7:13, 14, 22; 8:15, 32; and esp. 9:34, "When Pharaoh saw that the rain and the hail and the thunder had ceased, he sinned once more and hardened his heart, he and his officials").

Imitatio Dei. It has been customary for those treating the Old Testament as a resource for Christian ethics to focus on the concern for obedience to the revealed will of God. This tends to draw primary attention to the themes of covenant and commandment (esp. the Decalogue), and to the prophets. Thus, Thomas Ogletree, in his recent work, limits his consideration of the Old Testament primarily to the Pentateuch (reduced in meaning to covenant and commandment traditions) and the eighth- and seventh-century B.C.E. prophets. "The moral life of the ancient Israelites . . . is bound up with a sense of their concrete history. Within this basic frame of reference, deontological motifs are dominant. What we principally find are specification of those duties and obligations which are requisite to the ongoing life of the people."[55] Although Ogletree notes the concrete historical frame for Israel's covenant understanding, he fails to consider its content or its potential for a different moral norm than obedience to God's revealed commandments.

The history of Israel prior to Sinai and its covenant is presented in the canon as a history of the experience of God beginning with creation and coming to central focus for Israel in the Exodus experience. It is our contention that the character and actions of God in this story are not morally neutral observations. They are put forward as witness to divine character and conduct which is to be reflected in Israel as the people of God.

The community of faith is to live its life in *imitation of God* (*imitatio Dei*). In calling for greater investigation of the notion of imitation of God, John Barton notes Martin Buber's passionate claim, "The imitation of God—not of a human image of God, but of the real God, nor of a mediator in human form, but of God himself—is the central paradox of Judaism."[56] A number of scholars have recently called attention to the importance of the imitation of God as a moral norm in the Old Testament.[57]

Without proper attention to the moral claims of the narra-

tive framework within which the deontological (duty, obligation) elements of covenant and commandment are put
forward we run the risk of falling back into older law/gospel
caricatures of the Old Testament. Prior to the law is a long
narrative through which many elements of the basic character
and identity of the Israelite community are established in relation to understandings of what God has been about in the
world. We surely could not imagine focus in the New Testament on the moral resources of Jesus' teachings without attention to what God is doing and modeling for us in the life,
death, and resurrection of Jesus.

God is not just the source of divine commandment (and
other forms of revelation of the divine will calling for the community's obedience). God has already (before Sinai) acted out
the qualities which the community is to reflect in its life both
individually and corporately. One of the clearest and most direct examples of this type of moral norm in the Old Testament
material is God's statement, "For I am the LORD who brought
you up from the land of Egypt, to be your God; you shall be
holy, for I am holy" (Lev. 11:45).[58]

When we take seriously the self-revelation of God in creation, promise, and deliverance we can then properly understand covenant as response to what God has already done.
Obedience to the commandments of God is not submission to
divine fiat but response to divine grace. The community structured by the effort to discern God's covenantal will is to be in
harmony with the qualities revealed in God's graceful activity
to bring the community into being. The predominantly judicial language of covenant is preceded by the primarily relational language of creation, promise, and deliverance.[59] Both
languages are necessary for a full appropriation of the Old
Testament's moral resources.

Moses as Agent

It is proper to recognize the chief focus of the Exodus story
in the saving activity of God, but we would be seriously remiss
if we did not take note of God's designation of Moses (and
secondarily Aaron) as the human agent through which God
works. Moses' role and influence tower over the events of Exodus and over the formative years in the wilderness after the
departure from Egypt.[60]

It is significant that in the Exodus God's power does not

operate in isolation from human agency. Side by side with the drama of God's wonder-working power is the story of Moses' call to the vocation of liberating agent (Ex. 3–4), his face-to-face confrontations with a dreaded tyrant (Ex. 5–12), his abuse and rejection by an oppressed people reluctant to believe in the possibilities of their own freedom (e.g., Ex. 5:20ff. and 14:10–12), and his mediation of God's power in the decisive moment (Ex. 14:13ff.). If the elements of God's wonders remind us of divine power available beyond our rational hopes, then the role of Moses reminds us of familiar human and social struggles necessary as we live toward and in hope of God's deliverance.

It is important to note that Moses is said to have been raised in an Egyptian context. The agent of God's deliverance is nourished in the bosom of the oppressor.

> This motif reflects a social phenomenon recognized by revolutionary theorists down to our time, namely, that the masses of an oppressed people often are too drained of energy and broken of spirit to effect their own means of escape. A human catalyst, somehow spared from the depths of oppression, is required. Thus Moses, having benefited from a privileged upbringing, and yet having been nurtured within the ethnoreligious traditions of his kinsfolk by his nurse-mother, became the representative who stood firmly against both the grumbling skepticism of his broken people and the Pharaoh's hard heart.[61]

To take seriously the role of Moses is to abandon passive waiting for God's liberating action. Trust in God's promised future requires leadership in ways expressive of that trust and in confidence that God's purposes will be served. It requires involvement in the confrontations and struggles that lead to the freedom God has planned.[62]

The role of Moses also reminds us of struggles in mediating God's power to the liberated. Moses as mediator often stood between God and a rebellious people, demanding faithfulness and obedience from the people, imploring forgiveness and mercy from God. As S. Dean McBride, Jr., suggests, Moses in this role becomes a model for God's people. "Moses transmits to Israel the call of a God of incomparable power, and his intimate access to that power without being destroyed by it makes him not only mediator but model for the formation of a people set apart, holy to Yahweh."[63]

God does not liberate without also calling us to the vocation of liberation. God does not confront the powers without call-ing us to confront them in God's name. The roles of God and Moses are inextricably linked in the Exodus account. "Israel saw the great work that the LORD did against the Egyptians. So the people feared the LORD and believed in the LORD and in his servant Moses" (Ex. 14:31).

Salvation as Liberation

The Exodus story is perhaps the major biblical corrective to a spiritualized notion of God's salvation. God's salvation is liberation from the oppression of a tyrant. God's salvation is-sues forth in freedom within the sociopolitical order. "God did not begin saving in the spiritual order, not even from sin. God saves total human beings whose human fulfillment can be impeded not only by themselves (sin) but also by other human beings who abuse their power or their social status."[64] Both of the Hebrew terms that describe God's saving activity are used here, *nasal* and *yasa'*. Both include God's action to restore to wholeness in concrete, physical, sociopolitical terms as well as God's concern for wholeness in relationship and spirit. Since God's liberation of Israel to new life also establishes new rela-tionship with God and sets the stage for covenant, there is a religious and spiritual dimension to liberation, but it cannot be separated from the wider sociopolitical dimensions of the Exodus.[65]

There would be no better place in scripture on which to test the theological legitimacy of a "theology of liberation" than the book of Exodus. . . . The exodus from Egypt involved political activity in an historical arena for the sake of an oppressed people with the expectation of a new life. Yet Exodus also sets these events within the theological reality of human arrogance, divine judgment, and profound faith in the ultimate plan of God. The canonical shape of Exodus acts as a major deterrent against all forms of quietism, but offers no warrant for the politicizing of biblical redemption into a form of human self-fulfillment.[66]

The dual political-spiritual reality of God's liberation of Is-rael in the Exodus is paralleled by a constant intermixing of the ordinary with the wondrous, the natural with the supernat-ural. God's hand is seen at work in both, and the tradition resists efforts to separate them.[67] Historicist concerns for what *really* happened at the Sea of Reeds are doomed to failure because the biblical accounts themselves are not concerned to separate the so-called natural from the supernatural. As with our discussion on Moses, elements of both human and divine agency play a part, and human and divine agents participate in both natural and supernatural aspects of the story.[68]

Deliverance/Liberation as Paradigm

The full theological and moral significance of the Exodus experience for Israel cannot be grasped if we imagine that we are only seeking to understand the Exodus events in their original context. Already the narrative of Ex. 1–15 is representative of a constant process of claiming and reclaiming the Exodus story as in some sense the story of every generation in the community of faith.

Event and Response. We have already described the Exodus experience as the birth of Israelite community. We can now be more specific about what is constitutive of that community.

Israelite community is formed first and foremost by response to the deliverance the people have experienced at the hand of God and the newfound freedom they enjoy as the gift of God. The community of faith is therefore first constituted as a community of worship, and its initial hymn is in Ex. 15.[69]

The response in worship has a twofold character. Initially and spontaneously it is a bursting forth in *praise*.

> I will sing to the LORD, for he has triumphed gloriously;
>   horse and rider he has thrown into the sea.
> The LORD is my strength and my song,
>   and he has become my salvation;
> this is my God, and I will praise him,
>   my father's God, and I will exalt him.
>
> (Ex. 15:1–2)

The community of faithful response is first constituted in doxology.[70] Praise remained central to the Israelite community of faith. This can be especially seen in the Psalms where praise of God is constantly associated with recital of God's works including Exodus (e.g., Ps. 135).

This introduces the second element of Israel's response in worship which is *recital*. The Song of the Sea goes on to recount in marvelous poetic imagery the story of God's victory over pharaoh at the sea (Ex. 15:4–10). Worship becomes the vehicle for memory in the community of faith.[71] Through recital in the midst of the gathered community the formative encounters with God's grace in its behalf is passed on from generation to generation. This may be seen especially in the existence of several creeds, long seen as central expressions of Israel's basic faith identity. Deuteronomy 26:5–10 is especially revealing since it is to be recited with every presentation of the firstfruits of the harvest before the Lord (cf. also Josh. 24). These creeds give central prominence to the Exodus experience.

It is the constant remembrance of Exodus in recital and praise that keeps the Exodus experience available as a source of hope, but such remembrance is also to be a source of *humility*. "Remember that you were a slave in the land of Egypt, and the LORD your God redeemed you" (Deut. 15:15). In worship through praise and recital Israel is constantly reminded that its very existence is the gift of God. Without the basic foundation of the community in such faithful worship there grow the dangers of pride and exclusivism. More than once Israel fell victim to such dangers and had to be called back to authentic identity. The community of faith from biblical times onward has always found it tempting when it experiences prosperity to attribute success pridefully to its own efforts and worth. Remembrance of Exodus in praise and recital is a reminder of our roots among the dispossessed and the unmerited gift of life by which God constituted us. Exodus then acts as a constant corrective to pride and self-sufficiency.[72]

Event and Meaning. The meaning of the Exodus experience was not contained in the event itself, whatever its character. Exodus did not stay tied to its historical moorings in the past. It became the lens through which generation after generation read its own experience. In so doing each generation added its meaning to the growth of the meaning of Exodus.

J. Severino Croatto is especially helpful in understanding the dynamics of this process for the Exodus. Such foundational events as Israel's deliverance from bondage in Egypt become "reservoirs of meaning." The meaning of Exodus for Israel never resided primarily in the past.

> For the Hebrews the Exodus always signified the ontological origin of their present reality, or it became a challenging "memory" when they ceased to be free. . . . The Exodus is thus not the bald happening that took place around the thirteenth century B.C., but

rather represents the event as it was reflected upon, pondered, and explored by faith and grasped in all its projections. This explains why the narration of the book of Exodus "says" much more than what actually transpired at that time.[73]

Although this process of constant appropriation and addition to the meaning of Exodus may be seen in general by the wealth of Exodus allusion throughout the canon, it is especially evident in Deutero-Isaiah. In this prophet of the exile, remembrance of Exodus becomes the basis of hope for New Exodus (cf. Isa. 43:16–21 where images of deliverance at the sea and guidance through the wilderness are related to God's "new thing" and reference is made to Israel as "the people whom I formed for myself so that they might declare my praise"; see chapter 8).

This process does not end at the boundaries of the canon. The Exodus theme has continued to influence and be claimed by generation after generation of the church and by wide segments of Western society in general. Michael Walzer has chronicled the remarkable influence of the Exodus theme in Western political and social thought. He concludes that, in the West, the Exodus pattern of meaning has shaped the very alternatives among which we choose in shaping our communities.[74]

The Pattern of Exodus Faith. Growing out of the Exodus experience as it is claimed by succeeding generations is a pattern of faith, a paradigm, that may be seen as an Exodus shape to the basic faith of the community throughout the Old Testament, into the New Testament and the subsequent history of the church.

Rooted in the experience of deliverance at the sea, this pattern consists of three elements.

$$\text{Situation of Distress} \rightarrow \text{Unexpected Deliverance} \rightarrow \text{Response in Community}$$

In situations of distress we, like Israel at the sea, despair of hope for any way into the future. Death seems about to have the final word; we can see no possibilities for life. It is the faith growing out of the experience of those who walked through the midst of the sea to new life, that through God unexpected deliverance is made available. In God there is always a way into the future and a further word of life to be spoken over against the apparent finality of death. The shape of God's new future is unexpected and sometimes surprising. This pattern of faith does not mean that people of Exodus faith get what they wish for, but in God there will be a way forward to new life. In response to this word of deliverance out of distress the community is formed in worship and in faithful life. They are a people who know the gift of God's deliverance and the testimony to that gift handed down through generations of the faithful, and this makes a difference in the way they organize their life together and in the world. (We have talked about the response in worship; we will discuss the more comprehensive structuring of faithful community in covenant in the next chapter.)

This pattern of distress, deliverance, and community exerts its influence throughout the canon, but may particularly be seen in the Psalms. The psalms of lament speak movingly of a variety of distresses (both individual and corporate), but as is well known constantly move toward praise in anticipation of deliverance (see Ps. 77 where explicit reference to Exodus is made as a ground for such hope). The psalms of thanksgiving celebrate deliverance and look back on distress. Both genres are part of the corporate worship tradition of Israel which has preserved them for use in the gathered community.[75] These psalm types reflect a pattern of trustful hope which arises first out of the Exodus experience. The same pattern may be seen in many places in the canon, but for Christians it must be suggested that this pattern lies behind the central salvation drama of the New Testament. Crucifixion, resurrection, and Pentecost reflect the christological reenactment of the same Exodus-shaped pattern. Here God incarnate has experienced the deepest distress of the human condition, but unexpectedly the resurrection speaks a word of new life in the face of apparently triumphant death. In Pentecost, a new community has been called forth in response to God's salvation—the church. It is little wonder that baptism is associated in the early church both with resurrection (rising from death to new life) and with Exodus (passing through the waters to new life).

Beyond the numerous explicit references to the Exodus story this foundational experience of Israel's faith has become the source of a paradigmatic shaping of much in the faith understanding of subsequent generations of the biblical communities and the church. Brevard S. Childs concludes his theological treatment of the deliverance at the sea:

The church lives in the memory of the redemption from the past bondage of Egypt, and she looks for the promised inheritance. She now lives still in the desert somewhere between the Red Sea and the Jordan. "Therefore let no one think that he stands lest he fall, but God is faithful and will also provide for us the *way of escape*."[76]

Notes

1. See J. Severino Croatto, *Exodus: A Hermeneutics of Freedom*, trans. S. Attanasio (Maryknoll, N.Y.: Orbis Books, 1981), pp. 15–16, for a description of the dynamics of this hermeneutical effect of the Exodus event.

2. Early meanings to themes of promise as the guarantee of God's presence and purposes in the lives of the ancestors remain visible in the narratives of Gen. 12–50. These stories are, however, now shaped by the larger sense of promise pointing to the Exodus birth of a new people through God's deliverance. See Claus Westermann, *The Promises to the Fathers: Studies on the Patriarchal Narratives*, trans. D. Green (Philadelphia: Fortress Press, 1980), for a detailed and helpful treatment of the various dimensions of the promise motif in Genesis.

3. Croatto, *Exodus*, p. 15.

4. Among the most theologically helpful commentaries on Genesis are Gerhard von Rad, *Genesis, A Commentary*, rev. ed., trans. John H. Marks, OTL (Philadelphia: Westminster Press, 1973); Claus Westermann, *Genesis 12–36: A Commentary*, trans. John J. Scullion (Minneapolis: Augsburg Publishing House, 1985); and Walter Brueggemann, *Genesis*, IBC (Atlanta: John Knox Press, 1982).

5. There have been some recent efforts to date the whole of Gen. 12–50 to the late monarchical or the exilic period. See T. L. Thompson, *The Historicity of the Patriarchal Narratives*, BZAW 133 (Berlin: Walter de Gruyter, 1974), and John van Seters, *Abraham in History and Tradition* (New Haven, Conn.: Yale University Press, 1975). These arguments have not been widely convincing. The evidence of a long history of oral and

literary development seems clearly to extend prior to the monarchy in Israel, and the correlation of historical and archaeological evidence with the picture of society reflected in the ancestral stories of Genesis seem to suggest a background in the early second millennium. On this see W. G. Dever and W. M. Clark, "The Patriarchal Traditions," in *Israelite and Judaean History,* ed. John H. Hayes and J. Maxwell Miller, OTL (Philadelphia: Westminster Press, 1977), pp. 70–148.

6. Although he has organized his work in a different manner, Christopher J. H. Wright, *An Eye for an Eye: The Place of Old Testament Ethics Today* (Downers Grove, Ill.: Intervarsity Press, 1983), has made a constant and helpful use of this basic connectedness between creation and redemption themes in the Old Testament.

7. Claus Westermann, *What Does the Old Testament Say About God?* (Atlanta: John Knox Press, 1979), pp. 44–45.

8. See Westermann, *Promises to the Fathers,* pp. 95–163. "These promises are a component of the patriarchal religion even before any contact with the history and religion of Israel. These promises go back to traditional experiences of the patriarchs Abraham, Isaac, and Jacob in the context of their nomadic way of life. Here they had the function of attesting to the earliest association we can discover between what a god says (promise) and what he does (fulfillment). They were preserved because deliverance from deadly danger or preservation through mortal peril was experienced in relationship to God, as fulfillment of his word. In these promises is revealed the most important analogy between the religion of Israel and the religion of the fathers" (pp. 162–163).

9. Ibid., p. 162: "Clearly recognizable in its early stage in Genesis 12:1–3, in its late stage in Genesis 17 . . . the promises are viewed from the perspective of Israel after its encounter with Yahweh as the God who delivers (exodus tradition). They have the function of bringing coherence into the history of God with his people. The promises given to the fathers provide assurance that the God who promised in the past and fulfilled his promises of the land and of increase will remain faithful to his word, that one can rely for the future on the words and actions of this God. This assurance makes it possible to look back and see Israel's history as a coherent whole and to look forward trusting in God's future actions." See also Paul D. Hanson, *The People Called: The Growth of Community in the Bible* (San Francisco: Harper & Row, 1986), pp. 15–20.

10. "The book of Genesis offers a powerful example of a process of editing in which an eschatological framework was finally allowed to become the dominant force in its shaping." Brevard S. Childs, *Introduction to the Old Testament as Scripture* (Philadelphia: Fortress Press, 1979), p. 158.

11. Walter Brueggemann, *The Land*, OBT (Philadelphia: Fortress Press, 1977).

12. Wright, *An Eye for an Eye*, pp. 46–62, uses land as the central focus of Israel's concern for economic ethics. I consider this too narrow a use of the land theme in the Old Testament since land clearly has sociopolitical implications as well. Wright treats the social dimensions under the theme of Israel as a people. He does bring out well the broad meaning of land beyond mere physical geography.

13. Brueggemann, *The Land*, pp. 6–9, singles out the periods of ancestral sojourning, wilderness wandering, and Babylonian exile as such creative periods of landlessness. In these periods are defined some of the Israelite self-understandings of life as God's people which provide anchor in times of possessing the land and experiencing its temptation to self-sufficiency.

14. See Hans Walter Wolff, "The Kerygma of the Yahwist," *Int* 20 (1966): 131–158, argues persuasively for this theme as programmatically important in Israel's self-understanding.

15. Brueggemann, *Genesis*, p. 106.

16. See Brueggemann, *The Land*, pp. 6–7, on the matter of sojourning.

17. Two works that have consistently and insightfully explored the ethical insights of these stories and their applicability to our own experience are Arthur I. Waskow, *Godwrestling* (New York: Schocken Books, 1978), and Brueggemann, *Genesis*.

18. Abraham is not a complete paragon of virtue. His effort to save himself at the expense of Sarah (Gen. 12:10–20; 20) and his weak and equivocating role in the conflict between Sarah and Hagar (ch. 16; 20:8–18) show him as only too human.

19. See Brueggemann, *Genesis*, pp. 166–177, and von Rad, *Genesis, A Commentary*, pp. 210–215, for insightful treatments of this important text.

20. See the use of this story in Bruce C. Birch and Larry L. Rasmussen, *The Predicament of the Prosperous* (Philadelphia: Westminster Press, 1978), pp. 74–75, and in Waskow, *Godwrestling*, pp. 1–12.

21. George W. Coats, *From Canaan to Egypt: Structural and Theological Context for the Joseph Story*, CBQMS 4 (Washington, D.C.: Catholic Biblical Association of America, 1976), p. 89. Coats's work on Joseph gives access to a remarkable range of scholarship on these chapters and is an important contribution in its own right to understanding the Joseph story.

22. It was Gerhard von Rad, "The Joseph Narrative and Ancient Wisdom," *The Problem of the Hexateuch and Other Essays*, trans. E. W. T. Dicken (New York: McGraw-Hill Book Co., 1966), pp. 292–300, who first directed widespread attention to the ties of this story with wisdom. See the refinement of von Rad's argument in George W. Coats, "The Joseph Story and Ancient Wisdom: A Reappraisal," *CBQ* 35 (1973): 285–297.

23. See Brueggemann, *Genesis*, p. 293.

24. This dark side of the Joseph story is brilliantly exposed in Waskow, *Godwrestling*, pp. 34–42.

25. Brueggemann, *The Land*, pp. 9–10.

26. The most important and comprehensive commentary on the book of Exodus is by Brevard S. Childs, *The Book of Exodus; A Critical, Theological Commentary*, OTL (Philadelphia: Westminster Press, 1974). The influence of this seminal work is found throughout the remainder of this chapter.

27. Our focus will be on the account of Ex. 1–15 as a whole and not on analysis of its sources or the process of its composition. "A literary analysis of sources is frequently of great help in hearing precisely the different witnesses within a passage. However, when the attempt is made to treat the sources as separate theological entities, an assumption of an isolation between sources is at work which runs counter to the canonical traditioning process and which disregards the way the material was used authoritatively within a community of faith and practice." Childs, *Introduction to the Old Testament as Scripture*, p. 177.

28. It is widely agreed that it was during the reign of Rameses II (c. 1290–1224 B.C.E.) that a band of slaves made their escape from Egypt and experienced in the events of that escape the hand of their God Yahweh in deliverance. The lack of concern for historical detail in the Exodus narratives does not allow much more to be said historically, although some background material on conditions in Egypt might be cited. That this was of little concern to the biblical tradition may be seen by the failure to identify the pharaoh of the Exodus in the biblical account. See Hayes and Miller, eds., *Israelite and Judaean History*.

29. Croatto, *Exodus*, p. 17, writes of this verse: "This is not 'infidelity' to grace but a total human estrangement that annuls even hope, the last possibility of liberation. Perhaps this sentence—unique in the entire Bible—has not been given its due attention. . . . But it stands out in all its crushing violence when we 'rediscover' it in so many concrete cases of oppressed people. . . . This is what Paulo Freire makes so clear when he asserts that the oppressed internalize the oppressors—and consequently their own situation as oppressed people—in such a way that they cannot imagine any other possibility nor any change whatsoever that might 'liberate' them."

30. See J. Cheryl Exum, " 'You Shall Let Every Daughter Live': A Study of Exodus 1:8–2:10," *The Bible and Feminist Hermeneutics*, Semeia 28 (1983): 63–82.

31. See Walter Brueggemann, *The Prophetic Imagination* (Philadelphia: Fortress Press, 1978), pp. 20–22; Croatto, *Exodus*, pp. 17–20; and Dorothee Soelle, *Suffering* (Philadelphia: Fortress Press, 1975), pp. 72–74, all of whom stress the outcry of pain and grief as a necessary step toward liberation.

32. Brueggemann, *Prophetic Imagination*, p. 21.

33. Hanson, *People Called*, p. 18.

34. Terence E. Fretheim, *The Suffering of God: An Old Testament Perspective*, OBT (Philadelphia: Fortress Press, 1984), has particularly stressed the importance of recognizing both stories of God and generalizations about God that arise from and help interpret the stories. "Underlying these materials is a certain understanding of the kind of God who has been engaged in such activity on Israel's behalf. . . . Regarding the nature of the discussion of God in OT theology, it must be as attentive to the generalizations as to the history/story. It is the former which makes the latter intelligible and coherent. . . . Israel was both synchronic and diachronic in the way in which it developed and presented materials about God" (pp. 25, 28).

35. A similar emphasis on divine initiative out of which community is established in Israel may be found in Hanson, *People Called*, pp. 24–25.

36. Paul van Buren, *The Burden of Freedom: Americans and the God of Israel* (New York: Seabury Press, 1976), builds his theological consideration of the freedom of God around the three experiences of creation, promise, and Exodus.

37. Brueggemann, *Prophetic Imagination*, pp. 16, 17. Hanson, *People Called*, pp. 21–22, stresses a similar point: "In the deliverance from Egyptian slavery, Israel encountered a God

whose nature and whose corresponding plan for reality stood in diametric opposition to the gods of the Pharaoh. The latter were the divine sponsors of the ruling class, similar to the high gods of the Mesopotamian city-states. . . . In the exodus was revealed the heart of a God whose sovereignty spanned the heavens, but who at the same time embraced the cause of the most humble and oppressed members of society, a God neither impressed with nor influenced by the pedigrees, proud claims, or pompous displays of power, erudition and wealth of kings and other earthly potentates."

38. See Walter Brueggemann, "Presence of God, Cultic," *IDBSup*, ed. Keith Crim (Nashville: Abingdon Press, 1976), pp. 680–683, and *Prophetic Imagination*, pp. 35ff.; Walther Zimmerli, *Old Testament Theology in Outline* (Atlanta: John Knox Press, 1978), pp. 70–81. In *Prophetic Imagination* Brueggemann seems to have moved to a broader definition of God's freedom without seeing that this calls into question the narrower polarity with accessibility.

39. Fretheim, *Suffering of God*, pp. 67–70, has more fully discussed the inadequacies of the freedom-accessibility polarity. He has not fully developed the broader understanding of God's freedom that seems to me needed.

40. This formula is almost always in a context expressive of divine initiative and freedom, but is one of the chief expressions of divine presence and access. See H. D. Preuss, "Ich will mit dir sein," *ZAW* 80 (1968): pp. 139–173.

41. At the particular time of this writing one thinks especially of the attitude of some church people that those stricken with AIDS are not deserving of God's mercy.

42. Note also Jesus' parable of the workers (Matt. 20:1–16) where those who come to work the vineyard late in the day are paid the same wages as those who came early. Like the disciples we often feel this unfair, but the parable is again about the freedom of God to extend mercy even to those who come late to the kingdom. Of course, good church people always suspect they are among the early arriving, hardest workers. In its initial gospel context Jesus was speaking about the Jews and the Gentiles. That makes most of us descendants of the latecomers.

43. See Fretheim, *Suffering of God*, pp. 127–128. Although we have cited this work previously in the chapter, it is in connection with the theme of God's vulnerability that we must call particular attention to this important book. Over against the

usual attention to the power of God, Fretheim chronicles a remarkable Old Testament witness to the suffering of God. Much of what he gathers as witness to this theme would fall under the aspect of God's character that I am treating as the vulnerability of God. This whole section is indebted to Fretheim's work.

44. James A. Wharton, "Theology and Ministry in the Hebrew Scriptures," in *A Biblical Basis for Ministry*, ed. Earl E. Shelp and Ronald Sunderland (Philadelphia: Westminster Press, 1981), pp. 17–71.

45. See Fretheim, *Suffering of God*, pp. 127–137. Fretheim also cites a comment by Abraham J. Heschel that captures this theme well in a discussion of Jer. 12: "Israel's distress was more than a human tragedy. With Israel's distress came the affliction of God, His displacement, His homelessness in the land, in the world." *The Prophets* (New York: Harper & Row, 1962), p. 112.

46. See W. L. Moran, "The Ancient Near Eastern Background of the Love of God in Deuteronomy," *CBQ* 25 (1963): pp. 77–87.

47. The linguistic issues and the interpretive history related to this passage are exceedingly complex, and our brief treatment by no means does justice to this unique and important text. For a thorough discussion and assessment of the exegetical options, see Childs, *Book of Exodus*, pp. 60–65.

48. Fretheim, *Suffering of God*, pp. 100–101. On the significance of names and naming, see also James Barr, "The Symbolism of Names in the Old Testament," *BJRL* 52 (1969): 11–29.

49. This may be seen especially in the book of Deuteronomy where it is God's name that dwells in the midst of Israel as the symbol of God's presence (Deut. 12).

50. The bibliography on this theme is extensive. We can list only a few representative works: Norbert F. Lohfink, S.J., *Option for the Poor: The Basic Principle of Liberation Theology in Light of the Bible* (Berkeley, Calif.: Bibal Press, 1987), esp. pp. 27–52; Gustavo Gutiérrez, *The Power of the Poor in History* (Maryknoll, N.Y.: Orbis Books, 1983); Ronald J. Sider, *Rich Christians in an Age of Hunger: A Biblical Study* (New York: Paulist Press, 1977); Sharon H. Ringe, *Jesus, Liberation and the Biblical Jubilee: Image for Ethics and Christology* (Philadelphia: Fortress Press, 1985); and Bruce C. Birch, "Hunger, Poverty and Biblical Religion," *Christian Century* 92 (June 11–18,

1975): 593–599. See Douglas Meeks, *God, the Economist* (Philadelphia: Fortress Press, 1989), for an important work of systematic theology and ethics that builds on this biblical aspect of God's character.

51. Hanson, *People Called*, p. 22.

52. There has been a broad discussion of warrior imagery associated with Yahweh and the theological issues that arise from such imagery. Especially important are the following: Frank M. Cross, *Canaanite Myth and Hebrew Epic: Essays in the History of the Religion of Israel* (Cambridge, Mass.: Harvard University Press, 1973), pp. 91–144; Patrick D. Miller, Jr., *The Divine Warrior in Early Israel* (Cambridge, Mass.: Harvard University Press, 1973); Millard C. Lind, *Yahweh Is a Warrior* (Scottdale, Pa.: Herald Press, 1980).

53. See Croatto, *Exodus*, pp. 29–30, for a helpful discussion of the issue of violence in the Exodus story seen from the perspective of Latin American liberation concerns. It remains true that concern for the pharaoh and the fate he brings upon Egypt is primarily voiced among those who have not themselves experienced oppression and the violence it unleashes no matter the course of events. For a consideration of issues of violence, war, and peace in the Hebrew Bible, see Bruce C. Birch, "Old Testament Foundations for Peacemaking in the Nuclear Era," *Christian Century* 102 (Dec. 4, 1985): 115–119.

54. See Childs, *Book of Exodus*, pp. 170–175, for a detailed and helpful discussion of this perennial theological crux.

55. Thomas W. Ogletree, *The Use of the Bible in Christian Ethics* (Philadelphia: Fortress Press, 1983), pp. 47–48.

56. Martin Buber, *Kampf um Israel* (Berlin, 1933), p. 75, cited in John Barton, "Understanding Old Testament Ethics," *JSOT* 9 (October 1978): 60–61.

57. See Hanson, *People Called*, pp. 30, 44; Walter C. Kaiser, Jr., *Toward Old Testament Ethics* (Grand Rapids: Zondervan Publishing House, 1983), p. 143; Wright, *An Eye for an Eye*, p. 27; Harry P. Nasuti, "Identity, Identification, and Imitation: The Narrative Hermeneutics of Biblical Law," *Journal of Law and Religion* 4 (1986): 9–23.

58. Because God's holiness does not receive primary attention in the narratives of Genesis or of Ex. 1–15, which are the focus of this chapter, I have chosen to discuss the holiness of God in chapter 5. Additions to our understanding of the central moral significance of the character and activity of God will continue on through the discussion of the entire canon.

59. Alongside imitation of God and obedience to God's will as a source for moral norms there needs to be further exploration of the notion of natural law in the Old Testament. The natural functioning of the order of all things is, of course, encompassed by God's work as Creator, but stories such as Cain and Abel (Gen. 4) and the bargaining of Abraham with God ("Shall not the Judge of all the earth do what is just?" Gen. 18:25) suggest moral principles built into the creation completely apart from the explicit revealing of divine will, or the modeling of God. Likewise, the oracles of Amos (1:1–2:16) against the nations appeal to general standards of morality that are not based in a revealed Yahwistic tradition but are assumed to be generally known and acknowledged by all peoples. See John Barton, "Natural Law and Poetic Justice in the Old Testament," *JTS* 30 (1979): 1–14; F. Horst, "Naturrecht und Altes Testament," *EvT* 10 (1950–51): 253–273; and John J. Collins, "The Biblical Precedent for Natural Theology," *JAAR* Supplement 45 (1977): 39–40.

60. The most thorough and theologically sound treatment of Moses is George W. Coats, *Moses: Heroic Man, Man of God*, JSOTSup 57 (Sheffield: JSOT Press, 1988). See also Dewey M. Beegle, *Moses, The Servant of Yahweh* (Grand Rapids: Wm. B. Eerdmans Publishing Co., 1972), and Gerhard von Rad, *Moses*, World Christian Books (London: Lutterworth Press, 1960).

61. Hanson, *People Called*, p. 18.

62. See Croatto, *Exodus*, pp. 21, 27–28, for a discussion of the importance of this theme in a liberation hermeneutic.

63. S. Dean McBride, Jr., "Transcendent Authority: The Role of Moses in Old Testament Traditions," *Int* 44 (1990): 229.

64. Croatto, *Exodus*, p. 18.

65. Exodus is, of course, central to the many expressions of liberation theology, and from the beginning the best of the liberation works have recognized in the Exodus event the coming together of sociopolitical and spiritual concerns, both being necessary for the wholeness and freedom God intends for all people. See esp. James Cone, *A Black Theology of Liberation* (Philadelphia: J. B. Lippincott Co., 1970), and Gustavo Gutiérrez, *A Theology of Liberation: History, Politics and Salvation* (Maryknoll, N.Y.: Orbis Books, 1973). See Croatto, *Exodus*, p. 27, for a biblical theology of salvation as liberation. For a complete exegetical treatment of the book of Exodus from the

perspective of liberation concerns, see George V. Pixley, *On Exodus: A Liberation Perspective* (Maryknoll, N.Y.: Orbis Books, 1987).

66. Childs, *Introduction to the Old Testament as Scripture*, p. 178.

67. "The waters were split by the rod of Moses, but a strong wind blew all night and laid bare the sea bed. The waters stood up as a mighty wall to the left and the right, and yet the Egyptians were drowned when the sea returned to its normal channels. Yahweh produced panic with his fiery glance, but it was the mud of the sea bottom which clogged the wheels of the heavy chariots. The elements of the wonderful and the ordinary are constitutive to the greatest of Old Testament events. There never was a time when the event was only understood as ordinary, nor was there a time when the supernatural absorbed the natural." Childs, *Book of Exodus*, p. 238.

68. Pixley, *On Exodus*, p. 80, discusses the interaction of divine and human agency in the account and concludes, "In sum, God does nothing—if by 'do' we mean God is the exclusive agent of anything. On the other hand, God does everything—if by 'do' we mean that God is present in every event, prompting it to the realization of its fullest and best potential."

69. Both Childs, *Book of Exodus*, p. 238, and Hanson, *People Called*, pp. 24–26, have stressed the people's worship and praise as formative of community in response to God's salvation.

70. On the centrality of praise in the life of Israel see Walter Brueggemann, *Israel's Praise: Doxology Against Idolatry and Ideology* (Philadelphia: Fortress Press, 1988).

71. For the dynamics involved here see Bruce C. Birch, "Memory in Congregational Life," in *Congregations: Their Power to Form and Transform*, ed. C. Ellis Nelson (Atlanta: John Knox Press, 1988), pp. 20–47.

72. See Birch and Rasmussen, *Predicament of the Prosperous*, pp. 93–98, for the application of this theme to the American experience.

73. Croatto, *Exodus*, p. 14.

74. Michael Walzer, *Exodus and Revolution* (New York: Basic Books, 1985), pp. 134–135: "The Book of Exodus . . . is certainly the first description of revolutionary politics. . . . It isn't only the case that events fall, almost naturally, into an Exodus shape; we work actively to give them that shape. We complain

about oppression; we hope (against all the odds of human history) for deliverance; we join in covenants and constitutions; we aim at a new and better social order. . . . Within the frame of the Exodus story one can plausibly emphasize the mighty arm of God or the slow march of the people, the land of milk and honey or the holy nation, the purging of counter-revolutionaries or the schooling of the new generation. One can describe Egyptian bondage in terms of corruption or tyranny or exploitation. One can defend the authority of the Levites or of the tribal elders or of the rulers of tens and fifties. I would only suggest that these alternatives are themselves paradigmatic; they are our alternatives. In other cultures, men and women read other books, tell different stories, confront different choices."

75. See Walter Brueggemann, *The Message of the Psalms* (Minneapolis: Augsburg Publishing House, 1984), and Bernhard W. Anderson, *Out of the Depths: The Psalms Speak for Us Today,* rev. and exp. ed. (Philadelphia: Westminster Press, 1983), both of whom trace a similar pattern in the Psalms and treat it in greater detail than we are allowed here. See Bruce C. Birch, "The Psalter as Preaching Text," *Quarterly Review* 1 (1981): 61–93.

76. Childs, *Book of Exodus,* p. 239.

5

People
of the
Covenant

Although the experience of God's deliverance from bondage in Egypt forms the common experience out of which faith community was born, it requires the formative experience of covenant making at Sinai to make the community of Israel an ongoing reality. God's grace is manifest in the history of all humanity (cf. Amos 9:7), but it requires Israel's faithful response to God's initiative in its own experience to build the faithful community.

The special relationship of covenant is also God's initiative. "In accordance with these words I have made a covenant with you [Moses] and with Israel" (Ex. 34:27). In this brief verse are suggested all the crucial realities which must be discussed in order to understand the moral significance of covenant community for Christian faith. We will look first at the God who initiates covenant and the further dimensions of the divine character revealed in the covenantal themes. We will look then at the words (laws/commandments) and their significance, and finally we will examine the structures of community through which Israel tried to express the nature of its covenant calling.

It must be stressed that in the present shape of the book of Exodus we are intended to understand covenant and law as a response to God's initiative in the Exodus deliverance. Gerhard von Rad and Martin Noth had argued strenuously that the Exodus and Sinai traditions arose independently of one another, were nurtured at separate cultic shrines, and were combined secondarily by later editors of the Pentateuchal literary traditions.[1] This view has now been almost universally abandoned.[2] The opening of the Decalogue is clear about the importance of this connection. "I am the LORD your God, who brought you out of the land of Egypt, out of the house of slavery" (Ex. 20:2). The theological connection of the God of Exodus with the God of Sinai existed at the earliest periods of Israel's history and is not a late and artificial literary connection.

Israel arrives at the Sinai encampment in Ex. 19:1 and departs in Num. 10:12. This body of material contains some of the most ancient witnesses to the nature of covenant relationship and the oldest of the law codes, the Decalogue. It also, however, contains codes of law that clearly reflect the conditions of later periods of Israelite life (e.g., the Deuteronomic Code; the Holiness Code). Nevertheless, all of these have now been placed in the framework of the Sinai covenant making.

> The striking point . . . is that all of these materials now appear as elements in the events at Sinai. For the ancient Israelites, Moses is the prototypical lawgiver, and the covenant defines the framework within which the commandments, laws, and ordinances are to be understood.[3]

In order to fully understand the covenant relationship we will not be limited to the Sinai material in the Pentateuch but will also draw upon witnesses throughout the canon to Israel's understanding of the covenant relationship and the issues of Israel's community life which reflect that understanding.

The God Who Makes Covenant

God as Covenant Initiator

The God who delivered Israel from Egypt initiates a special relationship with Israel at Mt. Sinai.

> I will take you as my people, and I will be your God. You shall know that I am the LORD your God, who has freed you from the burdens of the Egyptians. (Ex. 6:7).

> You have seen what I did to the Egyptians, and how I bore you on eagles' wings and brought you to myself. Now therefore, if you obey my voice and keep my covenant, you shall be my treasured possession out of all the peoples. (Ex. 19:4–5)

As a part of this establishment of relationship God also gives commandments and statutes, the law (Heb. *torah*).

The Hebrew term for this relationship between God and Israel is covenant (Heb. *berit*). The term is used broadly in the Old Testament to refer to contracts or agreements (e.g., a treaty, Gen. 31:44; a friendship, 1 Sam. 23:18; an alliance, 1 Kings 20:34). It is used to refer to unconditional divine promises to Noah (Gen. 9:9) and Abraham (Gen. 15:18). Covenant, however, comes to have special meaning for defining the relationship between Yahweh and Israel, established at Sinai and including the giving of the law (Ex. 19:5; 24:7–8; 31:16; 34:10, 27–28; Lev. 24:8; 26:9, 15, 25, 44–45; Deut. 4:13; 29:1, 21).[4]

Beginning with the work of George Mendenhall,[5] it has become commonplace to relate the Israelite covenant to the formal structure of Hittite suzerainty treaties (fourteenth and thirteenth centuries B.C.E.). This thesis has usefully served to stress the initiative of the sovereign in establishing the treaty, and the basis for its acceptance in the recitation of benevolent acts already performed by the sovereign. Stipulations (laws) are then specified as the obligation of the weaker (vassal) party. These features have some obvious analogy to aspects of biblical covenant, but other features of the treaty form are notably missing in most covenant texts.

Recent scholarship has been increasingly critical of the treaty hypothesis.[6] No single biblical text displays all the features of the treaty form. Its closest analogies seem to be to the book of Deuteronomy. Further, the substance of the treaties does not correspond to that of biblical law, each governing quite different matters. It seems best at this point in the discussion not to rely heavily on the treaty analogy. It may suffice to simply note the uniform witness to covenant as established by divine, sovereign initiative and leave to further research the aptness of analogy to royal treaties.

In the Old Testament, God as the covenant initiator brings to the fore a terminology for the character of God that is especially related to God's role in covenant relationship. Terms descriptive of God's character such as holiness, steadfast love, righteousness, justice, and compassion are not limited to covenantal texts but may best be understood in the context of the relationship which covenant implies. Such aspects of the divine character are only properly understood as relational. They point to both the identity and the activity of God as understood in the context of the covenant relationship.

As we turn to discussion of these aspects of divine character and conduct we must be reminded of the long course of time from which the texts are drawn. The terms overlap and interrelate. There is no completely consistent usage. Each textual witness chooses emphases within the range of images available for understanding the divine character. Thus, an Amos may speak more of justice and righteousness, but a Hosea more of love and knowledge of God. Our task is to understand some of the basic covenant-related witnesses to the nature of Israel's God as they are now available to us in the collective witness of the canon.

The Holiness of God

"For I am the LORD who brought you up from the land of Egypt, to be your God; you shall be holy, for I am holy" (Lev. 11:45). No clearer statement exists in the Old Testament for the relationship of Israel's character to that of God. Israel is to exist in imitation of God, but this is now also reinforced by a divinely revealed commandment.[7] God's holiness is to be a central standard by which Israel's own life will be judged. Reference to God and the things of God as holy appear in every segment of the canon and every period of Israel's life.[8]

The holiness of God has been grossly misconstrued by some. It is not uncommon to find references suggesting that God's holiness relates only to cultic matters, or that God's holiness is an anachronistic or peripheral concern in the Old Testament.[9] As we shall see, neither is the case.

Because the holiness of God is such a comprehensive concept definitions are difficult. Holiness points to God's uniqueness (Isa. 40:25) and often contrasts divine perfection to sinful and fragile human nature (Isa. 6:1–5). James Muilenburg describes well the far-reaching meaning of holiness in reference to God:

> The "given" undergirding and pervading all religion; the distinctive mark and signature of the divine. More than any other term, "holiness" gives expression to the essential nature of the "sacred." It is therefore to be understood, not as one attribute among other attributes, but as the innermost reality to which all others are related. Even the sum of all the attributes and activities of "the holy" is insufficient to exhaust its meaning, for to the one who has experienced its presence there is always a plus, a "something more," which resists formulation or definition.[10]

Modern discussion of the nature of the holy is rooted in Rudolf Otto's classic work *The Idea of the Holy*.[11] He identified the element of the human religious experience which was suprarational[12] and called this "the numinous." John Gammie, in his important recent work, has shown how the account of the Sinai theophany in Ex. 19 contains all the distinct elements Otto identified with the numinous, the holy. These include "awefulness, dread" (Ex. 19:18c, 19b, 21–22), "majesty and unapproachability" (12, 21, 23), "energy, vitality, and movement" (18ab), "mystery" (9a), and "fascination" (24b).[13] Holiness is the very essence of the God who appears to make covenant on Sinai.

To Otto's description of the numinous, Gammie (drawing upon important recent work in anthropology and biblical studies) has added two important categories: "Nowhere does Otto sufficiently probe the notion that the holy calls for purity, cleanness, and that frequently purity is to be attained by means of separation."[14] To be holy is to be separate; to be holy is to be clean and pure. Each of these notions has ethical as well as cultic implications.

The holiness of God is a theme present in some of Israel's most ancient traditions. "Who is like you, O LORD, among the gods? Who is like you, majestic in holiness, awesome in splendor, doing wonders?" (Ex. 15:11). In the midst of this ancient recital of praise, this description of the numinous is followed by the vanquishing of the oppressor. "You stretched out your right hand, the earth swallowed them" (v. 12). God's holiness from earliest times in Israel is related to God's power to act as a moral agent in human history. "In the presence of this holy God, wickedness perished. . . . The holy God Yahweh did not look on injustice with indifference, but with incisive action. Neither the cries of the oppressed, nor the reveling of the oppressor were unheeded. . . . Yahweh, majestic in holiness, became the standard of righteousness within this nascent community."[15]

The same connection of God's holiness with God's moral activity in behalf of the dispossessed may be seen in the ancient poetry of the Song of Hannah, "There is no Holy One like the LORD. . . . The bows of the mighty are broken, but the feeble gird on strength. . . . He raises up the poor from the dust; he lifts the needy from the ash heap" (1 Sam. 2:2a, 4, 8).

From these references to God's holiness in early Israelite poetry there extends a constant witness to God's holiness throughout Israel's history. Out of this rich witness only a few observations can be made here.

1. Affirmation of God's holiness is a constant reminder of the separateness of God—and of the things of God. Thus, God's holiness is related to the divine freedom we discussed in chapter 4. God is "wholly other," and the presence of the Holy One in our midst is itself an act of grace and not something which even proper cultic observance can command. Indeed, God's holy presence or glory ("glory . . . is but holiness made manifest"[16]) can be withdrawn in the absence of the people's justice and righteousness (Ezek. 10–11; see chapter 8). If God's holiness extends to the things of God, then we must explore later in this chapter what it means to be God's holy people, separated from the world for a mission to the world.

2. Holiness is always related to cleanness and purity. God's holiness always confronts us with our own unworthiness. Isaiah's response to the vision of God's holiness is to cry out that he is a man of "unclean lips" (Isa. 6:1–5). It is out of God's holy grace that we are made pure and called to vocation. Isaiah's lips are purged and he is called to prophetic vocation. God's holiness is a constant reminder that our vocation to proclaim God's justice and righteousness and love arises out of God's worthiness and not our own.

Gammie reminds us that notions of cleanness associated with God's holiness were quite diverse.

> For the entire Old Testament/Hebrew Scriptures, holiness summoned Israel to cleanness. . . . Diversity within unity is to be discerned in the fact that for the different groups of religious persons within Israel—prophets, priests, and sages—the kind of cleanness required by holiness varied. For the prophets it was a cleanness of social justice, for the priests a cleanness of proper ritual and maintenance of separation, for the sages it was a cleanness of inner integrity and individual moral acts.[17]

3. Walter Kaiser suggests that "God's holiness had two distinct sides. One stressed his otherness, his so-called numinous character. This was picked up in the ceremonial and ritual laws of Israel. The other side of holiness expressed the righteousness and goodness of Yahweh and that became the basis for the morality and ethics taught in the Old Testament."[18]

Such a division has some practical usefulness. There are some contexts in which the holy presence of God is not directly associated with any moral content, for example, the references to the Ark as a holy palladium of divine presence. Israel itself did not make sharp separations between the cultic and the ethical, and the numinous character of God's holiness is as important to the explicit moral and ethical references as to the cultic. Awareness of God's holiness fostered in Israel's worship (however strange the specific practices may seem to us) formed a basis for understanding God's separation from the gods of the other ancient religions and for understanding God's call for Israel to be separate and clean, that is, holy. Psalm 15 can serve as a powerful reminder of the close association of God's holiness, celebrated in the cult, with God's ethical demands on the people.[19]

> O, LORD, who may abide in your tent?
>   Who may dwell on your holy hill?
> Those who walk blamelessly, and do what is right,
>   and speak the truth from their heart;
> who do not slander with their tongue,
>   and do no evil to their friends,
>   nor take up a reproach against their neighbors; . . .
> who do not lend money at interest,
>   and do not take a bribe against the innocent.
> Those who do these things shall never be moved.
>   (Ps. 15:1–3, 5)

Holiness describes the very foundations of the *divine being*. It is fundamental to divine character and identity, and out of God's holiness a variety of expressions for *divine activity* grow. Perhaps the most central of the terms expressive of divine activity within the covenant relationship is steadfast love (*ḥesed*). God *is* holy. God *acts* in steadfast love.

The Steadfast Love of God

In the context of theophany on Mt. Sinai, God allows the divine glory to pass by Moses and utters this remarkable self-confession.

> The LORD, the LORD,
> a God merciful and gracious,
> slow to anger,
> and abounding in steadfast love and faithfulness,
> keeping steadfast love for the thousandth generation,
> forgiving iniquity and transgression and sin,

>   yet by no means clearing the guilty,
>   but visiting the iniquity of the parents
>   upon the children
>   and the children's children,
>   to the third and the fourth generation.
>   (Ex. 34:6–7)

This remarkably propositional statement is reduplicated in some part (this is the only complete version) in eighteen other contexts in the Old Testament.[20] This may indicate its liturgical usage; it certainly indicates its importance.

The Hebrew word translated as "steadfast love" here is *ḥesed*. It is a difficult concept to capture in any one English word and has been represented variously by "mercy," "grace," "loyalty," "goodness," "loving-kindness," and "compassion."[21] This alone witnesses to the breadth of divine activity encompassed in the term.

Katharine Doob Sakenfeld's important work on *ḥesed*[22] helps focus several elements important to understanding the basic meaning of this aspect of God.

1. God's steadfast love is always demonstrated in the context of relationship, and most often in relation to the need of the other in relationship. It is not mere allegiance to a concept—even the concept of covenant. In covenant it is steadfast love shown to the covenant partner and the needs of that covenant partner, Israel.

2. God's steadfast love may be understood as an expression of fidelity in relationship. For that reason Sakenfeld has chosen to consistently translate *ḥesed* as "loyalty," but it is not loyalty in the abstract. "Loyalty is attitude made manifest in concrete action."[23] It is the well-known recurring refrain of Ps. 136 that best illustrates this. Throughout a recitation of God's activity from creation through Exodus to present needs, the refrain announces, "For God's steadfast love endures forever."

In the self-confession of Ex. 34 the fidelity of God's steadfast love is emphasized by its pairing with "faithfulness" (*'emet*), a frequent coupling in the Hebrew Bible.[24] The phrase "abounding in steadfast love" also emphasizes fidelity since it is used only of God and implies God's inexhaustible covenant love, whereas Israel's loyalty is more uncertain.

3. It is in the context of covenant relationship that *ḥesed* is used to characterize the relationship of God to Israel. "Divine

loyalty within covenant involved both God's commitment to Israel and the ever new free decision of God to continue to honor that commitment by preserving and supporting the covenant community. Divine freedom and divine self-obligation were held together in this single word."[25]

God's *hesed* points to God's actions of loving fidelity to the covenant relationship. In Ex. 34 steadfast love is related to actions of mercy, graciousness, and forgiveness, but also to a divine determination not to avoid accountability within the covenant framework.[26] In the ancient Song of the Sea, God's steadfast love appears (Ex. 15:13) as the sustaining love of God leading the people beyond the dramatic moment of their deliverance: "In your steadfast love you led the people whom you redeemed, you guided them by your strength to your holy abode."[27] It is not surprising that in time of catastrophe the writer of Lamentations returns to trust in God's steadfast love.

> The steadfast love of the LORD never ceases,
>   his mercies never come to an end;
> they are new every morning;
>   great is your faithfulness.
> (Lam. 3:22–23)

The Righteousness and Justice of God

God's holiness and God's steadfast love are expressed in their particular dimensions by a wide variety of biblical terms descriptive of the nature and work of God, especially in the covenant relationship to Israel. Perhaps the most important of these for the concerns of Christian ethics are God's righteousness (*sedeq*, masc.; *sedaqah*, fem.) and God's justice (*mišpat*). Both of these appear in the Old Testament as expressions of God's holiness and steadfast love. "But the LORD of hosts is exalted by justice, and the Holy God shows himself holy by righteousness" (Isa. 5:16). "I am the LORD; I act with steadfast love, justice, and righteousness in the earth, for in these things I delight" (Jer. 9:24).

Righteousness. It is this term, *sedeq/sedaqah*, understood in legalistic terms, which has most often led to the belief that the Old Testament is devoid of the grace depicted in the New. Although righteousness is the most common translation, it is also translated as vindication, deliverance, uprightness, right, and even prosperity.

Elizabeth Achtemeier helpfully sweeps aside some troubling and incorrect notions about righteousness.

> In the OT it is not behavior in accordance with an ethical, legal, psychological, religious, or spiritual norm. It is not conduct which is dictated by either human or divine nature, no matter how undefiled. It is not an action appropriate to the attainment of a specific goal. It is not an impartial ministry to one's fellow men. It is not equivalent to giving every man his just due.[28]

It was Gerhard von Rad (relying on and quoting from the earlier work of H. Cremer) who drew widespread attention to righteousness as a concept understood in the Old Testament only in terms of relationship.

> Ancient Israel did not in fact measure a line of conduct or an act by an ideal norm, but by the specific relationship in which the partner had at the time to prove himself true. "Every relationship brings with it certain claims upon conduct, and the satisfaction of these claims, which issue from the relationship and in which alone the relationship can persist, is described by our term *ṣdq*."[29]

When applied to God righteousness implies the covenant relationship which God has initiated with Israel. Although God's righteousness is sometimes described as manifest among the nations, it is from the perspective of the covenant relationship that this divine behavior is perceived.

Yahweh's righteousness was not an abstract norm but was seen in God's concrete acts to establish and preserve relationship.[30] For Israel this divine righteousness is known in God's actions to establish Israel in deliverance and preserve community in covenant. "The righteous deeds of Yahweh are his saving acts, his victories, all that he does to create, and establish and perpetuate community."[31] One of the oldest of Israel's poems, the Song of Deborah, speaks of "Yahweh's righteous acts" (*ṣedaqot*, pl.; Judg. 5:11; NRSV "triumphs") clearly meaning the acts of salvation by which God called Israel into being.

In preserving community Yahweh's righteousness is always experienced as God's gift, actions upholding and vindicating the community. It often appears coupled with the term "salvation" (Pss. 40:10; 51:14; Isa. 61:10). God's gift of the law is an action of God's righteousness, establishing terms under which relationship is preserved and maintained. "His commandments were not indeed any absolute 'law,' but a kindly gift rendering life orderly."[32] It is worth noting in connection with righteousness as a gift that the term is never used to refer to the punishment of sin or in any punitive meaning.[33] The term for justice can, however, be used in this way.

God's righteousness is expressed in the restoration of community in time of need. In this regard the righteousness of God often appears in a forensic context with God as the righteous judge (see Pss. 9:4, 8; 50:6; 96:13; 99:4; Isa. 5:16; 58:2; Jer. 11:20). God upholds the right and restores those who have had their right taken from them. God restores Israel to full life and relationship in times of need, affliction, and trouble as expression of divine righteousness. God is, therefore, also especially concerned with individuals denied their right.

"The LORD will give what is good. . . . Righteousness will go before him, and will make a path for his steps" (Ps. 85:12–13).

Justice. The Hebrew word *mišpaṭ* is usually translated as "justice" or "judgment" but can also indicate a law or a statute (in its plural it indicates a body of law or judgments). The noun is derived from the verbal root *špṭ*, which means "to judge" or "to render judgment." This, however, "must not be understood in the modern sense of the term, namely, as pronouncing a judgment, a 'sentence.' The primitive idea of *šapaṭ* was broader: it comprised all the actions which accompanied or immediately followed the primitive process that took place when two opposed parties presented themselves before the competent authority, each to claim its rights."[34]

It is clear that *mišpaṭ* has a more basic forensic character to its meaning than *ṣedaqah*, dealing with "judicial activity at every level"[35]; but it also has a broader meaning dealing with the rights due to every individual in the community, and the upholding of those rights. The prophets in particular used the term in a broad sense which went beyond the boundaries of judicial activity, and in combination with the term "righteousness" came close to approximating the broad meanings now associated with "justice" as an ethical concept.

Justice is a chief attribute of God's activity in the world. "The LORD of hosts is exalted by justice" (Isa. 5:16). Obviously God is not acting out of some abstract legal norm to be administered. God is the source of care for the right of every person, and the giver of the law which seeks to embody that right in structures of faithful community. Thus, the context for apprehending the activity of God as justice is the wider covenant community and not merely the structures of the judicial system. The prophets in particular appeal to this broad understanding of God's justice as a warrant for human justice (see chapter 7).

The *mišpaṭ* of God is experienced by the vulnerable in the community as "justice," the upholding of their rights, and the advocacy of their need (Deut. 10:18; Ps. 10:18; Jer. 5:28). To those who have denied or manipulated the rights of others God's *mišpaṭ* may be translated as "judgment," the activity of God to hold accountable those who exploit the rights of others.

Justice was understood by Israel as a fundamental aspect of the activity of God from its earliest history as can be seen in the ancient poem, the Song of Moses:

> The Rock, his work is perfect,
>   and all his ways are just.
> A faithful God, without deceit,
>   just and upright is he.
>   (Deut. 32:4)

Orientation to the Poor and the Afflicted. In the previous chapter we have already discussed God's special care for the dispossessed, experienced by Israel in God's care for them when they were slaves. In examples of God's justice and righteousness we have seen the continuation of that expression of the divine character. God's justice and righteousness is especially manifest in care for the poor, the hungry, the widow, the orphan, the oppressed, the troubled, the afflicted.[36] Here we simply add several observations concerning this divine bias.

Stephen Mott has helpfully pointed to the centrality of the principle of redress in the biblical concept of justice.[37] God does not just care for the weak and vulnerable in the human community but is active to redress the inequities when needs are unmet and rights are denied (Ps. 146:7–8).[38]

Covenant relationship is the framework within which Israel apprehends and relates to God's demands for righteousness and justice, and God's special concern for the dispossessed, but the covenant does not prescribe the boundaries for God's care. God is universal and sovereign over all creation/history. Thus, important recognition is made that "the LORD works vindication and justice for *all* who are oppressed" (Ps. 103:6, italics added).

Finally, special attention must be directed to Ps. 82 as a remarkable witness to the implications Israel attached to the recognition of its God as a God of righteousness and justice. This psalm opens in the heavenly council of the gods where Israel's God has taken a stand to render judgment (Ps. 82:1) and challenges the gods, "How long will you judge unjustly and show partiality to the wicked?" (v. 2). God goes on to make clear what is required of the truly divine, "Give justice to the weak and the orphan; maintain the right of the lowly and the destitute. Rescue the weak and the needy; deliver them from the hand of the wicked" (vs. 3–4). Then, remarkably, God pronounces a verdict on these failed deities, "You shall die like mortals, and fall like any prince" (v. 7). They are deposed from their claim to divinity. In Israel's conception the doing of justice and righteousness was defining of true divinity, and only its God could claim faithfulness to that statement. Such a God was not only Israel's God but the only true God of all the nations. "Rise up, O God, judge the earth; for all the nations belong to you!" (v. 8).[39] In effect Israel understands the God of its covenant relationship as an alternative to the gods of the surrounding cultures. This has important implications for life as the alternative community of God's people in the world.

The Moral Dynamics of Israelite Law

Contained within the Pentateuch are four important collections or codes of law. These "commandments," "statutes," "ordinances" are all presented as the direct revelation of God to Israel (although some are mediated through Moses). The oldest is the Decalogue, which appears in Ex. 20:2–17 and Deut. 5:6–21. Also dating to Israel's early life before the monarchy is the Book of the Covenant, Ex. 20:22–23:33. Leviticus 17–26 is known as the Holiness Code for its repeated references to God's holiness and the demand for Israel's holiness. Within the book of Leviticus the Holiness Code is surrounded by large sections of additional priestly legislation (Lev. 1–7; 11–16). In its present form these laws reflect late Israelite cultic practice prior to the exile. Deuteronomy 12–26 is a body of laws bracketed by the speeches of Moses to Israel before entry into the Promised Land. It is usually identified with the scroll of law found in the temple during the time of

Josiah which formed the basis of his reforms in 621 B.C.E. (2 Kings 22–23). The laws reflect conditions of Israel's life during the height of the monarchy (c. eighth–seventh centuries B.C.E.).

The Narrative Setting of Israelite Law

Israelite law is handed on to us in a narrative setting, and there is increasing attention to the importance of this narrative context in the interpretation of Israel's law.[40] All the legal material in Exodus and Leviticus appears now in the context of Israel's experience in the encampment and covenant making at Sinai. This is interpretively important in spite of the fact that some of these materials, the Leviticus legal material in particular, originated historically at a much later time. It has become important that these laws be read through the norm of the Sinai covenant.[41] Even the Deuteronomic law code is presented in the setting of Moses' speech to Israel before entry into the land, and specifically recalls Sinai and its covenant as the key to understanding Moses' communication of the divine will for those entering the land. "Not with our ancestors did the LORD make this covenant, but with us, who are all of us here alive today" (Deut. 5:3).

Even the laws themselves often include a narrative reference to Israel's experience or tradition.[42] For example, the Decalogue commandment on the Sabbath includes narrative reference either to creation (Ex. 20:8–11) or to Exodus (Deut. 5:12–15).

The narrative context makes clear that for Israel all law receives its authority from the belief that it has been divinely revealed as a part of the solemn covenant established by God with Israel and agreed to by Israel at Sinai. The Decalogue and the Book of the Covenant are bracketed by the announcement of covenant intent (Ex. 19:5–6), and by the solemn covenant ceremony (Ex. 24:3–8) which includes the people's commitment to the covenant and the announcement of law which it included. "All that the LORD has spoken we will do, and we will be obedient" (v. 7).[43]

Brevard Childs suggests that the wider narrative context of the whole Sinai complex is also theologically important.

It is theologically significant to observe that the events of Sinai are both preceded and followed by the stories of the people's resistance which is characteristic of the entire wilderness wanderings. The narrative material testifies to those moments in Israel's history in which God made himself known. For Israel to learn the will of God necessitated an act of self-revelation. Israel could not discover it for herself.[44]

Within the Sinai complex the Decalogue is narratively positioned to serve "as an interpretive guide to all the succeeding legal material."[45] It is introduced with reference back to the Exodus experience (Ex. 20:2), and in its present position serves as a simple statement of God's covenant will which the other law codes elaborate. In Deuteronomy when Moses interprets the covenant law for a new generation entering the land he begins again with the Decalogue (Deut. 5).

The Character of Israelite Law

The recent literature on Old Testament law has been rich and voluminous.[46] We can only touch on a few issues that seem especially important for understanding the moral significance of the Old Testament legal materials.

1. In 1934 Albrecht Alt published his landmark article on the form critical study of Israelite law.[47] He related all the Old Testament laws to two basic categories. The short, unconditional, and categorical statements of right and wrong he called apodictic law. This included both positive and negative imperatives such as found in the Decalogue (e.g., "You shall not steal"), and laws that incorporate prescribed punishment (e.g., "Whoever strikes father or mother shall be put to death," Ex. 21:15). He believed that these laws were characteristic and unique to early Israel, grew out of the uniqueness of Israel's religion, and were recited in the renewal of the covenant. The larger body of laws he labeled casuistic law based on their statement of a case with its carefully described conditions and announcement of penalties or remedies for each case. "If someone leaves a pit open, or digs a pit and does not cover it, and an ox or a donkey falls into it, the owner of the pit shall make restitution, giving money to its owner, but keeping the dead animal" (Ex. 21:33–34). Alt believed this form of law, common throughout the ancient Near East, was borrowed by Israel from its neighbors, was used in judicial settings, and bore little religious significance. Alt's views are now often cited as standard in texts and reference works.

Recent years have, however, seen considerable erosion of

Alt's hypothesis. The single most cogent criticism was leveled by Erhard Gerstenberger who made a strong case for separating, in both form and function, the apodictic laws which specify punishment from those that simply state a command. Perhaps more important, he demonstrated that there do exist significant parallels to the apodictic laws elsewhere in the ancient Near East in both wisdom and cultic materials as well as legal settings.[48] Others also believe that more than one distinct pattern should be distinguished in the casuistic laws.[49] It is sufficient simply to note that the moral distinctiveness of Israelite law does not lie in the form of categorical commandment per se.

2. Of particular importance to the understanding of the continuing moral significance of Israel's law has been the study of motive clauses attached to many of Israel's laws. Berend Gemser's influential work in 1953 called new attention to the clauses attached to many biblical laws which provide reasons or motives for performing the act commanded in the law.[50] "You shall not oppress a resident alien; you know the heart of an alien, for you were aliens in the land of Egypt" (Ex. 23:9; cf. also Deut. 10:18–19). Although the motive clauses are of several different types, many of them are religious in character and reflect specific norms drawn from Israelite experience with their God. Gemser argued that this type of motive clause was unique to Israel and the source of some of its humanitarian impulses.[51]

Paul Hanson, focusing on the Book of the Covenant, used the appearance of the motive clauses, which refer to Israel's faith experience, as one of the factors in distinguishing two different types of legal collections in that early code.[52] A body of case laws found in Ex. 21:1–22:16 (Eng. 22:17) reflects the common legal practices of Mesopotamia in the same period. It indicates the influence of a common ancient social system and its practices on the young Israelite society. This social system was highly stratified with males valued more highly than females and free men more highly than slaves. Women and slaves often appear treated as property in these laws. There are no specific references to Yahwistic faith in these laws.

By contrast, a collection of what Hanson terms Yahwistic laws in Ex. 20:22–26; 22:17 (Eng. 22:18)–23:19 "betray an intimate connection with the specific confessions of early Yahwistic faith. . . . The law draws its motivating force concretely from Israel's memory of its past bondage."[53] This can be illustrated in particular by laws dealing with the stranger, the widow, the orphan, and the poor. Concern for the legal protection of these vulnerable members of the community is specifically related to the people's memory of their own experience in Egypt and God's mercy in deliverance. This connection is sometimes made through use of the motive clause to which Gemser called attention (Ex. 23:9), but the connection is sometimes more directly to the activity of God already experienced by Israel. "You shall not abuse any widow or orphan. If you do abuse them, when they cry out to me, I will surely heed their cry; my wrath will burn, and I will kill you with the sword, and your wives shall become widows and your children orphans" (Ex. 22:21–23 [Eng. 22–24]). "If you lend money to my people, who are poor among you . . . you shall not exact interest from them. . . . If your neighbor cries out to me, I will listen, for I am compassionate" (Ex. 22:24–26 [Eng. 25–27]).

In the contrast between these two bodies of law we can see Israel inevitably affected by the social practices of surrounding culture, but placing those practices in tension with patterns of societal relationship which grow specifically out of the uniqueness of Israel's God and experience in relation to that God.

> On the one hand, we find the case laws, emphasizing an ordering of society largely in continuity with the other societies of the ancient world. On the other hand, we see laws articulating a community ideal dedicated to justice embracing all members and emphasizing compassion to those whose economic or social status make them vulnerable to abuse. Especially noteworthy is the source of the motivation for this latter community ideal, namely, the antecedent, gracious, saving activity of Yahweh.[54]

Development of the implications of Israel's faith for its social structure and practices continues to be reflected throughout the law codes. The Code of Deuteronomy clearly reflects a further stage of this development in a direction of increased sensitivity to the value of all. Laws related to slaves and women, for example, have moved in the direction of broadening rights and recognition for those exploited classes.[55] This is, however, only a hopeful movement. The subordinate role of women and the practice of slavery still reflect the overwhelmingly patriarchal character of Israelite society, and remind us that communities, Israel included, seldom fully actualize their most idealistic visions.

Although there is not space for a detailed survey of the
Israelite legislation,[56] we might note that Israelite law in its
concern for the vulnerable of society and the ideal of community it reflects is most remarkable. In many matters the concerns of the law are common to other ancient cultures as well:
protection of the family, adjudication of disputes, business
practices. But wherever there was a danger that some more
vulnerable members of the community might be exploited by
other stronger members the law sought to give protection, and
this protection was often directly attributed to insights and
experiences out of Israel's relationship to Yahweh. This concern was manifest in familial, economic, political, and social
contexts, although it must be stressed that Israel never embodied all that its religious vision implied.

Leon Epsztein in his detailed comparative study of Israelite and other ancient Near Eastern social legislation and social practice suggests that Israel was not unique in a concern
for justice. Israel, however, took that concern and developed
it more fully, consistently, and constantly than other ancient
cultures precisely because of the strength of Israel's empowering theological vision. "It is probably largely thanks to this
dynamism [of Israel's faith] that the quest for social justice,
which elsewhere came sharply to a halt (Mesopotamia) or
suffered a long eclipse (Egypt), was to be pursued by the
people of the Bible almost without interruption down to our
own day."[57]

3. One brief word must be added about the relationship between religious and ethical, cultic and social matters in the law
codes. Some interpreters, in an attempt to claim continuing
authority for some laws while dismissing others, have sharply
separated religious and cultic laws from those dealing with ethical and social matters. They argue that the cultic laws are
anachronistic while the ethical laws retain moral authority.[58]
The laws themselves and their covenant context do not allow
this separation. Cultic and social legislation is intermixed, and
their authority is interrelated. It is not accidental that the Decalogue contains commandments dealing with Sabbath observance and idolatry alongside those dealing with killing, stealing,
and the like. Because Israel's law is an attempt to give concrete
expression to the covenant relationship to Yahweh it requires
both the remembrance and the celebration in worship (cult) of
that relationship and its history, and it requires the embodiment of that relationship in concrete social structures. Thomas

Ogletree has aptly noted the moral importance of this intermixture:

> On the one hand, Israel's religious convictions themselves concern a moral relationship: a covenantal commitment between two parties. . . . One is thus *morally* obliged to incorporate the reality of the religious relation into the normal processes of life in some suitable fashion, that is, in cultic activity. . . . On the other hand, since the authority of the social laws presupposes not only the covenant, but also narrative accounts of the saving actions of God which first made the covenant possible, the rehearsal of these accounts in the context of the cult is itself integral to covenant fidelity. . . . A religious ethic which is wholly abstracted from the cult is a religious ethic without historical and social substance.[59]

4. Because it is so often used to characterize Old Testament law, indeed Old Testament religion as a whole, the talion formula (*ius talionis*) requires brief comment.[60] Popularly abbreviated to "an eye for an eye, and a tooth for a tooth" this formula is often used to reduce Old Testament morality to retribution and retaliation.

Variations of the talion formula appear in three places, Ex. 21:23–25; Lev. 24:18, 20; Deut. 19:21. "If any harm follows, then you shall give life for life, eye for eye, tooth for tooth, hand for hand, foot for foot, burn for burn, wound for wound, stripe for stripe" (Ex. 21:23–25). It is by no means uniquely Israelite, and is also known in other ancient legal codes, for example, the Code of Hammurabi.

In the context of ancient family, clan, and tribal life injury to any person was considered an injury to the entire group, and balance was often sought by inflicting damage on the family, clan, or tribe of the offender. This practice of blood vengeance could often lead to severe violence and bloodletting. This can be seen in the boastful song of vengeance by Lamech in Gen. 4:23–24:

> Adah and Zillah, hear my voice;
> > you wives of Lamech, listen to what I say:
> I have killed a man for wounding me,
> > a young man for striking me.
> If Cain is avenged sevenfold,
> > truly Lamech seventy-sevenfold.

In this context the talion formula is an effort to introduce the principle of proportionality into Israel's law. "The intention of the talion was not, therefore, to inflict injury—as it might sound to us today—but to limit injury. The talion was meant to contain the mechanism of blood-revenge triggered off by an injury within limits. . . . We can therefore paraphrase the talion formula as follows: only one life for a life, only one eye for an eye, only one tooth for a tooth, etc."[61]

The Moral Authority of Israelite Law

Several aspects of the nature and functioning of moral authority in Old Testament law deserve special comment.

Law and Community. Legal codes invariably reflect and derive some measure of their authority from the communities out of which they come. Israel's law codes are no exception. The legal materials reflect an understanding of Israel as a community initiated by the saving activity of God, and continued in ongoing covenant relationship with God.

With such a dynamic understanding of community it would be odd if the law codes were regarded as static, fixed, authoritative codes. There is ample evidence that the authority of Israel's law was not regarded in this way. The *Shema* (Deut. 6:4) is already treated in the text as a summary of the law in terms of loving God, and it is this central principle to which the law points which is to be passed on to future generations.

> The ability of Deuteronomy to summarize the Law in terms of loving God with heart, soul and mind is a major check against all forms of legalism. According to Deuteronomy, the whole Mosaic law testifies to the living will of God whose eternal purpose for the life of his people provides the only grounds for life and salvation.[62]

Recent studies of biblical law suggest that the laws are not considered the expression of ideals or timeless truths which are then enforced to define the community. Community is already formed in relation to Yahweh and the laws are for guidance and instruction in apprehending and living out the implications of such a community.

> For the period during which the legal tradition was in formation, the law of God was an unwritten Law. It was the sense of justice and right shared by the legal community and sharpened by lawgiv-

ers and judges. . . . The precepts and judgments of the codes were not prescriptions with statutory force but testimony to God's just and righteous will. . . . The lawbooks were intended not for judicial application but for instruction in the values, principles, concepts, and procedures of the unwritten divine Law. . . . [The written legal traditions serve the purpose of] inculcating the values and principles of the legal community. One might say that biblical law sought to create the conscience of the community. The auditors were being instructed in the sense of justice and right expected by their divine sovereign and embedded in the structure of the community.[63]

In a sense, the law codes in their narrative setting are themselves witnesses to the journey of the community Israel, constantly discovering God's will for them anew. This is a very different notion of authority for the law than that which sees the law as an authoritative end in itself.[64]

Law and Moral Identity. It has been customary to think of Israel's laws as specifying actions (frequently moral actions), but Old Testament laws often specify, even advocate, a particular identity for the reader (or hearer).[65] Their function is not just in the shaping of community conduct, but in the formation and maintenance of a particular community character.[66]

Harry Nasuti focuses on the sojourner formula and the slave formula as examples of this function of the law to specify identity for the reader.[67] The sojourner formula ("For you were sojourners [NRSV 'resident aliens'] in the land of Egypt," Ex. 22:20 [Eng. 22:21]; 23:9; Lev. 19:34; Deut. 10:19; 23:7) appears in motive clauses such as were discussed above. As a motive for receiving the law authoritatively the reader is reminded of an identity with a people who themselves were once sojourners (strangers). The slave formula appears primarily as a separate and distinct command: "Remember that you were a slave in the land of Egypt" (Deut. 5:15; 15:15; 16:12; 24:18, 22). There are a variety of other references in the laws which serve to remind the Israelite reader of an identity. For example, in a law specifying the use of unleavened bread in the cultic feast of Passover the identity statement is made, "because you came out of the land of Egypt in great haste." All these identity statements serve not simply to seek compliance with laws on slaves or sojourners or Passover, but to establish and perpetuate a community of memory.[68]

This role of the law in identity formation is especially evident in the credo statement of Deut. 26:5–10, to be recited at the offering of firstfruits. It begins with memory in the third person regarding the ancestor of the promise, "A wandering Aramean was my ancestor; he went down into Egypt"; but with the beginning of the Exodus recital the language shifts to the first person, "When the Egyptians treated us harshly . . . , we cried to the LORD. . . . The LORD brought us out of Egypt. . . . Now I bring the first of the fruit of the ground." Clearly the commandment for this cultic recital serves to establish an identity between the bringer of the offering and the faith memory of Israel brought to birth in God's deliverance.

Nasuti points out that in addition to identity with those who were former slaves and sojourners, the Israel of the faith story, the intended Israelite reader of the laws is asked to identify with and imitate God who acted with justice and compassion toward them when they were slaves[69]: "[God] who executes justice for the orphan and the widow, and who loves the strangers, providing them food and clothing. You shall also love the stranger, for you were strangers in the land of Egypt" (Deut. 10:18–19). Nasuti speaks of this as a command to act as God had acted toward Israel, an *imitatio Dei.*[70] We have already noted this dynamic in connection with our discussion of the character of the covenant God, especially in the command to be holy as God is holy (Lev. 19:2), and in God's special identification with the dispossessed (see chapter 4).

Thus, the laws function not simply to specify actions appropriate to the covenant relation but to establish and preserve an identity with Israel's memory of themselves as delivered slaves, and an identification with (imitation of) God in certain specified ways (identification with the oppressed, resting on the Sabbath, embodying holiness, etc.).[71] The need to urge this specificity of identity may itself imply that the actual reader the law codes has in mind is someone in the land, possibly holding slaves, and in a position to oppress the vulnerable. The need to establish an identity for such people is as morally urgent as the specification of particular actions.[72]

Law and Divine Will. It is important to stress that the covenant relationship and the law as an expression of that relationship are presented in the Old Testament as the revealed will of God. The laws of the Old Testament cannot be reduced to sociological evidence for the structures of ancient Israel. They are also evidence for the theological priority given in that community to the revelation of God's will as a central moral focus. "To know God is to know his will. . . . Israel does not first know God and then later discover what God wants. Knowledge of his person and will are identical, and both are grounded in his self-revelation."[73] Thus, the law cannot be fully understood if it is wrenched out of its context of theophany at Sinai.

For those who claim the Old Testament as scripture and seek resources there for the theological and ethical reflection of the church, the biblical community's own claim that its life has been initiated by the revelatory activity of God is of central importance. This claim has come under critical assault in the recent work of Norman Gottwald and his sociological approach to the Old Testament (which he terms a cultural-materialistic reading).[74]

For Gottwald and others who have followed his lead, religion is simply the symbolic expression of underlying social realities. These can be recovered to a certain degree using social scientific methods and a sociohistorical account of Israel's traditions can be written. This reduces theology (ideology) to a secondary symbolic expression intended to support prevailing social values or institutions. This approach gives no credence to the biblical community's own testimony to the priority of divine revelatory experience, but reduces the theological dimension of the text to realities no different from the realities that stand behind the other ancient religions.[75] There is no transcendent divine reality that stands behind the text. The text ultimately points, not to God, but to the social community alone.

For Christian ethics this would leave little reason to look to the Bible for moral resources in any way distinguishable from the broad resources of human history. For our discussion of covenant and law, we would be forced to disregard the community's own claim that something new has altered the course of their existence, and that new reality, God, has shaped their lives and community in ways they could not have shaped themselves. "The use of the term revelation within the context of the canon reflects the concern to be open to the theological dimensions of the biblical tradition which can never be either separated from or identified with the life of empirical Israel."[76] The laws themselves constantly bear testimony to this sense of the transcendent reality of God as a formative influence in the very heart of their social structures. It is our awareness of this testimony to God's self-revealing activity that helps create openness to such transforming realities beyond the sum of social forces in our own world.

The Decalogue

The Decalogue has played a significant role not only in the history of Jewish and Christian theology but in the shaping of Western law, social philosophy, and ethics. We cannot, in a short space, do justice to its central moral influence. Fortunately, we are blessed with a number of excellent commentaries and monographs on the Decalogue, and we will not attempt commentary on each commandment, but make some general observations about the Decalogue in its Old Testament context and as a moral resource.[77]

1. The Decalogue is clearly regarded as foundational by the biblical communities and within the biblical witness. Although in its present form the Decalogue reflects some development,[78] it is placed in the text of the Sinai theophany as the only words of God addressed directly to the people and not mediated through Moses (Ex. 20:1–17). Standing prior to all other law codes, the Decalogue appears not so much as a legal code itself as the foundational principles of the covenant on which subsequent legal codes may be based. This view is reinforced by the appearance of the Decalogue a second time in Deut. 5:6–21. Moses is here reinterpreting the covenant and the law for life in the Promised Land, and the necessary foundation is the recital once again of the Decalogue. Indeed, Deut. 4:13 equates the making of covenant with the giving of the Decalogue: "He declared to you his covenant, which he charged you to observe, that is, the ten words." That these remained centrally important to Israel's understanding of itself as God's covenant people can be seen by the frequency of reference to one or more provisions of the Decalogue in other texts in the canon (e.g., Ps. 81:8–10; Jer. 7:9; Hos. 4:2).

2. The Decalogue does not have the character of a law code in the sense found elsewhere in the Old Testament or in the ancient Near East. It is not legislative in tone and shows no concern for the nuances of particular cases. No sanctions or penalties are prescribed for the violation of its provisions.

The Decalogue seems more intended to lay out broad principles and general moral presumptions which require further legal application and refinement in particular contexts. Patrick Miller suggests that the function is "akin to what we encounter in constitutional law. The foundations are laid for the order of the community. Those foundations do not change. . . . The specifics of those basic guidelines, however, need to be spelled out again and again in changing circumstances and as new matters come up in the community."[79] Thus, many segments of the law codes appear to be giving legal specificity to the broad, general, though imperative, principles of the Decalogue. For example, it has been convincingly suggested that the entire Code of Deuteronomy (Deut. 12–26) is structured around the commandments of the Decalogue.[80]

3. Although there is not space for full commentary, several observations can be made about the structure and content of the Decalogue.

In both Exodus and Deuteronomy the Decalogue is introduced by an identification of God as the God of the Exodus deliverance. God's prior initiative of grace and freedom is the presupposition on which the Decalogue rests. Obedience to these commands will not establish relationship with God; they but spell out the framework of response in community to a relationship already initiated by God.

That response in community begins with exclusive commitment to and worship of God, Yahweh. The first two commandments[81] specify absolute loyalty to Yahweh and prohibit worship of idols. In their present form they seem redundant, and most scholars (noting the long expansion of text with the second commandment) believe that the second commandment originally prohibited images of Yahweh, but in the Israelite conflict over idolatry has been expanded to prohibit the worship of any image. The command to absolute loyalty in the first commandment is thus reinforced with a specific prohibition of idolatry.[82]

The provisions against misuse of God's name (third) and observance of the Sabbath (fourth) continue a concern with the things of God and the proper orientation of the community to God. The Sabbath commandment begins to bridge to the so-called second tablet of the Decalogue since it deals with the honoring of Yahweh's day and the work of God which it commemorates (the creation in Exodus; the Exodus deliverance in Deuteronomy), but it has implications for the activity of the community and relationships within the community (esp. in the Deuteronomic version).[83]

Commandments five through ten all deal with relationship to the neighbor, life in the social community. The close tie between obedience in the relation to God and obedience in the relation to neighbor in the Decalogue makes particularly appropriate Jesus' summary of the greatest commandment in Matt. 22:34–40 as the double commandment to love God and neighbor.

The commandments dealing with the human community begin with the positively formulated command to honor one's parents. This is not concerned with obedience but with protection of father and mother as they age beyond the ability to do productive work.[84]

The next three commandments prohibit the taking of the neighbor's life, wife, or property. In the command against killing a less common verb has been used (*raṣah*) and this has been subject to considerable discussion. It clearly does not apply in the Old Testament to all taking of life (e.g., war and capital punishment), nor can it simply be translated as "murder" since it is sometimes applied to unintentional killing. Childs, summarizing past research, concludes that the term originally "described a type of slaying which called forth blood vengeance. . . . An escape was provided in cities of refuge for the unintentional slayer. . . . The verb came to designate those acts of violence against a person which arose from personal feelings of hatred and malice. The command . . . rejects the right of a person to take the law into his own hands out of a feeling of personal injury."[85]

The command against adultery is aimed at the protection of marriage. Either a man or a woman can be the subject of the verb, but in the patriarchal society of the time a woman is regarded as the property of the husband, thus, as Johann Stamm and Maurice Andrew suggest, "the man can only commit adultery against a marriage other than his own, the woman only against her own."[86]

The commandment against stealing was thought by some originally to apply to the stealing of a person, that is, kidnapping. Whatever the merit of this view for the prehistory of the text, the present text and its widest reflections in the canon regard the eighth commandment as a prohibition of the illegal taking of another's property.[87]

The prohibition against false witness applies specifically to the integrity necessary to judicial processes, but is broadened elsewhere in the canon to include lying, particularly slander, that does injury to another (see Ex. 32:1a; Lev. 19:11; Ps. 15:2–3).[88]

The tenth commandment against coveting may be the most interesting. Both the verb used in Exodus and the different verb in Deuteronomy point to inner desires, feelings, and lusts. Although this can include the action to effectuate one's desire, recent study has supported the contention that this commandment intends to deal with inner motivation—with the moral effect of disposition as well as act.[89] Such a commandment is unenforceable in merely judicial terms, but it extends the moral demands of God's covenant to the human heart. Covetousness as a disposition of the human heart can and does lead to the violation of others seen in the previous commandments, thus, the heart cannot be left free of the moral claims of God's words. The Decalogue here points to a dimension of covenant obedience that cannot be reduced to legalist righteousness. Understood properly the demands of covenant and of the law cannot be reduced to external obedience. In a remarkable metaphor which recognizes this dimension of covenant Moses tells the Israelites "Circumcise, then, the foreskin of your heart" (Deut. 10:16). This foreshadows Jeremiah's hope, "I will put my law within them, and I will write it on their hearts" (Jer. 31:33). This is the necessary background to understand Jesus' opposition to those who treat covenant obedience as an external matter and to his own teachings on internalizing the law and extending it to matters of disposition as well as act (cf. Matt. 5:21–30).[90]

Law as Torah

In many ways our use of the term "law" is unsatisfactory because of the narrow definition this calls to mind for most persons. We have already begun to see the more expansive understanding of law in Israel even when applied to the legal codes.

The Hebrew term, however, is *torah*, and its basic meaning is not law (in our usual understanding) but "instruction" or "guidance." Torah was the teaching of God and its application in the Old Testament is much wider than the legal codes themselves. The term "Torah," in the late Old Testament period and in later Judaism, was applied to the whole of the Pentateuch, the five books of Moses. Thus, the first segment of the Hebrew canon is the Law, obviously not limited to legal codes as such, but referring to the whole of Israel's formative story.[91]

By this time, however, the term "Torah" had already received a broadened usage. It indicated a way of life, an ethical system, oriented to life in relation to God. God, as the giver of Torah, was seen as more than the giver of commandments, but the source of divine teaching and guidance which defined the life of the faithful community. Conversely, the commandments were seen less as stern rules of behavior than as the joyous gift of God's guidance, manifest in the commandments, but in other ways as well.

> The best way to approach the Old Testament ethical system as "Torah" is to remember that the purpose of the Old Testament is not primarily to give information about morality . . . but to provide materials which, when pondered and absorbed into the mind, will suggest the pattern or shape of a way of life lived in the presence of God. . . . *"Torah" is a system by which to live the whole of life in the presence of God, rather than a set of detailed regulations to cover every individual situation in which a moral ruling might be called for.* . . . Torah . . . is in another aspect the design according to which the world was created, and which makes sense of it; and by adhering to it human beings form part of God's plan, and enjoy a kind of fellowship with him. . . . In this sense ethics is not so much a system of obligations as a way of communion with God, which is a cause for joy: hence, the lyrical quality, so puzzling to us who use "law" in a much narrower sense, of such passages in praise of the law as Psalm 19 or Ecclesiasticus 24.23ff. And hence the existence of the text which has so often struck Christian readers as artificial, repetitive, and legalistic, but which could well serve as a complete statement in miniature of Old Testament ethics . . . Psalm 119: one hundred and seventy-six verses in praise of the Torah.[92]

The Shape of Covenant Community

Covenant community in the Old Testament is not just an abstract ideal. In response to the initiating activity of God and within the framework suggested by the legal materials Israel worked to embody covenant community in faithful societal structures and practices.

Covenant as Alternative Community

Recent study on the sociology of ancient Israel has led to a new appreciation for the radically different character of early Israel as a social system. Norman Gottwald,[93] who has written the most extensively in this area, labels the earliest Israelite community as egalitarian in character and stresses its intentional formation as a distinct alternative to the surrounding social systems: Egyptian empire, Canaanite city-states, the small kingdoms of Edom, Moab, and Ammon, and the Philistine military oligarchy. For Gottwald this alternative community was formed in a revolution against the prevailing social structures, and the religion of Yahwism developed as the ideological alternative to support this new social reality.[94]

Others have also noted the emergence of Israel as an alternative society, and while noting the social realities that made this possible, have taken seriously Israel's own claim that the initiating factor was theological. It was the emergence of a new understanding of God and how God is at work in the world that provided the necessary catalyst for the emergence of alternative community. The Old Testament itself is consistent in this claim, and it is important for those who understand the Old Testament as witness to a continuing reality of divine activity in the world not to reduce that claim to a rationalization of purely social forces.

Closer to our view of Israel's origins as an alternative community are these representative statements.

However [the] antecedents are finally understood, *the appearance of a new social reality* is unprecedented. Israel in the thirteenth century is indeed ex nihilo. And that new social reality drives us to the category of revelation. Israel can only be understood in terms of the new call of God and his assertion of an alternative social reality. . . . The participants in the Exodus found themselves . . . involved in the intentional formation of a *new social community* to match the vision of *God's freedom*. . . . Israel emerged not by Moses' hand—although not without Moses' hand—as a genuine alternative community.[95]

Thus a new notion of community was born with the exodus. In compromising it or denying it, as Israel repeatedly would, Israel would compromise or deny its own essential being as a people called by God, a community of freed slaves within which the pyramid of social stratification consigning certain classes to lives of ease and others to relentless suffering and deprivation was to be banned forever. . . . The notion of the alternative community would be kept alive and deepened in the resulting fray. . . . Within this community, every individual was equally precious to God, regardless of social standing, and thus to be protected from exploitation and oppression by the structures intrinsic to the covenant between God and people.[96]

Covenant Religion

Israel understood its own life as a community to be in response to God's saving activity. Thus, remembrance and celebration of that saving history, and praise of the God who called them into being was at the heart of community. Worship was the foundation of Israel as alternative community, and not a secondary expression. In Yahweh, Israel found "the true object of worship, and at the same time, the only dependable basis for human community."[97]

Israel's foundational understanding of itself was as a confessing community. Those who would continue to claim the covenant understanding of community as their own must take seriously the fundamental orientation of the community outside itself to the God it worships.

As a confessing community Israel remembers. One of the roles of covenant religion (worship/cultus) is to tell and retell the formative stories. Remembrance and rehearsal of the faith stories of Exodus, wilderness, and entry into the land (later also the promise to the ancestors) were crucial for establishing the character of Israel's God and for understanding Israel's life as response to that God. It is in the institutions and practices of Israelite worship that foundational identity is established for the covenant community. The cultic festivals of Passover, Weeks, and Booths had origins in the agricultural rhythms of the land, but were quickly adapted by Israel as occasions for remembering and retelling the important formative stories in liturgical form.

As a confessing community Israel praises. On the basis of its remembrance of the stories of God's deliverance and care Israel offers praise to God.[98] It celebrates and sings of all those aspects of the divine character we have discussed (see the entire Psalter). Praise is not simply an activity of Israel's worship life but a quality of life itself, acknowledged as the gift of God. To die was to be beyond the praise of God (Pss. 30:9; 88:11), and by implication the inability to praise God was to be as good as dead.

As a confessing community Israel expresses allegiance to its God as the one true God. This may be especially seen in the *Shema* (Deut. 6:4–5), "Hear, O Israel: The LORD is our God, the LORD alone. You shall love the LORD your God with all your heart, and with all your soul, and with all your might."[99] This central focus on Israel's God as the one God, and the sole object worthy of full love and loyalty was to be passed on as a precious gift to succeeding generations, and kept constantly before them (Deut. 6:6–9). It was the corrective to all forms of allegiance claimed by the world, for example, idolatry, nationalism. It is this focus on God which is the heart of all commandments and statutes attempting to express the covenant understanding; therefore, it is never the commandment itself which is ultimate but the God to which commandment points as the one to whom obedience is due.

As a confessing community Israel frames its social response. The covenant making, including the Decalogue, is bracketed by liturgical passages (Ex. 19:3–8 and 24:3–8) in which the formation of community is anticipated and then solemnized in ceremony before God. Throughout Israel's history the renewal of covenant is not a matter of political process but of liturgical gathering before God (Deut. 5; Josh. 3–5; 24), and was probably celebrated in an annual cultic festival.

As a confessing community religious institutions are prominently included in Israel's social structure from earliest times. The model of Israel as a religion-based league focused around a central sanctuary (as in the Greek amphictyonies) has been largely discredited.[100] Yet it is still clear that the early social organization of Israel included an important role for sanctuaries such as Gilgal, where traditions of exodus and entry into the land are confessionally preserved in the cult.[101] At Gilgal and other early sanctuaries a priestly class was supported for the maintenance of Israelite worship and its important identity-shaping role.

As a confessing community Israel understands itself as God's people. Perhaps the most important text for understanding Israel's own sense of uniqueness and its source in God is Ex. 19:4–6:

> You have seen what I did to the Egyptians, and how I bore you on eagles' wings and brought you to myself. Now therefore, if you obey my voice and keep my covenant, you shall be my treasured possession out of all the peoples. Indeed, the whole earth is mine, but you shall be for me a priestly kingdom and a holy nation.

Whatever the sociohistorical forces operative in the emergence of Israel as a social reality, it is clear from texts such as this that Israel's own sense of uniqueness was theologically grounded.[102] Once again the establishment of special relationship with God is grounded in the liberating action God has already taken in their behalf. God is now inviting to covenant relationship which if accepted will imply obligations on Israel's part; but in that relationship Israel is to be God's own possession, not because God is to be their parochial patron deity. Indeed, the testimony to the universality of God is remarkably expansive here ("the whole earth is mine"), but life as God's special possession implies a role. Israel is to be a "kingdom of priests" (NRSV "priestly kingdom"). This is a remarkably inclusive phrase in a world where priests were a subclass of privilege within society. It also implies that Israel is not separated from the nations for its own benefit alone, but will function among the nations as priests function in society—an entire people as mediator of divine will and blessing. Finally, to be God's holy nation implies life that reflects God's own holiness and all that we discussed earlier in relation to that conception of God.

Israel is indeed separated out for life as an alternative community in the world, but that alternative life is grounded in the alternative reality of Israel's God. Israel is not to be like the other nations because its God is not like the other gods. It is in worship that this theological foundation is remembered and renewed. This covenant religion would have little meaning if it had no reflection in the social organization of ancient Israel. If love of God is tied to love of neighbor, then Israel will live as an alternative community in respect to its societal structures and practices.

Covenant Society

The uniqueness of Israel's covenant relationship to God is reflected in the clear effort of early Israel (thirteenth–eleventh centuries B.C.E.) to embody that uniqueness in concrete social structures. Israel's efforts, however imperfect, model the effort to live as alternative community in the midst of the world.[103]

> There was . . . an organic connection between the exodus event and the communal structures. . . . That connection could not be preserved solely by abstract formulations of belief, but demanded a quality of life relating inextricably to systems of justice, land distribution, use of capital, treatment of vulnerable classes within the society, and the like. These institutions are not formal acci-

dents, but essential structures already implicit in the nature of the God revealed in the exodus.[104]

Righteousness and Justice. Israel's life as a concrete social reality is to reflect the qualities already modeled by God in Israel's experience. Righteousness and justice are the terms most often used to characterize what is called for in covenant society ("Let justice roll down like waters, and righteousness like an everflowing stream," Amos 5:24), but other terms are used as well. Israel is to be holy (Lev. 11:45; Ex. 19:6), to show steadfast love (Hos. 10:12), and to seek shalom (Jer. 29:7).

> He has told you, O mortal, what is good;
>   and what does the LORD require of you
> but to do justice, and to love kindness (*ḥesed*),
>   and to walk humbly with your God?
> (Micah 6:8)

These qualities of Israel's covenant calling are clearly all interrelated. They are modeled by Israel's God and framed by the law as God's gift, but they are lived out in relationships (with God and with neighbor) which require discernment and judgment. These qualities of faithful life cannot be reduced to merely performing the letter of the law. The most dramatic example of this is the story of Tamar to which we already referred in chapter 2. When Judah does not provide for the widowed Tamar and her household as custom required she dresses as a harlot and becomes pregnant by Judah himself. Accused of adultery and about to be executed Tamar reveals to Judah that he is the father of her child, and his response is "She is more in the right than I" (Gen. 38:26). Israel too, is called to conduct of loyalty in covenant relationship which calls for more than obedience to the mere letter of the law.

It goes without saying that for Israel a life characterized by justice and righteousness (and their related qualities) must show the same special regard for the poor, the weak, and the vulnerable that God's activity has already demonstrated and God's law urges. The concrete manifestation of such special concern toward the dispossessed is at the heart of identity as God's covenant people.

> Did not your father eat and drink
>   and do justice and righteousness?

Then it was well with him.
He judged the cause of the poor and needy;
  then it was well.
Is not this to know me?
  says the LORD.

                                   (Jer. 22:15–16)

Politics and Economics. Covenant faithfulness required of
Israel the effort to embody justice, righteousness, and steadfast love in systemic social structures and practices and could
not be left to abstract or episodic concern. The social reality of
Israel was an attempt to embody an alternative model of community consistent with the alternative Yahweh represented
over against the gods of the ancient world.

Politics deals with the manner in which communities organize to make decisions and to utilize (distribute) power.
Gottwald has argued that early Israelite society was a radical,
egalitarian departure from the feudal and hierarchically organized systems of the surrounding nations and city-states.

> The socioeconomic relations of Israelites were egalitarian in the
> sense that the entire populace was assured of approximately equal
> access to resources by means of their organization into extended
> families, protective associations of families (sometimes called
> "clans" . . .), and tribes, federated as an intertribal community
> called "Israel." . . . [These groupings] operated in various auton-
> omous or combined ways to provide mutual aid, external defense,
> and a religious ideology of covenanted or treaty-linked equals.
> . . . The defining feature of politics in old Israel was that political
> functions were diffused throughout the social structure or fo-
> cused in temporary ad hoc role assignments.[105]

In contrast to the hierarchically constructed political systems of the surrounding ancient world, Israel constructed a
social system that was to a considerable extent "grass roots
up" rather than "top down." Much of this seems due to a
valuing of every member of the community, even the weakest
or poorest, and thus, to an effort to remove severe class
distinctions.

We must, however, avoid romanticizing early Israel. Much
in Israelite society reflects and is in continuity with surrounding culture and the emergence of covenant alternative grows
rather than bursting full blown on the scene. There were distinctions of class, particularly seen in relation to slaves and

resident aliens. These were treated with care and respect (esp. compared to other ancient cultures) but not given the full rights of all Israelites. Family structure was patriarchal and hierarchical; women did not enjoy the full rights accorded free men in Israel. Some village and tribal structures seem to reflect power concentrated in the hands of a few. In short, Israel does not represent the full and perfect embodiment of the covenant vision, but a people living toward that vision.[106]

The judicial system was of special importance to a community living toward a vision that fully values all persons. It is to the structures for adjudicating disputes and securing jeopardized rights that the weak must be able to turn. Thus, Israel sought to ensure the equality of all before the law (Deut. 16:20; Lev. 19:15). Corruption of the courts, especially in favor of the rich or the powerful, is among the gravest of offenses (Ex. 18:21; 23:8; Deut. 16:18–19; 2 Chron. 19:7). Advocacy and representation of those who are weak and vulnerable is especially commended (Job 29:14–16). Mott describes this as "taking upon oneself the cause of those who are weak in their own defense."[107]

In the economic sphere[108] Israel's life as an alternative community is also made evident. It is Israelite understandings of the land itself, and its resources, that make the dispersed system of political order described above possible.

> There arose in early Israel the concept of the *nahălâ*, the sacred patrimony, according to which the land was to be divided equitably among the people. . . . The land Yahweh first promised and then conferred on Israel was Yahweh's own possession. No tribe or individual could claim private ownership. Nor were Israelites free to buy additional land or sell the portion allotted to them. . . . If the re-enslavement of parts of the community was to be prevented, each family had to be guaranteed a portion of land sufficient for its physical sustenance.[109]

Although this practice may have had a more limited beginning historically, the tradition now understands it as applicable to all of Israel and a condition of covenant life (Josh. 13–19). Each tribe received a portion in accordance with its size and need (Num. 26:52–56). Most important, God was regarded as the true owner of the land, and the use of the land was thus a sacred trust. "The land shall not be sold in perpetuity, for the land is mine; with me you are but aliens and tenants. Throughout the land that you hold, you shall provide for the redemption of the land" (Lev. 25:23–24). This final phrase seeks to ensure provision for those who lose their inheritance of land (*naḥalah*), through debt or exploitation, to have it restored.

Naturally those forces that are always opposed to justice and righteousness and seek their own wealth and power would be particularly opposed to such an egalitarian distribution of resources. When Ahab wished to buy the vineyard of Naboth he is told, "The LORD forbid that I should give you my ancestral inheritance (*naḥalah*)" (1 Kings 21:3). But, of course, he is falsely accused, executed, and his land is seized for the sake of royal greed. Numerous laws and prophetic utterances seek to protect and extend this foundational institution of covenant economics (Lev. 25–27; Num. 27; 36:6; Micah 2:1–2; Ezek. 47:2).

Economics in ancient Israel has to do with the production and distribution of resources necessary to meet basic human needs. Naturally the land was fundamental to those needs, but covenant concern extended to the resources drawn from the land and the structures necessary to make those resources accessible to all.

The manna story in Ex. 16, which is itself a reminder of God as the ultimate source of the resources that sustain us, included in the provisions for the gathering of the manna, "The Israelites did so, some gathering more, some less. But when they measured it . . . , those who gathered much had nothing over, and those who gathered little had no shortage; they gathered as much as each of them needed" (Ex. 16:17–18). This story is representative of a concern in Israelite covenant economics to provide equal access to basic resources *on the basis of need*. The apostle Paul comes back to this very story for his principle of equitable economic distribution in taking up the collection for the Jerusalem church.

> I do not mean that there should be relief for others and pressure on you, but it is a question of a fair balance between your present abundance and their need, so that their abundance may be for your need, in order that there may be a fair balance. As it is written, "The one who had much did not have too much, and the one who had little did not have too little." (2 Cor. 8:13–15)

Between these two witnesses lie a host of texts as testimony to the seriousness with which Israel sought to provide economic access to all, and to give special consideration and protection to those least capable of maintaining their own interests in the economic system. This remarkable statement from Deut. 15:4–5, 7–8, 10–11 is representative.

There will, however, be no one in need among you . . . if only you will obey the LORD your God. . . . If there is among you anyone in need, a member of your community in any of your towns within the land that the LORD your God is giving you, do not be hard-hearted or tight-fisted toward your needy neighbor. You should rather open your hand, willingly lending enough to meet the need. . . . Give liberally and be ungrudging when you do so. . . . Since there will never cease to be some in need on the earth, I therefore command you, "Open your hand to the poor and needy neighbor in your land."

This passage suggests that if the demands of the covenant were fully embodied, there would be no poverty and need, but since Israel, like all human communities, is a "stiff-necked" people, some of its inhabitants will inevitably be poor. Therefore, God's people are commanded to care for them. This task is part of what it means to be the people of God, and it is not an optional activity.

Adequate food was particularly regarded as an inherent right for every person in the covenant community.[110] Major attention in Israel's covenantal law codes is given to provision of food for those in need. The poor could pick grapes or pluck grain when passing by a field (Deut. 23:24–25; Matt. 12:1–8 and par.). They also had the right to glean in fields and vineyards and to take any sheaves left behind. Owners were urged, for the sake of the poor and hungry, not to be too efficient in their harvest (Deut. 24:19; Lev. 19:9–10; 23:22; Ruth 2:1–3). Anything that grew up in fallow fields belonged to the poor (Ex. 23:10–11), and they were to receive the tithe of every third year (Deut. 14:28–29; 26:12).

The law codes also provide for protection of the dispossessed in other areas of the socioeconomic system.[111] Persons were urged to lend money to the poor (Deut. 15:7–8), but the law prohibited the taking of interest (Ex. 22:25). Garments or other items necessary for survival, if taken from the poor as security for debts, were to be returned each night so that a person might not have to face the night without a cloak (Ex. 22:26–27; Deut. 24:10–13). So that the poor would not remain permanently in debt, the law called for the remission of debts after seven years (Deut. 15:1–2; Lev. 25:1ff.), and if a poor man sold himself into servitude because of debts, he was to be given freedom in the seventh year (Lev. 25:39–55), and he should not then be sent out empty-handed but given provision from the flocks and the harvest (Deut. 15:12–15).

A particular word must be said about the biblical concept of the jubilee year.[112] Israel knew that the covenant would be broken, and that societal structures for corporate care would be perverted and abused. Thus, the law included a provision for every seventh year to be a sabbath year, and after seven sabbath years, the fiftieth year was to be a year of jubilee (Ex. 23:10–14; Deut. 15; Lev. 25; Num. 36:4). In these years the inequities of the social order were to be rectified so that justice might be restored in the covenant community.[113]

In particular, the jubilee ideal called for letting the land lie fallow, the remission of all debts, the liberation of slaves, and the return of family property (the *nahalah*) to its original owner. Many scholars have debated whether such provisions were ever fully carried out. No doubt the jubilee represented an ideal standard of radical societal renewal to restore wholeness and equity. But even if utopian, jubilee represents the kind of daring vision called for on the part of God's people. There is considerable evidence that many faithful figures of the Old and New Testaments, such as Jeremiah (Jer. 34:14) and Jesus himself (who announces his public ministry with a jubilee passage, Luke 4:18–19; cf. Isa. 61:1–2),[114] took this ideal standard of jubilee seriously as the just society for which God calls us to work even if society at large refuses the vision.[115]

Exodus requires Sinai if deliverance is to issue forth in enduring community. Both are the gift of God but it is the gift of covenant, the establishment of ongoing relationship, that requires Israel's response. "Exodus frees us from the forced labor that builds the pharaoh's cities, but Sinai calls us to the covenantal labor that is necessary to build the righteous community."[116]

The Struggles of Covenant Community

Israel's life as God's covenant people was not an unmitigated success story. The narratives that bridge from Sinai to the establishment of monarchy in the mid-eleventh century B.C.E. are stories of struggle. In Exodus, Leviticus, and Numbers narratives record the difficult challenge of the period of wilderness wanderings. The book of Joshua preserves traditions of settlement in the land, some of them reflecting attitudes toward that settlement shaped by the strident nationalism of a later period in Israel's life. The book of Judges gives us stories of crises and heroes, interpreted for us by a historian's framework of apostasy and deliverance—a way of understanding this difficult period of triumphs and tragedies. Space considerations do not allow a detailed treatment of all these narratives and their diverse themes. We can offer only a few programmatic comments.

1. In many ways these stories of Israel's early history are but variations on the themes already introduced in the stories of Israel's origins in Exodus deliverance and Sinai covenant. But these are the stories of the drama which unfolds in trying to live faithfully as the delivered and covenanted people of God. The vision of a vocation as God's people is always somehow in view within these narratives, but the struggles to live that vision let us know that vocation to alternative community in the world is no easy task. Almost immediately following the covenant-making experience itself at Sinai there unfolds the tragic story of idolatry and apostasy in the building and worshiping of the golden calf (Ex. 32–34).[117] It is the first and foremost commandment that is broken in this initial drama of covenant people as sinful people. We are given to know that covenant relationship is no guarantee of privileged virtue before God. Even God's covenant people go forward only as a forgiven people, still dependent on God's grace.

Life as the covenant community remains a challenge. The wilderness stories give rise in Israel to two different images. One is the positive image of life lived in radical awareness of our dependence on God (manna, water, guidance); the other is the negative image of life lived as God's stiff-necked people, stubbornly rebellious and complaining.[118]

2. In dealing with the narrative traditions of Israel's struggles to be the faithful community we should be reminded that we have here stories of Israel's failures as well as its successes in fulfilling its calling as God's covenant people. In Josh. 3–5 the crossing of the Jordan and the commemoration at Gilgal clearly parallel and recall Israel's Exodus origins. In Gilgal we have witness to the places of worship where the identity stories were nurtured and handed on, and we are reminded that land comes to God's people as gift.[119] In the detailed listing of

boundaries we are reminded of the importance to Israel of broad and equitable allocation of land so that all possess an inheritance (*naḥalah*), and in the covenant renewal of Josh. 24 we understand anew the importance of the salvation story as the basis of community. But alongside these important themes stand the exaggerated claims of a tradition of armed conquest. Though largely the traditions of Benjamin and Ephraim, they are now claimed for all Israel and chauvinistically picture all of the Canaanites as swept out of the land (Josh. 11–12). Elsewhere (esp. Judg. 1 but throughout Judges and the books of Samuel) we see a more accurate picture of Israel living in the midst of and surrounded by Canaanite peoples and their settlements. Joshua becomes a reminder of the way in which nationalism can distort the memory of one's own tradition to heighten one's own sense of importance and power.

In the dramatic stories of Judges we find God's purposes able to move forward through diverse human instruments: a faithful and wise leader in Deborah, a foolish and untrusting Jephthah, a man of unfettered passions in Samson. And here, in the story of Gideon, we see the first impulse to move away from the pattern of alternative community posed by covenant. "Rule over us, you and your son and your grandson also" (Judg. 8:22). Although rejected, the impulse to dynastic kingship, common to the ancient world of Israel's time, has made its appearance in Israel. Life as an alternative community is never easy. The pressures are always to conform to the patterns of the world. Perhaps we should not be too surprised that there came a day when the elders approached the prophet Samuel and in revealing words demanded, "Appoint for us, then, a king to govern us, like other nations" (1 Sam. 8:5). The establishment of kingship introduces a new chapter into the Old Testament drama of relationship to God with important ethical implications for covenant life in tension with prevailing cultural influences.

Notes

1. Gerhard von Rad, *The Problem of the Hexateuch and Other Essays,* trans. E. W. T. Dicken (New York: McGraw-Hill Book Co., 1966), pp. 13–26; Martin Noth, *A History of Pentateuchal Traditions,* trans. Bernhard W. Anderson (Englewood Cliffs, N.J.: Prentice-Hall, 1972; German ed. 1948). Their argument is based on the absence of reference to Sinai in some of the credo statements (e.g., Deut. 26:5ff.) and other literary tensions between Exodus and Sinai traditions.

2. See Ernest W. Nicholson, *Exodus and Sinai in History and Tradition* (Richmond: John Knox Press, 1973), pp. 1–32, for a detailed treatment of this debate and its resolution against the views of von Rad and Noth. See also Brevard S. Childs, *Introduction to the Old Testament as Scripture* (Philadelphia: Fortress Press, 1979), pp. 171–172, for a discussion of this issue and the apt observation, "It seems a priori unlikely that traditions so basic to the faith of Israel as the exodus and Sinai could have existed apart from one another in complete isolation for such a long period."

3. Thomas W. Ogletree, *The Use of the Bible in Christian Ethics* (Philadelphia: Fortress Press, 1983), p. 53.

4. For a readable survey of the scholarly discussion of covenant, see Ernest W. Nicholson, *God and His People* (Oxford: Oxford University Press, 1986).

5. George E. Mendenhall, *Law and Covenant in Israel and the Ancient Near East* (Pittsburgh: Biblical Colloquium, 1955); see also Klaus Baltzer, *The Covenant Formulary: In Old Testament, Jewish and Early Christian Writings,* 2nd ed., rev., trans. D. Green (Philadelphia: Fortress Press, 1971).

6. Dennis J. McCarthy, *Treaty and Covenant: A Study in Form in the Ancient Oriental Documents and in the Old Testament*, AnBib 21 (Rome: Pontifical Biblical Institute, 1963), effectively raised serious doubts about the treaty hypothesis and concluded that only Deuteronomy showed serious signs of treaty form influence and that more on the model of first millennium Hittite treaties. See also Erhard Gerstenberger, "Covenant and Commandment," *JBL* 84 (1965): 38–51. Detailed discussion of the treaty hypothesis and its critics can be found in Nicholson, *Exodus and Sinai in History and Tradition*, pp. 33–52; Nicholson, *God and His People*; and Dennis J. McCarthy, *Old Testament Covenant: A Survey of Current Opinions* (Richmond: John Knox Press, 1972).

7. The expressed will of God is made clear in the commandment to be holy, but the nature of that divine holiness cannot be made clear from the commandment alone. It requires knowledge of how God's holiness has been experienced in Israel's encounters with the divine. Obedience to God's revealed will and imitation of God (*imitatio Dei*) cannot be too sharply separated as modes of moral authority.

8. Walter C. Kaiser, Jr., *Toward Old Testament Ethics* (Grand Rapids: Zondervan Publishing House, 1983), pp. 139–143, has made holiness (of God and Israel) the central organizing focus of Old Testament ethics. I have learned much from him about the moral significance of holiness, but I am not prepared to make it the sole category for understanding the moral character of God or Israel. I certainly am prepared to argue the central importance of holiness alongside several other important biblical categories. Kaiser seems also to imply that any effort to systematically treat the ethics of the Old Testament based on its whole shape as scripture requires the identification of some single overarching moral category (see pp. 141–142). With this I simply disagree.

9. Werner H. Schmidt, *The Faith of the Old Testament: A History* (Philadelphia: Westminster Press, 1983), pp. 152–156. His argument seems to hinge on holiness as a late concept in Israel, and therefore not central to the Old Testament message. Both parts of this assertion are incorrect.

10. James Muilenburg, "Holiness," *IDB*, ed. George A. Buttrick (Nashville: Abingdon Press, 1962), 2:616. For a classic discussion of basic vocabulary, etymologies, and definitions related to God's holiness, see Norman H. Snaith, *The Distinctive*

Ideas of the Old Testament (New York: Schocken Books, 1964), pp. 21–50.

11. Rudolf Otto, *The Idea of the Holy*, 9th ed., trans. J. Harvey (Oxford: Oxford University Press, 1928).

12. Otto also believed it was nonethical which more recent studies of holiness in the Old Testament clearly dispute.

13. John G. Gammie, *Holiness in Israel*, OBT (Philadelphia: Fortress Press, 1989), pp. 5–7. Gammie's work is the most important and comprehensive recent study of God's holiness. It is especially noteworthy for bringing out the ethical dimensions of the concept.

14. Ibid., p. 7. Gammie points to Ex. 19:10–12 for an example.

15. Paul D. Hanson, *The People Called: The Growth of Community in the Bible* (San Francisco: Harper & Row, 1986), p. 27.

16. Gammie, *Holiness in Israel*, p. 195.

17. Ibid., pp. 195–196.

18. Kaiser, *Toward Old Testament Ethics*, p. 143.

19. See John T. Willis, "Ethics in a Cultic Setting," in *Essays in Old Testament Ethics*, ed. James L. Crenshaw and John T. Willis (New York: KTAV Publishing House, 1974), pp. 147–163.

20. A sampling of the reduplication of Ex. 34:6–7: Num. 14:18; Deut. 5:9–10; 7:9; 1 Kings 3:6; Neh. 9:17; Pss. 86:15; 103:8, 17; 145:8; Jer. 32:18–19; Joel 2:13; Jonah 4:2; Nahum 1:3. See R. Dentan, "The Literary Affinities of Exodus XXXIV:6ff.," *VT* 13 (1963): 34–51. See also Terence E. Fretheim, *The Suffering of God: An Old Testament Perspective*, OBT (Philadelphia: Fortress Press, 1984), pp. 25–27, and Phyllis Trible, *God and the Rhetoric of Sexuality*, OBT (Philadelphia: Fortress Press, 1978), pp. 1–5.

21. I have chosen to use "steadfast love" because it is the usual translation in the NRSV text I am using for most biblical citations, and because it does convey the dual elements of fidelity and graceful gift that are a part of the meaning of *ḥesed*.

22. Katharine Doob Sakenfeld, *Faithfulness in Action: Loyalty in Biblical Perspective*, OBT (Philadelphia: Fortress Press, 1985). This excellent study is the most thorough available, and the most helpful theologically. She cites a number of earlier, important works, including her own *The Meaning of Ḥesed in the Hebrew Bible* (Missoula, Mont.: Scholars Press, 1978).

23. Sakenfeld, *Faithfulness in Action*, p. 131.

24. See Snaith, *Distinctive Ideas of the Old Testament,* p. 100.

25. Sakenfeld, *Faithfulness in Action,* p. 132.

26. The statement of Ex. 34 holds "in tension God the lover and God the punisher." Trible, *God and the Rhetoric of Sexuality,* p. 1. We shall discuss God's judgment as an expression of God's steadfast love in chapter 7 on the prophets.

27. See Hanson, *People Called,* pp. 27–28, for a discussion of this.

28. Elizabeth R. Achtemeier, "Righteousness in the OT," *IDB* 4:80–85 (quotation on p. 80). An extensive bibliography and history of research on both righteousness and justice in the Old Testament and the ancient Near East may be found in Leon Epsztein, *Social Justice in the Ancient Near East and the People of the Bible* (London: SCM Press, 1986).

29. Gerhard von Rad, *Old Testament Theology,* vol. 1 (New York: Harper & Row, 1962), p. 371. See also Elizabeth R. Achtemeier, "Righteousness in the OT," p. 80: "Righteousness is in the OT the fulfilment of the demands of a relationship, whether that relationship be with men or with God."

30. See von Rad, *Old Testament Theology,* p. 373, and Snaith, *Distinctive Ideas of the Old Testament,* p. 77.

31. James Muilenburg, *The Way of Israel: Biblical Faith and Ethics* (New York: Harper & Row, 1961), p. 60. See also Stephen Charles Mott, *Biblical Ethics and Social Change* (Oxford: Oxford University. Press, 1982), p. 63.

32. Von Rad, *Old Testament Theology,* vol. 1, p. 374. Von Rad points here to Zeph. 3:5 where the prophet speaks of God's righteousness as the daily renewal of divine guidance "like the light which does not fail."

33. This is particularly stressed by Henri Cazelles, "A propos de quelques textes difficiles relatifs à la justice de Dieu dans l'Ancien Testament," *RB* 58 (1951): 185–188. See also Elizabeth R. Achtemeier, "Righteousness in the OT," p. 83.

34. Epsztein, *Social Justice in the Ancient Near East,* p. 46. See also Stephen Charles Mott, "Justice," *HBD,* ed. Paul J. Achtemeier et al. (San Francisco: Harper & Row, 1985), pp. 519–520.

35. Christopher J. H. Wright, *An Eye for an Eye: The Place of Old Testament Ethics Today* (Downers Grove, Ill.: Intervarsity Press, 1983), p. 134.

36. This aspect of God's character has been especially stressed in the liberation theologies. See as representative José Porfirio Miranda, *Marx and the Bible: A Critique of the Philos-*

ophy of Oppression (Maryknoll, N.Y.: Orbis Books, 1974), pp. 109–160, and Gustavo Gutiérrez, *A Theology of Liberation: History, Politics and Salvation* (Maryknoll, N.Y.: Orbis Books, 1973).

37. Mott, *Biblical Ethics and Social Change*, pp. 67–70.

38. Snaith, *Distinctive Ideas of the Old Testament*, p. 70, writes of justice as "vindication by God of those who cannot themselves secure their own right." Mott, *Biblical Ethics and Social Change*, p. 220, adds that "normally, God's justice is implemented by means of human justice, but when human institutions fail in this purpose God acts directly (Isa. 59:12–16)."

39. Hanson, *People Called*, p. 68, also calls attention to the importance of Ps. 82.

40. Bernard S. Jackson, "Law," *HBD*, pp. 548–551, makes a particular point of the renewed attention to this area of study.

41. "The laws of Leviticus which stemmed originally from very different periods, and which reflected remarkably different sociological contexts, are subordinated to the one overarching theological construct, namely, the divine will made known to Moses at Sinai for every successive generation. This hermeneutical move is not to be characterized as simply a dehistoricizing of the tradition. Rather, . . . one historical moment in Israel's life has become the norm by means of which all subsequent history of the nation is measured. If a law functions authoritatively for Israel, it must be from Sinai." Brevard S. Childs, *Old Testament Theology in a Canonical Context* (Philadelphia: Fortress Press, 1985), pp. 54–55.

42. Harry P. Nasuti, "Identity, Identification, and Imitation: The Narrative Hermeneutics of Biblical Law," *Journal of Law and Religion* 4 (1986): 9–23.

43. Nasuti, ibid., p. 11, observes that for Israel "the narrative situates the law and gives it the context from which it receives its significance." Stanley Hauerwas, *A Community of Character: Toward a Constructive Christian Social Ethic* (Notre Dame, Ind.: University of Notre Dame Press, 1981), pp. 67, 91, has argued more generally that the non-narrative material of the Bible gains its intelligibility from the narrative material.

44. Childs, *Introduction to the Old Testament as Scripture*, p. 174.

45. Ibid.

46. Some of the general works on Israelite law that have been especially helpful are Dale Patrick, *Old Testament Law* (Atlanta: John Knox Press, 1985); Joseph Blenkinsopp, *Wis-*

dom and Law in the Old Testament: The Ordering of Life in Israel *and Early Judaism* (Oxford: Oxford University Press, 1983); Hans Jochen Boecker, *Law and the Administration of Justice in the Old Testament and Ancient East* (Minneapolis: Augsburg Publishing House, 1980); G. Quell, "The Concept of Law in the Old Testament," *TDNT,* ed. Gerhard Kittel and Gerhard Friedrich (Grand Rapids: Wm. B. Eerdmans Publishing Co., 1966), 2: 174–178; Martin Noth, *The Laws of the Pentateuch and Other Studies,* trans. D. R. Ap-Thomas (Edinburgh: Oliver & Boyd, 1966); David Daube, *Studies in Biblical Law* (New York: KTAV Publishing House, 1969); Anthony Phillips, *Ancient Israel's Criminal Law* (Oxford: Basil Blackwell Publisher, 1970).

47. Albrecht Alt's 1934 article is now available in English translation "The Origins of Israelite Law," *Essays on Old Testament History and Religion,* trans. R. A. Wilson (Oxford: Basil Blackwell Publisher, 1966), pp. 79–132. Alt's views were refined and made more broadly influential by his student Martin Noth, *Laws of the Pentateuch and Other Studies.*

48. Erhard Gerstenberger, *Wesen und Herkunft des "Apodiktischen Rechts,"* WMANT 20 (Neukirchen-Vluyn: Neukirchener Verlag, 1965), and "Covenant and Commandment," n. 6 above. Gerstenberger argued because of the wisdom connections that apodictic law originated with patriarchal instruction in the clan and was later adapted by Israel to the legal setting. This view of origin has not received widespread support.

49. See Patrick, *Old Testament Law,* pp. 23–24.

50. Berend Gemser, "The Importance of the Motive Clause in Old Testament Law," VTSup (Leiden: E. J. Brill, 1953), 1: 50–66.

51. Gemser identified four types of motive clause: explanatory, ethical, religious, and historical. There are, however, theological dimensions to all of the last three listed. Rifat Sonsino, *Motive Clauses in Hebrew Law: Biblical Forms and Near Eastern Parallels* (Chico, Calif.: Scholars Press, 1980), disputes Gemser's contention that the motive clause is unique to Israel, but is forced to admit a different character to parallels he finds in the ancient Near East and to note the rarity of such clauses elsewhere compared to the high percentage of motive clauses in Israel's social legislation. See also G. Chirichigno, "A Theological Investigation of Motivation in Old Testament Law," *JETS* (1981): 303–314.

52. Paul D. Hanson, "The Theological Significance of Contradiction Within the Book of the Covenant," in *Canon and*

Authority, ed. G. W. Coats and B. O. Long (Philadelphia: Fortress Press, 1977), pp. 110–131. See also Hanson, *People Called*, pp. 44–52.

53. Hanson, *People Called*, pp. 45–46.

54. Ibid., p. 50. On the laws related to slaves see Anthony Phillips, "The Laws of Slavery: Exodus 21:2–11," *JSOT* 30 (1984): 51–66.

55. See Hanson, "Theological Significance of Contradiction," p. 127.

56. Kaiser, *Toward Old Testament Ethics*, has organized his book in some of its major sections around a survey of the contents of the great law codes and then around particular topics or arenas of moral concern addressed out of this moral legislation. This alternative pattern of organization greatly supplements my own approach. See also the thorough discussion of the codes in Patrick, *Old Testament Law*. His treatment is especially admirable for its accessibility to the nonspecialist.

57. Epsztein, *Social Justice in the Ancient Near East*, p. 140.

58. For a recent example see Kaiser, *Toward Old Testament Ethics*, pp. 44–48, where he distinguishes Israel's moral law from its civil and ceremonial law and argues for normative precedence in the moral laws. See Robert R. Wilson, "Approaches to Old Testament Ethics," in *Canon, Theology, and Old Testament Interpretation: Essays in Honor of Brevard S. Childs*, ed. Gene M. Tucker, David L. Petersen, and Robert R. Wilson (Philadelphia: Fortress Press, 1988), pp. 66–67, for a brief critique of this view. In my opinion, the problems Kaiser is attempting to treat arise only if the primary focus is on the prescriptive authority of Israel's laws.

59. Ogletree, *Use of the Bible in Christian Ethics*, pp. 54–55.

60. A helpful discussion and references to the wider literature on the talion formula are found in Boecker, *Law and the Administration of Justice in the Old Testament and Ancient East*, pp. 171–175.

61. Ibid., pp. 174–175.

62. Childs, *Old Testament Theology in a Canonical Context*, p. 56.

63. Patrick, *Old Testament Law*, pp. 189–190, 198, 200. Patrick further argues that with the fixing of the canon the authority of the law codes moved in the direction of identifying the divine Law solely with the written rules of the codes, but that Jesus and later New Testament traditions "revived the idea that God's law is an unwritten law" (p. 190).

64. Stanley Hauerwas, *The Peaceable Kingdom: A Primer in Christian Ethics* (Notre Dame, Ind.: University of Notre Dame Press, 1983), p. 119, writing on the formation of character in community, notes: "For the telos in fact is a narrative, and the good is not so much a clearly defined 'end' as it is a sense of the journey on which that community finds itself."

65. Nasuti, "Identity, Identification, and Imitation." I am deeply indebted to Nasuti's work in this section. In part, he is applying contemporary literary theory on the nature and identity of the reader to biblical law. "Whereas biblical narrative might imply (or invite) a reader, biblical law specifies a reader" (p. 12).

66. Stanley Hauerwas has stressed the role of Israel's narrative and legal traditions in shaping identity. This identity is dependent on both Israel's remembering and Israel's imitating of God's actions in its behalf. In his stress on the priority of narrative he has not fully seen the narrative function of the law in Israel, but his views are obviously along the same lines as this discussion. See Hauerwas, *Peaceable Kingdom*, pp. 77f.

67. Nasuti, "Identity, Identification, and Imitation," pp. 12–14.

68. See Bruce C. Birch, "Memory in Congregational Life," in *Congregations: Their Power to Form and Transform*, ed. C. Ellis Nelson (Atlanta: John Knox Press, 1988), pp. 20–47. See also Brevard Childs, *Memory and Tradition in Israel* (London: SCM Press, 1962), esp. pp. 52–54.

69. Nasuti, "Identity, Identification, and Imitation," pp. 16–18. He also notes the central use of this dynamic in the liberation theologies. "Israel's identity as a community of liberated slaves demands a different relationship with the oppressed, a relationship similar to that which God had with the Israelites in their own oppressed state" (p. 22). He cites Gutiérrez, Cone, and Miranda as examples of this imitation of God motif in liberation theology.

70. Hanson, *People Called*, p. 44, also refers to this dynamic in the law codes as an *imitatio Dei*.

71. There are limits to the imitation of God. See Dale Patrick, *The Rendering of God in the Old Testament*, OBT (Philadelphia: Fortress Press, 1981).

72. In the light of the identity-shaping function of the law, and the wider significance of relationship to the covenant God, it seems to me that we should avoid describing Old Testament ethics prior to the exile as primarily deontological in

character. So Ogletree, *Use of the Bible in Christian Ethics*, pp. 47–48.

73. Childs, *Old Testament Theology in a Canonical Context*, p. 51.

74. His methodology and its implications are thoroughly spelled out in Norman K. Gottwald, *The Tribes of Yahweh: A Sociology of the Religion of Liberated Israel, 1250–1050 B.C.E.* (Maryknoll, N.Y.: Orbis Books, 1979), and *The Hebrew Bible: A Socio-Literary Introduction* (Philadelphia: Fortress Press, 1985).

75. Brevard Childs, *Old Testament Theology in a Canonical Context*, p. 25, writes of Gottwald's method, "Gottwald's position results in a massive theological reductionism. Certainly lying at the heart of Christian theology is the confession that God has brought into being a new reality which is different in kind from all immanental forces at work in the world (Isa. 65:17; Rom. 4:17). . . . The Bible bears testimony to a divine activity which breaks into human society in countless unexpected ways. . . . To propose that theology and social reality can be simply identified destroys any possibility of doing justice to the complex tensions within the Bible between the ways of God and the world."

76. Ibid., p. 25.

77. Of particular importance I would note the following: Walter Harrelson, *The Ten Commandments and Human Rights*, OBT (Philadelphia: Fortress Press, 1980); Eduard Nielsen, *The Ten Commandments in New Perspective*, SBT (Chicago: Alec R. Allenson, 1968); Johann Jakob Stamm and Maurice E. Andrew, *The Ten Commandments in Recent Research*, SBT (Chicago: Alec R. Allenson, 1967); Brevard S. Childs, *The Book of Exodus; A Critical, Theological Commentary*, OTL (Philadelphia: Westminster Press, 1974), pp. 385–439; Brevard S. Childs, "The Theological Significance of the Decalogue," *Old Testament Theology in a Canonical Context* (Philadelphia: Fortress Press, 1985); Moshe Greenberg, "Decalogue," *EncJud* 5 (Jerusalem: Keter Publishing House, 1971), cols. 1435–1446; Patrick D. Miller, Jr., "The Place of the Decalogue in the Old Testament and Its Law," *Int* 43 (1989): 229–242; Walter C. Kaiser, Jr., *Toward Old Testament Ethics* (Grand Rapids: Zondervan Publishing House, 1983), pp. 81–95.

78. For example, the commandment on the Sabbath is different in Ex. 20 than in Deut. 5. Probably the original list was composed of short, direct commands without the comment and elaboration that now accompanies some of the command-

ments. That such development has occurred does not argue against the Mosaic origin of the original list. See Harrelson, *Ten Commandments and Human Rights*, pp. 19–48.

79. Miller, "Place of the Decalogue," p. 231.

80. Although building on earlier suggestions, Stephen A. Kaufman, "The Structure of the Deuteronomic Law," *Maarav* 1 (April 1979): 105–158, has argued this case most convincingly in the modern discussion. His view is adopted by Kaiser, *Toward Old Testament Ethics*, pp. 127–137.

81. It is well known that different Christian and Jewish traditions have utilized conflicting systems for numbering the commandments. Tables showing these numberings are standard in Bible reference works. I am following the numbering system which treats "no other gods before me" as the first commandment, "no idols" as the second, and which treats all of the "no coveting" provisions as a single, tenth commandment.

82. For this and all subsequent reference to the historical and literary development of the commandments into their present form, see the detailed discussions on each commandment in Stamm and Andrew, *Ten Commandments in Recent Research*.

83. So Miller, "Place of the Decalogue," p. 233.

84. Childs, *Book of Exodus*, p. 418.

85. Ibid., p. 421.

86. Stamm and Andrew, *Ten Commandments in Recent Research*, p. 100. See Henry McKeating, "Sanctions Against Adultery in Ancient Israelite Society, with Some Reflections on Methodology in the Study of Old Testament Ethics," *JSOT* 11 (1979): 57–72.

87. See Harrelson, *Ten Commandments and Human Rights*, pp. 138f.

88. Miller, "Place of the Decalogue," p. 241.

89. See Childs, *Book of Exodus*, pp. 425–428; Harrelson, *Ten Commandments and Human Rights*, pp. 148–154.

90. See esp. Harrelson, *Ten Commandments and Human Rights*, for the extension of the Decalogue and its pertinence to the church and issues of the modern world.

91. See James A. Sanders, *Torah and Canon* (Philadelphia: Fortress Press, 1972).

92. John Barton, "Approaches to Ethics in the Old Testament," in *Beginning Old Testament Study*, ed. John Rogerson (Philadelphia: Westminster Press, 1982), pp. 128, 130. See

also Ronald E. Clements, *Old Testament Theology: A Fresh Approach* (Atlanta: John Knox Press, 1978), pp. 104–130.

93. Gottwald, *Tribes of Yahweh* is an extensive application of social scientific method to the data for Israel's social formation and structure in this early period.

94. Gottwald, *Hebrew Bible*, pp. 284–286.

95. Walter Brueggemann, *The Prophetic Imagination* (Philadelphia: Fortress Press, 1978), pp. 16, 17, 19.

96. Hanson, *People Called*, pp. 22–23.

97. Ibid., p. 69.

98. On the central importance of praise in the life of Israel, see Walter Brueggemann, *Israel's Praise: Doxology Against Idolatry and Ideology* (Philadelphia: Fortress Press, 1988).

99. Patrick D. Miller, Jr., "The Most Important Word: The Yoke of the Kingdom," *Iliff Review* 41 (1984): 17–29; J. Gerald Janzen, "On the Most Important Word in the Shema (Deut. VI 4–5)," *VT* 37 (1987): 280–300, and "The Yoke That Gives Rest," *Int* 41 (1987): 256–268.

100. See the discussion of this debate and a convenient chart of comparative features in Gottwald, *Hebrew Bible*, pp. 280–284. The amphictyony model was popularized by Martin Noth; see his *The History of Israel* (New York: Harper & Brothers, 1960), pp. 85–109.

101. See J. Alberto Soggin, "Gilgal, Passah und Landnahme," VTSup 15 (1966): 263–277; Frank M. Cross, Jr., *Canaanite Myth and Hebrew Epic: Essays in the History of the Religion of Israel* (Cambridge, Mass.: Harvard University Press, 1973), pp. 103–105, 137–139.

102. See Childs, *Book of Exodus*, p. 367.

103. Several recent works have suggested tripartite models for understanding covenant community as alternative community. I have been greatly instructed by each of them, but in the end have not found the threefold division convincing. Wright, *An Eye for an Eye*, pp. 19–20, suggests an "Old Testament ethical framework" composed of a triangular relationship between God, Israel, and the land. He then discusses these as "the theological angle, the social angle and the economic angle." Similarly, Brueggemann, *Prophetic Imagination*, pp. 11–27, relates religion, economics, and politics. In the Mosaic model he finds a distinct character to each of these: a religion of God's freedom, an economics of equality, and a politics of justice. I find both of these treatments very congenial to my

own, but I have had trouble making this sharp a distinction between Israel's covenant economics and its sociopolitical life. They are interrelated in the social system of early Israel. Further, I do not wish to use terms like justice to apply only to the political dimension of Israel's life since there is also an obvious understanding of economic justice in the covenant model. In Wright I find people as a social reality too abstract when discussed apart from the land and the socioeconomic institutions of life in the land. It seems to me that the dominant contrast in the covenant model of alternative community is between religious life (focused on love of God) and societal life (focused on love of neighbor), and the necessary interrelationship of these two in the covenant model of community. Covenant society will obviously have political and economic dimensions. Hanson, *People Called*, pp. 30–86, speaks of a triadic model composed of worship, righteousness, and compassion as the qualities of the covenant community. As with Wright, Brueggemann, and myself, worship places the originating focus of the community on God. Hanson uses righteousness to represent the role of faithful order in the community and compassion to indicate the quality of heart which guards against rigid legalism. Righteousness counterbalances what might be a free-wheeling romanticism if left to compassion alone. I do not find that righteousness and compassion are used in the Hebrew Bible in this way. Righteousness might issue forth in the law but might require breaking of the law as with Tamar (Gen. 38). Compassion can be an expression of righteousness. In Hanson's work justice crops up as a term in relation to both righteousness and compassion. Although sympathetic with his intent I do not find the terminology to correspond with the way in which the community of Israel describes itself.

104. Hanson, *People Called*, p. 23.

105. Gottwald, *Hebrew Bible*, pp. 285, 286. See also George E. Mendenhall, "Social Organization in Early Israel," in *Magnalia Dei: The Mighty Acts of God. Essays on the Bible and Archaeology in Memory of G. Ernest Wright*, ed. Frank M. Cross, W. E. Lemke, and Patrick D. Miller (Garden City, N.Y.: Doubleday & Co., 1976), pp. 132–151.

106. See Childs's critique of Gottwald on this issue in *Old Testament Theology in a Canonical Context*, pp. 176–177.

107. Mott, *Biblical Ethics and Social Change*, p. 72.

108. See the fuller discussions in Christopher J. H. Wright, *God's People in God's Land: Family, Land and Property in the Old*

Testament (Grand Rapids/Exeter: Eerdmans/Paternoster, 1990); Wright, *An Eye for an Eye*, pp. 67–102; Bruce C. Birch and Larry L. Rasmussen, *The Predicament of the Prosperous* (Philadelphia: Westminster Press, 1978), pp. 85–89.

109. Hanson, *People Called*, p. 64.

110. For a survey of basic biblical material dealing with hunger and poverty, see Bruce C. Birch, "Hunger, Poverty and Biblical Religion," *Christian Century* 92 (June 11–18, 1975): 593–599, and Ronald J. Sider, ed., *Cry Justice! The Bible on Hunger and Poverty* (New York: Paulist Press, 1980).

111. See Roland de Vaux, *Ancient Israel: Its Life and Institutions* (London: Darton, Longman & Todd, 1961), pp. 164–177.

112. Ibid., pp. 173–177. Much of the current interest in jubilee has been stirred by André Trocme, *Jesus and the Nonviolent Revolution* (Scottdale, Pa.: Herald Press, 1974).

113. Miller, "Place of the Decalogue," pp. 237–238, gives an especially helpful statement on the sabbatical and the jubilee years as an outgrowth of the principle embodied in observance of the Sabbath in the Decalogue.

114. See John Howard Yoder, *The Politics of Jesus* (Grand Rapids: Wm. B. Eerdmans Publishing Co., 1972).

115. The enduring quality of that vision might be noted in the fact that some of the founders of a new nation in the American colonies chose to inscribe the Liberty Bell with a passage from the jubilee laws of Leviticus, "Proclaim liberty throughout all the land unto all the inhabitants thereof" (Lev. 25:10, KJV).

116. Birch and Rasmussen, *Predicament of the Prosperous*, p. 89.

117. See Childs, *Book of Exodus*, pp. 553ff.

118. See George W. Coats, *Rebellion in the Wilderness* (Nashville: Abingdon Press, 1968), and *Moses: Heroic Man, Man of God*, JSOTSup 57 (Sheffield: JSOT Press, 1988). This later includes an extensive recent bibliography on literature related to this period. For a helpful theological view of this period see Walter Brueggemann, *The Land*, OBT (Philadelphia: Fortress Press, 1977), p. 28.

119. See Hanson, *People Called*, pp. 31–34.

6

Royal Ideal
and
Royal Reality

Around 1000 B.C.E., Israel, under social and military pressure (particularly from the Philistines), established a kingship. After a shaky start under Saul, this experiment in monarchy developed into a strong and influential nation under David and Solomon. Although this move to monarchy relieved some political tensions and perhaps secured the very existence of Israel as an independent entity, it also created serious theological problems with social repercussions. These centered on the proper conception of the community in its relationship to God and neighbor. What adaptations were necessary and possible for the covenant community of Yahweh to accommodate a kingship which borrowed much of its trappings from surrounding Canaanite culture? As a united kingdom the Israelite monarchy was short-lived. In 922 B.C.E. the kingdom divided into northern and southern kingdoms, Israel and Judah, due to many of the pressures introduced by the rapid changes under David and Solomon. Kingship continued in the north until 722 when Israel was conquered by the Assyrians, and in the south until 587 when Jerusalem was destroyed and Judah subjugated by the Babylonians.

Reconstruction of the history of this period and of the development of the literary sources (primarily the books of Samuel and the books of Kings) is notoriously complex.[1] Although we may have occasion to refer to these historical and literary problems from time to time, they are not our primary focus. Our focus will be on the theological-ethical address of the text in its present, final shape.[2] It is our contention that the biblical text, though preserving disparate voices and perspectives, has not passed them on to us at random. The text is organized in order to give us the witness of the biblical community on this important period as it has finally evaluated diverse viewpoints and rendered its own judgment on God's will and work in the midst of these events.

Attention to the crucial importance of the transition to monarchy for Israel's history has led to some neglect of the theological importance of the historical books of Samuel and of Kings.[3] It cannot be overemphasized that the political crisis of kingship resulted in a crisis for Israel's moral and theological vision as well. Important and perennial ethical issues come to the fore: the relationship between divine will and human leadership; tension and accommodation between religious and sociopolitical institutions; the role of theological and ethical discernment in the shaping of public policy. These are among the issues that occupy our attention as we look at this crucial chapter in the biblical story.

God as Divine Sovereign

It is not possible to assess the literature on Israel's monarchy without first giving attention to the affirmation throughout the Old Testament of the sovereignty of God. If there is to be an earthly ruler, what is the relationship to the reign of the divine sovereign?

We have waited until this point in Israel's story for a full discussion of this rich image of God for obvious reasons, but we have encountered the imagery of God's sovereign rule in passing at several earlier points in our discussion. In Gen. 1 it is God's sovereignty as Creator and ruler that we represent in our humanity as bearers of the image of God. In Ex. 15:18 the victory of God, the Divine Warrior, over the forces of an oppressive pharaoh to bring deliverance to Hebrew slaves, is concluded by the proclamation of divine reign: "The LORD will reign forever and ever." In discussion of the covenant relationship of Yahweh to Israel some of the imagery is taken from the treaty relationship of kings to their subjects now applied to a divine ruler and the people of that ruler, Israel.

Throughout much of the Old Testament literature the reign of God as divine sovereign is a common image. In addition to the contexts already encountered we will also draw in our discussion on the preaching of the prophets, and especially on the enthronement psalms. There are two distinct foci to the claim that God is sovereign: God is sovereign over the cosmos; God is sovereign over the people, Israel.

Sovereign Over the Cosmos

The foundation for affirmation of God as sovereign over the whole of creation is laid in the testimony to God as Creator in the priestly account of Gen. 1 (see chapter 3). The portrait of God in general is one of power and majesty. In picturing creation as the overcoming of chaos the priestly creation tradition appropriates the battle with chaos tradition known elsewhere in the ancient Near East. In those traditions victory over chaos ended in the establishment of the cosmos and the enthronement of the creator God as sovereign over the ongoing cosmos (e.g., Marduk in the *enuma elish* or Baal in the Canaanite texts). The commission of humankind to its task in the creation comes in delegated royal terms, to "have dominion" (Gen. 1:28). Created in the image of God, humankind exercises dominion as representative of God's sovereignty.

It is in the enthronement psalms that we find the clearest affirmation of Yahweh as ruler over the whole of creation. The liturgies of the Psalms proclaim that God (Yahweh) is king over the gods, and this ascendancy is related to God's rule over all creation as both its originator and sovereign.

> For the LORD is a great God,
>   and a great King above all gods.
> In his hand are the depths of the earth;
>   the heights of the mountains are his also.
> The sea is his, for he made it,
>   and the dry land, which his hands have formed.
>   (Ps. 95:3–5)

> Ascribe to the LORD, O sons of gods. . . .
> The LORD sits enthroned over the flood;
>   the LORD sits enthroned as king forever.
>   (Ps. 29:1a, 10)

Israel's liturgies preserve the ancient view of a council of gods, each ruler over a particular people. "When the Most High apportioned the nations, when he divided humankind, he fixed the boundaries of the peoples according to the number of the gods" (Deut. 32:8).

Yahweh's ascendancy over the gods and their nations is based on Yahweh's role as Creator and ruler over the whole of the cosmos. The language of the *Chaoskampf*, the battle of God with the forces of chaos (the sea, the waters, the flood, Rahab, Leviathan) to establish the order of creation, is prominent in the psalms which celebrate Yahweh's enthronement as king.[4] In these themes the enthronement psalms obviously draw on a common tradition in the royal cultus of the ancient Near East.[5]

> Let the heavens praise your wonders, O LORD,
>   your faithfulness in the assembly of the holy ones.
> For who in the skies can be compared to the LORD?
>   Who among the heavenly beings is like the LORD,
> a God feared in the council of the holy ones. . . .
> You rule the raging of the sea;
>   when its waves rise, you still them.
> You crushed Rahab like a carcass;
>   you scattered your enemies with your mighty arm.
> The heavens are yours, the earth also is yours;
>   the world and all that is in it—
>   you have founded them. . . .
> For the LORD is yet our shield;
>   the Holy One of Israel is yet our king.
> > > (Ps. 89:5–7a, 9–11, 18 [author's
> > > translation for v. 18]; cf. also
> > > Ps. 74:12–17)

Thus, the language of God's enthronement as king is closely related in many texts to God's sovereignty over all creation. Typical is Ps. 93.

> The LORD is king, he is robed in majesty;
>   the LORD is robed, he is girded with strength.
> He has established the world; it shall never be moved;
>   your throne is established from of old;
>   you are from everlasting.
> The floods have lifted up, O LORD,
>   the floods have lifted up their voice;
>   the floods lift up their roaring.
> More majestic than the thunders of mighty waters,
>   more majestic than the waves of the sea,
>   majestic on high is the LORD!
> > > (Ps. 93:1–4)

God's kingship over the cosmos is not a morally neutral matter. We have already seen in our discussion of Ps. 82 in chapter 5 that it is because of Yahweh's concern for justice and
righteousness that the other gods are judged, found wanting,
and virtually deposed from divine status. The enthronement
psalms celebrate the moral qualities which God's kingship establishes as foundational in the creation itself. Psalm 89 follows celebration of the victory over Rahab (chaos) with:

> Righteousness and justice are the foundation of your
>   throne;
>   steadfast love and faithfulness go before you.
>   (Ps. 89:14; see a parallel
>   statement in Ps. 97:2)

Psalm 96 suggests that God's reign includes God's judging of
the cosmos by standards of justice and righteousness.

> Say among the nations, "The LORD is king!
>   The world is firmly established;
>   it shall never be moved.
> He will judge the peoples with equity." . . .
> He will judge the world with righteousness,
>   and the peoples with his truth.
>   (Ps. 96:10, 13b)

Such celebrations of justice and righteousness as a part of
God's reign established in the order of creation suggest a concept not unlike natural law since it envisions moral dimensions
to the very nature of the created order. The source is still
divine but the existence of this moral dimension of God's
reign is apart from embodiment in any form of revealed will or
law. It is on this basis that even the nations may recognize the
true sovereignty of God.

Sovereign Over Israel

Yahweh also appears in the tradition as the divine Ruler of a
particular people, Israel.[6] God's sovereignty is recognized and
celebrated in Israel, both by individuals (cf. Ps. 5:2) and by the
corporate community. Contrary to earlier opinion, this understanding of God as king with reference to Israel seems to develop early in the Israelite tradition in connection with
Exodus-Sinai traditions.[7] The victorious Song of the Sea concludes its celebration of God's Exodus victory over pharaoh

with a reference to God's reign and the establishment of a divine abode (Ex. 15:17–18). This is an element of divine kingship themes elsewhere in the ancient Near East but is here related to God's sovereignty over Israel. In Balaam's second oracle God's kingship is related to Israel and the victory won, not over chaos, but over oppression in history.

> The LORD their God is with them,
>   acclaimed as a king among them.
> God, who brings them out of Egypt,
>   is like the horns of a wild ox for them.
>   (Num. 23:21b–22) `

Even in the Jerusalem cultus from which the enthronement psalms come, the older connection of God's kingship to Exodus-Sinai traditions is preserved.

> The LORD is king; let the peoples tremble!
>   He sits enthroned upon the cherubim. . . .
> Mighty King, lover of justice,
>   you have established equity;
> you have executed justice
>   and righteousness in Jacob. . . .
> Moses and Aaron were among his priests,
>   Samuel also was among those who called on
>   his name.
>   (Ps. 99:1, 4, 6)

Here again Yahweh's kingship is the basis for justice and righteousness but as established in relation to God's history with Israel.

The two traditions of God as king of Israel and of the cosmos (and the nations) come together in a number of texts as well.

> For the LORD, the Most High, is awesome,
>   a great king over all the earth.
> He subdued peoples under us,
>   and nations under our feet.
> He chose our heritage for us,
>   the pride of Jacob whom he loves. . . .
> God is king over the nations;
>   God sits on his holy throne.
> The princes of the peoples gather
>   as the people of the God of Abraham.
>   (Ps. 47:2–4, 8–9)

Matitiahu Tsevat also points to Isa. 24:21–23 as such a text which he paraphrases, "The one who commands mythical, cosmic, and historical forces will rule as king in Zion amidst his people Israel."[8]

Walter Brueggemann reminds us of the broad ethical implications to the description of God in a political metaphor such as kingship. "That Yahweh is a royal power serves to destabilize every other royal power and to relativize every temptation to absolutize power. This kingship is a gift of freedom, for allegiance to this liberating God tells against every other political subservience (cf. Lev. 25:42)."[9] Of course, the significance is not in God's kingship alone, but in relation to the establishment of an earthly kingship in Israel.

Relationship to Kings and Kingdoms

It is clear that in Israel until the time of the prophet Samuel there was a widespread belief that earthly kingship was not acceptable in the light of God's kingship. The two were considered to be in conflict.

When Gideon led the coalition of northern Israelite tribes to victory over the Midianites he was approached with an invitation to become king, "Rule over us, you and your son and your grandson" (Judg. 8:22). His reply is a refusal on theological grounds, "I will not rule over you, and my son will not rule over you; the LORD will rule over you" (v. 23). One of Gideon's sons, Abimelech, establishes a short-lived kingship over the city of Shechem. The story is told with a clear bias against kingship, seen especially in the antimonarchical parable of Jotham (Judg. 9:7–21) and the untimely death of Abimelech, treated as a just reward for his arrogant usurping of the kingly role his father refused (vs. 22–57).

This bias against earthly kingship is the context for much of the tension in the time of the establishment of kingship under Saul and is reflected in the diverse attitudes of the literary sources. David must deal with the same tensions although he does so more successfully. We shall be looking at these periods in detail below.

It is under David and his successors on the throne of Judah that a new theology develops which couples the reign of God positively with the reign of an earthly king, namely, the dynasty of David. In this royal theology of David and Zion, cultivated in the Jerusalem cultus, there is, of course, the desire to legitimate the dynastic claims of the Davidic line; but it should also be recognized that the kingship of Yahweh and its long tradition exercises a moral influence on the defining of the king's role in Israel.[10] The king is considered to be Yahweh's regent. Thus, the qualities of God's rule are to be reflected in the rule of the earthly king. Yahweh's kingship remains the source of a royal ideal even when the royal reality of Israelite and Judean kings sought to turn the religious tradition to self-serving ends. This is made abundantly clear in royal psalms like Ps. 72.

> Give the king your justice, O God,
> and your righteousness to a king's son.
> May he judge your people with righteousness,
> and your poor with justice. . . .
> May he defend the cause of the poor of the people,
> give deliverance to the needy,
> and crush the oppressor.
>
> (Ps. 72:1–2, 4)

In the struggle with the legitimacy and authority of earthly power the political metaphor of God's kingship provides an ethical norm for judging earthly kings and any other form of earthly political power. It is to the tradition's judgments on its own kings that we will turn to see this norm in operation.

One final word is necessary to note the trajectory of the theme of God's kingship into the New Testament. It is the kingdom of God that Jesus comes announcing in the Gospels, not his own kingdom. Although Jesus is the Messiah, a royal title, his own messiahship is but representative of God's kingship and in the service of God's kingdom. It should be obvious that if we are to understand the moral significance of this central New Testament theme, we shall have to first understand the roots of that theme in the traditions of Yahweh's kingship in the Old Testament.[11]

The Promise and Threat of Kingship

As we shall see, kingship in Israel introduced elements of Canaanite culture and ideology that were antithetical and deeply threatening to the Exodus-Sinai covenant tradition. Yet, the Old Testament story is not simply a story of this threat; it is also the story of God's ability to work through the circumstances of disobedient and prideful human choices to work the divine will. Kingship becomes the context for a new envisioning of divine promise. Even this institution, presented as a sinful request of the people, can become the locus of God's graceful working in the midst of human history. Thus, the royal ideal of the king as God's king always looms larger than the often sordid and sinful story of royal reality in the history of Israel's kings. Measured by the standards of pragmatic political reality, kingship in Israel is often judged a failure; but measured by the moral vision of leadership truly accountable to God's ultimate reign, and the role that vision plays in understanding the obedience of Jesus as God's anointed one (Messiah), kingship in Israel becomes the context through which some of the most important and perennial theological and ethical themes are introduced in the Old Testament.

Saul: The Promise Aborted

In the mid-eleventh century B.C.E. the Philistines, an aggressive, militarily organized coalition of city-states occupying the coastal plain, cast an eye on the territory held by the loosely organized Israelite tribal coalition. In a climactic battle the Philistines defeated an Israelite volunteer army, captured the Ark of the Covenant (symbol of Yahweh's presence among the people), destroyed the central sanctuary at Shiloh, and occupied Israelite territory west of the Jordan River (see 1 Sam. 4–6). Most historians believe that it was this urgent set of historical circumstances that led Israel to seek in Saul a centralized military leadership capable of coping with this threat.[12] Whether or not this was initially conceived as kingship, it is clear that Saul eventually came to conceptualize it as such, even to the extent of hoping for the dynastic succession of his son Jonathan to the throne.

The presentation of these events in the biblical text is more complex. The text of 1 Samuel includes perspectives that regard Saul's kingship as sinful, as well as those which celebrate Saul as God's anointed king. It is widely agreed that both of these perspectives are historically rooted in the tensions introduced by the establishment of kingship in Israel. In the present shape of the tradition in 1 Samuel these diverse witnesses have been organized to pass on a witness from the biblical community to the important theological and ethical issues raised by this crucial time of transition from tribal federation to monarchy. It is to the shape of that final witness that we will primarily attend.[13]

The Dangers of Kingship. In 1 Sam. 8 the elders of Israel approach the prophet Samuel and ask for a king. It is in the narrative of this encounter that we get our first perspectives on the kingship soon to be embodied in Saul. This first glimpse of kingship is largely a warning of its dangers.

It is extremely important to note that there is no word in 1 Sam. 8 about the Philistines, or any allusion to an urgent political crisis. For the most part we are asked in this chapter to consider kingship first as a theological-ethical matter and not as a political-military expediency. As a pretext for the meeting allusion is made to the corruption of Samuel's sons who are his successors as judge (1 Sam. 8:1–3, 5), but beyond the opening line of the elders nothing more is heard of this matter. It is the challenge kingship represents to the whole Israelite religious tradition that is the focus. Not even the historical reality of the Philistines will be allowed to obscure the important issues at stake.

We have earlier discussed the nature of covenant community as alternative community in the world (see chapter 5). This alternative model and all it represents is implicitly challenged by the terms of the elders' request, "Appoint for us, then, a king to govern us, like other nations" (1 Sam. 8:5). Even after Samuel's warning of the dangers, they persevere in their desire to conform to the patterns of community among their neighbors: "No! but we are determined to have a king over us, so that we also may be like other nations, and that our king may govern us and go out before us and fight our battles" (vs. 19–20). Kingship raises the issue of accommodation to the world over against the call of God to alternative community in the world. This will remain a central issue in the whole history of Israel's kings.

Earthly kingship is also presented as a threat to the kingship of God. After Samuel prays to God, God answers, "They have not rejected you, but they have rejected me from being king over them. Just as they have done to me, from the day I brought them up out of Egypt to this day, forsaking me and serving other gods" (1 Sam. 8:7b–8). The notion that God's kingship excludes earthly kingship we have already seen in the Gideon story, and this was undoubtedly the view that led many in Israel to oppose the establishment of kingship. The text forces us to consider the danger of earthly centers of political authority that usurp God's ultimate sovereignty. Verse 8 (which may be from the later hand of the Deuteronomic historian) suggests that this is nothing more than the issue of idolatry. Leaders can become like gods displacing the loyalty owed to God alone.[14]

Samuel is charged by God to warn the people and recite for them the "ways of the king" (1 Sam. 8:9). Over against the covenantal demand for obedience in Israelite tradition is here laid a consequentialist element. If you insist on this sinful and idolatrous course, the people are told, then these are the potential consequences. Samuel's recitation (vs. 11–18) is dominated by the verb "take." His portrait is of the king as one who takes the sons, daughters, produce, and livestock of the citizenry and puts them to the use of the king in establishing a militia, a royal bureaucracy, a royal court and household, and a life-style of luxury for himself and his courtiers.[15] The most devastating critique comes at the end.

> And you shall be his slaves. And in that day you will cry out because of your king, whom you have chosen for yourselves; but the LORD will not answer you in that day. (1 Sam. 8:17b–18)

In kingship is the danger of reversing the Exodus deliverance. The people risk becoming slaves again. Whereas God heard their cry in Egypt (Ex. 2:23–24; 3:7), this is the people's own choosing, and God will not hear their cry. The danger of the kingship is the potential for introducing a social system that is antithetical to the very notion of community to which they were called by God's deliverance.

The narrative on the dangers of kingship in 1 Sam. 8 has what we suggest is a surprise ending. God says to Samuel, "Listen to their voice and set a king over them" (1 Sam. 8:22). Kingship may be a sinful request by the people, but if there is to be a king then it will be God's king. If kingship is in danger of self-justifying authority, then kings will be made through God's prophet as a reminder of God's authority. If there are dangers ahead, God will nevertheless be present to ensure the possibilities of grace as well.

The Possibilities of Kingship. Having been warned of the dangers of kingship we can now also know its possibilities. Following in quick succession on Samuel's warning in 1 Sam. 8

are stories of Saul's encounter with and commissioning by the prophet Samuel (1 Sam. 9:1–10:16); his selection by lot for the kingship in the assembly of the people (10:17–27); and his charismatic deliverance of the people of Jabesh-gilead (11:1–15). Except for a brief reiteration of the theme of the rejection of God in 10:18–19 these episodes are very positive to Saul and his role as God's anointed one. The stories are filled with possibilities for the future of God's king and God's people.

In the story of the young Saul seeking his father's asses but finding instead a kingdom, the biblical story allows the urgency of the Philistine crisis to come into view. Samuel is instructed to anoint Saul as ruler (*nagid*) because "he shall save my people from the hand of the Philistines; for I have seen the suffering of my people, because their outcry has come to me" (1 Sam. 9:16). The language is reminiscent of Exodus deliverance. Saul's call to this role is formally reminiscent of the call narratives of Moses and the prophets.[16] We are clearly dealing here with a story of God's grace toward Israel in the midst of trouble. Saul is anointed by God's prophet (10:1), and when he leaves Samuel the text says that God "gave him another heart" (v. 9), and that the "spirit of God possessed him" so that he prophesied among the prophets (v. 10).

Designation by Yahweh is followed by acclamation by the people in the episode of Saul's selection by lot in 1 Sam. 10:17–27.[17] The role of the people (they appear again in the parallel Gilgal reference in 11:14–15) and the reference in some traditions to Saul as *nagid* (commander) rather than *melek* (king) suggests that at least in the beginning kingship in Israel was of a limited variety. Frank Cross comments, "Certainly Saul's exaltation to the office of *nagid* or *melek* . . . was conceived by the tribesmen as a conditional appointment or covenant, so long as the 'Spirit of God' was upon him, and so long as he did not violate the legal traditions or constitution of the league."[18]

In 1 Sam. 11 we have what may be the most reliable account of the circumstances leading to Saul's kingship. His leadership and victory over the Ammonites in rescuing the people of Jabesh-gilead leads to the people's acclamation of him as king in Gilgal (and presumably with the hope he could aid them as well against the Philistines). The account is in the style of the stories of Judges with the spirit of the Lord seizing Saul and empowering him to lead in deliverance of the people. His elevation to kingship is reminiscent of the offer which Gideon refused. In the present organization of the text this account is not, however, the beginning of Saul's story. Chapter 11 now functions to confirm the designation of God and the selection by the people which are reported in chs. 9 and 10. Saul's charismatic acts in ch. 11 demonstrate the power of the spirit of God already given to Saul following his anointing by Samuel.

What appears in the present shape of the text is an emergent theology of God's anointed one (Hebrew *mašiaḥ* > Messiah), a theological-moral perspective on this newly emergent institution in Israel.[19] There may be kings in Israel but they are to be designated by God and anointed by God's prophet; they will receive and be bearers of God's spirit; they will be presented to and affirmed by the people; and they will demonstrate the power of God's spirit in mighty deeds. Their career as God's anointed one will be judged by faithfulness to the demands of God's covenant and will be monitored by the prophets. In 1 and 2 Samuel we seem to have in Saul one who was judged and failed, in David one who was judged and confirmed in kingship. Like Saul, David is anointed by Samuel, receives God's spirit (while at the same time it is taken from Saul), makes his public debut in the service of Saul and the people, performs a mighty deed in the killing of Goliath, and eventually is confirmed in perpetual kingship by Nathan (2 Sam. 7). Perhaps the central point to emphasize here is that the text as it now stands is clear that not even kings are exempt from the ultimate authority which rests in God. Kings in Israel serve as the vessels of God's spirit at work in the people's midst, and that spirit may be withdrawn if the king is not worthy, a lesson Saul learns to his grief.

The Tragedy of Saul. The farewell address of the prophet Samuel in 1 Sam. 12 is perhaps from the late hand of the Deuteronomic historian but occupies a pivotal position in the narrative as it now stands.[20] The kingship arose in disobedience which here the people acknowledge, "We have added to all our sins the evil of demanding a king for ourselves" (1 Sam. 12:19). But God will not turn aside from them if they "serve the LORD with all [their] heart" (v. 20).

There will be kings, but there must also now be prophets. It is not accidental that prophets and kings make their appearance together in Israel's story.[21] In 1 Sam. 12:23 Samuel, the first prophet, defines what is to be the prophet's role in the era of kingship. "Moreover as for me, far be it from me that I should sin against the LORD by ceasing to pray for you; and I will instruct you in the good and the right way." With the guidance of the prophets faithful life will be possible in the new political order. If a new political office inspired by the surrounding cultures is to emerge, then a new spiritual office to represent the inheritance of the covenant tradition must also make its appearance.[22]

However, the danger is still great. "If you still do wickedly, you shall be swept away, both you and your king" (1 Sam. 12:25). What follows is the story of Saul's sin and rejection in the immediate context, and in the longer sweep of Israel's history what is foreshadowed is the destruction of Jerusalem and the end of the kingship in Babylonian exile (587 B.C.E.).

In 1 Sam. 13:7–15 Saul grows impatient waiting for Samuel and offers the sacrifice before battle himself. In ch. 15, against the instructions of Samuel, Saul returns from battle with the Amalekites with booty and the captured king. Both of these actions assert Saul's authority into areas of sacral responsibility guarded by Samuel, and for both he is denounced and rejected. In 13:13–14 he is rejected for dynasty and confirmation of his kingship forever; in 15:26 Saul is himself rejected as legitimate king over Israel.

Readers and interpreters over the centuries have been torn in their response to Saul's plight. Saul is indeed a tragic figure. Unable to simply shrug off this rejection and strike his own course Saul increasingly appears in the remainder of 1 Samuel as a plagued man, jealous of David, given to rages and uncontrolled actions, and pathetically calling for comfort from the ghost of Samuel on the eve of his own death (1 Sam. 28). It is easy to be sympathetic to Saul when Samuel is a somewhat petulant character and the violations of holy war ritual strike us as insignificant because we have little sympathy for the holy war institutions. We must be clear, however, that what is at stake here is the danger of autonomous political authority extending its control even into the realm of sacred and religious institutions. Is the self-interest of the political authority to take priority even over the sacred institutions of the community of faith and therefore to define morality in its own interests?[23] It was not compatible with the religion of Yahweh that a political leader could assume that "any war he orders is to be sanctioned by the highest authority."[24] Although the institutional structures are different the issue is little different from the questions of civil religion and the usurping of religious role and authority by purely civil and political interests in our own society. The whole history of Israel's kings is influenced by this tension between the religious traditions inherited from the tribal league and the ideology of kingship borrowed in large measure from Israel's neighbors. Can Yahwism be accommodated in the new order? How is its integrity to be guarded?

In the drama of 1 Samuel it seems almost inevitable that Saul will fail, unable to reconcile the needs of an emerging kingship with the demands of the covenant tradition and its representative in Samuel. David Gunn has suggested that in spite of the divine role Saul was the people's king ("make a king for *them*," 1 Sam. 8:22) but David is to be God's king ("I have provided, among his sons, a king for *myself*," 16:1; "a man after his [God's] own heart," 13:14).[25] The people's repentance in ch. 12 was not enough. The king born of their sin, and rejected because of his own sin, must be swept away for David's story as God's king to show more fully the possibilities in the royal ideal as well as the dangers in the royal reality.

David: The Promise Glimpsed

Interpretation of the material on David in the books of Samuel has largely focused on identification of two major narratives: the Rise of David, 1 Sam. 16–2 Sam. 1;[26] the Succession to the Throne of David, 2 Sam. 8–20; 1 Kings 1–2.[27] It has been the second of these which has attracted greatest theological interest. Gerhard von Rad[28] developed the thesis that this material was the product of a Solomonic Enlightenment which introduced genuine history writing into the ancient world. Yahweh's work is seen through the human and political order rather than breaking supernaturally into it. Although von Rad's view has not held up in all of its particulars (esp. the thesis of a Solomonic Enlightenment), he did succeed in drawing attention to the importance of the radical shifts taking place in the David material, both historically and theologically.

Recent interpretation has shown renewed interest in the shape and emphases of the David narrative as a whole.[29] Attention to the two great narrative complexes tended to ignore 2 Sam. 2–6 and 21–24 except for historical purposes. The great dynastic oracle in 2 Sam. 7 was treated in separation from the rest of the David story. In keeping with recent emphasis on the David story as a whole we will focus on matters of theological and ethical importance that emerge from the David story in its present canonical shape. This is rich material, both historically and theologically, and our discussion is informed by the especially insightful works of Brueggemann, Gunn, and McCarter.[30] In the limited space here, we can lift up only a few crucial matters for attention.

The Promise of David. In contrast to Saul's failure David's story is one of unparalleled success, due not only to his own shrewd capabilities, but through a sense of God's favor which begins with his anointing by Samuel (1 Sam. 16) and culminates in his confirmation in the dynastic promise by Nathan (2 Sam. 7).

The narrative of *David's rise* to kingship (1 Sam. 16–2 Sam. 1) is not a document of developed royal ideology. It is more a narrative of populist partisanship, celebrating the rise of David from a nobody to the leadership of all Israel.[31] It is uncritical storytelling to celebrate the courage and resourcefulness of David, and the inevitability of his destiny. It is anti-Saul storytelling to celebrate the manner in which one of those outside the boundaries of state power became the legitimate holder of power.

David appears in several aspects in this story, all contributing to an overall image of David as a man of resourcefulness and destiny. He is portrayed as hero. As a mere boy he vanquishes the gigantic Philistine warrior, Goliath (1 Sam. 17), and thereby wins a place in the infant military structure of Saul. He quickly distinguishes himself as a capable and popular young warrior and commander. The young women sing of his feats, a turn of events which rouses Saul's jealousy and endangers David (1 Sam. 18). Mendenhall reminds us that there are deep implications to these events. From celebration in Israel of Yahweh as warrior, there is a movement to celebrate the exploits of a human professional warrior. It is the beginning of a royal ideology which is in deep tension with the resistance to kingship and professional militarism which was part of the ideology of God's kingship in Israel.[32]

What gives this story of David's rise a part of its unique power is that David is not only hero but also one of the dispossessed. His story begins as one of the least regarded sons of

Jesse, an unlikely choice by Samuel for king (1 Sam. 16). His
rise to heroic status is that of the unlikely underdog, the man
out of the ranks of the nobodies who gives hope to the aspira-
tions of others like him without status or power. Although
David achieves initial success and fame, Saul, out of jealousy,
seeks to kill him and David is forced to flee. He lives in the
wilderness, dodging the pursuit of Saul and living by his courage and daring. He gathers a band of men who themselves are
refugees from legal society, the impoverished, the marginal,
the outlawed (22:1–2). Mendenhall cites this portrait of David
as the best example of the Habiru (a socially marginal group in
the ancient Near East often cited as background for those
Israelites who escaped as slaves from Egypt).[33] To escape the
reach of Saul, David hires his band out to the Philistines as
mercenaries, but uses his position in Ziklag to do favors and
build support among the elders of Judah (1 Sam. 27). David is
glorified here, but not as any paragon of virtue. He is clever,
rough, capable, ambitious, and courageous. He does what he
must to survive, and the story seems to celebrate this as if this
were the story of those who themselves know about survival.

Through the story also survives a glimpse of David as more
than capable and ambitious warrior. There are stories of David as loyal friend, seen especially in his friendship with Jonathan, a moving story of loyalty and love (1 Sam. 18–20).[34]
David is loved by Michal, Saul's daughter, as well and she becomes his wife. Both son and daughter help David escape from
Saul's wrath. Even when he has Saul's life in his hands (twice, 1
Sam. 24 and 26) David acts with compassion and respect toward Saul as God's anointed. It is fitting that our first glimpse
of David after Saul's tragic death is not of David, the political
opportunist, but of a grieving David, singing an eloquent and
moving lament over the death of Saul and Jonathan (2 Sam.
1:19–27).

In 2 Sam. 2–6 we move to the narrative account of the
consolidation of *David's kingdom*. The drama of this material is
set by what has preceded it. Saul has come to grief over his
inability to handle the tensions set in motion by the transition
from league to kingdom. How will David fare with these same
challenges?

The details of the events whereby David consolidated his
kingdom are too complex to rehearse here in detail. He becomes king first over Judah, and only later over the tribes of
northern Israel. The later division of the kingdom is already

foreshadowed. He proves himself a capable politician through these difficult events. He wins significant victories over the Philistines and extends the kingdom's borders, and he establishes a stronger economic base through treaties with Tyre.

Two of David's actions are of special importance for the political and theological future of Israel. The first of these was the capture of Jerusalem (2 Sam. 5:6–12). This, of course, gave David a politically neutral capital, neither in northern Israel nor in southern Judah, but more important it gave David an urban center with its special capabilities necessary to the growth of a successful royal bureaucracy. Mendenhall writes:

> It has been suggested by many others, and reiterated here, that David's regime at Jerusalem was possible only because he temporarily brought about a unity between the old Israelite population (who furnished the population base) and the urban Canaanite population who furnished at least a minimum of specialist skills that any empire would have to command in order to exist.[35]

Literacy was not widely needed as a skill in village-based Israel before. Essential to David's empire were scribes, tradesmen, architects, and managers. He found the nucleus for this in Jebusite Jerusalem, but eventually incorporated into his empire most of the other Canaanite urban city-states in the region. Israel had no experience with kings or their bureaucracies, so it makes sense that David would use the existing Canaanite models as his own.

The danger, of course, is that cultures come with their own ideologies. Would this embracing of Canaanite royal patterns and practices drive out those things distinctive of Israel and its Yahwistic faith? This was the danger feared by those in Israel who opposed kings as antagonistic to God's kingship. It was the tension that brought Saul's rejection. David dealt with this in the immediate context by searching for and bringing the Ark of the Covenant to Jerusalem, where he established it in a place of honor (1 Sam. 6).[36] This brilliant move made David the patron of the older covenant league tradition which had centered at Shiloh before its destruction and the capture of the Ark by the Philistines (1 Sam. 4–6). It also in effect made Jerusalem, David's own capital, the central sanctuary. At least for the duration of David's reign he managed to convince the village population of Israel that his kingship could be compatible with Yahwism and serve its covenant faith. This hope and promise, as we will see, is still preserved as a part of the royal ideal reflected in the royal psalms and other texts.

This already begins to suggest that David's kingdom began the development and emergence of a *Davidic theology* which sought both to justify the Davidic dynasty and to develop lines along which Davidic kingship could find common existence with the older traditions of Israel's faith.

Psalm 132 represents this emergent Davidic theology in an appealing way. It tells the story of David's search for the Ark in its opening verses (Ps. 132:1–7) and depicts David's zeal and concern for a resting place for Yahweh. Verses 11–18 go on to describe the "sure oath" which the Lord swore to David. It involves the promise of dynasty to David's sons and the promise of divine habitation on Mt. Zion. These are to be new signs of God's grace in the ongoing story of Israel's faith. Significantly there is a condition.

> One of the sons of your body
>   I will set on your throne.
> If your sons keep my covenant
>   and my decrees that I shall teach them,
> their sons also, forevermore,
>   shall sit on your throne.
>   (Ps. 132:11–12)

The king is to be the servant of the covenant and its decrees. Royal ideology is not to be directed to its own purposes alone.

The most important text for the Davidic theology is 2 Sam. 7. This complex text shows evidence of development long beyond the time of David; thus it reflects both emergent and fully developed royal ideology reflected in a new theology of God's promise to David.[37] In this text we have the reflection of the state on David, not the traditions of the populace from which David came.[38]

David wishes to build a house for Yahweh. Temple building was a common ancient Near Eastern practice through which kings legitimized their reign. Nathan, the prophet, receives a vision and message from Yahweh that forbids David to do this (2 Sam. 7:4–7). The God of Israel dwells in a tent. The tension here is between the freedom of God represented by the Ark (brought to Jerusalem in the preceding chapter) and the fixity (even the possession) of God suggested by a royal sanctuary.

In this the text surely represents opposition during David's time to the Canaanization of Israel's faith that the building of a temple would necessarily represent.

In 2 Sam. 7:8–16 God, through Nathan, remarkably promises instead to build a house (dynasty) for David. David's sons will rule after him forever. Unlike Ps. 132 there are no conditions expressed. The king, if disobedient, may be chastised (2 Sam. 7:14), but the kingdom cannot be taken away as with Saul (v. 15). This surely reflects a later stage of development in the royal ideology than seen in Ps. 132. Davidic kingship is now an eternal, unconditional promise. Solomon is explicitly reflected in vs. 12–13 as one who will build the temple so the text is vested in his interests.

On the one hand, Davidic theology as expressed here in 2 Sam. 7 reflects the effort of earthly power to justify itself by appeal to divine authority, but this remarkable text will not so easily be captured. In this appearance of unconditional promise is a sign of divine grace that cannot be deterred even by the sins of a royal ideology and its wielders.[39] There may be sanctions and consequences, but God's promise will not be revoked. This does indeed make David a powerful new sign of God's promise in the ongoing story of God's grace to Israel. The promise of God's grace to David outlasts the Judean throne and is the root of Jewish messianism. In this text lies the trust that one in the line of David will surely always be coming and that has kindled hope through generations of hopelessness. It is to this promise that the early church looked to aid them in understanding Jesus as God's gift of grace in faithfulness to that promise. The boldness of the promise in 2 Sam. 7 is matched by the boldness of David's prayer in which he claims that promise (vs. 18–29).

The Humanity of David. The David material in the books of Samuel are not all stories of unparalleled success. In 2 Sam. 11–12 unfolds the tragic story of David's adultery with Bathsheba and his murder of her husband, Uriah, to cover his misdeed. Royal power is asserted in willful and violent ways to enable royal privilege. The episode is not to be overlooked. Nathan the prophet confronts David with his crime, "You are the man!" The prophet's oracle of judgment on David is the prologue to the unfolding of a sad and tragic series of episodes in David's own family, all involving the violent use of power for the sake of self-interested privilege. Rape, murder, rebellion, sedition, war, palace intrigue all appear in the story of David's own family in 2 Sam. 13–20; 1 Kings 1–2.[40]

The remarkable element in this material is the full humanness of its portrait of David.[41] This is no longer predominantly the heroic storytelling of the populace, or the self-interested ideology of the state. It is David, the man. It shows his folly, his weakness, his vacillation; but it also shows his courage, his grief, his compassion. It is perhaps the ability of the biblical community to preserve for us this human being alongside the hero and the king that gives the David tradition its extraordinary power. It is in looking at this entire scope of the David story that some of the most helpful and suggestive theological perspectives on David have been advanced. Gunn has traced a constant dynamic of gift and grasp throughout the entire drama of David. "It is when David's mode of action [is] most attuned to giving that he is most successful. His grasping (especially in the Bathsheba scene), on the other hand, brings in its train a series of disasters in both political and private spheres."[42] The kingdom, received as God's gift, can be faithful, but the kingdom, as power to be grasped, is sinful and self-destructive. Brueggemann has found throughout the David story witness to a willingness on God's part to risk human freedom with its possibilities and its consequences. He speaks of David as a model for our own lives as God's trusted creatures, and finds purposeful echoes of the David story in the primeval history stories of freedom and responsibility in Genesis.[43]

We should take note in this encounter with David's painful humanness of the crucial role played again by God's prophet Nathan. Not even the king is beyond the reach of God's judgment. Kings in Israel are not intended to be self-justifying authority but are answerable to God's authority. At least during David's reign this is accepted. David receives Nathan's indictment as just. When in later stories of Israel's kings prophets are forced outside the court or co-opted by the king it is clear that royal ideology is running in a direction not acceptable or compatible with Yahwistic faith.

The Role of God's Kings. In Israel the David tradition did not function simply to illuminate a particular, though important, period of its history. As we have seen with the Exodus tradition, David became the model of the messianic ideal in Israel. During the time of kings David served to model the role

God's kings were to play. This idealized David appears in the liturgically influenced portrait of the books of Chronicles where the rough edges of the David story are less in view and the role of David in the religious life of Israel is enhanced. He is clearly God's representative and the chief patron of Israel's religious life.

Even in 2 Samuel this movement of the tradition toward a modeling of faithful kingship can be seen. Brevard Childs has observed insightfully that 2 Sam. 21–24, usually treated as interruptive appendixes, are actually placed very intentionally to end David's story with a review of his career that moves away from personal glorification to the glory of God who works through David as the righteous king. It "pictures the ideal ruler of Israel as a righteous one" and "provides a theological programme for the future of his royal dynasty."[44]

> The God of Israel has spoken,
>   the Rock of Israel has said to me:
> One who rules over people justly,
>   ruling in the fear of God,
> is like the light of morning,
>   like the sun rising on a cloudless morning,
>   gleaming from the rain on the grassy land.
>   (2 Sam. 23:3–4)

Childs suggests that these chapters strike some of the same themes as the Song of Hannah which opens the Samuel-Saul-David story.

> In sum, the final four chapters offer a highly reflective, theological interpretation of David's whole career as adumbrating the messianic hope. These chapters in conjunction with the story of Hannah establish an eschatological, messianic perspective for the whole; God will exalt the poor and debase the proud in his rule of righteousness. Although David's human weaknesses are not suppressed within the tradition, his final role as the ideal, righteous king emerges with great clarity.[45]

Growing out of the David tradition is a royal ideal that even under the most sinful and faithless of Israel's kings kept alive the demand and the hope for kings who are truly the righteous servants of Yahweh. Sigmund Mowinckel has found this ethical emphasis distinctive of Israel's ideal conception of kingship. "Two points express what is distinctive of the Israelite ideal:

the king is absolutely subordinate to Yahweh and in everything dependent upon Him and His covenant blessing; and the king's essential task is to be the instrument of Yahweh's justice and covenant blessing among men."[46] This royal ideal is most visible in the royal psalms.[47] We have already cited Ps. 72 above. Here we will let Ps. 101 stand as representative of the character of these portraits of the king's moral responsibility as God's representative. It is a king's pledge, perhaps on the occasion of his enthronement.

> I will sing of loyalty and of justice;
>   to you, O LORD, I will sing.
> I will study the way that is blameless.
>   When shall I attain it?
> I will walk with integrity of heart
>   within my house;
> I will not set before my eyes
>   anything that is base. . . .
> Perverseness of heart shall be far from me;
>   I will know nothing of evil.
> One who secretly slanders a neighbor
>   I will destroy.
> A haughty look and an arrogant heart
>   I will not tolerate
> I will look with favor on the faithful in the land,
>   so that they may live with me;
> whoever walks in the way that is blameless
>   shall minister to me.
> No one who practices deceit
>   shall remain in my house;
> no one who utters lies
>   shall continue in my presence.
> Morning by morning I will destroy
>   all the wicked in the land,
> cutting off all evildoers
>   from the city of the LORD.
>   (Ps. 101:1–3a; 4–8)

There is one attempt in Israelite tradition to embody this royal ideal in covenant legislation. Deuteronomy 17:14–20 gives us a law for the king which attempts to set the boundaries and the conditions under which kings may rule in Israel.[48] The passage reflects the language of the warning by Samuel in 1 Sam. 8. The law begins by citing the people's demand to have a king "like all the nations" (Deut. 17:14) and indicates they may have a king whom "God will choose" and who must be one of their "own community," not a foreigner (v. 15). The king is prohibited from the practices of economic privilege common to ancient kings (vs. 16–17). Further,

> when he has taken the throne of his kingdom, he shall have a copy of this law written for him in the presence of the levitical priests. It shall remain with him and he shall read in it all the days of his life, so that he may learn to fear the LORD his God, diligently observing all the words of this law and these statutes, neither exalting himself above other members of the community nor turning aside from the commandment. (Deut. 17:18–20)

The king's central role is defined as the reading and keeping of Torah. One can imagine this passage as significant in the reform effort of Josiah in 621 B.C.E.

With Solomon's accession this royal ideal is deeply challenged by a royal reality removed from the influence of the people, seemingly absent of any prophetic influence (in spite of Nathan's role at the accession), and reflective of Canaanite models of kingship and ideology.

Solomon and His Successors: The Promise Broken

The biblical tradition in 1 Kings 1–11 and much subsequent interpretation is of a divided mind in the assessment of Solomon. He brought tiny Israel to a position of unparalleled prominence in the world of his time. The splendor of his court and his monuments is often a matter of pride to those who look on his era as a golden age. Much in the biblical tradition celebrates his achievements, including his personal wisdom, but the tradition also knows and finally reports with brutal honesty that Solomon's reign deeply compromised the Israelite covenant faith and led to the division of the kingdom.

Current assessment of Solomon is deeply influenced by a fuller understanding of the social models of Canaanite royal culture that Solomon borrowed and infused fully into his own royal system. Mendenhall expresses it with characteristic economy: "It must be emphasized as strongly as possible that by the end of Solomon's regime the Jerusalem state was a thoroughly paganized Syro-Hittite regime and was condemned as intolerable by the prophets, who represented the continuity of the Yahwist tradition."[49] To put it in the terms of our previous discussion, Israel under Solomon ceases to live as an alternative community in the world (although some kept this tradition alive), and instead adopts a model of royal ideology and management borrowed from surrounding Canaanite culture. It is this royal model opposed to the covenant alternative which we will seek to describe as fully emerged under Solomon and continued by most of his successors in the northern and the southern kingdoms.[50]

The Economics of Privilege. Under Solomon the covenantal economics of equality was replaced by an economics of privilege. No longer were the community's resources distributed equitably on the basis of need, but a larger share of wealth in all forms went to the king and those in privileged positions around the king.[51]

> Solomon's provision for one day was thirty cors of choice flour, and sixty cors of meal, ten fat oxen, and twenty pasture-fed cattle, one hundred sheep, besides deer, gazelles, roebucks, and fatted fowl. . . . Solomon also had forty thousand stalls of horses for his chariots, and twelve thousand horsemen. Those officials supplied provisions for King Solomon and for all who came to King Solomon's table . . . ; they let nothing be lacking. (1 Kings 4:22–23, 26–27)

These are not the provisions or trappings of the average Israelite. The increase of wealth and prosperity under Solomon was not distributed equitably. In keeping with the pattern of Phoenician and Egyptian royal courts Solomon created a new hierarchy of elite classes. Cross describes the new Solomonic pattern:

> Solomon introduced chariotry in Israel and with it a new class of military nobility. [See 1 Kings 5:6–8; 10:26–29.] In fact, a whole new elite emerged made up of officers of the court, the *'abdê hammélek*, who administered the new royal cartels, the expanded corvée, and fiscal systems. Solomon followed the familiar pattern of rewarding military and administrative services with land, bringing into being a landed aristocracy with loyalties directly bound to the court.[52]

The growth of this elite class was a threat to the tradition of inheritance of land through families (the *naḥalah*). Solomon's penchant for ostentatious consumption and the building of monumental structures (well attested by archaeology) led also to increased tax burdens. At the bottom of the economic hierarchy was a growing class of the poor, some of whom were forced into indentured servitude by their indebtedness.[53] Israelites were slipping back into bondage under an Israelite king!

In the atmosphere of wealth and well-being that surrounded the king, Solomon was not spending his time reading and studying Torah (as the later "law of the king" in Deut. 17 suggests), but he cultivated the practice of wisdom associated with and in imitation of the courts in Egypt and Phoenicia. The specific traditions of Yahwism, including prophets as representatives of that tradition, are rendered invisible during Solomon's reign and are replaced by the tolerant, international traditions of wisdom teaching. In this Solomon became adept and well known (1 Kings 4:29–34; 10:1–25).

The Politics of Power. Under Solomon the covenant politics of justice are replaced by the politics of power. This power was wielded in the self-interest of the king and the privileged classes surrounding him, and often took the form of oppressive social policy for those lacking in privilege and position.

The changes under Solomon are evident from the time of his accession. He comes to power not as the result of prophetic designation or the acclaim of the people, but through internal court intrigue. Following David's death, Solomon consolidates his position as the deathbed choice of David (influenced by Solomon's mother Bathsheba, herself a non-Israelite). In a brutal show of power he executes Adonijah, Joab, and Shimei. Abiathar, the high priest connected to the priesthood at Shiloh, is banished, thus removing a link to the older covenant traditions.[54] Zadok, a priest with only tenuous claims to Israelite lineage, is elevated to privileged position and his family are made permanent and sole priests of Solomon's temple when it is built. Control of both the kingdom and the religious institutions of Israel is decided by power at the start of Solomon's reign.

With his chief opponents dispatched Solomon is free to structure the kingdom along what all agree are the lines of a typical Syro-Hittite kingdom of the region. The royal politics of Solomon concentrate power in the king and his surrounding elite, and it is removed from the people (1 Kings 4:1–19).

Solomon made a direct attack upon the organization of the league by dividing his realm on arbitrary lines into suitable fiscal districts over which he appointed officials attached to the crown. Hence,

the tribal divisions and the tribal representatives used still by David were overthrown.[55]

The expansion of the military and the extent of Solomon's
building enterprises introduced conscription into Israel. Some
now lost their freedom to the royal interests. Especially hated
was the corvée, the conscription of forced labor for Solomon's
building projects (1 Kings 5:13–18). It is ironic to come to a
point where Israelites are engaged in forced labor for an Israelite king. At a later point when Rehoboam, Solomon's son,
sends the taskmaster over the forced labor to negotiate for
him with northern Israel the Israelites stone this official to
death (12:18).

Ironically and tragically rebellion breaks out in Israel toward the end of Solomon's reign (1 Kings 11:26–40). Although it is unsuccessful, its leader Jeroboam escapes to Egypt
only to return after Solomon's death and lead the elders of
northern Israel in negotiations with Rehoboam to roll back
the oppressive policies of his father. In his famous and intem-
perate reply Rehoboam declares, "My father made your yoke
heavy, but I will add to your yoke; my father disciplined you
with whips, but I will discipline you with scorpions" (12:14).
Whereupon the northern tribes withdrew from the kingdom.
"What share do we have in David? We have no inheritance in
the son of Jesse. To your tents, O Israel! Look now to your
own house, O David" (v. 16). The kingdom is then permanently divided in 922 B.C.E.

The Domestication of God. It is unlikely that a kingdom organized around economic privilege and oppressive power
could have tolerated the covenant religion of the radically free
Yahweh. The covenant God of Israel was identified with the
dispossessed and uncontrolled by earthly power. It should not
surprise us to find that under Solomon the religion of Israel
moved in the direction of the royal religion of the surrounding pagan cults. The radical freedom of God is replaced by the
domestication of God.

Mendenhall refers to the entire Solomonic enterprise as the
"paganization of Israel": "The entire ritual-political system of
Jerusalem by 922 B.C. had nothing to do with the Yahwist
revolution of 1200 B.C. other than a few linguistic items, especially the name of the official god of the state."[56] We have
already noted some elements of this in the religious sphere.

Zadok and his family after them are priests by virtue of royal patronage. Prophets are absent from Solomon's court and support the rebellion of Jeroboam (1 Kings 11:29–39).

It is the Jerusalem temple, that most epitomizes Solomon's attack on the covenant religion of Yahweh. Brueggemann refers to the temple as "the quintessence of Canaanization in Israel."[57] In the style of other Near Eastern kings Solomon built an acropolis on Mt. Zion with the palace and the temple side by side (1 Kings 9:15), and this was done with the forced labor of the corvée. The cult is now directly under the sponsorship of the king. The temple is built with skilled workmen and materials from the Phoenician city-state of Tyre and is modeled completely after the design of Canaanite temples of the period. The temple is intended as both royal chapel and imperial shrine, both purposes in tension with the conception of Israel's tabernacling God.[58]

As with the kingship itself, there is an important element of the tradition on the temple that sought to preserve a connection to authentic Yahwism. Many of the psalms referring to the temple suggest its possibilities as a place of authentic worship of Yahweh. Well-known and loved psalms such as 100 and 121 reflect the joy of the pilgrim traveling to Jerusalem for worship. But this was temple ideal over against the temple reality as a place co-opted by the interests of kings, and compromised through much of its existence by the presence of idols. It was this reality that finally led to its destruction.

The domestication of God from Solomon onward is reflected in the effort to control both the activity and the access to God.[59] In the history of Israel with its kings from Solomon onward this tends to take two primary forms: idolatry and nationalized religion.

Because of his practice of treaty marriage Solomon came to have seven hundred wives and three hundred concubines (1 Kings 11:3). Although this was considered a mark of Solomon's prestige among the nations, it is considered by the biblical tradition the beginning of Solomon's most grievous sin. In his cosmopolitan tolerance Solomon allowed these wives to bring their foreign gods and their cultus with them. He even erected shrines and supported priests in the service of these gods. Still worse, the text is very clear that Solomon himself became a worshiper of some of these gods, thus, an idolater (vs. 4–13). The central commandment of loyalty to Yahweh is violated in the very leadership of Israel. It is clear that from

Solomon onward most of the kings tolerated idols, even in the temple, and some were themselves idol worshipers.[60] Such worship was a matter of expedience. Idolatry always held out the promise of manipulating the divine to one's own favor and advantage. The radical freedom of an undepicted God is not a comfortable prospect for kings. Why not box the presence of that God in a royal temple and surround it with other idols? Is it little wonder that the conflict of the prophets with Baalism in the days ahead is also a conflict with kings?

The domestication of the radically free God of covenant is also accomplished through the creation of a nationalized religion where the interests of God are considered inseparable from the interests of the king. Davidic royal theology preserved the notion of conditional elements to the promise of dynasty. The king is called to obedience in relationship to God. It is from the Solomonic ideology and its development beyond Solomon's time that the unconditional promise is advanced. In the Solomonic redaction of 2 Sam. 7 not only is an unconditional eternal dynasty promised to Solomon but he is to be regarded as a divine son. "He shall build a house for my name, and I will establish the throne of his kingdom forever. I will be a father to him, and he shall be a son to me" (2 Sam. 7:13–14).

This exalted position of the king is reflected in some of the psalms from the Jerusalem liturgy.

> I will tell of the decree of the LORD:
> He said to me, "You are my son;
>   today I have begotten you.
> Ask of me, and I will make the nations your
>   heritage,
>   and the ends of the earth your possession.
> You shall break them with a rod of iron,
>   and dash them in pieces like a potter's vessel."
>   (Ps. 2:7–9)

The king comes to be regarded as a priest-king.

> The LORD sends out from Zion your mighty scepter. . . .
> The LORD has sworn and will not change his mind,
>   "You are a priest forever according to the
>   order of Melchizedek."
>   (Ps. 110:2, 4)

Psalm 45 in a particularly flourishing celebration and even veneration of the king addresses the king himself as God: "Your throne, O God, endures forever and ever" (Ps. 45:6a). It further ends with a vow that would seem more appropriate directed to God: "I will cause your name to be celebrated in all generations; therefore the peoples will praise you forever and ever" (v. 17).

The identification of the royal interests with God's interest becomes a frequent target of prophetic indictment in later times. The idea of the temple as the place where a domesticated God is controlled and accessible in the national interests is really the focus of Jeremiah's harsh indictment in his temple sermon (Jer. 7). For his attack on the temple he is placed on trial and the implied capital offense is sedition.

Israel's Experience with Kings. The kingdom is divided in 922 B.C.E. following Solomon's death. Although the northern kingdom is initially established with prophetic support (Ahijah of Shiloh expresses this in 1 Kings 11:29–39), it too quickly falls into some of the patterns of royal ideology described above. Probably the northern kingdom tried to return to the limited kingship conception attempted under Saul and to some degree continued under David, with designation by the prophets and acclamation by the people. The result was a series of unstable reigns, some very brief. The dynasty of Omri seems to represent the same decisive move toward more Canaanite models of kingship than we saw under Solomon. The Deuteronomic historian gives us this cryptic assessment of Omri, that he "did more evil than all who were before him" (1 Kings 16:25).

It was under Omri's son Ahab that occurred the episode which most epitomizes the continuation of royal ideology in its Solomonic form through the ranks of Israel's kings, north and south. It is the story of Naboth's vineyard (1 Kings 21).[61] When Ahab seeks to exercise the prerogatives of wealth and privilege to buy a vineyard he desired, he is told by its owner Naboth, "The LORD forbid that I should give you my ancestral inheritance (*nahalah*)." Royal privilege comes up against the covenant notion of Yahweh as the owner of the land who has apportioned it equitably to all the families of Israel. It is Jezebel, his queen and a Phoenician princess who zealously promoted Baalism and persecuted the prophets, who finds the king sulking and reminds him of the possibilities of royal

power. "Do you now govern Israel?" She takes the matter in
hand, arranges to have Naboth falsely accused and executed.
The vineyard is then seized to become royal property and
Ahab goes to take possession only to find Elijah, Yahweh's
prophet, there to pronounce judgment in the name of the
covenant God.

Much of the story of Israel, in both kingdoms, from Solomon to the exile can be understood as the struggle between
the calling to be the alternative community of covenant and
the pattern of royal ideology which sought to make Israel "like
all the other nations." The implication of the biblical story is
that this is a perennial moral struggle. The temptation is always to believe that the patterns of community put forward by
the world can be indulged to some degree without compromising the covenant. Many of Israel's kings sought to indulge the
prerogatives of privilege and power while imagining that they
can still serve the covenant God, Yahweh. Only the covenant
reformers Hezekiah and Josiah are judged by Israel's own historians to have been faithful. Privilege and oppressive power
and domesticated religion are linked and appear together in
the biblical story. The implication is that they are wedded together in the ongoing story of the church seeking to be faithful in a world that tempts them to be "like all the other
nations."

It was the prophets who pointed to these realities with an
unwavering resolve, and who defended the integrity of covenant faithfulness with a courageous commitment. We will take
a fuller look at prophetic activity and message in the following
chapter.

Messiah: The Promise Postponed

The Emergence of Israelite Messianism. Our consideration
of the themes of kingship in Israel would not be complete if
we did not consider the relationship of the Davidic ideal to the
emergence of messianic hope in Israel. In contrast to the disobedient and sinful rule of Israel's earthly kings the prophets
began to hope for the eschatological reign of God's true king
and the establishment of God's kingdom in its fullness.[62] Several prophets offer portraits of this ideal king that suggest
attributes of God's divine kingship made manifest in the line
of David.

He is named
Wonderful Counselor, Mighty God,
    Everlasting Father, Prince of Peace.
His authority shall grow continually,
    and there shall be endless peace
for the throne of David and his kingdom.
    He will establish and uphold it
with justice and with righteousness
    . . . forevermore.

(Isa. 9:6–7)

A shoot shall come out from the stump of Jesse. . . .
The spirit of the LORD shall rest on him,
    the spirit of wisdom and understanding,
    the spirit of counsel and might,
    the spirit of knowledge and the fear of the LORD. . . .
With righteousness he shall judge the poor,
    and decide with equity for the meek of the earth; . . .
    with the breath of his lips he shall kill the wicked.
Righteousness shall be the belt around his waist,
    and faithfulness the belt around his loins.

(Isa. 11:1–2, 4–5)

The days are surely coming, says the LORD, when I will raise up for David a righteous Branch, and he shall reign as king and deal wisely, and shall execute justice and righteousness in the land. (Jer. 23:5)

I will set up over them one shepherd, my servant David, and he shall feed them: he shall feed them and be their shepherd. And I, the LORD, will be their God, and my servant David shall be prince among them. (Ezek. 34:23–24)

It is important to notice that David is the source of this eschatological ideal and not Solomon.

Not only is this hope for the messianic king but also for the messianic kingdom, the time when God's reign will be truly established. The imagery for this coming kingdom is rich with hope for the future and has served throughout the generations of the church as a source for renewal in times that seem barren of hopeful signs. The hope for the messianic king in Isa. 11 is followed by the image of the peaceable kingdom (Isa. 11:6–9). In Ezekiel the messianic shepherd will establish the "covenant of peace" (Ezek. 34:25). Both Isaiah (2:2–4) and Micah (4:1–5) envision a day when peoples "shall beat their swords into plowshares," and "nation shall not lift up sword against nation, neither shall they learn war any more." Micah (4:4) includes in this vision a redistribution of land where "they shall all sit under their own vines and under their own fig trees, and no one shall make them afraid."

In the postexilic period, when the Psalter received its final editing and there were no longer Israelite kings, there is evidence that the royal psalms of the Jerusalem cultus were heard in a new way as the anticipation of God's eschatological reign.[63] The promise had been postponed, and earthly kings had not proved to be the realm of its fulfillment, but the promise of God's reign was nevertheless trustworthy and the community lived in the sure hope that the reign of God would be consummated in God's own time.

The royal ideal, far from being compromised by the royal reality of Israelite kings, lived on as God's promise, rooted in the ultimate reign of God.

Jesus and the Kingdom of God. It should be obvious that the themes we have been discussing have important implications for the way in which the early church received and interpreted the ministry of Jesus. This is not the appropriate place to give these New Testament themes full explication. We will only make brief indications in two areas: Jesus as the Messiah, and Jesus' preaching of the reign (kingdom) of God.[64]

1. In the claim that Jesus is Messiah, the New Testament church lays claim to the tradition of hope for the coming of God's true king, the anointed One (Messiah). Jesus is presented as one in the line of David. He is anointed by a prophetic figure (the baptism by John) at which time he receives the spirit of God and is announced as God's son in the language of Ps. 2 (Matt. 3:13–17; Mark 1:9–11; Luke 3:21–22). His ministry is a demonstration of the power of that spirit, and he is acclaimed by the people in the royal entry into Jerusalem at the beginning of his passion week. But his kingdom is not that of earthly kings. His crown is of thorns and his throne a cross. He ascends into heaven after his resurrection, there to receive his true throne as one with the God who reigns over the heavens and the earth.

2. Jesus' preaching constantly announced, not the beginning of his own reign, but the present and yet to be consummated reign of God. The authority of earthly powers and the standards of earthly communities of self-interest are thereby

relativized. The presence and the approach of God's kingdom laid a new and urgent moral imperative on Jesus' hearers to live a life of discipleship in keeping with the ethical demands of the kingdom. It is our contention that these are in harmony with the covenant ideal advanced by Moses, defended by the prophets, and anticipated in its fullness by the visionaries. It is none other than the God who reigns as king in the proclamations of the Old Testament, whose kingdom is brought near in the preaching of Jesus.

Notes

1. For helpful discussions of the literary sources for this period and their relationship to the historical course of events see Bruce C. Birch, *The Rise of the Israelite Monarchy: The Growth and Development of I Samuel 7–15*, SBLDS 27 (Missoula, Mont.: Scholars Press, 1976); Bruce C. Birch, "I and II Samuel," in *Books of the Bible*, ed. Bernhard Anderson (New York: Charles Scribner's Sons, 1989), pp. 127–140; P. Kyle McCarter, *I Samuel*, AB (Garden City, N.Y.: Doubleday & Co., 1980), pp. 12–30; Baruch Halpern, *The Constitution of the Monarchy in Israel*, HSM 25 (Chico, Calif.: Scholars Press, 1981), pp. 149–175; T. N. D. Mettinger, *King and Messiah: The Civil and Sacral Legitimation of Israelite Kings* (Lund: Gleerup, 1976), pp. 80–98. On the history of this period see George E. Mendenhall, "The Monarchy," *Int* 29 (1975): 155–170; A. D. H. Mayes, "The Period of the Judges and the Rise of the Monarchy," and J. Alberto Soggin, "The Davidic-Solomonic Kingdom," in *Israelite and Judaean History*, ed. John H. Hayes and J. Maxwell Miller, OTL (Philadelphia: Westminster Press, 1977), pp. 285–331, and 332–363.

2. Consideration of the final form of the text must always be informed by critical analysis and judgments concerning the prior stages in the development of the text. These will sometimes affect our understanding and evaluation of the final witness of the text as a whole.

3. There have been recent signs of renewed attention to the theological importance of the books of Samuel. Especially noteworthy are two recent commentaries: Walter Brueggemann, *First and Second Samuel*, IBC (Louisville, Ky.: John

Knox Press, 1990), and Ralph W. Klein, *I Samuel*, WBC (Waco, Tex.: Word Books, 1983).

4. Halpern, *Constitution of the Monarchy in Israel*, pp. 61–84, has a detailed and helpful discussion of the theme of God's kingship in the enthronement psalms in which he particularly stresses the prominence of Divine Warrior language, both in cosmic and historical terms. See also Matitiahu Tsevat, "King, God as," *IDBSup,* ed. Keith Crim (Nashville: Abingdon Press, 1976), pp. 515–516.

5. See the classic work of Sigmund Mowinckel, available in English primarily in *The Psalms in Israel's Worship* (Nashville: Abingdon Press, 1962). See also S. H. Hooke, ed., *Myth, Ritual and Kingship* (Oxford: Clarendon Press, 1958), as well as the works by Halpern and Tsevat cited in n. 4.

6. Although dated in some of its particulars, Martin Buber, *The Kingship of God* (New York: Harper & Row, 1967), remains a classic on this subject. George E. Mendenhall, "Early Israel as the Kingdom of Yahweh," *The Tenth Generation* (Baltimore: Johns Hopkins University Press, 1973), pp. 1–31, makes a strong case that the kingship of Yahweh was the ideological focus which accounts for the entirely different social character of the early Israelite constitution compared to surrounding cultures. The functions of administering the law, waging war, and ensuring the economic well-being of the people are all functions elsewhere of kings but in early Israel directly attributed to Yahweh. See also Halpern and Tsevat, cited in n. 4.

7. Tsevat, "King, God as," p. 515, argues vigorously for early dating of this tradition. He also cites personal names incorporating the affirmation of God as king (e.g., Abimelech, Judg. 8:31).

8. Tsevat, "King, God as," p. 515.

9. Walter Brueggemann, *The Message of the Psalms* (Minneapolis: Augsburg Publishing House, 1984), p. 151.

10. See Keith Crim, *The Royal Psalms* (Richmond: John Knox Press, 1962), and Aubrey Johnson, *Sacral Kingship* (Cardiff: University of Wales Press, 1967).

11. See Herman Ridderbos, *The Coming of the Kingdom* (Philadelphia: Presbyterian and Reformed Publishing Co., 1962), and Rudolf Schnackenburg, *God's Rule and Kingdom*, trans. J. Murray (Freiburg: Herder, 1963). See Stephen Charles Mott, *Biblical Ethics and Social Change* (Oxford: Oxford University Press, 1982), pp. 82–106, for an ethical appropriation of king-

ship and kingdom of God themes in contemporary Christian ethics.

12. See Mendenhall, "Monarchy," p. 158.

13. In addition to those resources mentioned in n. 1 we should also observe that renewed application of literary-critical methods to Old Testament narrative in particular has resulted in several important works which stress the literary integrity of the books of Samuel as a whole and make a strong case that whatever earlier stages of development (sources) may be discerned, they have been incorporated into a unified narrative witness with its own describable perspective. See David M. Gunn, *The Fate of King Saul*, JSOTSup 14 (Sheffield: University of Sheffield Press, 1980), and Robert Polzin, *Samuel and the Deuteronomist* (San Francisco: Harper & Row, 1989).

14. This was a particular danger in the ancient world with respect to kings who were in many of the ancient Near Eastern cultures regarded as gods themselves by nature (Egypt) or by adoption (Mesopotamia). See Henri Frankfort, *Kingship and the Gods* (Chicago: University of Chicago Press, 1948), and Ivan Engnell, *Studies in Divine Kingship in the Ancient Near East*, 2nd ed. (Oxford: Basil Blackwell Publisher, 1967).

15. Most commentators have seen in this ominous list a reflection of the later experience of Israel under Solomon and thus, a critique of Solomonic power, but Isaac Mendelsohn, "Samuel's Denunciation of Kingship in Light of Akkadian Documents from Ugarit," *BASOR* 143 (1956): 17–22, makes a strong case that this also reflects the common pattern of kingship known in the Syro-Palestinian region. This only strengthens the contention we will make later that Solomon's kingship was largely in imitation of surrounding Canaanite models. In either case, 1 Sam. 8 is a devastating critique of royal power.

16. Bruce C. Birch, "The Development of the Tradition on the Anointing of Saul: 1 Samuel 9:1–10:16," *JBL* 90 (1971): 55–68.

17. Albrecht Alt, in his classic essay, "The Formation of the Israelite State in Palestine," *Essays on Old Testament History and Religion*, trans. R. A. Wilson (Oxford: Basil Blackwell Publisher, 1966) pp. 171–239, greatly stressed the coupling of designation by Yahweh and acclamation by the people as crucial to the character of the newly emerging institution of leadership. Paul D. Hanson, *The People Called: The Growth of Community in the Bible* (San Francisco: Harper & Row, 1986),

pp. 90–92, has placed renewed emphasis on these elements in understanding the early kingship.

18. Frank M. Cross, *Canaanite Myth and Hebrew Epic: Essays in the History of the Religion of Israel* (Cambridge, Mass.: Harvard University Press, 1973), p. 221. See also Hanson, *People Called*, p. 92.

19. For a full discussion of this view in relation to the Saul material, see Birch, *Rise of the Israelite Monarchy*, and the provocative article by Rolf Knierim, "The Messianic Concept in the First Book of Samuel," in *Jesus and the Historian*, ed. F. Thomas Trotter (Philadelphia: Westminster Press, 1968).

20. See Dennis J. McCarthy, "The Inauguration of the Monarchy in Israel. A Form-Critical Study of I Samuel 8–12," *Int* 27 (1973): 401–412.

21. See Cross, *Canaanite Myth and Hebrew Epic*, pp. 223ff. "It is fair to say that the institution of prophecy appeared simultaneously with kingship in Israel and fell with kingship. This is no coincidence: the two offices belong to the Israelite political structure which emerged from the conflict between league and kingdom" (p. 223).

22. We will discuss prophets and prophecy in greater detail in the next chapter.

23. See Cross, *Canaanite Myth and Hebrew Epic*, p. 221: "All our sources, whatever their attitude towards the nascent monarchy, are in accord in reporting that Saul forfeited the kingship, for himself and his house, by his breach of old law, namely by attempts (in one way or another) to manipulate the fixed forms of holy war in his own interests."

24. The phrase is from Mendenhall, "Monarchy," p. 159, who makes a convincing case for Saul's tragedy as rooted in his inability to harmonize a village population with an emerging kingship forced to turn to Canaanite urban models of organization and management.

25. Gunn, *Fate of King Saul*, pp. 125–131.

26. See Niels Peter Lemche, "David's Rise," *JSOT* 10 (1978): 2–25, for a thorough discussion of the interpretive literature.

27. Leonhard Rost first identified and named this material as a succession narrative and his work is the starting point of the modern discussion: "Die Überlieferung von der Thronnachfolge Davids," BWANT 3 (1926), E.T., *The Succession to the Throne of David* (Sheffield: JSOT Press, 1982). See David M. Gunn, *The Story of King David: Genre and Interpretation* (Shef-

field: JSOT Press, 1978), pp. 17–34, for a thorough discussion of the diverse interpretive treatments given to the so-called succession narrative.

28. Gerhard von Rad, "The Beginnings of Historical Writing in Ancient Israel," *The Problem of the Hexateuch and Other Essays*, trans. E. W. T. Dicken (New York: McGraw-Hill Book Co., 1966), pp. 166–204. This essay was first published in German in 1944.

29. See Brevard S. Childs, *Old Testament Theology in a Canonical Context* (Philadelphia: Fortress Press, 1985), pp. 117–119, for his strong criticism of Rost and von Rad. Robert Alter, *The Art of Biblical Narrative* (New York: Basic Books, 1981), p. 119, argues solely on literary-critical grounds that the David story should be treated as a single, imaginative, literary piece.

30. Walter Brueggemann, *David's Truth in Israel's Imagination and Memory* (Philadelphia: Fortress Press, 1985); Brueggemann, *First and Second Samuel*; Gunn, *Story of King David*; P. Kyle McCarter, *II Samuel*, AB (Garden City, N.Y.: Doubleday & Co., 1980).

31. Brueggemann, *David's Truth*, pp. 19–40, calls this portion of the David story the "trustful truth of the tribe," and characterizes it as the uncritical literature of those outside the boundaries of state power who celebrate the rise to power of one of their own.

32. Mendenhall, "Monarchy," p. 159.

33. Mendenhall, *Tenth Generation*, pp. 135–136: "The clearest example is David. He lost status in the Israelite community by flight caused by the enmity of the king. There gathered about him other refugees motivated by economic as well as other concerns. All were similarly without legal protection and had to maintain themselves by forming a band under the leadership of David, which was then able to survive by cleverness combined with a considerable degree of mobility." See also Lemche, "David's Rise," p. 23.

34. See Katharine Doob Sakenfeld, *Faithfulness in Action: Loyalty in Biblical Perspective*, OBT (Philadelphia: Fortress Press, 1985), pp. 8–15.

35. Mendenhall, "Monarchy," p. 160.

36. Patrick D. Miller, Jr., and J. J. M. Roberts, *The Hand of the Lord* (Baltimore: Johns Hopkins University Press, 1977), is the most helpful recent treatment of the Ark narrative in 1 and 2 Samuel.

37. See McCarter, *II Samuel*, for a full discussion of this text.

38. See Brueggemann, *David's Truth*, pp. 67–86, where he discusses this and other texts as "the sure truth of the state."

39. Brueggemann, *First and Second Samuel*, p. 257, calls 2 Sam. 7 "the root of evangelical faith in the Bible."

40. Scholars are less certain now than was Rost that 1 Kings 1–2 belong with 2 Sam. 11–20 as part of a succession narrative. See McCarter, *II Samuel*, for a full discussion of the opinions on this. Nevertheless, the palace intrigue and Solomon's treacherous dealings before and after David's death continue the theme of violence within David's own household which begins with David's taking of Bathsheba and murder of Uriah.

41. Brueggemann, *David's Truth*, pp. 41–66, calls this portion of David's story "the painful truth of the man."

42. Gunn, *Story of King David*, p. 95. See also his earlier article "David and the Gift of the Kingdom (2 Sam. 2–4, 9–20, 1 Kgs. 1–2)," *Semeia* 3 (1975): 14–45.

43. See Walter Brueggemann, "David and His Theologian," *CBQ* 30 (1968): 156–181; "The Trusted Creature," *CBQ* 31 (1969): 484–498; "On Trust and Freedom: A Study of Faith in the Succession Narrative," *Int* 26 (1972): 3–19; *In Man We Trust: The Neglected Side of Biblical Faith* (Richmond: John Knox Press, 1972).

44. Childs, *Old Testament Theology in a Canonical Context*, pp. 118–119.

45. Ibid., p. 119.

46. Sigmund Mowinckel, *He That Cometh: The Messiah Concept in the Old Testament and Later Judaism* (Nashville: Abingdon Press, 1954), p. 94.

47. See Crim, *Royal Psalms*.

48. See the discussion in Walter Brueggemann, *The Land*, OBT (Philadelphia: Fortress Press, 1977), pp. 75–79.

49. Mendenhall, "Monarchy," p. 160.

50. Walter Brueggemann, *The Prophetic Imagination* (Philadelphia: Fortress Press, 1978), pp. 28–43, and Hanson, *People Called*, pp. 105–127, have especially helpful discussions of this royal ideology which emerges under Solomon. Mendenhall, "Monarchy," paints a powerful portrait of this period in historical and sociological terms, a period he calls the "paganization of Israel." See also Cross, *Canaanite Myth and Hebrew Epic*, pp. 237–241.

51. Brueggemann, *Prophetic Imagination*, pp. 32–33.

52. Cross, *Canaanite Myth and Hebrew Epic*, p. 239.

53. See Hanson, *People Called*, pp. 115–116.

54. Mendenhall, "Monarchy," pp. 164–166, believes that the struggle between Adonijah and Solomon reflects the struggle of Yahwistic and Jebusite elements of the court. Following a suggestion made by numerous others he also understands the elevation of Zadok to high priest and his family to sole priesthood in the temple to be the installation of a Jebusite rather than an Israelite levitical priesthood.

55. Cross, *Canaanite Myth and Hebrew Epic*, p. 240. See the detailed treatment of this subject in G. Ernest Wright, "The Provinces of Solomon," ErIsr, 8 (1967): 58–68.

56. Mendenhall, "Monarchy," p. 164.

57. Brueggemann, *Prophetic Imagination*, p. 31. Much of the data on the Canaanite background to the temple can be found in G. Ernest Wright, *Biblical Archaeology* (Philadelphia: Westminster Press, 1957), ch. 3.

58. See Hanson, *People Called*, p. 106.

59. Brueggemann, *Prophetic Imagination*, pp. 37–38, discusses royal religion primarily in terms of the accessibility of God. I am not in disagreement with any of the aspects of royal religion to which he points. I do not, however, think the concept of accessibility is broad enough to encompass the full scope of royal religion I am suggesting in the domestication of God, and it runs the risk of suggesting that the radically free God of covenant religion is inaccessible.

60. Both the covenant reform kings Hezekiah and Josiah clean various idolatrous objects out of the temple as a part of their purification of the covenant cultus. Kings such as Omri and Ahab in the north, and Manasseh in the south are reported as idol worshipers and often as persecutors of the prophets.

61. See the fuller discussion of this episode as an example of royal, anti-Yahwistic ideology in Hanson, *People Called*, pp. 143–146.

62. Hanson, *People Called*, p. 126, writes of this prophetic response to the disappointment with earthly kings: "God's people came to be understood as a remnant, God's kingdom as an eschatological reign, and God's king as an eschatological messiah. All three of these developments were actually expressions of a return to the early Yahwistic belief in God's sole sovereignty and the accompanying relativization of all earthly

norms and powers." See also Childs, *Old Testament Theology in a Canonical Context*, pp. 119–120.

63. See Brevard S. Childs, *Introduction to the Old Testament as Scripture* (Philadelphia: Fortress Press, 1979), pp. 515–518, for a compelling presentation of this argument.

64. See Mott, *Biblical Ethics and Social Change*, pp. 82–106, for an ethical appropriation of the themes of this chapter in both their Old and New Testament contexts.

7
Prophetic Confrontation

The importance of the Hebrew prophets is obvious for any effort to assess biblical resources for Christian ethics. Their preaching constantly champions the moral dimensions of Israel's life which are implied by commitment in relationship to God, and they courageously oppose all those forces which might diminish or distort that commitment.

Unfortunately, consideration of the prophetic contribution to Christian ethics has often isolated the prophets' message from its context in the rest of the Old Testament, almost as if the prophets were an aberration from rather than an expression of the Old Testament faith traditions. Julius Wellhausen's notion of the prophets as a moment of creative innovation from which the Israelite tradition devolves into legalistic Judaism[1] has been discredited critically but continues to find modern expression. It is important in our consideration of the prophets to see them in relation to their social contexts historically and their literary and theological contexts as a part of the Hebrew canon.

The origins of prophecy in Israel are unclear. The biblical text shows little concern to clarify the distinctions between seer, visionary, and prophet either as vocabulary or as social role in early Israel.[2] Comparative studies have found prophet-like functionaries in other ancient Near Eastern societies and other studies have focused on the psychology and ecstatic behavior of the prophets.[3] Although research on such matters can help us understand the role of the prophet more fully, the theological evaluation of the prophetic literature focuses on the content of the prophetic message. In reclaiming the prophetic witness for Christian ethics in the life of the church, we will also focus on the prophetic message.

Prophetic message cannot be understood apart from attention to the social contexts in which the prophets' words were originally heard. New attention to sociological and historical method has produced valuable research important in recovering and understanding the social contexts within which the prophets worked.[4] Since this brief chapter must address the prophetic movement and prophetic literature as a whole, it can only address that social context in the broad terms of large periods of Israelite history. The work of this chapter must be complemented by attention to the particular context within which each prophet preached.

Attention to the prophets' social context must be supplemented by attention to the canonical context of the prophetic literature. Most often a prophet's words are collected and edited into their present literary form by later generations. This process may supplement as well as organize the prophetic message as this is felt necessary to make it accessible as a word to succeeding generations. Thus, the meaning and address of the prophetic literature is not limited to its meaning in an original social context. It may take on new dimensions of meaning as it is shaped and passed on in the canonical process. Brevard Childs sums it up, "Prophetic oracles which were directed to one generation were fashioned into Sacred Scripture by a canonical process to be used by another generation."[5] In assessing the prophetic message as a moral resource, one must avoid fragmenting the witness as the community has handed it on while at the same time being aware of the process through which the literature has been shaped and reclaimed by generations beyond that of the prophet's initial hearers.

In chapter 6 we spoke of the emergence of Hebrew prophets in response to the particular dangers of the monarchy for Israel's faith tradition. In these early periods of the kingship in Israel we see the prophets primarily through the narrative traditions which record their activities and witness in Israel's story (e.g., Samuel, Nathan, Elijah, Elisha). In this chapter we will focus on the classical prophets beginning with Amos in the mid-eighth century. The focus shifts from stories about prophets to collections of their preached oracles; from activities to message. Only for Jeremiah do we have extensive biographical material in addition to the collected oracles. Thus, our focus here will also be primarily on the content of the prophetic message. We will include the great prophets of the exile, Ezekiel and Deutero-Isaiah, in discussions where they share features and emphases in common with the pre-exilic prophets, but we will discuss features unique to their setting in the experience of the Babylonian exile in the next chapter. We may also take some note of Deuteronomic texts here, since the Deuteronomic reform of Josiah in 621 B.C.E. and its associated book of law are widely recognized to reflect the influence of earlier prophets, and the Deuteronomic reform in turn influences the preaching of subsequent prophets (esp. Jeremiah).

The God of Judgment and Hope

To understand the message of the Israelite prophets one must be clear that their message was always centered in the character and will of God.

> The ethical foundations of the prophetic proclamation may be stated in [this] way. One God, and only one God, is Lord over history, and wills to make himself known in history. This one God manifests his holiness in justice and righteousness, but is also compassionate and faithful. . . . *Prophetic faith is faith in a singular, transcendent, holy, absolutely righteous God,* a God who wills to live in community and to create his community among men [sic].[6]

The Prophet as Divine Representative

The prophets did not speak their own word to Israel, but spoke as the representatives of Yahweh, mediating a divine word to Israel. They not only spoke in the name of God, but for the most part presumed to speak the very words of God.

> For you shall go to all to whom I send you,
> and you shall speak whatever I command you. . . .
> Now I have put my words in your mouth.
> See, today I appoint you over nations and over kingdoms,
>   to pluck up and to pull down,
>   to destroy and to overthrow,
>   to build and to plant.
>
> (Jer. 1:7b, 9b-10)

The prophetic literature is constantly punctuated with the phrase "Thus says the LORD (Yahweh)." Form critical work identified this phrase as a messenger formula, and scholars quickly drew the conclusion that the prophets were less authors, poets, or preachers (common conceptions of the prophets before World War II) than messengers of God.[7] Some legitimate questions have been raised about the identification of "Thus says Yahweh" solely as a messenger formula.[8] Nevertheless, it is clear in the prophetic literature that this phrase serves as a constant reminder that the source of the prophet's authority is in God and not in himself, and that what follows is to be considered the direct address of God.

James Muilenburg made the influential observation that the prophets serve as covenant mediators in the tradition of Moses and other earlier figures.[9] They represent the covenant demands of God to the people and call them to task when those demands have been ignored or broken. This sense of formally mediating the covenant has been shown to be more prominent in the northern traditions than in those prophets who reflect a Judean tradition.

Robert Wilson, reflecting categories drawn from anthropology, has suggested that the prophets be considered intermediaries between God and people.[10] This more general term then allows him to observe and characterize different forms of intermediation. The result is a more complex and nuanced picture of the relationship between prophet, God, and society than the picture of a simple messenger allows. Considering the complex interrelationships of prophets like Isaiah, Jeremiah, and Ezekiel with the events and societies of their time this view is more adequate to the complexities of prophetic role.[11]

Lest we think of the prophets' relationship to God in terms of social role alone we would do well to recall Abraham Heschel's classic treatment of the prophets as those who communicated "insight into the present pathos of God." As representative of God's pathos the prophets were making known a God who refused to be neutral to the course of history, but was passionately and intentionally involved on the side of justice. For Heschel, God's pathos was the relational ground out of which God's word could be addressed to God's people.[12]

What is important at this stage in our discussion is to note the broad and general agreement that the prophets are the representatives of God, standing between the divine and human realms, to communicate the divine word and will.

Imagery for God

Because of their central focus on the word and will of God the prophets draw upon an extraordinary range of images for relationship to God. All of the aspects of the divine character we have discussed thus far make their appearance in the prophets, although each individual prophet has his own distinctive preferences from the spectrum of divine imagery.

The role of God as divine sovereign (see chapter 6) is especially important in the prophets since the role of messenger or intermediary in the ancient world is most often conceived in terms of the communications of a sovereign with the people. Isaiah, for example, is called to his task in a vision of the enthroned, holy God (Isa. 6:1–8; cf. also 1 Kings 22:19). The prophets are in the service of a divine king and not an earthly one, a conception that frequently places the prophets in tension with Israelite kings who are often uneasy with or opposed to the notion of a divine kingship which supersedes their own.

God as Creator, maker of promises to the ancestors, deliverer out of bondage, giver of the law—all these ways of speaking about God's relationship to Israel and to all of humankind are present in the prophetic corpus. To be sure, some of these are more prominent in some prophets or some periods of prophetic activity than in others. Although briefly present in prophetic preaching before the exile, God's role as Creator is not fully utilized by the prophets until Deutero-Isaiah during the Babylonian exile.

Some additional images for the divine-human relationship come into prominence in the prophets. Familial images are important in a number of the prophets. God's relationship to Israel is pictured as the relationship between a husband and a wife, intended by God as loving relationship, but broken by Israel's unfaithfulness. This image is, of course, central to Hosea, whose own marriage provided the metaphor for his understanding of God's relationship to Israel (see esp. Hos. 1–3). This imagery can reflect tender and loving relationship between God and Israel (e.g., Isa. 54:5–8). It is also reflected in other prophets (e.g., Jeremiah and Ezekiel) where conflict with Baalism leads to characterization of Israelite unfaithfulness as harlotry. The result is often the depiction of God's judgment on Israel as the violent punishment of a harlotrous wife in terms that are brutal and unacceptable for what they imply about ancient Israelite conceptions of women, marital relationship, and husband's rights.[13]

Relationship between God and Israel is also depicted as parent-child. One of the most moving of these is in Hos. 11:1: "When Israel was a child, I loved him, and out of Egypt I called my son." Israel is sometimes depicted as a son (Jer. 31:20) and sometimes as a daughter (v. 22). God is most often depicted as a father but is sometimes clearly described in mother images (e.g., Isa. 42:14; 49:15).

In the prophets God is frequently characterized as a judge.[14] We have seen elements of this image in our earlier discussion since the rendering of judgment is one of the functions of a king, and since the making of covenant carries with it the possibility of judgment on those who would break covenant. God the judge is also God the king and giver of covenant. "For the LORD is our judge, the LORD is our ruler, the LORD is our king; he will save us" (Isa. 33:22). Because the prophets prior to the exile are announcing God's word of judgment on a sinful people, the role of judge comes more sharply in focus, sometimes explicitly, at other times by implication (see Isa. 2:4; Jer. 11:20; Ezek. 7:3, 8, 27; 18:30; Joel 3:12; Micah 4:3). In keeping with their role as representatives of God the judge, the prophets often draw upon vocabulary and forms of speech taken from the law courts, "Hear the word of the LORD, O people of Israel; for the LORD has an indictment against the inhabitants of the land" (Hos. 4:1a; see also Micah 6:1–8). In this announcement of God's judgment the prophets serve in effect as agents of God in litigation against Israel for breaking and violating relationship to God and neighbor.

Covenant as Context

Should the relationship with God which Israel has broken be thought of as covenant relationship? Something of a debate on this issue has taken place in the scholarly literature over recent years.[15] In the preexilic prophets the term "covenant" (*berit*) appears only in Hos. 6:7; 8:1 and Isa. 24:5 as a term for Israel's relationship to Yahweh. This has led some to argue that the covenant imagery was not introduced into Israel until the Deuteronomic reform in 621 B.C.E. and was not the basis of earlier prophetic indictment against Israel.[16] Others argued that the presence of covenant-related vocabulary (e.g., justice and righteousness) and the imagery of Exodus and desert experiences imply the covenant relationship.[17] There is general agreement that the greater prominence of explicit references to covenant in Jeremiah and subsequent prophets is due to the influence of the Deuteronomic theology on the prophets and later Israelite tradition in general. Because of the greater prominence of covenant-related terms in Hosea, a northern prophet, and the ties of Deuteronomy to northern tradition, it may well be that historically the covenant concept was developed and preserved in the northern or Ephraimitic kingdom of Israel while the southern or Judean prophets relied on David-Zion imagery which does not give prominence to the Sinaitic covenant.[18]

It is clear that the prophets are concerned with the divine-human relationship, and with the announcement from God's perspective that this relationship has been broken and violated. The assumption in prophetic judgment speeches is that relationship to God entails responsibility and that this responsibility has not been upheld. Covenant is only one image for speaking about that divine-human relationship, and as we have seen, it relies on legal and contractual metaphors. When the prophets speak of justice and righteousness, appeal to obligations we know to be present even in the earliest law codes, use forms of speech drawn from the law courts, interpret and reinterpret the theme of Israel's election, then it is hard not to note the congruence of these concerns with the covenant concept of community. It may well be that the term "covenant" itself was not a common summation term for this matrix of community concepts until Deuteronomy, but this should not prevent us from noting the prophets' role in advocating a conception of obligation in relationship to God that is covenantal in character.

Indeed, apart from consideration of the historical development of these concepts, the canon as it now stands does not allow us to read the prophets without a full awareness of covenant relationship, established at Sinai, made concrete in the law, and used as a standard for judging Israel's history. In canonical terms there never was a time when appeal was made simply to "the prophets." Appeal was only to "the law and the prophets." The canonical collection of the prophetic literature was intended to be read in the light of and in concert with the law, the Torah.[19] We would argue that it is legitimate to speak of the prophets as representatives of God in the covenant relationship even in the eighth century when the term "covenant" is rarely used, but values and perspectives at home with the covenant concept are commonly appealed to. At the same time, our discussion of the wide range of imagery for God and relationship to God used in the prophets should caution us not to reduce everything to covenantal terms. The prophets used many ways of presenting divine-human relationship, and covenant was only one of those. Thus, broken relationship and responsibility for that brokenness is presented in both covenantal and noncovenantal images.

Judgment, Hope, and Broken Relationship

At the risk of oversimplification the prophetic message can be summarized as follows: God has been faithful to the relationship with Israel and has fulfilled the divine obligations within that relationship, but Israel has been unfaithful, has failed to carry out its obligations to the relationship. The relationship is now broken and the prophets announce God's necessary judgment on Israel's sin. Yet, relationship is not ended. Beyond judgment still lies hope for future restored relationship (although for some prophets this meant beyond the present sinful generation). God continues faithful to that relationship in spite of Israel's sin and will act to renew it.

God's Faithfulness. The prophets give testimony to God's faithfulness in relationship to Israel. God has demonstrated the qualities called for in the covenant established on Sinai.

> Let those who boast boast in this, that they understand and know me, that I am the LORD; I act with steadfast love, justice, and righteousness in the earth, for in these things I delight, says the LORD. (Jer. 9:24)

In Israel's own experience these qualities of God's faithfulness have been made known.

> Hear this word . . . , O people of Israel, against the whole family that I brought up out of the land of Egypt:
> > You only have I known
> > of all the families of the earth.
> > (Amos 3:1–2)

> > O my people, what have I done to you?
> > In what have I wearied you? Answer me!

For I brought you up from the land of Egypt,
    and redeemed you from the house of slavery;
and I sent before you Moses, Aaron, and Miriam.
                                    (Micah 6:3–4)

God has been a faithful covenant partner, a loving parent
(Hos. 11:1ff.; Isa. 1:2), a faithful and generous husband
(Jer. 2:2; Hos. 2:8). In Israel's own election God's faithful-
ness has been made known in special measure.

Israel's Unfaithfulness. The prophets announce God's angry indictment. Israel has broken the covenant, failed in the
obligations of relationship. God's justice and righteousness
have not been reflected in the people's justice and righteousness. The sinful effects of broken covenant are identified by the prophets as known to God.

There is no faithfulness or loyalty,
    and no knowledge of God in the land.
Swearing, lying, and murder,
    and stealing and adultery break out;
    bloodshed follows bloodshed.
                                    (Hos. 4:1b-2)

He expected justice,
    but saw bloodshed;
righteousness,
    but heard a cry!
                                    (Isa. 5:7b)

God's judgment is the accompanying result of Israel's indictment by the prophets. This judgment is to be in the
form of Israel's immanent destruction and suffering, a fate
not desired by God but executed by a divine, righteous
judge because of Israel's sin.

For they have transgressed laws,
    violated the statutes,
    broken the everlasting covenant.
Therefore a curse devours the earth,
    and its inhabitants suffer for their guilt.
                                    (Isa. 24:5b-6a)

This judgment is often pictured as the death of Israel although the imagery for this is very broad: earthquake, pesti-
lence, flood, and in particular, destruction by one's enemies.

> The end has come upon my people Israel;
> I will never again pass them by.
>
> (Amos 8:2b)
>
> Ah, Assyria, the rod of my anger—
> the club in their hands is my fury!
>
> (Isa. 10:5)

God's judgment amounts to Israel's choosing of death by disregard to the covenant and its promise of life in relationship to God (see Deut. 30:15–20).

> Because you have said, "We have made a covenant with death,
> and with Sheol we have an agreement;
> when the overwhelming scourge passes through
> it will not come to us;
> for we have made lies our refuge,
> and in falsehood we have taken shelter";
> therefore thus says the Lord GOD. . . .
> I will make justice the line,
> and righteousness the plummet;
> hail will sweep away the refuge of lies,
> and waters will overwhelm the shelter.
> Then your covenant with death will be annulled,
> and your agreement with Sheol will not stand;
> when the overwhelming scourge passes through
> you will be beaten down by it.
>
> (Isa. 28:15–16a, 17–18)

This often means a reversal of Israel's expectations. Relationship to God had come by many to be understood as privileged position. Amos startles his listeners by announcing that Israel's sin had transformed the Day of Yahweh from a day of privileged reward to a day of judgment on Israel.

> Alas for you who desire the day of the LORD!
> Why do you want the day of the LORD?
> It is darkness, not light. . . .
> Is not the day of the LORD darkness, not light,
> and gloom with no brightness in it?
>
> (Amos 5:18, 20)

In spite of Isaiah's suggestions to the contrary, Micah and later Jeremiah make clear that even Jerusalem and the temple are not to be exempt from or protected from God's judgment (Micah 3:12; Jer. 7:1–15). Even the relationship of covenant is rendered void by Israel's sin; from God's people they have become "Not my people" (Hos. 1:8–9).

God's Continued Faithfulness. Judgment is not the final word of God which the prophets have to announce. In spite of sin and judgment God remains faithful to relationship with Israel, and will act to initiate and make renewal and restoration possible. The prophets have a word of hope as well as of judgment, and both arise out of God's faithfulness.

In Amos this hope seems but a faint possibility. "Hate evil and love good, and establish justice in the gate; it may be that the LORD, the God of hosts, will be gracious to the remnant of Joseph" (Amos 5:15). Even in Amos a chapter of promise (ch. 9) has been added by later redactors so that Amos' announcement of judgment will not be taken as the final word. The imagery of hope is rich and varied.

> I will take you for my wife forever; I will take you for my wife in righteousness and in justice, in steadfast love, and in mercy. I will take you for my wife in faithfulness; and you shall know the LORD. (Hos. 2:19–20)

> See, a king will reign in righteousness,
>   and princes will rule with justice.
>   (Isa. 32:1)

> The days are surely coming, says the LORD, when I will make a new covenant with the house of Israel and the house of Judah. . . . I will put my law within them, and I will write it on their hearts; and I will be their God, and they shall be my people. (Jer. 31:31, 33b)

We shall have more to say of the prophetic message of hope later, but here we must note that God's justice and righteousness are manifest not only in divine judgment but in divine compassion. Indeed, God's compassion finds explicit reference in the prophets.

> For a brief moment I abandoned you,
>   but with great compassion I will gather you.
> In overflowing wrath for a moment
>   I hid my face from you,
> but with everlasting love I will have compassion on you,

> says the LORD, your Redeemer. . . .
> For the mountains may depart
> and the hills be removed,
> but my steadfast love shall not depart from you,
> and my covenant of peace shall not be removed,
> says the LORD, who has compassion on you.
>
> (Isa. 54:7–8, 10)

The Hebrew word for God's compassion here and elsewhere is related to a noun (*reḥem*) which means "womb" or "uterus." Phyllis Trible has demonstrated how an entire vocabulary of divine compassion reflects a metaphor of the womb.[20] God's compassion is an indication of the vulnerability of God alongside of the wrath and judgment of God which indicates a relationship of God to the people as intimate as that of a mother carrying a child, separate and yet one. As a mother participates in the life of the child and makes birth possible, so God's compassion indicates divine participation in human experience, and it is through God's compassion that new life is possible even beyond judgment.

The Universality of God

For the prophets God is not simply the God of Israel, while other peoples have their gods. The broad scope of events involving the Israelite kingdoms force the prophets to a radicalized understanding of the universal sovereignty of God— God's reign over all of human history. Here the prophets are drawing the implications inherent in the notion of a God who both creates the cosmos (see chapter 3) and rules over the cosmos (see chapter 6). Such a God cannot be a mere local deity, but must be understood in universal terms.

Amos opens his preaching with a series of oracles against the immediately surrounding nations which imply that God's judgment extends to them as well as to Israel (Amos 1–2). The books of Isaiah, Jeremiah, and Ezekiel all contain collections of oracles against the nations as well as those intended for Judah. Isaiah describes Assyria as an instrument of God's judgment (Isa. 10:5–11); Jeremiah and Ezekiel see Babylon in similar fashion (Jer. 20:1–6; 42:9–17; Ezek. 17:11–21);[21] Cyrus is seen as God's instrument of deliverance during the exile by Deutero-Isaiah (Isa. 45:1ff.). God's salvation and the peace of God's kingdom extend to all peoples (Isa. 2:1–4 ‖ Mic. 4:1–4).

One of the implications of this radical vision of divine sover-

eignty is that Israel's conception of election cannot be con-
strued as a matter of privilege, exclusive possession of God, or
moral superiority among the nations. Time and again the
prophets compare the sins of Israel with those of the nations.
The prophets point toward a new inclusiveness that does not
receive fullest expression until the time of the exile and restoration.[22] "I will give you as a light to the nations, that my
salvation may reach to the end of the earth" (Isa. 49:6b).

Prophetic preaching here addresses one of the central
moral dilemmas of the doctrine of election—its tendency to
exclusivism. By radicalizing the notion of God's universal
reign, the prophets are able to be clear that God is not the
exclusive possession of Israel, without surrendering the particularity of Israel's experience of God in their own salvation
story. God's people are especially chosen for a role in God's
story, but God's story will not be exhausted by Israel's story.
The prophets see clearly the radical implications of divine
freedom. Thus, the prophet Amos can make the startling
statement:

> Are you not like the Ethiopians to me,
>   O people of Israel? says the LORD.
> Did I not bring Israel up from the land of Egypt,
>   and the Philistines from Caphtor and the Arameans from Kir?
>   (Amos 9:7)

This notion of divine freedom and universal sovereignty allows
the prophets to scan the horizon looking for the activity of
God in human history and to seek to align God's people with
that divine activity in the world. The moral implications of this
conception of God's universality are obvious and radical for
the church in our own time where the tendency is often to
think of God as obligated to special presence in the church's
institutional forms and activities, and the conception of divine
activity is often narrow and parochial.

The prophetic radicalizing of God's universality has obvious
connections to the notion of God as Creator and to the full
statement of radical monotheism. Although these themes are
briefly touched upon in the preexilic prophets, it is Deutero-
Isaiah in the context of Babylonian exile who fully develops
them, and we will discuss these themes in the following chapter. The canonical joining of Isa. 40–55 (and 56–66) with Isa.
1–39 should remind us, however, that it was the judgment of

the community that Deutero-Isaiah's preaching should be read in the light of and as an extension of the preaching of Isaiah in eighth-century Jerusalem.

Foundations of Prophetic Ethics

Completely apart from the content of their message the prophets share certain characteristics that seem central both to the matter of prophetic identity and to the nature of prophetic ethics.

The Authority of God's Word

The central and exclusive authority for the prophet's role is in God, and it is God's word which he speaks. It is through the prophet that God's word is mediated to the people, calling (recalling?) them to exclusive loyalty to the God with whom they are covenanted. When Jeremiah identifies the three offices of priest, sage, and prophet it is by association with God's word that the prophet is identified (Jer. 18:18). Likewise Deut. 18:18 promises prophets to follow Moses as those who will speak God's word, "I will put my words in the mouth of the prophet, who shall speak to them everything that I command." Indeed, most of the prophets' message is in the form of the direct address of God, introduced and punctuated by "Thus says the LORD."

This exclusive claim of God upon the people mediated through the prophet as the bearer of God's word serves to relativize all other claims for loyalty and allegiance. "The word of our God will stand forever" (Isa. 40:8b). If the divine demands for obedience to the covenant responsibilities of the community to God and neighbor are not met, then no appeal to other authority will serve as justification. King, Zion, temple, religious practices, leaders, even Israel's own sense of election—none of these sources of authority were self-justifying apart from obedience to God's covenant demand. The prophetic announcement of God's word makes all of these secondary to the divine will.

> This extraordinary relativizing of all the structures of the common life, including the religious structures that provided a place for the prophets to speak . . . is of immense import for ethics. It assured a critical dimension to Israel's religious ethics, requiring

that the prophets defend with passion and with argument the radical positions they often took. This in turn means that prophetic ethics . . . was under continuing review, challenge, and elaboration, and was kept relevant to changing times and circumstances. It also preserved the community and its members from authoritarian ethical pronouncements and systems, or at least offered the leverage for such freedom. It is a democratizing principle—this relativizing of all the structures and figures of the society—and the community of Israel and the Christian community have taken advantage of it abundantly.[23]

In a sense the prophets were made necessary by the rise of two central challenges to God's exclusive claim for Israel's loyalty: the monarchy and Baalism.[24] In both of these developments central challenges were raised to the character of Israel's religious and social life. These challenges were antagonistic to Israel's conception of covenant community and relationship to the God who called them into that community. The prophets, as bearers of God's word to the people, reassert the authority of God's exclusive claim on the community, and announce God's word of judgment on the abuses and distortions which monarchy and Baalism have introduced into the community. We shall discuss the specifics of the prophetic indictment at a later point.

Calling and Vocation

The prophets are clear that they come to their task not out of personal initiative or by virtue of institutional office. They have been called by God, indeed, often compelled by God into the vocation of speaking God's word.[25] "The LORD took me from following the flock, and the LORD said to me, 'Go, prophesy to my people Israel' " (Amos 7:15). In the narratives that report the call experience for many of the prophets (Amos 7–9; Isa. 6; Jer. 1; Ezek. 1–3; Isa. 40:3–8; Zech. 1:7–6:8) the experience is described in different ways, but all testify that God's summons has brought them to the prophetic task, and many resisted that calling. The call is to the proclamation of God's word and many felt unworthy or inadequate to the task (Isaiah, Jeremiah, Ezekiel). God's word, however, does not depend on human resources alone. Isaiah's lips are purified with a burning coal; Jeremiah is told "Now I have put my words in your mouth"; Ezekiel is commanded to eat a scroll. The prophets are in agreement. The word they pro-

claim is from God, and the call to proclaim it cannot be refused. "The Lord GOD has spoken; who can but prophesy?"
(Amos 3:8b).

The call to prophetic vocation is often accompanied by visionary or charismatic experience. Many have focused on ecstatic experience as central to prophetic identity,[26] but it must
be emphasized that the prophets themselves "never emphasize
the means of revelation, but only its reality and contents."[27]
The prophets do not surrender their own consciousness and
identity to ecstatic experience but receive and respond to
God's summons.[28] "Here am I; send me!" (Isa. 6:8). The focus
is on God's word which the prophet called to proclaim it must
shape and focus through his own individuality for his own time
and place. The focus is never on revelatory experience as an
end in itself or a proof of divine authority. "I have heard what
the prophets have said who prophesy lies in my name, saying,
'I have dreamed, I have dreamed!' . . . Let the prophet who
has a dream tell the dream, but let the one who has my word
speak my word faithfully" (Jer. 24:25, 28).

The vocation of prophet is not just a calling to act as the
mouthpiece of God's word, but involves the prophet himself
in the embodiment of God's word. "The prophet's life was
reflective of the divine life. . . . God is seen to be present not
only in what the prophet has to say, but in the word as embodied in the prophet's life. To hear and see the prophet was to
hear and see God, a God who was suffering on behalf of the
people."[29] The vocational calling and the personal life of the
prophet are increasingly interrelated through the period of
classical prophecy. Hosea marries at God's command, and his
children's names are part of the prophetic message. Isaiah also
has symbolically named children. With Isaiah and Jeremiah it
is prophetic actions as well as speech through which they embody the word of God for their times. Ezekiel's dramatic actions and visionary experience is intertwined with his oracles.
It is perhaps in Jeremiah's confessions (found in Jer. 11; 12;
15; 17; 20) that we see both the interrelationship of personal
life with vocational calling and the deep struggles, even suffering, that this entails. To be called to the proclamation of God's
word in life and speech is often to be placed in tension and
conflict with the normal patterns of one's life and community.[30] To be the servant of God's word when the community
has departed from God's word is a perilous calling, and the
prophets' experience should serve as a warning to the church

in its prophetic ministry that it cannot preserve its comfort and still serve the word of God. Walter Brueggemann suggests that prophetic ministry in the mode of the Hebrew prophets automatically commits one to a consciousness arising out of the vocation of God's word which is alternative to the dominant consciousness of culture in any time and place.

> *The task of prophetic ministry is to nurture, nourish, and evoke a consciousness and perception alternative to the consciousness and perception of the dominant culture around us.* . . . . The alternative consciousness to be nurtured, on the one hand, serves to *criticize* in dismantling the dominant consciousness. . . . On the other hand, that alternative consciousness to be nurtured serves to *energize* persons and communities by its promise of another time and situation toward which the community of faith may move.[31]

Tradition and Creativity

To what extent are the prophets the proponents of a new and radical morality in ancient Israel? Or are they simply the conservators of earlier Israelite moral traditions? This has been the subject of considerable debate in the study of Israel's prophets.

Julius Wellhausen and Bernhard Duhm popularized a view in the early part of the century which saw the prophets as the producers of a new and higher theology and morality in Israel.[32] The prophets were portrayed as theologians and innovators rather than as proclaimers of God's word already made known in the traditions of Israel. This view of the prophets as creative reformers was popular and influential in Protestant social gospel circles because of its antilegal bias. Even some recent works on the prophets tend to emphasize this creative and innovative element.[33]

It was Gerhard von Rad who gave most definitive voice to an increasing chorus of criticism for the Wellhausen-Duhm emphasis.[34] On the one hand, he argued that every prophet was indebted to a received tradition (with religious and social aspects) which he used in his preaching to conserve and to reinterpret to his own context. For Amos, Hosea, and Jeremiah this was the Exodus-Sinai tradition; for Isaiah and Micah it was the David-Zion tradition; for Ezekiel and Deutero-Isaiah it tended to be a combination of these. On the other hand, von Rad was concerned to affirm the freedom of the prophets. They often reinterpreted the traditions they received, or broke with the prevailing understandings of those traditions (e.g., Amos on the Day of Yahweh, Amos 5:18–20, or Jeremiah's temple sermon, Jer. 7).

Some have criticized von Rad for overreacting to Wellhausen since he tended to argue that the prophets thought exclusively within the framework of received tradition.[35] The prophets are also the representatives of God who is acting anew in Israel's midst. However, few, if any, would now challenge the notion that the prophets speak to the people on behalf of a God who has already made known the obligations of covenant relationship (whether in the framework of Exodus-Sinai or David-Zion). In calling the people to accountability, the prophets drew upon the traditions of Israel's received faith and interpreted those traditions in the light of the present situation they found. "The problem is not that Israel did not know, but that Israel did not do. So the prophets introduce no new and higher morality, and do not even appear to radicalize the old laws, which were sufficiently demanding to begin with."[36]

This need not reduce our respect for the new in prophetic preaching. Although rooted in tradition the prophets clearly announce the word of a living God who is active in new ways in the people's midst, and they often found themselves as the announcers of God's new future for the people—both in judgment and in hope. Although God's word may be known through the traditions of the past, the prophets believed in the power of God's word to change history for the future. The people could receive or refuse God's word, but in either case the future would be affected by the entry of God's word into their midst. Thus, the prophets were both renewers of a faith tradition and discerners of God's "new thing" (Isa. 43:19). Those in the church who would appeal to the prophets as a moral resource would do well to note this dialectic. Calls for radical change apart from rootedness in the faith tradition are likely to express only our own desires and not the divine will. Preaching of our historic moral traditions as an end in itself robs us of participation in what God is doing anew in our time, and suggests that we do not believe in the power of God's word to affect the course of history anew.

Concreteness and Social Context

The prophets were not given to abstract formulations of good and evil. When Amos cries out, "Hate evil and love good," he adds, "and establish justice in the gate" (Amos 5:15a). Prophetic ethics is concerned for concrete realities in the midst of history. God's word was not a theological abstraction but an expression of divine rule in the concreteness of human community.

1. The prophets were acutely concerned for historical reality as the arena for their preaching of God's word. They preached to Israel as a people who had known the reality of God in the history of their own salvation experiences, and as a community called to reflect relationship to God in the concrete patterns of their life together. Hence, they assumed that God's will and activity would be manifest in the concrete realities of the present history. God's rule was over history, not beyond it.

The prophets were acute observers of their world. The politics of the nations, the practices of the leaders, the structures of economic life, the welfare of the most vulnerable, the institutions of cult and court—these are the arenas where God was active and the divine will was to be served; these were the focus of prophetic preaching. Covenant faithfulness, relationship to God, was to be found in attention to these concrete realities of human experience, not in pious practices, religious formulations, or ethical principles separated from such particularities.

2. The prophets spoke to Israel as a community, a social reality, rather than as a collection of individuals. This is in keeping with the corporate consciousness which is consistently present in the Israelite faith tradition, but the prophets reclaim this sense of corporate solidarity in a time when individuals and groups are tempted to pursue their own welfare apart from concern for the welfare of the people as a whole. Thomas Ogletree finds in this social solidarity one of the most distinctive contributions of the Old Testament to ethics.

> According to Israelite understandings, it is not as isolated individuals, but as members of a community that we realize our being. . . . Consequently, our wholeness as moral beings cannot be abstracted from the moral soundness of the community to which we belong. The moral soundness of the community, moreover, is most clearly manifest in its treatment of its most vulnerable members. . . . Individual responsibility is not ruled out by this sense of solidarity; yet it gains an essentially social meaning. I act not simply for myself, but for the well-being of the whole people. I am

answerable not simply to myself and my own principles, but to the whole people and its foundational principles.[37]

Even when the prophets single out individuals (such as the king) or groups within Israel (such as the wealthy), the judgment of God they announce is often on the people as a whole, for they know all of the community as interdependent. Moral responsibility is a corporate responsibility of the entire community, and the lack of justice and righteousness on the part of some can bring consequences for all.

In our own time and setting the tendency to define faith in individualistic terms suggests that we would do well to hear the prophets anew at this point. We cannot pursue our own righteousness apart from our interrelationship with the whole of God's people, and in the context of the concrete social and historical realities of our lives.

The Prophetic Indictment

The concreteness that was characteristic of the prophets led them to state God's indictment of Israel in very specific terms. Of course, each prophet addressed this indictment to the social context of a particular time and place, so each prophetic message has its own individual character. Nevertheless, many of the particulars of the prophetic indictment recur in slightly varied form throughout the preexilic period. Thus, it is possible to sketch a composite picture while realizing that no one prophet encompassed all the elements discussed. Many of these issues are perennial and universal issues for the faith community, thus, the prophets often seem to be speaking as freshly to a new generation as to their own.

Justice and Righteousness

These two terms appear throughout the body of prophetic literature, and often in close association. For prophetic ethics these concepts are foundational.

We have already discussed the basic meaning of these Hebrew terms in chapter 5. Justice (*mišpaṭ*) relates to the claim to life and participation by all persons in the structures and dealings of the community, and especially to equity in the legal system. Righteousness (*ṣedaqah*), a more personal term, refers to the expectations in relationship for intentions and actions that make for wholeness in that relationship.

These qualities are rooted in the character of God who has acted in justice and righteousness toward the people. God then expects these qualities to be reflected in the life of God's people, in their relationships to one another and to God. The prophets announce that God has not found this expectation met.

> For the vineyard of the LORD of hosts
>   is the house of Israel,
> and the people of Judah
>   are his pleasant planting;
> he expected justice,
>   but saw bloodshed;
> righteousness,
>   but heard a cry!
>   (Isa. 5:7)

Justice and righteousness are also the moral values which are to characterize covenant obedience. They are basic to the identity of the covenant community if it is to be faithful to its relationship with God. Obedience to God's law as expressed in the moral demands of the Decalogue and the Covenant Code (and the Deuteronomic law for Jeremiah) seems to be a part of what the prophets understand as the divine expectation (cf. Hos. 4:2; Jer. 7:9–10). But justice and righteousness in the prophets go beyond mere attention to the letter of the law. They are associated with the general moral task of doing good while turning from evil, and the measure is to be the welfare of the most vulnerable.

> Cease to do evil,
>   learn to do good;
> seek justice,
>   rescue the oppressed,
> defend the orphan,
>   plead for the widow.
>   (Isa. 1:17)

It is because justice and righteousness are ignored or despised that the prophets must announce that the covenant is broken; relationship to God is sundered; the community suffers from this sin. "Where someone cries out for justice, all hear in that word a claim that something has gone wrong in the relation between a society and its members."[38] Something has also gone wrong in the relation to God. In the absence of these moral qualities, acts of piety and devotion are meaningless, even repugnant to God.

> I hate, I despise your festivals,
>   and I take no delight in your solemn assemblies.
> Even though you offer me your burnt offerings and grain
>   offerings,
>   I will not accept them. . . .
> But let justice roll down like waters,
>   and righteousness like an everflowing stream.
>   (Amos 5:21–22a, 24)

It is important to note that for the prophets God's demand of justice and righteousness was not a utopian fancy. They believed it was possible to embody these moral qualities in relationships to others and to God. The concreteness of their indictment of Israel's sin was designed to make clear the particulars of justice and righteousness as they should and could be expressed in faithful community. What God asks is capable of fulfillment.

> He has told you, O mortal, what is good;
>   and what does the LORD require of you
> but to do justice, and to love kindness,
>   and to walk humbly with your God?
>   (Micah 6:8)

Economic Issues

The prophets found ample evidence in the economic sphere for the brokenness of covenant relationship, and much of their indictment focuses on economic issues.

The chief structural issue was ownership of the land and the benefits that accrue from such ownership.[39] As we have seen, the economic structures of the covenant community sought wide distribution of land ownership to every family through the institution of the "inheritance" (*naḥalah*, see chapter 5). God was the true owner of the land, and each family was to possess an inheritance to manage as God's steward. The whole of the land was Israel's "possession" as the gift of God who brought them out of Egypt and gave them the land as a sign of salvation.

Monarchy introduced a new social system that was not harmonious with the conception of land as continual "inheritance" (see chapter 6). Land was needed as the basis for royal patrimony. Land was used to reward royal service, and was accumulated as the basis of new, wealthy classes. This meant the loss of "inheritance" to those deprived of land. Traditional Israelite society depended on small family-based agricultural plots organized around villages, with common land held for grazing and water. Loss of family land or of common land raised serious issues of material welfare and reduced many to poverty.

In addition to loss of material support these Israelites lost identity and benefits. Land was the sign of God's salvation, the basis of participation in assemblies, cultic festivals, mutual defense. It was the basis of freedom as members of God's people; those who lost their land were reduced to slaves, debtors, and wage earners. The law courts provided no protection and were often manipulated to benefit a growing wealthy class (cf. Naboth's vineyard, 1 Kings 21). James L. Mays describes this shift in Israel as "the shift of the primary social good, land, from the function of support to that of capital; the reorientation of social goals from personal values to economic profit; the subordination of judicial process to the interests of the entrepreneur."[40]

The prophets saw this situation clearly, both in its consequences for the exploited poor and in its structural basis in an exploitive system for the accumulation of land and wealth.

> Alas for those who devise wickedness
>   and evil deeds on their beds!
> When the morning dawns, they perform it,
>   because it is in their power.
> They covet fields, and seize them;
>   houses, and take them away;
> they oppress householder and house,
>   people and their inheritance.
>   (Micah 2:1–2)

> Ah, you who join house to house,
>   who add field to field,
> until there is room for no one but you,
>   and you are left to live alone
>   in the midst of the land!
>   (Isa. 5:8)

The prophets saw the results of such accumulation of land and wealth in the plight of the poor. It was an offense to Israel's God who is especially identified with the dispossessed (see chapters 4 and 5).

For three transgressions of Israel,
  and for four, I will not revoke the punishment;
because they sell the righteous for silver,
  and the needy for a pair of sandals—
they who trample the head of the poor into the dust of the earth,
  and push the afflicted out of the way.

(Amos 2:6–7a)

The LORD enters into judgment
  with the elders and princes of his people:
It is you who have devoured the vineyard;
  the spoil of the poor is in your houses.

(Isa. 3:14)

The poor and the needy are defrauded by corrupt business practices and aggressive exploitation of their need.

Hear this, you that trample on the needy,
  and bring to ruin the poor of the land,
saying, "When will the new moon be over
  so that we may sell grain;
and the sabbath,
  so that we may offer wheat for sale?
We will make the ephah small and the shekel great,
  and practice deceit with false balances,
buying the poor for silver
  and the needy for a pair of sandals,
  and selling the sweepings of the wheat."

(Amos 8:4–6)

Can I tolerate wicked scales
  and a bag of dishonest weights?
Your wealthy are full of violence;
  your inhabitants speak lies,
  with tongues of deceit in their mouths.

(Micah 6:11–12)

For the prophets those who enjoyed the fruits of wealth and luxury without regard to the plight of the poor and the needy are as guilty as those who actively exploit them.

Alas for those who lie on beds of ivory,
    and lounge on their couches,
and eat lambs from the flock,
    and calves from the stall;
who sing idle songs to the sound of the harp,
    and like David improvise on instruments of music;
who drink wine from bowls,
    and anoint themselves with the finest oils,
but are not grieved over the ruin of Joseph!
                                          (Amos 6:4–6)

Amos, Isaiah, and Micah all have harsh words for the excesses of a wealthy class that seeks its own luxury when social ills are obvious and widespread (Amos 4:1–3; Isa. 3:16–17; 5:11–13; Micah 3).

> There was a kind and degree of wealth which they [the prophets] held to be incompatible with justice, and the nature of its incompatibility can be inferred from the way in which they describe it. If its acquisition and possession cost the economic freedom and welfare of others, they called it violence and oppression. If it fostered conspicuous consumption at a level of luxury that was enjoyed in heedless unconcern for the needs of others, it was wrong. If it was gained by violation of the rules of righteousness which set the values of personal relations above profit, it was iniquitous. If wealth became the dominant motivation of those responsible for social well-being because they held power, that was sin.[41]

Sociopolitical Issues

The economic exploitation which the prophets indict was made possible by corruption, abuse, and self-seeking power in the sociopolitical institutions of Israel.

The administration of justice had itself become corrupted. It was the judicial system, both the local justice in the gates and the larger judicial apparatus of the monarchy, that should have provided the place for redress of injustice and protection for those who might be exploited by the self-serving interests of others. The greed of judicial officials for wealth, the self-serving bias toward the powerful, and outright bribery are all observed and condemned by the prophets.

Ah, you who are heroes in drinking wine
    and valiant at mixing drink,

> who acquit the guilty for a bribe,
>> and deprive the innocent of their rights!
>>> (Isa. 5:22–23)

> Ah, you that turn justice to wormwood,
>> and bring righteousness to the ground! . . .
> For I know how many are your transgressions,
>> and how great are your sins—
> you who afflict the righteous,
>> who take a bribe,
> and push aside the needy in the gate.
>>> (Amos 5:7, 12; cf. also Isa. 1:21–26;
>>>> Micah 7:3; Ezek. 22:12)

The corruption of leadership indicted by the prophets goes far beyond the law courts. At every level those in leadership have failed in their responsibility to serve justice and righteousness. Their loyalties have been turned from God to the lure of wealth and power. From rulers and nobles to prophet and priest—at every level the covenant has been forgotten and corruption is evident. Micah's sweeping indictment can serve as representative:

> Listen, you heads of Jacob
>> and rulers of the house of Israel!
> Should you not know justice?—
>> you who hate the good and love the evil,
> who tear the skin off my people,
>> and the flesh off their bones;
> who eat the flesh of my people,
>> flay their skin off them,
> break their bones in pieces,
>> and chop them up like meat in a kettle,
>> like flesh in a cauldron.
> Then they will cry to the LORD,
>> but he will not answer them. . . .
> Thus says the LORD concerning the prophets
>> who lead my people astray,
> who cry "Peace"
>> when they have something to eat,
> but declare war against those
>> who put nothing into their mouths. . . .
> Hear this, you rulers of the house of Jacob,
>> and chiefs of the house of Israel,
> who abhor justice
>> and pervert all equity,

who build Zion with blood
and Jerusalem with wrong!
Its rulers give judgment for a bribe,
its priests teach for a price,
its prophets give oracles for money;
yet they lean upon the LORD and say,
"Surely the LORD is with us!
No harm shall come upon us."
Therefore because of you
Zion shall be plowed as a field;
Jerusalem shall become a heap of ruins,
and the mountain of the house a wooded height.
(Micah 3:1–4a, 5, 9–12)

Even kings are not exempt from this indictment. Hosea believes the whole institution of kingship to be sinful (Hos. 8:4;
13:10–11) and includes them in God's judgment (5:1). Jeremiah excoriates Jehoiakim for collecting wealth by injustice,
for failing to pay fair wages, for violence against the innocent,
for failure to champion the cause of the needy, and for general disregard of justice and righteousness (Jer. 22:13–19).

In particular the prophets indict the kings and their advisers
for trust in diplomacy and military might in their quest for
extended power rather than trust in God.

You have plowed wickedness,
you have reaped injustice,
you have eaten the fruit of lies.
Because you have trusted in your power
and in the multitude of your warriors,
therefore the tumult of war shall rise against your people.
(Hos. 10:13–14)

Alas for those who go down to Egypt for help
and who rely on horses,
who trust in chariots because they are many
and in horsemen because they are very strong,
but do not look to the Holy One of Israel
or consult the LORD!

(Isa. 31:1)

In their narrow nationalism and pursuit of personal power the
kings seek to silence critics and avoid accountability. They
command the prophets to speak only "smooth things" and to
"prophesy illusions" (Isa. 30:10). Their supporters cry,
" 'Peace, Peace,' when there is no peace" (Jer. 6:14; 8:11).

When exile and destruction come Ezekiel preaches against the kings and leaders of Judah who were the shepherds of Israel but have failed in their duties and brought disaster on the flock.

> You have not strengthened the weak, you have not healed the sick, you have not bound up the injured, you have not brought back the strayed, you have not sought the lost, but with force and harshness you have ruled them. (Ezek. 34:4)

Cultic Issues

The realm of Israel's religious life did not escape prophetic indictment. The most obvious violation of covenant obedience to God is idolatry. Throughout the time of the prophets the temptation to worship other gods (esp. the Baals) alongside or in place of Yahweh was a threat. Hosea focuses particularly on this arena of Israel's sin:

> My people consult a piece of wood,
>   and their divining rod gives them oracles.
> For a spirit of whoredom has led them astray,
>   and they have played the whore, forsaking their God.
>   (Hos. 4:12; cf. also 2:1–13)

Isaiah, Micah, and Jeremiah all include idolatry among Israel's sins, and this threat to Yahweh's claim for Israel's exclusive loyalty seems to persist even into the exile experience as seen in Deutero-Isaiah's biting satire on the folly of worshiping a piece of wood (Isa. 44:9–20; cf. also Jer. 10:1–10).

The prophets also indict Israel for the degree to which their religious life has been influenced by the breakdown of covenantal justice and righteousness. Priests, especially charged with the preservation and dissemination of the knowledge of God, have neglected this duty and engaged in the general desire for privilege, wealth, and power. Thus, they are especially singled out for prophetic announcement of divine wrath.

> My people are destroyed for lack of knowledge;
>   because you have rejected knowledge,
> I reject you from being a priest to me.
>   (Hos. 4:6; cf. also Micah 3:11)

In the absence of justice and righteousness piety, sacrifice, and cultic observance had become hypocritical. The covenant

faith of Israel was to promote and defend justice and righteousness. Religious practice was not to be an end in itself.

> For I desire steadfast love and not sacrifice,
>   the knowledge of God rather than burnt offerings.
> (Hos. 6:6)
>
> I hate, I despise your festivals,
>   and I take no delight in your solemn assemblies. . . .
> But let justice roll down like waters,
>   and righteousness like an everflowing stream.
> (Amos 5:21, 24)
>
> I cannot endure solemn assemblies with iniquity.
> (Isa. 1:13b; cf. 1:12–17; Jer. 6:20)

The prophets denounce the domesticated religion of monarchy and its service to royal power rather than to divine
power. The temple, which should have been a place for covenant remembrance and renewal, had become a part of the
royal system of oppression and injustice. Jeremiah is forced to
confront those who look on the temple as a sign of privileged
protection and declare that in the absence of covenant faithfulness even the temple is under God's judgment and will be
destroyed (Jer. 7; 26; cf. Micah 3:12).

Special Concern for the Vulnerable

It has not been possible to discuss the prophetic indictment
of Israel without already noting the special prophetic concern
for the weakest and most vulnerable members of the community. Indeed, this was a special concern of the covenant and
the covenant legal collections. In the face of economic exploitation, maladministration of the legal system, corrupt and self-
serving leadership, and an inward turning cultus, the most
vulnerable members of Israelite society (the poor, the needy,
the widow, the orphan, the weak) were in need of advocates.
The prophets became those advocates, and in so doing suggested that these most vulnerable and their welfare are the
most adequate measure of justice and righteousness in the
community. It is the task of covenant community to secure
value and place for full life to those most unable to secure it
for themselves. That Israel had failed to do this is the subject
of some of the prophets' harshest indictment and most ener-
getic advocacy.

What do you mean by crushing my people,
> by grinding the face of the poor? says the Lord GOD of hosts.
>> (Isa. 3:15)

> Cease to do evil,
>> learn to do good;
> seek justice,
>> rescue the oppressed,
> defend the orphan,
>> plead for the widow.
>>> (Isa. 1:16c–17)

The prophetic ethic at this point seeks a societal order that values the worth of every person before God. Therefore, when any member of the community is denied the resources of full life and worth, the entire community is diminished and broken.

> In the prophetic oracles . . . it is apparent that principles of justice like "To each according to his merit" or "To each according to his societal contribution" or "Similar treatment for similar cases" are not adequate. The justice they advocated must be capable of exception, of responsiveness to the individual's needs, of an estimate of worth based on the simple existence of a person.[42]

The Prophetic Hope

The prophets clearly announced God's judgment on Israel as an already accomplished reality. God had rendered a verdict on Israel's sin, and the community's imminent destruction is the penalty. But in the prophets there is a further word from the Lord. Judgment is not to be the only or the final word.

The Possibility of Repentance

Can God's judgment be averted? Is the prophets' word intended to evoke repentance, and can a heeding of their word alter the reality of coming disaster?

There is some indication that the prophets held out some hope of repentance to avert or at least to survive the impending judgment.

> If you return, O Israel,
>> says the LORD,
> if you return to me,

if you remove your abominations from my presence,
   and do not waver,
and if you swear, "As the LORD lives!"
   in truth, in justice, and in uprightness,
then nations shall be blessed by him,
   and by him they shall boast. . . .
Circumcise yourselves to the LORD,
   remove the foreskin of your hearts,
   O people of Judah and inhabitants of Jerusalem,
or else my wrath will go forth like fire,
   and burn with no one to quench it,
   because of the evil of your doings.

                              (Jer. 4:1–2, 4)

At times the prophets seem to suggest that a faithful remnant might be preserved, although this seems to mean through the judgment rather than an alternative to it.

A remnant will return, the remnant of Jacob, to the mighty God. (Isa. 10:21)

   Hate evil and love good,
      and establish justice in the gate;
   It may be that the LORD, the God of hosts,
      will be gracious to the remnant of Joseph.
                              (Amos 5:15)

Prophetic admonitions, such as quoted earlier from Isa. 1:17, seem to imply a belief by the prophets that appeals to obedience and conscience are meaningful, and God's demands are capable of fulfillment. Change is possible, and a different pattern to the community can be meaningfully called for.

Nevertheless, the prophets for the most part believe that calls to repentance will not be heeded, and that admonitions to faithfulness will fall on deaf ears.

      Their deeds do not permit them
         to return to their God.
      For the spirit of whoredom is within them,
         and they do not know the LORD.
                              (Hos. 5:4)

      Can Ethiopians change their skin
         or leopards their spots?
      Then also you can do good
         who are accustomed to do evil.
                              (Jer. 13:23)

The prophets submitted their announcement of God's judgment to history and grieved over the failure of the people to heed their words. They were not reformers or revolutionaries, for they held little hope that judgment could be averted; but they persisted in articulating a vision of what faithful community could be in the simple trust that even through and beyond judgment this vision of community as God's people was capable of fulfillment and should also be understood as God's word. It was perhaps this trust that led them to the conviction that judgment was not the end of relationship to God.

The Emergence of Eschatological Hope

If God's judgment could not be averted, the prophets nevertheless dared to speak of God's future in dramatic and hopeful images that introduced a genuinely eschatological element into Israelite faith for the first time.[43] God was not through with Israel. Beyond judgment and in harmony with God's saving activity in the past God will act redemptively to restore relationship in the future. In Hosea, Israel will return to the wilderness to begin the relationship of husband and wife anew in love (Hos. 2:14–23). In Isaiah, God's future promises a new Davidic king who will reign in justice and righteousness (Isa. 11:1–5; 32:1). In Jeremiah broken covenant shall be replaced by new covenant (Jer. 31:31).

The prophets also understood that God's future with Israel would not be simple renewal of Israel's past. Israel's hope lay in incorporation in new visions of God's reign, and new understandings of the role of God's people in that future vision. Jeremiah's new covenant will not be like the old, but a new covenant written upon the heart (Jer. 31:33). God's salvation will extend divine renewal to the nature of sinful humanity itself and make possible new and hopeful beginnings within the human heart, not just in the history of social institutions.

Likewise, in Isaiah genuinely eschatological pictures of God's future kingdom provide hopeful visions of God's future that are more than the hope for a more responsive king on the Davidic throne in Jerusalem.

Then justice will dwell in the wilderness,
  and righteousness abide in the fruitful field.
The effect of righteousness will be peace,
  and the result of righteousness, quietness and trust forever.

My people will abide in a peaceful habitation,
in secure dwellings, and in quiet resting places.
(Isa. 32:16–18; see also the peaceable kingdom in 11:6–9)

In both Isaiah and Micah this vision of God's future defines Israel's role in broader inclusiveness of God's purposes for the nations and not Israel alone.

He shall judge between the nations,
and shall arbitrate for many peoples;
they shall beat their swords into plowshares,
and their spears into pruning hooks;
nation shall not lift up sword against nation,
neither shall they learn war any more.
(Isa. 2:4 ‖ Micah 4:3)

This articulation of God's hopeful future is taken much further by Ezekiel and Deutero-Isaiah under the impetus of the Babylonian exile and the sense that God's judgment had already been experienced in devastating terms. In the next chapter we shall discuss their fuller development of prophetic hope in its immediate word for the exile community and in continued development of this eschatological motif in prophetic preaching.

The moral significance of this development of prophetic eschatological vision should not be underestimated.[44]

1. It represents a radical affirmation of God's sovereignty over all of human history. Against the backdrop of a time when the human community seems incapable of embodying justice and righteousness in concrete human community, the prophets declare that God's purposes will not be thwarted. God's kingdom will come because it does not depend on our efforts alone. Hope becomes possible in the midst of seemingly hopeless conditions because of divine promises and not because we believe our efforts can build the kingdom. The alternative is despair or acquiescence in the present order which even in the face of immanent judgment the prophets refuse.

2. It summons the community to a quality of life appropriate to the coming of God's kingdom, perhaps even contributing to the movement of God toward its realization. Justice and righteousness are the pathways of those who live toward this vision even when the prevailing society around them refuses it.

The prophets understood that without the articulation of such vision it is not possible to survive in the present order with its brokenness, and faithfully live and wait in trust for the coming of God's new day. To choose, as did the prophets, to live in the tension between the no longer which is under judgment, and the not yet which awaits consummation, is often to face suffering and hardship. It is the articulation of hopeful vision that makes faithful endurance possible, and enables the faithful community of God's people to choose qualities of moral life which are not characteristic of other communities.

3. The early church consistently read the Hebrew prophets in an eschatological framework. The prophetic warnings of judgment were amply justified by the course of Israel's history and they could be taken as instructive for assessing God's demands for obedience in any generation. But it was the element of prophetic promise which moved ever into the future of each succeeding generation of readers.[45] For the early church the prophets provided insights into the events of the Gospel story of Jesus Christ as the inbreaking of the divine promise of God's kingdom while still luring the community into faithful living toward the final consummation of that kingdom.

The church was encouraged in this eschatological reading by the canonical shape of the collected prophetic corpus. In the process of canonization the elements of promise were highlighted, perhaps in the belief that divine judgment had already been experienced but the promises still moved toward fulfillment. Even the unrelieved judgment of Amos was given the added word of hope, "I will destroy . . . except that I will not utterly destroy" (Amos 9:8b and the following oracle of hope, vs. 9–15). To Isa. 1–39 with its few oracles of Isaiah's hopeful vision are appended the later oracles of chs. 40–55 and 56–66 giving the entire book a decided movement from judgment to promise.

Each book has its own canonical shape by which to render the traditions. Yet there are consistent theological patterns, and in all a message of forgiveness and future promise is voiced. When later Old Testament editors and Hellenistic authors, including the New Testament writers, read the prophets both as a unity and as pointing to a future hope, it was because indices of this holistic construal of promise have been built into the canonical structure of the books which they simply pursued.[46]

The experience of Babylonian exile introduced in sudden and catastrophic fashion a new impetus in the prophets and in Israel to think about relationship to God and God's working in history in new ways. It is to this decisive experience that we turn next.

Notes

1. Julius Wellhausen did not work extensively on the prophets, but their place in his evolutionary understanding of Israelite religion may be seen in *Prolegomena to the History of Ancient Israel*, trans. J. Black and A. Menzies (Cleveland: Meridian, 1957), pp. 397–399.

2. The note in 1 Sam. 9:9 that a prophet was previously called a seer in Israel is merely a note to keep the reader from becoming confused about Samuel's appearance in the story, and offers no clues to earlier distinctions between these terms. For a full discussion of recent understandings of early Israelite prophecy, see Robert R. Wilson, "Early Israelite Prophecy," in *Interpreting the Prophets*, ed. James L. Mays and Paul J. Achtemeier (Philadelphia: Fortress Press, 1987), pp. 1–13 (reprinted from *Int* 32 [1978]).

3. See David L. Petersen, "Ways of Thinking About Israel's Prophets," in *Prophecy in Israel*, ed. David L. Petersen (Philadelphia: Fortress Press, 1987), pp. 1–21, for a very helpful survey and typology of recent research and approaches to the Hebrew prophets. This collection of essays is an excellent orientation to the study of Israel's prophetic literature in general.

4. For example, see the important work of Robert R. Wilson, *Prophecy and Society in Ancient Israel* (Philadelphia: Fortress Press, 1980).

5. Brevard S. Childs, "The Canonical Shape of the Prophetic Literature," in Mays and Achtemeier, eds., *Interpreting the Prophets*, p. 42 (reprinted from *Int* 32 [1978]).

6. James Muilenburg, *The Way of Israel: Biblical Faith and Ethics* (New York: Harper & Row, 1961), pp. 75, 76.

7. It was Ludwig Koehler, "Der Botenspruch," *Kleine Lichter*, Zwingli Bücherei 47 (Zurich: Zwingli Verlag 1945), pp. 13–17, who first identified "Thus says Yahweh," as the messenger formula. Claus Westermann, *Basic Forms of Prophetic Speech*, trans. H. C. White (Philadelphia: Westminster Press, 1967, German ed., 1960), used this as a key element in his classic discussion of the announcement of judgment as the basic form of the messenger proclamation. James F. Ross, "The Prophet as Yahweh's Messenger," in *Israel's Prophetic Heritage: Essays in Honor of James Muilenburg*, ed. by Bernhard W. Anderson and Walter Harrelson (New York: Harper & Row, 1962), pp. 98–107, reprinted in Petersen, ed., *Prophecy in Israel*, pp. 112–121, drew the full implications of this form critical work for the understanding of prophetic identity and role.

8. See Robert R. Wilson, "Form Critical Investigation of the Prophetic Literature: The Present Situation," SBLSP 1973 (Cambridge, Mass.: Society of Biblical Literature, 1973), 1:100–121.

9. James Muilenburg, "The 'Office' of the Prophet in Ancient Israel," in *The Bible in Modern Scholarship*, ed. J. Philip Hyatt (Nashville: Abingdon Press, 1967), pp. 74–97.

10. Wilson, *Prophecy and Society in Ancient Israel*, see esp. pp. 21–88.

11. David L. Petersen, *The Roles of Israel's Prophets*, JSOTSup 17 (Sheffield: JSOT Press, 1981), uses contemporary role theory to discuss the complex roles that prophets play.

12. Abraham J. Heschel, *The Prophets* (New York: Harper & Row, 1962), pp. 221–231.

13. See Renita J. Weems, "Gomer: Victim of Violence or Victim of Metaphor?" *Semeia* 47 (1989): 87–104; T. Dvorah Setel, "Prophets and Pornography: Female Sexual Imagery in Hosea," in *Feminist Interpretation of the Bible*, ed. Letty M. Russell (Philadelphia: Westminster Press, 1985), pp. 86–95; and Gale A. Yee, "Spreading Your Legs to Anyone Who Passed: The Pornography of Ezekiel 16" (unpublished paper, Consultation on Feminist Theological Hermeneutics of the Bible, Society of Biblical Literature Annual Meeting, New Orleans, 1990).

14. See K. Nielsen, *Yahweh as Prosecutor and Judge*, JSOTSup 9 (Sheffield: JSOT Press, 1979).

15. See Eryl W. Davies, *Prophecy and Ethics: Isaiah and the Ethical Tradition of Israel*, JSOTSup 16 (Sheffield: JSOT Press,

1981), pp. 12–39, for an extended discussion of this debate in the scholarly literature.

16. L. Perlitt, *Bundestheologie im Alten Testament*, WMANT 36 (Neukirchen-Vluyn: Neukirchener Verlag, 1969).

17. Ronald E. Clements, *Prophecy and Covenant*, SBT, First Series, 43 (London: SCM Press, 1965). He later modified these views somewhat in *Prophecy and Tradition* (Oxford: Oxford University Press, 1975).

18. This was the view of Gerhard von Rad, *Old Testament Theology*, vol. 2, trans. D. M. G. Stalker (New York: Harper & Row, 1965), pp. 139–140.

19. On this matter see the discussion in John Barton, *Oracles of God: Perceptions of Ancient Prophecy in Israel After the Exile* (New York: Oxford University Press, 1986).

20. Phyllis Trible, *God and the Rhetoric of Sexuality*, OBT (Philadelphia: Fortress Press, 1978), pp. 31–59. Related to the noun *reḥem*, are a plural noun usually translated as "compassion, mercy, or love," a verb meaning "to show mercy," and an adjective translated as "merciful."

21. The role of Babylon in the biblical tradition is quite complex. Particularly during the exile and after, Babylon was not simply an image of God's judgment, but a coming to terms with the reality represented by Babylon was a part of God's redemptive purposes for God's people. These themes are richly addressed in Walter Brueggemann, "At the Mercy of Babylon: A Subversive Rereading of the Empire," JBL 110 (1991): 3–22. We shall have more to say of this in chapter 8 on exile.

22. Thomas W. Ogletree, *The Use of the Bible in Christian Ethics* (Philadelphia: Fortress Press, 1983), pp. 72–73, points to this development as one of the most important contributions of the prophets to Christian ethics.

23. Walter Harrelson, "Prophetic Ethics," *Westminster Dictionary of Christian Ethics*, ed. James F. Childress and John Macquarrie (Philadelphia: Westminster Press, 1986), p. 511.

24. So also Ogletree, *Use of the Bible in Christian Ethics*, p. 64.

25. On prophetic call and vocation see esp. Gerhard von Rad, *The Message of the Prophets* (New York: Harper & Row, 1967), pp. 30–49; Hans Walter Wolff, "Prophecy from the Eighth Through the Fifth Century," in Mays and Achtemeier, eds., *Interpreting the Prophets*, pp. 17–19; Norman Habel, "The Form and Significance of the Call Narratives," ZAW 77 (1965): 297–323.

26. See, e.g., Johannes Lindblom, *Prophecy in Ancient Israel* (Philadelphia: Fortress Press, 1962).

27. Gene M. Tucker, "The Role of the Prophets and the Role of the Church," in Petersen, ed., *Prophecy in Israel*, p. 161, originally published in *Quarterly Review* 1 (1981).

28. On this matter see esp. Wolff, "Prophecy from the Eighth Through the Fifth Century," p. 17.

29. Terence E. Fretheim, *The Suffering of God: An Old Testament Perspective*, OBT (Philadelphia: Fortress Press, 1984), p. 149. In this section I am particularly indebted to Fretheim's chapter entitled "Prophet, Theophany and the Suffering of God."

30. See Wolff, "Prophecy from the Eighth Through the Fifth Century," pp. 25–26.

31. Walter Brueggemann, *The Prophetic Imagination* (Philadelphia: Fortress Press, 1978), p. 13.

32. Wellhausen, *Prolegomena to the History of Ancient Israel* (1957; original German ed., 1883); Bernhard Duhm, *Die Theologie der Propheten* (Bonn, 1875).

33. E.g., Klaus Koch, *The Prophets*, vol. 1: *The Assyrian Period*, vol. 2: *The Babylonian and Persian Periods* (Philadelphia: Fortress Press, 1983, 1984), and Neils Peter Lemche, *Ancient Israel: A New History of Israelite Society* (Sheffield: JSOT Press, 1988), pp. 238–252.

34. Von Rad, *Old Testament Theology*, vol. 2: *The Theology of Israel's Prophetic Traditions* (original German ed., 1960).

35. See Georg Fohrer, "Remarks on Modern Interpretation of the Prophets," *JBL* 80 (1961): 309–319; and "Tradition und Interpretation im Alten Testament," *ZAW* 73 (1961): 1–30.

36. Tucker, "Role of the Prophets and the Role of the Church," p. 167.

37. Ogletree, *Use of the Bible in Christian Ethics*, p. 80; see also Tucker, "Role of the Prophets and the Role of the Church," p. 165.

38. James L. Mays, "Justice: Perspectives from the Prophetic Tradition," in Petersen, ed., *Prophecy in Israel*, p. 146, originally published in *Int* 1983.

39. See John A. Dearman, *Property Rights in the Eighth-Century Prophets: The Conflict and Its Background*, SBLDS 106 (Atlanta: Scholars Press, 1988).

40. Mays, "Justice: Perspectives from the Prophetic Tradition," p. 148.

41. Ibid., p. 154.

42. Ibid., p. 155.

43. Von Rad, *Old Testament Theology*, vol. 2, pp. 185ff., particularly stresses this element of the prophetic message.

44. For similar assessments of prophetic eschatology see Harrelson, "Prophetic Ethics," p. 511, and Ogletree, *Use of the Bible in Christian Ethics*, pp. 70–71.

45. See the suggestive discussion of Ronald E. Clements, "The Old Testament as Promise," *Old Testament Theology: A Fresh Approach* (Atlanta: John Knox Press, 1978), pp. 131–154.

46. Brevard S. Childs, *Old Testament Theology in a Canonical Context* (Philadelphia: Fortress Press, 1985), p. 131. See also Childs, "Canonical Shape of the Prophetic Literature," pp. 41–49.

8
Exile
and
Return

The beginning of the Babylonian exile in 587 B.C.E. is considered by most biblical scholarship to be a turning point event. However, many treatments of the exile and the period of return suggest that the prophetic traditions of Ezekiel and Deutero-Isaiah were final creative outbursts from the prophetic tradition before a descent into less important and less interesting forms of religious expression. "It [exile] is usually considered a watershed event, but often (since Wellhausen, at least) is seen to herald a steady decline from the pristine greatness of Prophetic-Deuteronomic religion to 'priest-dominated, legalistic religiosity.' "[1] Since this period represents the formative roots out of which early Judaism emerges, this viewpoint represents a continuing attitude of Christian superiority toward its sister religion. Even the widely used term "restoration" for the period following the exile suggests that what is most desirable is to restore what was lost prior to the exile. Although the hopes and dreams of restoration might be valued, there is little sense in many treatments of this period that any creative new expressions of Israelite religion are taking place. Among Christians the Jewish designation of this period as the Second Temple period and the positive valuation of its importance are relatively unknown.

The alternative we wish to suggest as a way of reclaiming the ethical resources of this segment of the biblical tradition is to regard the period of exile and return as a time of unusual creativity called forth in the face of severe threats to the integrity and survival of the Israelite community and its religious traditions. The problems of historical reconstruction of this period are notoriously difficult, and we will offer no new solutions to those difficulties.[2] However, the theological voices out of this time of crisis in Israel's story are clear witness to the capacity for hope, creativity, renewal, and survival of the faith community even when it is forced to live as a permanent cultural minority in an environment hostile to some of its basic values and perspectives. Such a witness surely has obvious value as a moral witness pertinent to many modern challenges faced by the church.

The Meaning of Exile

The catastrophic events of 587 B.C.E. shook the Israelite (Judean) community and its faith to the core. The experience of those events looms as the overwhelming reality against which several succeeding generations (before and after the return) sought to reformulate their basic understandings of relationship to God, God's ways of working in the world, and the nature of their own life as the people of God.

Sociopolitical Dimensions

The term "exile" itself has sometimes suggested to the casual church reader a geographic reality alone. Indeed, some scholarly treatments of exile imply that Babylonian policy of allowing exiles to live collectively in Babylon made the fate of Judah's exiles relatively easy. These casual views do not do justice to the wrenching character of the Babylonian exile experience.

In 587 B.C.E., following a siege by the Babylonian army under Nebuchadnezzar, Jerusalem was destroyed, the temple left in ruins, the Davidic kingship ended, the surrounding land devastated, and a significant portion of the surviving population was deported into exile in Babylon (the second such deportation; the earlier was in 597).[3] This was more than a matter of geographic removal. "For Israel exile was a cultural, political and religious upheaval. Exile was a calling into question of Israel's way of life, its institutions of leadership and its faith."[4] All the secure centers of meaning were called into question. A crisis as catastrophic as the exilic experience affects "the sense that one has of meaning and order."[5]

The book of Lamentations gives evidence of desperate conditions of physical need, exploitation by neighboring peoples, and emotional despair among those who remained behind in the land. Those who were carried away to Babylon faced forced removal from their own homeland, resettlement as a permanent minority in a foreign land, loss of their own symbols of identity, and subjection to Babylonian symbols and systems of subordination. Even though imprisonment was not a mentioned penalty in any of Israel's legal codes, it becomes a major metaphor for stories and texts from the exile experience (e.g., deliverance as release from prison in Isa. 49 and 61). Daniel Smith, drawing upon this material, suggests that "confinement became an established symbol for the exiles who reflected on their fate in Babylon" not as a punishment for crimes but as a confinement for political purposes.[6] Exile was not just a relocation but, as the common phrase accurately reflects, a Babylonian "captivity."

Theological Dimensions

Exile was also a spiritual crisis.[7] With the temple destroyed the chief symbol of God's presence in Israel's midst was gone. The people feared that God had abandoned them in anger.

> Why have you forgotten us completely?
>   Why have you forsaken us these many days?
> Restore us to yourself, O LORD, that we may be restored;
>   renew our days as of old—
> unless you have utterly rejected us,
>   and are angry with us beyond measure.
>
> (Lam. 5:20–22)

Others believed that Israel's God had been defeated by superior Babylonian gods. Deutero-Isaiah seems to be countering this view in passages that ridicule the idols of the foreign gods (Isa. 44:9–20; 46:1–5). Neither of these viewpoints is upheld in the texts of the canonical witnesses to this period, but a view held by the prophets of the exilic and return periods alike is that exile was God's judgment on Israel's own arrogance, injustice, and unfaithfulness. God's love had not failed, nor had God forsaken the people, but in keeping with earlier prophetic warnings Israel's breaking of covenant would be judged. There are consequences to such behavior on the part of nations.

> Who gave up Jacob to the spoiler,
>   and Israel to the robbers?

> Was it not the LORD, against whom we have sinned,
>> in whose ways they would not walk,
>> and whose law they would not obey?
>>> (Isa. 42:24)

Perhaps the mood of religious crisis and the theological meaning of the exile is best captured by the poignant language of Ps. 137.

> By the rivers of Babylon—
>> there we sat down and there we wept
>> when we remembered Zion.
> On the willows there
>> we hung up our harps.
> For there our captors
>> asked us for songs,
> and our tormentors asked for mirth, saying,
>> "Sing us one of the songs of Zion!"
> How could we sing the LORD's song
>> in a foreign land?
>>> (Ps. 137:1–4)

The implied answer to the final question of this text is "We can't. Don't ask us to sing God's songs here." Exile as a crisis of the spirit alongside the sociopolitical crisis is the abandonment of hope that our religious symbols retain any power or reality. Exile becomes the time when lips may open but the songs do not come; the captives are rendered voiceless. How remarkable it becomes that such a time should be the context for the creative and hopeful voices that do come forth to sing the Lord's song. "Sing to the LORD a new song" (Isa. 42:10).

Exodus, Exile, and Babylon

The image of exile as a theological symbol has often been subordinated to the image of Exodus. It is assumed that the goal of exile theology is simply that of Exodus in another historical context, namely, the deliverance (Exodus) or restoration (exile) of a captive people to its own land and nationhood. The goal of God's salvation is understood as a bringing of the dispossessed and the powerless to possession and empowerment. It is not surprising that this Exodus imagery has recommended itself to various forms of liberation theology that seek foundation for the church's involvement in struggles for freedom and justice against oppressive forces. That such biblical witness is valuable we have already indicated in chapter 4. Here we want simply to suggest that exile offers not a new setting for Exodus theology but its own models of exile theology which speak to radically different alternatives for understanding God and God's people than does Exodus.

Daniel Smith argues that the key to understanding the exile model for God's people is to approach the materials of exile and return through the "perspective of the exiled themselves." Even after return to rebuild Jerusalem the Jews of exile lived as permanent minorities in empires they could not control or hope to escape. Smith calls this a "Fourth World Perspective"—"the theology of those 'migrants' and 'refugees' who choose to live without power, yet as a people."[8] For those who must live as permanent minorities in larger cultural realities that dehumanize, devalue, and exploit, the exile traditions offer models for creative life in the midst of the empire as God's people.

In our opinion Exodus and exile stand as two great moments for creative reflection on God's activity in the world and on the nature of the community of God's people. John Howard Yoder suggests that Christian theology has reflected too much on the Exodus model and too little on that of exile.

> Instead of following only the pattern of going out into the wilderness—which the Exodus taken alone really was—and instead of dreaming of a theocratic takeover of the land of bondage by the brickmakers—which ideological exegesis has sought to do with the Exodus imagery—we work more creatively to describe what can best be done by creative minorities in a society they don't control.[9]

As we shall see in our later discussion these two images do not need to be treated as polar opposites diametrically opposed to one another.[10] Indeed the Exodus imagery is reappropriated to new and dramatic purpose in the midst of exile. But the social context of Exodus and exile must be recognized as radically different and therefore the theologies of Exodus and exile speak to different dimensions of the contemporary church's experience.

One of the chief differences is that Egypt in the biblical (Exodus) tradition is a reality to be escaped, left behind through God's power to defeat the powers of the world; but Babylon (from exile onward) becomes the symbol for all earthly empire. Its reality is not escaped, and God's power appears not to vanquish it but to subvert it.

> In the Old Testament, the theological struggle concerning public power and divine purpose remains focused on the reality, memory, experience, and symbolization of Babylon. . . . Israel's speech about God requires and permits Israel to say that the empire is not what it is usually thought to be. It is not what it is thought to be by Israelites who fear and are intimidated by the empire. Conversely, it is not what it is thought to be by the wielders of power themselves, in their presumed self-sufficiency. . . . It is odd and telling that the . . . rhetoric of Israel is not employed in the same way for any of the other great powers which dominate Israel's political horizon, not Egypt, not Assyria, not Persia. . . . Babylon functions in this regard as a metaphor for all such power. . . . In the Bible Israel would never finish with Babylon.[11]

An exile theology is promising as an available alternative for the church in the modern world. On the one hand, there are those for whom liberation as an "exodus" from pharaoh's land is not an option.

> A theology of Exodus has little meaning to Fourth World peoples who have no "promised land" to dwell in after escaping "pharaoh." What does Exodus mean for the Cheyenne, the Navajo, the Hopi, the Blackfoot . . . ? But Babylon is an image understood only too well.[12]

The themes of exilic theology may offer radical and creative possibilities for singing the Lord's song in a foreign land.

On the other hand, exile as an image for the modern church suggests creative possibilities for those who might have lived in participation in the realities of the empire (choosing like some exiles to accommodate), but who choose instead to live as an alternative community in the midst of the empire and even for the sake of the empire. "The first image for a contemporary theology of exile is the realization that we are not 'home,' we live in Babylon."[13] Judaism has used the exile experience as a central shaping experience for its life and self-understanding in subsequent generations,[14] and one might suggest that the entire New Testament is set in a framework of exile, minority community in the midst of the Roman Empire. These two great sister faiths find their origins intimately tied to a sense of living as alternatives within the public power of worldly empires—Babylon. Exile theology may thus open up new options for faithful and subversive alternatives even within the majority churches of the first world.

It is to the literature of exile and return in the Hebrew Bible that we must look for clues to the ethical perspectives and resources that would shape the character and conduct of such exilic communities of creative subversion in the midst of empire. In the following sections we will discuss the reimaging of God, the sources of hope in the midst of hopelessness, and the strategies for preservation of identity and faithful survival as we find these evidenced in the biblical materials handed on from the period of exile and return.

The God Who Forgives and Redeems

The harshness of exile and of the later conditions for the returned surely caused many to turn from trust that Israel's God had any further pertinence to their situation. God had either abandoned them or proved to be powerless in their behalf. It was primarily the prophets Jeremiah, Ezekiel, and Deutero-Isaiah who spoke in confidence that God was still at work even in the terrible events of exile. They drew on the rich imagery of testimony to God in the past tradition, but not simply to repeat it. They recast what they knew of God in the light of present exilic experience, heightening some elements, juxtaposing past testimonies in new ways, and adding their own rich images of God's grace even in exile.

The Exile and Return of God

The pain and dislocation of exile raised questions for Israel's faith about the presence and the absence of God. Where was God in this? The prophets' bold answer was that God was in the midst of their experience. God suffered the pain of their fate along with them. In this response the prophets are drawing upon the old tradition of God's vulnerability which we discussed in chapter 4. God participates in our suffering and out of that participation will act to make new life possible. The God of power emphasized by royal theology (see chapter 6) does not seem pertinent to the pain of exilic experience.

It is Ezekiel who gives us our most striking image for this. In Ezek. 10–11 the prophet sees a vision of God's glory rising out of the temple and departing the city. In his indictment of Israel for its apostasy and sin against the neighbor (see Ezek. 8

and 22) the prophet makes clear his understanding of God's departure. "Mortal, do you see what they are doing, the great abominations that the house of Israel are committing here, to drive me far from my sanctuary?" (Ezek. 8:6). Yahweh has become an exile. If Israel must suffer in exile for the sins of the nation, then so too will Israel's God suffer homelessness; but God will not remain an exile. Jerusalem will be restored as a faithful city named "The LORD is There" (48:35). Then God's glory will return to the temple and dwell in the midst of a restored people. God too is an exile, but will return and so will God's people.

It is clear that the prophets both during and after the exile understood God to have suffered along with Israel, and that divine suffering is itself a way of understanding God's presence and activity in a time when many fear God has abandoned them.[15] Jeremiah echoes the imagery of Ezekiel:

> I have forsaken my house,
>   I have abandoned my heritage;
> I have given the beloved of my heart
>   into the hands of her enemies.
>   (Jer. 12:7)

In Jer. 9:17–18 the first person plural includes God with Israel among those for whom lamentation is to be raised in the coming destruction and exile: "Thus says the LORD of hosts: . . . Let them quickly raise a dirge over us." Isaiah 63:9 (margin), looking back on the anguished events of exile and return, says, "In all their distress he was distressed; the angel of his presence saved them." God has been wounded by the events of Israel's exile. In a text later used by the early church with christological meaning, Zechariah speaks for God,

> I will pour out a spirit of compassion and supplication on the house of David and the inhabitants of Jerusalem, so that, when they look on me[16] whom they have pierced, they shall mourn for him, as one mourns for an only child. (Zech. 12:10)

Abraham Heschel captures this aspect of God in the exilic events well:

> Israel's distress was more than a human tragedy. With Israel's distress came the affliction of God, His displacement, His homelessness in the land, in the world. . . . Should Israel cease to be

home, then God, we might say, would be without a home in the world.[17]

If God, too, has gone into exile with Israel, then the prophets understood the radical implications of this in terms of the universal presence of God. God was not limited to Jerusalem. Building upon the conceptions of God's universality in the earlier prophets (see chapter 7) the prophets of the exile speak to fears of the absence of God by declaring the universal presence of God.

Once again Ezekiel provides the most striking image. In his call vision (Ezek. 1) what the prophet sees is nothing more than God's enthroned presence (similar to the Ark of the Covenant) mounted on wondrous wheels, like a mighty chariot, arriving to be present even in Babylon.

Deutero-Isaiah chided his hearers in the great disputation oracle of Isa. 40:12–31:

> Have you not known? Have you not heard?
> The LORD is the everlasting God,
>   the Creator of the ends of the earth.
>   (Isa. 40:28)

Israel's God is the God of all times (everlasting) and all places (the ends of the earth). This radical sense of the universality of God's presence leads the prophet to look for the saving activity of God on the broadest possible scale, thus, finding God's hopeful possibilities at work in Cyrus of Persia (Isa. 44:28; 45:1–13). This sense of universal presence and activity is further tied to the most straightforward and radical statements of monotheism in the Old Testament:[18]

> I arm you [Cyrus], though you do not know me,
> so that they may know, from the rising of the sun
>   and from the west, that there is no one besides me;
> I am the LORD, and there is no other.
>   (Isa. 45:5b-6)

> Turn to me and be saved,
>   all the ends of the earth!
> For I am God, and there is no other.
>   (Isa. 45:22)

Since the collection of the psalms received its final shape in the period during or after the exile one can readily imagine that Ps. 139 must have had special meaning to those who feared God's permanent absence from them.

> Where can I go from your spirit?
>   Or where can I flee from your presence?
> If I ascend to heaven, you are there;
>   if I make my bed in Sheol, you are there.
> If I take the wings of the morning
>   and settle at the farthest limits of the sea,
> even there your hand shall lead me,
>   and your right hand shall hold me fast.
> If I say, "Surely the darkness shall cover me,
>   and the night around me become night,"
> even the darkness is not dark to you;
>   the night is as bright as the day,
>   for darkness is as light to you.
>   (Ps. 139:7–12)

Initiatives of Grace

In the midst of exile the prophets proclaimed a word of uninterrupted hope which was grounded in trust that God's saving grace was still operative. In exile God has once again taken the initiative in salvation.

Forgiveness. Unlike the Exodus experience those in exile are in need of God's forgiveness as well as God's deliverance.[19] Even in this, God's initiative of grace has preceded the action of the people. The prophetic announcement of God's care for those in exile already includes announcement of God's forgiveness.

> Comfort, O comfort my people,
>   says your God.
> Speak tenderly to Jerusalem,
>   and cry to her
> that she has served her term,
>   that her penalty is paid.
>   (Isa. 40:1–2a)

Forgiveness is a part of the graceful character of God and not simply a result of Israel's payment of a penalty or serving of a sentence. Forgiveness is necessary to the inherent character of God and given freely for the sake of God's integrity.

I, I am He
  who blots out your transgressions for my own sake,
  and I will not remember your sins.

> (Isa. 43:25)

I will forgive their iniquity, and remember their sin no more. (Jer.
31:34b)

Of course, this initiative of God's grace in forgiveness calls for
response from Israel. Forgiveness, in and of itself, implies that
God has already judged Israel for its sin. In this the prophets
of the exile assume the message of judgment characteristic of
the preexilic prophets (see chapter 7), but the time of judgment is past. God's initiative is to restore relationship, but
Israel too must respond. Israel is freed from guilt by God's
forgiveness, but called to repentance. The Hebrew verb for
repent is *šub*, which means "to turn or return." It means to
move in a new direction. Thus, repentance is not mired in a
past of regret, but oriented to the new future God's forgiveness makes possible.

I have swept away your transgressions like a cloud,
  and your sins like mist;
return to me, for I have redeemed you.

> (Isa. 44:22)

Now you, mortal, say to the house of Israel, Thus you have said:
"Our transgressions and our sins weigh upon us, and we waste
away because of them; how then can we live?" Say to them, As I
live, says the Lord GOD, I have no pleasure in the death of the
wicked, but that the wicked turn from their ways and live; turn
back, turn back from your evil ways; for why will you die, O house
of Israel? . . . None of the sins that they have committed shall be
remembered against them; they have done what is lawful and
right, they shall surely live. (Ezek. 33:10–11, 16)

Seek the LORD while he may be found,
  call upon him while he is near;
let the wicked forsake their way,
  and the unrighteous their thoughts;
let them return to the LORD, that he may have mercy on them,
  and to our God, for he will abundantly pardon.

> (Isa. 55:6–7)

Redemption. The prophets of the exile are especially vigorous and creative in their announcement of God's redemption in the midst of exile. God has not abandoned Israel, but is already at work to redeem them. Jeremiah writes to the exiles in Babylon,

> For surely I know the plans I have for you, says the LORD, plans for your welfare and not for harm, to give you a future with hope. (Jer. 29:11)

In the face of the deadening and deenergizing dislocations of exile the prophets announce God's redemptive activity in an unusual array of creative and captivating images. They seem particularly aware of the role of vision in activating and empowering the moral community (see chapter 1).[20]

On the one hand, the prophets juxtapose themes from Israel's past recital of God's activity in ways that suggest new and creative dimensions of God's work in the midst of exile. Particularly noteworthy in this regard is Deutero-Isaiah's juxtaposition of creation and deliverance themes.[21] For the most part witnesses to these have been separate in the canon, but the prophet brings them together. Israel can trust in the possibilities of God's deliverance (for which the prophet often uses Exodus imagery) because God is also Creator of the whole earth (Isa. 45:12) as well as of Israel (43:1, 7; 44:2); of the primordial cosmos (40:12) as well as of miraculous new life in the desert (41:20). In a well-known hymn Deutero-Isaiah celebrates the continuity of divine redemptive action seen in victory over chaos, deliverance out of Egypt, and return to Zion of the exile captives.

> Awake, awake, put on strength,
>   O arm of the LORD!
> Awake, as in days of old,
>   the generations of long ago!
> Was it not you who cut Rahab in pieces,
>   who pierced the dragon?
> Was it not you who dried up the sea,
>   the waters of the great deep?
> who made the depths of the sea a way
>   for the redeemed to cross over?
> So the ransomed of the LORD shall return,
>   and come to Zion with singing.
>   (Isa. 51:9–11a)

The prophets of the exile also filled their proclamation with new and sometimes dramatic images of God's redemptive activity. We can only name and sample a few of these. In the midst of the siege of Jerusalem, Jeremiah buys a field to signal hope for God's future even as catastrophe falls on Israel (Jer. 32). Ezekiel's vision of the valley of dry bones which can live again through the breath of God is directly interpreted as an image for the new life of exiles (Ezek. 37:1–14), and his imagery of God as the true shepherd places even captive Israel in God's care for healing and renewal (ch. 34). Deutero-Isaiah chooses to use the intimate term of Redeemer (Hebrew *go'el*) seventeen times for God.[22] This term from Israelite family customs and legal practice refers to the kinsman who seeks in situations of crisis to redeem the family member from danger or threat. The effect is to make God's graceful activity that of God as family member to restore Israel to family relationship. Deutero-Isaiah also uses some striking feminine imagery for God in describing both divine suffering and the new birth which God brings for the exiles.

> For a long time I have held my peace,
>   I have kept still and restrained myself;
> now I will cry out like a woman in labor,
>   I will gasp and pant.
>   (Isa. 42:14; cf. also 46:3–4)

While acknowledging that Israel's fate does have to do with God's judgment, the prophets nevertheless make clear that God is not through with Israel. Judgment will be tempered by compassion.

> For a brief moment I abandoned you,
>   but with great compassion I will gather you.
> In overflowing wrath for a moment
>   I hid my face from you,
> but with everlasting love I will have compassion on you,
>   says the LORD, your Redeemer.
>   (Isa. 54:7–8)

The Renewal of Prophetic Hope

We have already seen the hopeful portrait which the exilic prophets painted of God's activity. What made hope possible for the prophets in the midst of those who could not sing the

Lord's song in a strange land? What would make hope concrete in the lives of the exile community if they were to heed the prophets' preaching? We must look further in these prophets to find the clues they give us for the empowerment of moral community as hopeful community in the midst of brokenness.

God's Past and God's Future

One of the dynamics operative in the prophets of the exile enabling their hopeful voices was a rootedness in faith memory on the one hand, and a visionary anticipation of God's future on the other hand. It was this grounding in memory and vision, God's past and God's future, that helped free the prophets from the tyranny and paralysis of present crisis.[23]

The Role of Memory. The prophets sought to remind Israelite captives in Babylon that in the memory of their own tradition lay resources for hope in their present circumstances. God had acted to bring new life in death-dealing crises in the past; God's promises of presence and care had proved trustworthy in the past; God's covenant relationship with Israel had not been broken from the divine side. In remembering, Israel had resources that could rekindle the hope that God was present and active in their behalf even in exile. God had been the source of salvation before and would be again.

> Look to the rock from which you were hewn,
>   and to the quarry from which you were dug.
> Look to Abraham your father
>   and to Sarah who bore you.
>   (Isa. 51:1b–2a)

Deutero-Isaiah is particularly rich in images that summon the exiles to remember their own tradition. He uses the language of creation and Exodus. He refers to the promises given to Abraham and Sarah, Noah (Isa. 54:9), and David (55:3). Jeremiah speaks of the promise to David (Jer. 30:9; 33:14–26), God's love for Jacob and Ephraim (30:10; 31:20), God as Creator (31:35). Ezekiel uses elaborate Exodus and wilderness tradition language to speak of Israel's restoration (Ezek. 20:33–38), speaks of a Davidic shepherd to renew righteous reign (34:25; 37:24), and draws on his own priestly back-

ground in the Jerusalem temple to draw a magnificent vision
of a new Jerusalem (chs. 40–48).

God's New Thing. Memory alone would not have been
enough on which to base hope for exiles. As an end in itself it
becomes preoccupation with the past. The prophets understood that memory had to be coupled with hopeful anticipation of God's future.

> See, the former things have come to pass,
>   and new things I now declare;
> before they spring forth,
>   I tell you of them.
> Sing to the LORD a new song,
>   his praise from the end of the earth!
>   (Isa. 42:9–10a)

> I am about to do a new thing;
>   now it springs forth, do you not perceive it?
>   (Isa. 43:19)

Memory served to enable discernment of God's new thing
for Israel's future. That future was to be no mere repeat of the
past. Even when the prophets use a familiar image or theme
from the tradition it was often transformed in keeping with
trust that God was doing a "new thing."

Thus, Jeremiah spoke of the renewal of covenant, but it was
not to be a covenant like that of the past. The image is
transformed.

> The days are surely coming, says the LORD, when I will make a
> new covenant with the house of Israel and the house of Judah. It
> will not be like the covenant that I made with their ancestors when
> I took them by the hand to bring them out of the land of Egypt—
> a covenant that they broke. . . . But this is the covenant that I will
> make with the house of Israel after those days, says the LORD: I
> will put my law within them, and I will write it on their hearts; and
> I will be their God, and they shall be my people. (Jer. 31:31–33)

Likewise, Deutero-Isaiah's appropriation of Exodus language and imagery is transformed as God's "new thing." New
Exodus is in continuity with the God known in the Exodus
tradition, but New Exodus will not be simply a repeat of the
old.[24] Although the prophet voices Israel's call for God to act
in vengeance against the enemy in imagery taken from the
vanquishing of pharaoh's army (Isa. 51:9–10; 43:16–18), the

prophet speaking for the Lord explicitly tells Israel not to remember these former things (43:18). God's New Exodus will not involve war and destruction; enemies will be transformed (51:12–16), and they too will be brought to recognize the sovereignty of God for their own salvation (45:22–23). Even Israel's suffering they will recognize as the suffering of God's servant for their own sake (52:13–53:12). The New Exodus will not be a battle but a wondrous way through the wilderness to new life (40:3–5; 41:17–20). God retains the power and freedom to deal harshly with those who oppose divine purposes (see ch. 47), but this is not the divine plan for Israel's salvation in this New Exodus.

Some developments of God's "new thing" do not rely upon transforming images from Israel's tradition but involve the prophet's discernment of God's activity in the world in new ways. The theme of Cyrus as God's anointed one (Isa. 45:1) already discussed is an example of this. The prophet is able to recognize in Cyrus a historical development through which God is seen at work bringing hopeful possibilities even though Cyrus does not know or acknowledge Israel's God.

> I call you by your name,
>   I surname you, though you do not know me.
>   (Isa. 45:4b)

Such discernment of divine activity in surprising and unorthodox forms does not seem acceptable to some as the prophet's apparent rejoinder to his critics would imply (45:9–13). It would seem that the prophet is reasserting the theme of God's radical freedom (see chapter 4) in the context of exile. God's saving purposes will be exercised in divine freedom to choose the means and instruments of divine grace.

Community and Individual Responsibility

In the profound moral crisis that exile represents, the prophets Jeremiah and Ezekiel suggest that in addition to the brokenness of covenant as a problem of social structures and public obedience there is an anthropological basis to sin and evil. As we have already seen, Jeremiah announces a new covenant written on the heart. Likewise Ezekiel calls for a "new heart . . . and a new spirit."

> A new heart I will give you, and a new spirit I will put within you; and I will remove from your body the heart of stone and give you a heart of flesh. I will put my spirit within you, and make you follow my statutes and be careful to observe my ordinances. (Ezek. 36:26–27; cf. also 18:31)

The problem is no longer idolatry or monarchy as institutions that corrupt covenant faithfulness. The problem is located in the human heart as well; it is a part of human nature which covenant faithfulness cannot address as an external matter alone.[25]

It has been commonplace to argue that Ezekiel in ch. 18 (and Jeremiah to a lesser degree in 31:27–30) introduces the moral principle of individual responsibility to deal with this issue of human nature: "It is only the person who sins that shall die" (Ezek. 18:4b). Some have treated it as a radical innovation in Israel's thought; others as the culmination of a developmental process from primitive to more sophisticated thought forms. These ways of viewing Ezek. 18 have been largely discredited.[26]

H. Wheeler Robinson was largely responsible for the widely accepted view that early Israel was possessed of a "corporate personality" which reflected a primitive psychology incapable of the consistent distinguishing of individual personality, and of course, individual moral responsibility from that of the group to which one belonged.[27] For those who followed Robinson's view Ezek. 18 was a revolutionary text, whether viewed as a sudden innovation or as a developmental climax, but Robinson's notion that the Hebrews operated out of a psychology essentially different from ours has been widely discussed and rejected.[28]

It is true that Hebrew conceptions of community are quite strong, and it is not possible to speak of the individual apart from communities that he or she is a part of. This is not, however, to say there is no notion of individual responsibility until Ezekiel.[29] The Yahwist portions of the primeval history (Gen. 1–11) had already suggested an anthropological basis for understanding sin and evil (see chapter 3) which included clear notions of individual responsibility both in the consequences for disobedience in the garden (Gen. 3) and in the implied affirmative answer to Cain's arrogant question, "Am I my brother's keeper?" (4:9). Law codes as early as the Book of the Covenant clearly imply individual responsibility in their use of individual penalties for violations. Such notions of individual moral responsibility are, however, within the framework of community as the context for meaning and accountability for the actions of individual moral agents and as the context within which moral agency is shaped. Although there is a clear role and conception of the individual in the Old Testament, there is no evidence of individualism.

Closer examination of Ezek. 18 suggests that the prophet is not elevating the individual so much as he is seeking to reconstitute moral community in the face of exilic sentiment that they are simply the victims of the sins of a previous generation. No longer are they to use the proverb "The parents have eaten sour grapes, and the children's teeth are set on edge" (Ezek. 18:2-3). Ezekiel criticizes the notion of inherited guilt in order to call the present generation of exiles to repent, turn, and live (vs. 20-29). It is not to individuals that Ezekiel speaks but to a generation in exile.[30] "Therefore I will judge you, O house of Israel, all of you according to your ways, says the Lord GOD. Repent and turn from all your transgressions; otherwise iniquity will be your ruin" (v. 30). Certainly Ezekiel is reclaiming earlier notions of individual responsibility rather than inherited guilt, but only in the context of the community of exiles, all of whom are addressed by Ezekiel's message.

The Servant Who Suffers

The Servant Songs of Deutero-Isaiah (42:1-4; 49:1-6; 50:4-9; 52:13-53:12) put forward a radical new image for God's way of acting in the world. In contrast to the claim of royal theology that God was present in history through kings, the prophet suggests God enters history through a servant who willingly suffers for the sake of righteousness. The generation of Israel in exile "cries for vengeance [against Babylon], but in reply God puts forward the picture of the Suffering Servant who, by renouncing power and accepting suffering, becomes a witness to the power of reconciliation and love that can change the world."[31]

The identity of the Servant figure has long been a vexing problem.[32] The Servant Songs use both individual and corporate language to describe the Servant, thus, proposals have divided among those who see the Servant as an individual and those who see the Servant as the personification of some group or community. Recent scholarship seems to be moving away from individual theories and increasingly to suggest that the Servant represents, not all of Israel, but a minority within the exile community who came to see their own suffering as an expression of God's righteous work in behalf of Israel and all the nations. This ties the Servant's story to the effort to find meaning in the experience of exile itself, and serves to emphasize the importance of reading the Servant Songs in the context of the whole of Deutero-Isaiah's message to the exilic community.[33]

Daniel L. Smith has recently made the intriguing suggestion that the experience of the Servant is to be seen as a variation on the stories of diaspora heroes (e.g., Joseph and Daniel, stories of heroes who were faithful while in exile) who suffer for their righteousness and are ultimately vindicated. Like the Servant the suffering of such heroes is understood to have redemptive meaning not only for the heroes' own people but often for the rulers of the nations who subject them to suffering.

> The theme of the righteousness of *one* sparing the *whole nation* was common and should remind readers of this same motif in the diaspora hero stories. . . . Because of the *social* significance of the hero stories, both in the trials the hero must undergo and his God-given success for himself and his people, it becomes clear that the Suffering Servant can take on an individual image as well as a social image and still remain a meaningful theme for the exilic period. In the same way, Daniel, Joseph, Mordecai, and Esther became social heroes. Seen in this manner, the urgency of separating individual from collective theories is overcome, and the entire context of the message of Deutero-Isaiah is allowed to teach us the meaning and significance of the Servant.[34]

Thus, the prophet's vision of God's work in history through the designation of a Servant is put forward as an understanding which allows exiles to move beyond the initial understanding of exile as judgment alone to a meaning for exile in the carrying out of God's redemptive purposes in the world. The Servant models the prophet's understanding of Israel's call to use its own experience of exile as a divine commission to a new understanding of its task in the world.[35]

The mission to which the Servant is called is the establishment of justice.

> I have put my spirit upon him;
>> he will bring forth justice to the nations. . . .
>
> He will not grow faint or be crushed
>> until he has established justice in the earth;
>> and the coastlands wait for his teaching (*torah*).
>>> (Isa. 42:1b, 4)

The justice and law which characterize the covenant community are here extended to the "nations" and "coastlands" (cf.
also 51:4), but the instrument through which this is to be done
is not the king anointed by God's spirit (see chapter 6), but
Yahweh's Servant. Unlike the royal way of power, the Servant's way will be gentle enough for a "bruised reed" or a
"dimly burning wick" (42:3). The extension or comment on
this Servant Song in 42:6–7 rightly interprets the implications
of this mission of justice.

> I have given you as a covenant to the people,
>> a light to the nations,
>> to open the eyes that are blind,
> to bring out the prisoners from the dungeon,
>> from the prison those who sit in darkness.
>>> (Isa. 42:6–7)

The scope of the Servant's mission is universal. Israel's suffering in exile is transformed into a vehicle for God's salvation
to reach all the nations.

> It is too light a thing that you should be my servant
>> to raise up the tribes of Jacob
>> and to restore the survivors of Israel;
> I will give you as a light to the nations,
>> that my salvation may reach to the end of the earth.
>>> (Isa. 49:6)

Those who would identify with the call of the Servant must,
however, also know that the Servant's path is one of obedient
suffering. This suffering is introduced in Isa. 50:4–8, but its full
meaning is made clear in 52:13–53:12. In the Servant the nations (perhaps many in the exile community itself) see one they
could not have imagined as God's instrument. In fact, the
marred and disfigured appearance of the Servant was associated
with those rejected by God. Nevertheless, this one is now revealed as the means whereby God's deliverance is being worked.
Those who despised the Servant now recognize the Servant's

suffering to have been in their own behalf. In this recognition is a new way of understanding God's work in the world, and a new model for the community that would align itself with God's work.

> He was despised and rejected by others;
>   a man of suffering and acquainted with infirmity;
> and as one from whom others hide their faces
>   he was despised, and we held him of no account.
> Surely he has borne our infirmities
>   and carried our diseases;
> yet we accounted him stricken,
>   struck down by God, and afflicted.
> But he was wounded for our transgressions,
>   crushed for our iniquities;
> upon him was the punishment that made us whole (*shalom*),
>   and by his bruises we are healed.
> All we like sheep have gone astray;
>   we have all turned to our own way,
> and the LORD has laid on him
>   the iniquity of us all.
>
>   (Isa. 53:3–6)

The nature of moral community in its covenantal commitment to justice, righteousness, and shalom has not changed, but its way of being in the world is changed. Its suffering in the midst of the empire is for the sake of the empire and not for Israel alone. This is to have profound implications for future generations of the faithful community of God's people because the way of national, political power for that community was not to be possible. Thus, the image of God's Servant who suffers for God's justice is appropriated by succeeding generations who see their story in the Servant's story. Their suffering was not a sign of God's wrath, but the necessary path of their mission as God's people.

The Servant was interpreted as the righteous remnant in Third Isaiah (56–66), the martyr of a persecuted community in Second Zechariah (12:10), and Jesus of Nazareth in the Gospels. This polyvalence was fully in keeping with Yahwistic faith, according to which God was involved and present in the events of history in the form of human agents.[36]

Visions of a New Community

Vision plays an important role in kindling hope among those who despair of new life. We have already seen the prophets of exile envisioning God's work in new ways that empowered the community to new efforts at discerning God's "new thing." Moral community is also empowered by visions of the goal toward which God is working and toward which the community joins its own moral effort (see chapter 1). Through vision we dare to project the implications of our present moral course, and the challenge of new vision often reorients us on the course we have chosen. For each of the prophets of the exile there is a dimension of their message that goes beyond imagery for what God is doing in the midst of exile to imaginatively envision what God is doing in the whole course of human history, and in so doing they challenge the community to examine its own life against that vision.

For Jeremiah this meant the envisioning of a time when the wounds of war would be healed and the desolated land restored (Jer. 33:1–13). The time would come when, in contrast to the kings who brought the destruction of exile upon the land, a truly righteous anointed one would reestablish the community of covenant faithfulness.

> The days are surely coming, says the LORD, when I will fulfill the promise I made to the house of Israel and the house of Judah. . . . I will cause a righteous Branch to spring up for David; and he shall execute justice and righteousness in the land. In those days Judah will be saved and Jerusalem will live in safety. And this is the name by which it will be called: "The LORD is our righteousness." (Jer. 33:14–16)

Ezekiel was himself a priest of the temple in Jerusalem carried into exile, therefore it is not surprising that his vision of the new Jerusalem is dominated by temple and priestly concerns. Ezekiel 40–48 is almost a blueprint for the returned community[37] but with elements of wonder and imagination as well (e.g., the River that flows from beneath the temple to renew the wilderness, 47:1–12). Much of the concern is with the restoration of the temple to central place in the community and to the necessary cultic provisions that would ensure its sacral purity, but beyond this cultic concern lies the concern for the restoration of God to central place in the community. The new Jerusalem is to be named "Yahweh is There" (Ezek. 48:35). Many of the concerns for covenant community we have seen earlier find renewed place in Ezekiel's vision. The land is to be apportioned to the tribes and therefore to the people once again (47:13–48:29), and the moral demands of covenant are to be evidenced in this land.

> Thus says the Lord GOD: Enough, O princes of Israel! Put away violence and oppression, and do what is just and right. Cease your evictions of my people. . . . You shall have honest balances, an honest ephah, and an honest bath. (Ezek. 45:9–10)

Ezekiel also envisioned a "covenant of peace (*shalom*)" where all would live in harmony with nature and nations. Captives would be freed and no longer subject to the plunder of the nations. There would be no more want and God would dwell in the midst of God's people (Ezek. 34:25–31).

Deutero-Isaiah drew on images from the Noah story and on language out of the covenant tradition to suggest a renewed age of restored relationship with God, release from captivity, and joyous embracing of a new future.

> This is like the days of Noah to me:
>   Just as I swore that the waters of Noah
>   would never again go over the earth,
> so I have sworn that I will not be angry with you
>   and will not rebuke you.
> For the mountains may depart
>   and the hills be removed,
> but my steadfast love shall not depart from you,
>   and my covenant of peace shall not be removed,
>   says the LORD, who has compassion on you.
>   (Isa. 54:9–10)

> For you shall go out in joy,
>   and be led back in peace;
> the mountains and the hills before you
>   shall burst into song,
>   and all the trees of the field shall clap their hands.
>   (Isa. 55:12)

It is important to take note of these visions of a new age for those who lived in the desolation of exile. We must now turn to the experience of those who returned from exile to rebuild their community. The struggle to embody the new community is fraught with tensions and conflict. Perhaps it is easier to dream of restored community than to build it, but surely without the power of great and hopeful visions toward which to move, the building would not have become possible.

The Survival of Community

The extension of Cyrus' Persian empire to Babylon brought enthusiasm and hope to many in exile, especially when the Edict of Cyrus in 538 B.C.E. (Ezra 1:1–4) allowed for the return of exiles to rebuild Jerusalem and the temple, even providing for financial support. With the return of the first group of exiles under Sheshbazzar it became quickly apparent that the challenges were difficult and the obstacles many. The literature for this period makes detailed historical reconstruction difficult, but the nature of many of the struggles is clear. It is apparent that the struggle for community survival was not left behind in Babylon but is fully present in the returned community who are little more than refugees returned to a land where they are no longer welcome.

It has been customary to treat the literature of the postexilic returned community as a degeneration from the high water mark of preexilic prophetic religion. The history of this period of return has often been treated as the less than fully successful attempt to reconstruct preexilic models of community. Increasingly these views are recognized as inadequate. The returned exiles are still struggling as a radical minority in a larger imperial reality, but it is now Persia rather than Babylon. In addition they face hostility from neighboring peoples (Samaritans, Edomites) and from Judean descendants of those left behind in the land. The literature that reflects this period of the biblical story is occupied with the realities of minority identity and existence. The literature is evidence, not of the degeneration of Israelite religion, but of the creative mechanisms of survival[38] and integrity of religion developed in the face of a hostile majority social and religious context.

Structures of Identity and Survival

Out of the diverse and complex biblical witnesses to the efforts at preserving the identity and survival of community (social and religious) we can only single out some elements that seem especially revealing of the moral demands upon and responses of Israel in this period. Despite the problems of historical reconstruction, the present canonical shape of these witnesses is suggestive of the issues and strategies facing efforts of those in the church who would choose to live as creative minorities in the prevailing cultures of the modern world rather than to accommodate to them.

The Welfare of Babylon. Prophetic visions of new community were important for keeping hope alive in the exilic community, but the actual building of new community calls for concrete creative response to challenging circumstances. The ability of the returned community to live its life in the midst of the ongoing reality of empire (Persian and later Greek) has its roots in response to Babylon during the exile itself.

Jeremiah gives early evidence of the changed nature of community in the face of exilic and later postexilic realities. He writes a letter to those taken to Babylon in the first deportation (Jer. 29). In it he urges them to refuse the false optimism of those who suggest a quick restoration to Jerusalem. The task in exile, according to Jeremiah, is to build community there, in the midst of Babylon. They are to build houses, plant gardens, conduct marriages, and have children (vs. 5–6).[39] But Jeremiah's advice takes an even more surprising turn.

> But seek the welfare of the city where I have sent you into exile, and pray to the LORD on its behalf, for in its welfare you will find your welfare. (Jer. 29:7)

In the place of the vengeance many would desire (see Ps. 137:8–9) the prophet sets the task not only of becoming community in the midst of the empire but of learning to live there for the sake of the welfare (*shalom*) of the empire. The prophet suggests a vocation of creative minority in the larger social realities of the world that remains pertinent through the remainder of the biblical period (Old Testament and New), for seldom after the period of exile was the Jewish community or the early church able to live a political existence apart from the reality of a larger political empire. Such a model is, of course, suggestive for modern Christian life in the midst of larger sociocultural realities. The role of intentional creative minority is an option open to those who feel that the church is endangered by more accommodationist models of community; but Jeremiah's words stand as a warning that such community in the midst of empire (majority culture) must be for the sake of that majority culture.

The Bet 'Abot. Exile disrupted the social structures of preexilic community and made necessary new ones capable of maintaining identity and cohesiveness. In preexilic Israel the basic biological family unit was called the *bet 'ab*, "house of the father." With the return of exiles from Babylon to Jerusalem it is clear that this smaller, biologically based family unit has been altered to provide a structure of community for life in exile, and subsequently for the returned community. The basic unit of social organization in the returned community appears to be the *bet 'abot*, "house of the fathers" (mentioned nineteen times in Ezra-Nehemiah alone, e.g., Neh. 7:70–71).[40]

There are significant differences in the exilic "fathers' houses" (NRSV, "ancestral houses"). They are as large as three thousand individuals, more akin to the size of the preexilic clan. It is clear that there can no longer be a biological familial base for this social unit, but genealogical lineages, sometimes clearly fictive, have been preserved for each "fathers' house." Although dealing with a larger unit, it seems clear that the family language and close community nature it supplies were found necessary for the survival of groups living in exile, and they brought this structure with them when they returned to Judah (see the lists of "sons of the exile" in Ezra 2 = Neh. 7 and the later list of those who returned with Ezra, Ezra 8).

In the returned community the "fathers' houses" provided community leadership through their "heads" (*rošim*), held the land inheritances (*nahalah*) which it subdivided among its members, and provided sociopolitical organization to the community. In time it becomes clear that the "fathers' houses" provided for the integration of those who had not been in Babylon with the returned community of exiles since the later lists include those who remained in the land (Neh. 7:61–62).

> An aspect of post-exilic identity is the consciousness of having been part of an exilic event, either by being a "son" of a returning collective, or by separating oneself from the "others" and becoming one of these "sons." . . . The *Bet 'Abot* expanded the familial fiction, even to encompass *all the people* as "sons" of the Golah [exile], as "sons of Israel." This is best understood as a socio-psychological response to the crisis of exile.[41]

These structural changes in postexilic Israel make clear the importance of structures of community capable of maintaining identity and relationship in the face of disintegrating cultural pressures.

The Temple. Joel Weinberg has argued convincingly that, in keeping with a pattern widely testified in the Achaemenid em-

pire, the postexilic Yahwistic community was organized as a
"Citizen-Temple-Community."[42] While the basic unit of social
structure was the "fathers' house," it was the temple which
was the focal center of the returned community, and ultimately for the Jewish community in diaspora as well.

The rebuilding of the temple in Jerusalem was not a return
to institutionalized forms of religion antithetical to the prophetic tradition as some scholars have suggested. In keeping
with much of the earlier tradition of Israel, the temple is the
most potent symbol of the placing of the presence and will of
God at the center of the returned community in Jerusalem.[43]
That this is certainly continuous with the prophetic tradition is
made clear by the vigorous support of the prophets Haggai
and Zechariah, at whose urging the rebuilding of the temple is
resumed. Haggai in particular (Hag. 1) poses the issue in
moral terms. The people enjoy the comforts of their own restored houses and community, but have no thought of restor-
ing the worship of Yahweh to central place by providing an
appropriate house of worship, the temple. For him it is a question of ethical priorities.

Under the leadership of Zerubbabel, the Persian-appointed
governor, and Joshua, the high priest (prodded and supported
by the prophets Haggai and Zechariah), the temple was rebuilt
between 520 and 515 B.C.E. In time the temple becomes not
only the religious center for Judah and the diaspora but assumes much of the governance and economic leadership of the
community through the high priest and his staff. The history of
the books of Chronicles with its stress on David as the layer of
foundations for the temple cult makes clear the shift that has
taken place from nation-state to cultic community. The Zion
psalms come to have new meaning as the temple focuses the
sense of God's presence in the midst of God's people even for
those at great geographical distances from the temple.

The Leadership. In addition to the "heads" of the "fathers'
houses" and the priestly leadership associated with the temple,
there were several important figures in the period of the returned community whose authority came from outside of the
community by appointment of the Persian officials.

Zerubbabel was appointed governor of the Persian province
of Judah and gave important leadership in the rebuilding of
the temple. His authority and leadership in the Jerusalem
community was clearly shared by the high priest Joshua (see

Zech. 1–8). Zerubbabel was also a descendant of the Davidic line, and he becomes the focus of messianic hopes in Haggai and Zechariah for the restoration of the Davidic kingship and national autonomy (see Hag. 2:20–23; Zech. 3:1–7; 4:1–5, 10b-14). The sudden disappearance of Zerubbabel from the textual traditions has caused many to speculate that he was removed because of Persian fears over Judean nationalism. In the references to Zerubbabel and the time of his leadership one senses an expectation of restored community among the nations, indeed preeminence among the nations, and the prophets are preparing the way for this.[44]

By the time of Ezra and Nehemiah, however we opt to re-construct their chronology relative to one another,[45] it is clear that the concept of leadership has changed, at least in the Chronicler's record as it now stands.

> When the record resumes with the narrative of the mission of Ezra, the messianic themes of the earlier narrative are no longer to be heard. Hierocracy supplants the diarchy of king and high priest. We hear nothing of the Davidic prince either in the Ezra-narrative or in the memoirs of Nehemiah.[46]

Under Ezra and Nehemiah we sense a more beleaguered community, struggling with its minority status in the sur-rounding world. Concerns of identity, purity, and integrity of the community and its worship come to the fore, as well as the physical security of the community under Nehemiah. This is leadership for survival and identity, not for leadership among the nations and manifest destiny.

Torah, Purity, and Separation. Ezra, a Zadokite priest and a scribe skilled in the law of Moses (Ezra 7:1–5), was sent with Persian support and authority to establish the law of his God as the law of the land (cf. esp. Ezra 7:25–26). In Ezra 8 we are told that Ezra read a law book before the assembled people and it was affirmed as the binding law of the land. It is unclear what the precise character of this law book was, but most are agreed that it has some relationship to the Torah, the Penta-teuch, thus, we are dealing here with a milestone in the pro-cess of canonization. What is clear is that the Persians were happy, for purposes of stability, to lend authority to the estab-lishment of a body of law out of Judah's own traditions as the basis for civil and religious jurisprudence.[47] It is also clear that, whether this was just a portion of the Torah or a substantial early edition of it, the role of Torah as central authority in the religious life of the community is also firmly established.

The establishment of Ezra's law book as constitution of the community probably resolved disputes over leadership and direction in the returned community in favor of a Zadokite-Aaronid group willing to move in a more exclusive and authoritarian direction for the sake of stability and identity. Both Ezra and Nehemiah in their reform policies rely on this Torah foundation.[48] In doing so they are able to address the abuses of leadership and religious life reflected in Malachi and Isaiah 56–66. Particularly under Nehemiah, economic reforms recall the covenantal concerns for equitable distribution of family lands and rejection of exploitive economic practices (Neh. 5:11). Other reforms relate to the purity and integrity of ritual practices, temple regulations, Sabbath practices, and the prohibition of marriage to non-Israelites (including forced dissolution of such marriages).

The seeming harshness and exclusivism of some of these practices have led to commonly held opinions that Ezra and Nehemiah represent a degeneration from authentic biblical religion.[49] During the exile the priestly traditions of the Pentateuch also receive final form, including the priestly legislation dealing with questions of purity and defilement. These priestly concerns may provide some of the basis for the reforms of Ezra and Nehemiah. It is in relation to Ezra-Nehemiah and the priestly laws that the common characterization of postexilic religion as legalistic and preoccupied with matters of ritual purity and exclusion is based.

Daniel Smith suggests that we may need to reassess these judgments in the light of a clearer understanding of the returned community as a minority community struggling for its very survival in the context of an oppressive majority culture.[50] He cites the work of Mary Douglas,[51] who "has shown how the priestly concerns with ritual, especially with regard to purity and pollution, are especially evident in situations of danger, i.e. threats to the continued existence of a minority group."[52] Smith relates this concern for ritual purity as a protection from pollution to the concern for separation in Ezra-Nehemiah and other exilic or postexilic texts. He argues that the concept of a separated and pure people is both characteristic and necessary to the identity and survival of minority groups who sense that their own future is in danger. Actions to effect such separation and avert the dangers of pollution are to be seen not as regressive but as creative and perhaps the only effective means to avoid community disintegration. In the light of Smith's argument we should perhaps take more seriously the nature of social behavior in radical minority settings where community identity and integrity are at stake. In this light the policies of Ezra and Nehemiah and the intent of the priestly ritual laws become more understandable. Majority cultures do not often understand or appreciate the efforts of minority or disenfranchised communities to preserve distinctive cultural identities and maintain group cohesiveness. The charge leveled against such efforts is usually that of exclusivism or separatism.

Reflections of Conflict and Heroism

Some of the literature out of the Second Temple period reflects points of view that did not prevail in the returned community, but survive as significant voices of dissent. Some narrative accounts also seem to have functioned as stories of heroic moral example in the face of conflict.

The Divided Community. It is clear that the arrival of returnees to Judah created immediate tensions. The land was in the hands of a new class of landholders, many of whom were among the disenfranchised before exile. Some returnees apparently intermarried and reestablished themselves, but the majority seemed to have formed a separate community and considered these new "people of the land" as illegitimate (see the attitude reflected in Ezek. 11:14–18 and 33:23–27).

There were, of course, the well-known conflicts with neighboring groups such as the Samaritans. Opposition to the rebuilding of the temple (Ezra 4) and meddling in temple politics later created tensions throughout the period.

Isaiah 56–66 seems to reflect the viewpoint of a powerless group pushed outside the boundaries of postexilic community who refer to themselves as God's servant, believe themselves persecuted and disenfranchised (65:13), are incensed at various abuses in the cult (57:1–13), and appeal to God for divine intervention in their behalf. Paul Hanson has found here evidence for a conflict between two groups over control of the Jerusalem cultus.[53] The hierocratic party of the Zadokite priests is represented in Ezek. 40–48, Haggai, and Zechariah while Isa. 56–66 represents the visionary party of Levites who are shut out of influence and limited in their role. Because of the appeal to God in terms of cosmic eschatology ("For I am about to create new heavens and a new earth," Isa. 65:17) Hanson sees here the early roots of apocalyptic literature. Hanson has certainly done us a service by calling attention to the sharp conflicts in the postexilic community. Certainly the tensions he exposes help us better to understand the struggles and dangers of community building. The effort to establish one minority community results in the marginalization of another group. The tensions he exposes sensitize us to the dangers of community definitions that are too narrow in scope. In particular, Hanson helps us reclaim the universal element of the tradition at a time when the tradition otherwise turns particularistic, for example, the imagery of the temple as "a house of prayer for all peoples" (Isa. 56:7) and the vision of all nations contributing children to the priesthood (66:18–21).

Most, however, would see the postexilic conflicts as more complex than the two parties Hanson traces,[54] and most would not limit the visionary traditions to only one of these. After all, Haggai and Zechariah also contain visionary eschatological elements, and while they may seem the establishment to the "servants" of Isa. 56–66, they are a relatively powerless minority in the context of the Persian empire, thus, they too appeal to God for divine intervention.

Protests and Heroes. The period of the returned community also produced some very interesting pieces of narrative literature. Two of these must be seen as exceptions to the notions of purified and separated community which prevail in the reforms of Ezra and Nehemiah. Both Ruth and Jonah represent alternative visions evidently valued broadly enough in the community that they have been preserved in the canon and act as correctives to uncritical and continued institutionalization of the attitude reflected in Ezra-Nehemiah.

Ruth is a story of women in a man's world, and its central heroine is a foreigner as well.[55] Through the resourcefulness and courage of Ruth and Naomi, and the openness of Boaz, community is recovered from fragmentation. The child born of this unlikely union is the ancestor of David himself (Ruth 4:17). The marginal have been brought into the center, and the community is enriched.

In Jonah a Yahwistic prophet is sent to preach judgment to the Assyrians and refuses. From the sea he is swallowed up as in death (or exile) and is restored to accept his mission only to be dismayed when the Assyrians, including the king, repent. In Jonah's rebuke by God (4:9–11) is the reassertion of the radical freedom of God (see chapter 4), who will extend salvation to whomever it pleases God to redeem. The narrow attitude of Jonah and those who would limit God's grace is exposed as a problem with the very character of God. The unacceptable have been made acceptable in God's eyes.

Other narrative traditions from the late Israelite period may be classed as diaspora hero stories.[56] The stories of Daniel and Esther serve as stories of role models for whole communities forced to live as minorities in foreign populations. In these and other such stories (Tobit, Joseph) the hero or heroine rises from lowly status to success through perseverance, cleverness, and piety. The majority population usually poses some threat and the hero or heroine is vindicated before the ruler. All of these figures face imprisonment which Smith treats as a major symbol of exile, absent from Israelite legal institutions before exile. In these stories the disenfranchised and the persecuted become the empowered and model this hope for the powerless in every generation.

The Emergence of Apocalyptic Vision

Near the end of the Old Testament period the book of Daniel represents the emergence of apocalypticism in ancient Israel. The main body of generally agreed upon apocalyptic literature falls outside of the Hebrew canon in the period 200 B.C.E. to 100 C.E.

There is little consensus on definitions or terminology for apocalyptic literature or apocalypticism. There is also a wide diversity of views on its origins.[57] We have already seen the emergence in prophetic literature of eschatological visions which serve to engender hope in the midst of situations that might otherwise give rise to hopelessness. The focus of eschatology is sometimes national (a new age for Israel) and sometimes cosmic (a new age for the world). Although these visions anticipate apocalyptic themes, they should at best be regarded only as protoapocalyptic in character.

In Dan. 7–12 we see the features of fully developed apocalyptic in its presentation as a revelatory vision, mediated by divine beings, focused on a cosmic eschatology in which the world is transformed, the dead are raised and judged, the present evil powers are vanquished. Apocalyptic is rich in mythological imagery and usually attributed to some ancient hero.

This is not the place for a full discussion of apocalyptic in general or the book of Daniel in particular. Our concern relates to the outright dismissal of apocalyptic by many in the church as fantastic and superstitious, having little value for the theologically sophisticated. Its image is often shaped by those who misuse apocalyptic literature as a device for making predictions about the course of history and luring the gullible with apocalyptic based scenarios.

Several features deserve our serious consideration. First, many apocalyptic books and Daniel in particular arise as a response to historical crisis. Daniel is widely viewed as reflective of the desperate circumstances in the mid-second century. Jews were undergoing persecution at the hands of Hellenistic authorities, religious practices were proscribed, the Jewish community itself was divided in response. On the one hand, the stories of Dan. 1–6 urge faithfulness in the face of pressures to accommodate, but it is the visions of Dan. 7–12 which assure the community that in the face of persecution and death God's righteousness will ultimately prevail, and the faithful who die will be vindicated. Beyond the crisis which produced Daniel these visions serve to express confidence that history is still directed by God's sovereignty and the divine purposes for the course of history will be fulfilled.

At the same time, there is a weariness with the world expressed in Daniel and other apocalyptic writings. The hope is usually for the end of history and the ushering in of a new age in which God's reign will be directly experienced. Thus, Daniel and apocalyptic remind us of our human need to understand the disparities between historical reality and God's promises. It is sometimes this radical vision which sustains us not simply in the dramatic moment of persecution, but in the ongoing oppressive and debilitating existence that is the lot of some groups in every generation. Apocalyptic is seldom appreciated by those who experience full and fulfilling lives. It is the literature of the powerless and the persecuted.

Apocalyptic envisions alternatives to life's brutalities that are not limited to the "realistic." Daniel and apocalyptic represent imaginative literature aimed at the affirmation of transcendent reality.

The language of the apocalypses is not descriptive, referential newspaper language, but the *expressive* language of poetry, which uses symbols and imagery to articulate a sense or feeling about the world. Their abiding value does not lie in the pseudoinformation they provide about cosmology or future history, but in their affirmation of a transcendent world. Even if the physical universe were to endure forever, there is no doubt that the social and cultural worlds we inhabit are constantly crumbling. Christianity inherited from the Jewish apocalypses a way of affirming transcendent values, those things we should affirm even when the world around us collapses.[58]

Apocalyptic was never the prevailing or majority voice in Israelite tradition and certainly not in the wider cultural world of the empires. It is countercultural in character. Thus, its voice is a reminder that for some groups the reality of life brutally denies them a place, even in the religious communities through which we try to live faithfully in the world. For such groups their vision must seek a place for them in the new age of God when even the dead may be raised to new and full life. Books like Daniel remind us that even our most faithful efforts to live in the world are an accommodation that some cannot make.

Exile called into reexamination every facet of Israel's faith. In the literature of exile and return we see the diversity of reflection that reexamination engendered, each category of literature contributing to the reassessment of relationship to God and world. As scripture this witness challenges us to the fresh examination of our own moral presumptions as we too attempt to live faithfully in the midst of the empires.

It was in the context of the returned community that the final segment of the Hebrew canon began to take shape. The Writings (*ketubim*) are a diverse collection, and many of the books included there do not fit well into the narrative course of Israel's story. It is to some of these witnesses within the canon that we turn in our final chapter.

Notes

1. Daniel L. Smith, *The Religion of the Landless: The Social Context of the Babylonian Exile* (Bloomington, Ind.: Meyer-Stone Books, 1989), p. 5. See also the call for reevaluation among those Old Testament scholars who write as if the Old Testament ends with the exile in Peter R. Ackroyd, *Exile and Restoration: A Study of Hebrew Thought of the Sixth Century B.C.*, OTL (Philadelphia: Westminster Press, 1968).

2. See Norman K. Gottwald, *The Hebrew Bible: A Socio-Literary Introduction* (Philadelphia: Fortress Press, 1985), pp. 409–456, for a cogent treatment of the difficulties and the options in reconstructing the history of this period.

3. The exact details of the destruction and deportation are difficult to reconstruct. 2 Kings 25:11 suggests wholesale depopulation while Jer. 52 uses more modest figures. On the reconstruction of the historical situation both in Judah and in Babylon during the exile, see Ackroyd, *Exile and Restoration*, pp. 17–38, and K. Galling, *Studien zur Geschichte Israels im persischen Zeitalter* (Tübingen, 1964).

4. Bruce C. Birch, *Singing the Lord's Song: Isaiah 40–55* (Nashville: Abingdon Press, 1990; 1st ed., 1981), p. 15. Included there is a fuller discussion for a lay audience of exile as a challenge to seemingly secure centers of meaning and the pertinence of this crisis to the modern world.

5. Smith, *Religion of the Landless*, p. 50, uses this phrase in summarizing the work of M. Barkun (*Disaster and the Millennium*; New Haven, Conn.: Yale University Press, 1974) as it applies to the exile. Barkun suggested that crises do not evoke significant ideological and sociological responses in communi-

ties unless they are extensive enough to affect the "mazeway" or structure of meaning and order which is formative of community identity. As Smith suggests, the biblical experience of exile certainly falls into this category.

6. Smith, *Religion of the Landless*, pp. 173–174.

7. Especially helpful on the theological meaning of exile are Ralph W. Klein, *Israel in Exile: A Theological Interpretation*, OBT (Philadelphia: Fortress Press, 1979), and Walter Brueggemann, *Hopeful Imagination: Prophetic Voices in Exile* (Philadelphia: Fortress Press, 1986).

8. Smith, *Religion of the Landless*, pp. 8–10.

9. John Howard Yoder, "Exodus and Exile: The Two Faces of Liberation," *Cross Currents* 23 (Fall 1973): 308.

10. Smith, *Religion of the Landless*, p. 205: "Exodus is the road to nationalism and power. But there is another biblical paradigm. It is a warning against Exodus theology. In the place of Joshua the revolutionary conqueror, it points to Jeremiah the prophet of subversive righteousness and Ezra the priest of a radically alternative community. In the place of David the emperor, it points to Daniel the wise. In the place of Solomon's great Temple, it points to the perseverance of singing the Lord's song in a foreign land. It is a religion of the landless, the faith of those who dwell in Babylon." See the criticism of Smith's dichotomizing of Exodus and exile by Norman Gottwald in the preface to Smith's book, p. xv.

11. Walter Brueggemann, "At the Mercy of Babylon: A Subversive Rereading of the Empire," JBL 110 (1991): 3, 15–16. Basing his theological claims on the analysis of eight exilic and postexilic texts (Jer. 6:23; 2 Chron. 36:7; Isa. 47:6; Jer. 42:12; 1 Kings 8:50; 2 Chron. 30:9; Dan. 1:9; 4:27), Brueggemann argues that Israel's rhetoric is able to envision Babylon, and thus the empire in all times, as a locus for God's mercy.

12. Smith, *Religion of the Landless*, p. 214.

13. Ibid., p. 206.

14. See Jacob Neusner, *Understanding Seeking Faith* (Atlanta: Scholars Press, 1986), pp. 137–141.

15. Terence E. Fretheim, *The Suffering of God: An Old Testament Perspective*, OBT (Philadelphia: Fortress Press, 1984), p. 108, chooses to discuss texts on the suffering of God under a threefold pattern: God who suffers because of the people, with the people, and for the people. Many of the pertinent texts are from the prophets including those of the exile and

return. If time allowed I believe these same nuanced divisions could be traced in the divine response to exile.

16. Reading with the Hebrew text. The NRSV emends at this point to read "on the one" which seems influenced by the later christological use of this text and is not at all necessary in the context of Zechariah.

17. Abraham J. Heschel, *The Prophets* (New York: Harper & Row, 1962), p. 112.

18. The positive statements of monotheism and divine universality for Yahweh are coupled in Deutero-Isaiah with attacks and ridicule on the ineffectual idols that represent other gods (cf. esp. Isa. 41:21–24; 44:9–20; 46:1–2).

19. See also the discussion on this theme in Birch, *Singing the Lord's Song*, pp. 33–40.

20. Klein, *Israel in Exile*, treats each of the voices of the exilic period in separate chapters that bring out well the richness of imagery which characterized the testimony out of the exile. In this chapter we can only briefly sample this richness. See also Brueggemann, *Hopeful Imagination*.

21. See Klein, *Israel in Exile*, pp. 114–116. See also P. H. Harner, "Creation Faith in Deutero-Isaiah," *VT* 17 (1967): 298–306.

22. See the full discussion of this term in Carroll Stuhlmueller, *Creative Redemption in Deutero-Isaiah*, AnBib 43 (Rome: Biblical Institute Press, 1970), pp. 99–123.

23. See Bruce C. Birch, "Memory in Congregational Life," in *Congregations: Their Power to Form and Transform*, ed. C. Ellis Nelson (Atlanta: John Knox Press, 1988), pp. 20–47, for an application of this same dynamic to the life of congregations in the modern church.

24. My thinking on this matter has been especially helped by Terence E. Fretheim, "Suffering God and Sovereign God in Exodus: A Collision of Images," *HBT* 11 (1989): 31–56, and by an article which Fretheim discusses by Erich Zenger, "The God of Exodus in the Message of the Prophets as Seen in Isaiah," in *Exodus—A Lasting Paradigm*, ed. B. van Iersel and A. Weiler (Edinburgh: T. & T. Clark, 1987), pp. 22–33. See also Bernhard W. Anderson, "Exodus and Covenant in Second Isaiah and Prophetic Tradition," in *Magnalia Dei: The Mighty Acts of God. Essays on the Bible and Archaeology in Memory of G. Ernest Wright*, ed. Frank M. Cross, W. E. Lemke, and Patrick D. Miller (Garden City, N.Y.: Doubleday & Co., 1976), pp. 338–360.

25. See Thomas W. Ogletree, *The Use of the Bible in Christian*

Ethics (Philadelphia: Fortress Press, 1983), p. 71, for a similar argument.

26. Gordon Henry Matties, *Ezekiel 18 and the Rhetoric of Moral Discourse*, SBLDS (Atlanta: Scholars Press, 1990), treats the issues and the literature related to the interpretation of Ezek. 18 in a helpful and thorough manner. It includes extensive bibliographic citations.

27. H. Wheeler Robinson, *The Christian Doctrine of Man* (Edinburgh: T. & T. Clark, 1911), and "The Hebrew Conception of Corporate Personality," in *Werden und Wesen des Alten Testaments*, ed. P. Volz, F. Stummer, and J. Hempel (Berlin: Alfred Topelmann, 1936), pp. 49–62.

28. See Matties, *Ezekiel 18*, esp. ch. 5, pp. 113–158; John W. Rogerson, "The Hebrew Conception of Corporate Personality," *JTS* 21 (1970): 1–16; George E. Mendenhall, "The Relation of the Individual to Political Society in Ancient Israel," in *Biblical Studies in Honor of H. C. Alleman*, ed. J. M. Myers (Locust Valley, N.Y.: J. J. Augustin, 1960), pp. 89–108; Paul M. Joyce, "The Individual and the Community," in *Beginning Old Testament Study*, ed. John Rogerson (Philadelphia: Westminster Press, 1982), pp. 74–89; and Denise Dombkowski Hopkins, "Biblical Anthropology, Discipline of," *Dictionary of Pastoral Care and Counseling*, ed. Rodney J. Hunter (Nashville: Abingdon Press, 1990), pp. 85–88.

29. See the strong statement by Walter C. Kaiser, Jr., on this matter, *Toward Old Testament Ethics* (Grand Rapids: Zondervan Publishing House, 1983), pp. 70–72.

30. My view of Ezek. 18 is close to that of Paul M. Joyce, "Individual Responsibility in Ezekiel 18?" in *Studia Biblica 1978: Papers on Old Testament and Related Themes*, ed. E. A. Livingstone, JSOTSup 11 (Sheffield: JSOT Press, 1979), pp. 185–196. Ezekiel 18 is not preoccupied with "the *unit* of responsibility . . . but rather the urgent need for his audience to accept responsibility as such" (p. 187).

31. Zenger, "God of Exodus in the Message of the Prophets as Seen in Isaiah," p. 28.

32. See C. R. North, *The Suffering Servant in Deutero-Isaiah* (London: Oxford University Press, 1948), for a classic discussion of the various options and proposals.

33. In an important recent work Tryggve N. D. Mettinger, *A Farewell to the Servant Songs: A Critical Examination of an Exegetical Axiom* (Lund: Gleerup, 1983), argues for a collective minority view of the Servant and insists that the meaning of

these Servant Songs can only be understood by not removing them from their context in the whole of Deutero-Isaiah. "It would be . . . difficult to imagine an historical individual whose ignominy and humiliation would have been capable of making the sort of impression on the Gentiles as that represented by Is. 53:1–6" (p. 38). See also the discussions in Paul D. Hanson, *The People Called: The Growth of Community in the Bible* (San Francisco: Harper & Row, 1986), pp. 240–246; and Daniel Smith, *Religion of the Landless*, pp. 166–170. Even a recent vigorous defense of the identity of the Servant as the prophet himself by R. N. Whybray in *Thanksgiving for a Liberated Prophet: An Interpretation of Isaiah Chapter 53* (Sheffield: JSOT Press, 1978) agrees that the testimony is preserved and passed on only because of its meaning for a significant segment of the exile community as a whole.

34. Smith, *Religion of the Landless*, pp. 168, 169.

35. See Birch, *Singing the Lord's Song*, pp. 109–130.

36. Hanson, *People Called*, p. 241.

37. There are some late additions to these chapters, but their basic pattern is from Ezekiel himself. Among the additions are those which enhance the Zadokite authority while attacking the Levites (Ezek. 44 and 48:11). Ezekiel himself was probably a Zadokite and restored them to prominent place in his own vision, but later conflict over Zadokite authority in the returned community led to these ideological additions. See Paul D. Hanson, *The Dawn of Apocalyptic*, rev. ed. (Philadelphia: Fortress Press, 1979).

38. This is the phrase used by Daniel Smith in *Religion of the Landless*, see p. 11. This extraordinarily important book sheds new light on the literature of exile and return by studying patterns and mechanisms for survival among modern exiled peoples and looking for similar patterns in the experience of the exilic and postexilic Jewish community. The results are illuminating and reflected in some of our subsequent discussion in this section.

39. We should not take the tone of Jeremiah's letter as an indication that conditions were not at all oppressive in Babylon. There are ample indications of harsh conditions and continued hostility toward Babylon as an oppressor. See the evidence cited by J. M. Wilkie, "Nabonidus and the Later Jewish Exiles," *JTS* 2 (1951): 6–44.

40. For detailed discussions of these matters see J. Weinberg, "Das *beit 'abot* im 6.–4. Jh. v.u.Z.," *VT* 23 (1973):

400–414; Smith, *Religion of the Landless*, pp. 93–126; David L. Petersen, *Haggai and Zechariah 1–8*, A Commentary, OTL (Philadelphia: Westminster Press, 1984), pp. 30–31.

41. Smith, *Religion of the Landless*, p. 116.

42. See Weinberg, "Das *beit 'abot*," and his later study "Die Agrärverhältnisse in der Bürger-Tempel-Gemeinde der Achämenidenzeit," in *Wirtschaft und Gesellschaft im Alten Vorderasien*, ed. J. Harmatta and G. Komoroczy (Budapest: Ib Akademiai Kiadbo, 1976), pp. 473–486.

43. See Ronald E. Clements, *God and Temple: The Idea of the Divine Presence in Ancient Israel* (London: Oxford University Press, 1965), pp. 135–140, and Ackroyd, *Exile and Restoration*, pp. 248–251.

44. Frank M. Cross, "A Reconstruction of the Judean Restoration," *JBL* 94 (1975): 4–18, believes there are three editions of the Chronicler's history. The first one significantly supports the restoration of a royal ideology centered on Zerubbabel, but this is absent from the editions that separately add the records of Ezra and Nehemiah.

45. See Gottwald, *Hebrew Bible*, pp. 432–438.

46. Cross, "A Reconstruction of the Judean Restoration," p. 16.

47. Gottwald, *Hebrew Bible*, pp. 436–438.

48. This view tends to support the opinion that Ezra's work came prior to that of Nehemiah. However, Donn F. Morgan in *Between Text and Community: The Writings in "Canonical" Interpretation* (Minneapolis: Fortress Press, 1990), pp. 64–66, makes a strong case that whatever the historical chronology of Ezra and Nehemiah, the books of Chronicles-Ezra-Nehemiah reflect an awareness and conversation with Torah and Prophets in their present canonical form. In the Ezra-Nehemiah material it is the Torah which is most influential. "The primary value of Ezra-Nehemiah is not to be found in the history it presents. Rather, the roles of Ezra and Nehemiah as Torah-centered leaders, obedient and committed to the values of the authoritative texts of the community, are crucial to the purpose of this literature. In this sense, this literature is more concerned to present a biblical ethics than a history of the postexilic period" (p. 66).

49. Even Hanson in *People Called*, pp. 293–296, who for the most part positively reassesses the value of the postexilic period, is forced to conclude that of his three marks of community Ezra and Nehemiah do well for worship and righteous-

ness, but are lacking in compassion. He sees Jonah and Ruth as protests against this narrowing of compassion to exclude the foreigner.

50. Smith, *Religion of the Landless*, pp. 139–151.

51. Mary Douglas, *Purity and Danger* (London: Routledge & Kegan Paul, 1966).

52. Smith, *Religion of the Landless*, p. 82.

53. Hanson, *Dawn of Apocalyptic*. See also Hanson, *People Called*, pp. 253–290.

54. Smith, *Religion of the Landless*, pp. 179–200, traces a broad range of evidence and interpretation dealing with conflict in the postexilic community.

55. See esp. Phyllis Trible, *God and the Rhetoric of Sexuality*, OBT (Philadelphia: Fortress Press, 1978), pp. 166–199.

56. See Smith, *Religion of the Landless*, pp. 153–178, and W. Lee Humphreys, "A Lifestyle for Diaspora: A Study of the Tales of Esther and Daniel," *JBL* 92 (1973): 213–226. Smith also includes a late edition of the Joseph story and the Suffering Servant in the model.

57. Paul D. Hanson distinguishes three levels of definition, apocalypse as genre, apocalyptic eschatology, and apocalypticism as a religiosocial movement. See "Apocalyptic Literature," in *The Hebrew Bible and Its Modern Interpreters*, ed. Douglas Knight and Gene Tucker (Philadelphia: Fortress Press, 1985). Hanson focuses on cosmic eschatology as characteristic of apocalyptic (see his *Dawn of Apocalyptic*) and thus sees its beginnings in later prophetic visionary literature. By contrast John J. Collins focuses on the introduction of personal eschatology, raising and judging of the dead, as the mark of true apocalyptic and thus sees Daniel as the first full expression of apocalyptic. See "Apocalyptic Eschatology as the Transcendence of Death," *CBQ* 36 (1974): 21–43, and "Old Testament Apocalypticism and Eschatology," *NJBC*, ed. R. E. Brown, J. A. Fitzmyer, and R. E. Murphy (Englewood Cliffs, N.J.: Prentice-Hall, 1990), pp. 298–304. A good collection with a spectrum of viewpoints is Paul D. Hanson, ed., *Visionaries and Their Apocalypses* (Philadelphia: Fortress Press, 1983).

58. John J. Collins, *The Apocalyptic Imagination* (New York: Crossroad, 1989), p. 214.

9
Wisdom and Morality

In the third and final section of the Hebrew canon, three books are usually regarded as wisdom literature: Proverbs, Job, and Ecclesiastes. In the apocrypha the books of Sirach and Wisdom of Solomon are also classed as wisdom. Although these books came into their final form during the postexilic and intertestamental periods (the Second Temple period), most scholars agree that they represent a wisdom tradition which arose much earlier in Israel, a tradition which exerts an influence on portions of the canon that are not formally to be classed as wisdom literature. Although the extent of this influence and its nature are debated, most would class a number of psalms as wisdom psalms, and many have found wisdom influences in the Joseph story (Gen. 37–50), prophets such as Amos and Isaiah, Esther, and elsewhere throughout the canon. The criteria for identifying such wisdom influences have often been somewhat loose.[1]

Wisdom literature and the wisdom tradition it represents arises within the framework of Israel's history, but is itself unconcerned with that historical tradition. Thus, it represents a strain of Israel's faith traditions quite unlike those we have been discussing.

The origins of this tradition as a formal literature probably go back to the Solomonic court and its adoption of practices common to royal courts elsewhere in the ancient world. Wisdom literature regards Solomon as its patron well into the intertestamental period, and its many similarities (even borrowings, e.g., Prov. 22:17–24:22 parallels the Egyptian Instruction of Amenemope) to the wisdom materials of other

321

ancient cultures are well known.[2] It was in the court that
formal schools for the training of the young seem to have
developed, but earlier roots of the sapiential (wisdom) tradition seem to lie in the advice passed on in families from
parent to child. Many examples of this "popular wisdom"
are reflected in stories throughout the Old Testament and in
sayings addressed to "my son" in the book of Proverbs.[3]

Most critics believe that the nurturing of this wisdom tradition and its development toward a formal literature was the
concern of a professional class of sages which developed in
Israel during the period of the monarchy. "For instruction
shall not perish from the priest, nor counsel from the wise,
nor the word from the prophet" (Jer. 18:18). These wise
teachers were probably attached to schools associated with
the Jerusalem court, but after the exile became more associated with the development of schools free of royal connection.[4] A certain amount of instruction certainly also went on
in the family and clan alongside the more formal schools.
Only over time did collections of the instruction passed on
from parent to child, teacher to student become gathered
into collections and preserved by a professional class of wise
teachers.

In all the evidence for this developing wisdom tradition it is
clear that we are dealing not only with the growth of a wisdom
literature but with the development of wisdom as a way of
thinking, an outlook on life.[5] The influence of this way of
thinking may be found in places where the features of formal
wisdom literature are not fully to be found. This makes a definition of "wisdom" in the Old Testament notoriously difficult.
The Hebrew word for wisdom (*ḥokmah*) and its derivatives appears in a wide range of contexts and with an equally wide
range of nuances, although the overwhelming majority of oc-
currences are in the five agreed upon wisdom books named
above.[6] A representative definition for our purposes is the following from James Crenshaw:

> Formally, wisdom consists of proverbial sentence or instruction,
> debate, intellectual reflection; thematically, wisdom comprises
> self-evident intuitions about mastering life for human better-
> ment, gropings after life's secrets with regard to innocent suffer-
> ing, grappling with finitude, and quest for truth concealed in
> the created order and manifested in Dame Wisdom. When a

marriage between form and content exists, there is wisdom literature.[7]

The wisdom literature, especially the book of Proverbs, bears a natural relationship to the concerns of Christian ethics. Older theologies of the Old Testament saw the collections of proverbs as the ethics of the Old Testament since they were didactic and concerned with both character formation (primarily instruction of the young) and codes of conduct (the behavior of the wise and the foolish).[8]

More recently (through the middle decades of the twentieth century) the wisdom literature and tradition was severely criticized and discounted as lacking in value for any authentic biblical theology. It was primarily considered too secular, highly pragmatic and individualistic, elitist in tone and intent, and out of step with the prevailing interest in Israel's salvation history. As we shall see, there is some basis in fact for these assessments, but these elements hardly do justice to the breadth and complexity of Israelite wisdom. Most recently there has been a revival of interest in the place and importance of wisdom in the Israelite tradition.[9] It is this recent work which most informs our discussion. Whatever the contribution of Israelite wisdom to the biblical resources for Christian ethics they must be assessed in the context of the wider Hebrew canon of which the wisdom books are now a part. Within that context a new appreciation of the wisdom tradition has arisen which recognizes the limitations of the wisdom perspective but appreciates its contributions.

> It would be easy to criticize this teaching [Proverbs] as at best pedestrian and at worst complaisant and ethically insensitive on a whole range of issues. . . . And, in general, much of it seems to be aimed at getting on, or sometimes just getting by, in life. . . . We must bear in mind that it started out as strictly vocational instruction, restricted to a very small class of aspirants to public office. Its inculcation of the virtues of truth, honesty, and self-control in public life has nothing to fear from comparison with standards which have come to be accepted, or tolerated, in our contemporary societies. In its search for order behind the apparent chaos of experience, its endeavour to teach how to discriminate between options and make reasonable choices, its delineation of human types, it laid the basis for a genuine social ethic applicable outside the class to which it was first addressed.[10]

God as the Source of Wisdom

Since Israel's early wisdom literature (Proverbs, Job, Ecclesiastes) takes human experience and well-being as the central focus, and shows no interest at all in the theological traditions of Israel's salvation history, these traditions have often been characterized as secular or humanistic in nature. But "wisdom identifies human good with divine intention."[11] In its present form wisdom does have a theological foundation. "The fear of the LORD is the beginning of knowledge" (Prov. 1:7a).

Wisdom, Order, and Life

At the heart of wisdom theology lies a belief in order, imbedded in the cosmos and discernible by human reason.[12] This is not a uniquely Israelite concept. Its similarity to the Egyptian concept of Ma'at has often been noted. Like Ma'at, this order can be discovered in the natural or the social world. To become wise, and thereby successful in life, was to discover this order and live in harmony with it. Unlike Ma'at this order was not an impersonal cosmic principle. Order in society and creation for Israelite wisdom finds its origin in God. To discern order in the world is to attune oneself to the divine intention and sustaining of order.

Five times in the wisdom literature the fear of Yahweh is cited as the foundation of wisdom and knowledge.

> The fear of the LORD is the beginning of knowledge;
>   fools despise wisdom and instruction.
>   (Prov. 1:7)

> The fear of the LORD is the beginning of wisdom,
>   and the knowledge of the Holy One is insight.
>   (Prov. 9:10)

> The fear of the LORD is instruction in wisdom,
>   and humility goes before honor.
>   (Prov. 15:33)

> The fear of the LORD is the beginning of wisdom;
>   all those who practice it have a good understanding.
>   (Ps. 111:10)

> Truly, the fear of the LORD, that is wisdom;
>   and to depart from evil is understanding.
>   (Job 28:28)

In each of these it is clear that wisdom grows out of and attests to a reality founded in God. Wisdom is not itself the impersonal principle of order on which the world is founded.[13] All the good things in life flow out of an order which God intended and established.

> The order of life is characterized in wisdom in many ways. . . .
> Whatever it is called, it is a remarkable confession of faith in the benevolence of life, in the staying power of our world, in the possibility of wholeness, in the health of right relations in right community, in the security every man may have without seizing what is his neighbor's. Moreover, in Israel's faith this orderliness to which man may conform himself is not an accident, but is the knowing arrangement of a generous, benevolent god.[14]

Some scholars (Roland E. Murphy in particular[15]) have challenged the notion of an all-encompassing principle of order, even if divine in origin, on grounds that it is in conflict with divine freedom. One cannot retain belief in a God who acts freely and believe in a fixed order of life to be discovered.[16] Murphy argues that "one would do better to speak of human's imposing an order (however provisory) upon the chaotic experiences of life, by analysis and classification."[17] God is experienced in the *search* for order. Despite its tension with divine freedom most would find wisdom concerned with divine intentions in the order of things to be discovered and not simply divine presence in the discovery process itself.

Wisdom is not only a search for order but can be described as a search for life.[18] Order stresses the divinely established foundation of existence, but life stresses the goal toward which harmony with order moves.

> Whoever heeds instruction is on the path to life,
> but one who rejects a rebuke goes astray.
> (Prov. 10:17)

To become wise is to choose for life and against death (Prov. 9:18). Such life is to be embraced in the immediate present. Proper relationship to God is necessary for life; indeed, life might be considered the gift of God made available in the order which God has established.

> The fear of the LORD prolongs life,
> but the years of the wicked will be short.
> (Prov. 10:27)

The life sought in wisdom is more than biological existence but involves well-being and wholeness.

> She [wisdom] is a tree of life to those who lay
>   hold of her;
>   those who hold her fast are called happy.
> (Prov. 3:18)

> Whoever finds me [wisdom] finds life
>   and obtains favor from the LORD;
>   but those who miss me injure themselves;
>   all who hate me love death.
> (Prov. 8:35–36)

Wisdom and the Creator

Most scholars would now agree with Walther Zimmerli's oft-quoted statement, "Wisdom thinks resolutely within the framework of a theology of creation. Its theology is creation theology."[19] God does not appear in wisdom as the God of Israel's history (although the divine name Yahweh is used), but as Creator.[20] God the Creator is responsible for the order built into creation, and it is God the Creator who has made humans with the capacity to discern the clues to that order and live in harmony with it. Although wisdom is often described as secular in character, it is clear that even in its most intense interest in and focus on human experience it was understood that God was the *source* of order and values in the creation, and therefore the *source* of the wisdom which sought to discern that order.

> For the LORD gives wisdom;
>   from his mouth come knowledge and understanding;
>   he stores up sound wisdom for the upright;
>   he is a shield to those who walk blamelessly,
>   guarding the paths of justice
>   and preserving the way of his faithful ones.
>   Then you will understand righteousness and justice
>   and equity, every good path;
>   for wisdom will come into your heart,
>   and knowledge will be pleasant to your soul.
> (Prov. 2:6–10)

It follows that creation (both the social and the natural world) is the medium within which God is experienced, in the very order which God originated and sustains (see the mixture of references to Yahweh and "worldly" things in Prov. 16:7–12). "The experiences of the world were for her [Israel] always divine experiences as well, and the experiences of God were for her experiences of the world."[21]

The created world was viewed in wisdom as good (in keeping with the picture of creation in Gen. 1, see chapter 3), and as a source of understanding for our own role and potential in the world; for example, Prov. 30:15–31 draws on the animal world for a series of comparisons to aid in understanding our humanness. Creation could also serve as a source of divine communication as in the opening of Ps. 19, a late wisdom psalm:

> The heavens are telling the glory of God;
>   and the firmament proclaims his handiwork.
> Day to day pours forth speech,
>   and night to night declares knowledge.
>   (Ps. 19:1–2)

Life in the created world was life in God's presence. Job struggling with issues of God's presence in the midst of suffering is pointed in the Yahweh speeches back to creation (Job 38–41).

Wisdom understands that God has created the world in such a way that wisdom and righteousness are rewarded while folly and evil are punished. Belief in God's creation for wisdom is always tied to issues of God's justice and not a simple affirmation of divine ordering. The order of God's creation is the framework within which good and evil can be sought by human reason. James Crenshaw[22] has argued that behind creation, chaos always threatened, thus, human actions in harmony with God's created order helped maintain the fabric of the universe. Manifestations of chaos in human experience (suffering, conflict, human struggles) make it all the more imperative that God's justice be undergirded by reasserting the fundamental creation theology behind wisdom (as in Job 38–41). It is the integrity of God at stake as well as the well-being of persons. "Creation and justice are intimately connected both in regard to the primordial creation and in the continual victory of order over chaos within each person and within society as a whole."[23]

It can only be observed that in such a view there is indeed little room for notions of divine freedom or divine grace to operate. This is part of what led to skepticism (in Job and Ecclesiastes) on the one hand, and to the eventual theologizing of the wisdom tradition which brings it into conversation with the rest of Israel's faith tradition and identifies wisdom with Torah. We will discuss these matters further at a later point.

The Personification of Wisdom

In an effort to explicate the nature and source of divine order associated with the wisdom tradition, the figure of Dame Wisdom emerges as the personification of divine order in the world, and the active agent urging persons toward the path of wisdom.[24] This figure appears in the late texts of Prov. 1, 8, and 9, and further in the intertestamental texts of Sir. 24 and Wisd. 7–10.

Personified as a female figure, Wisdom appears in Proverbs to promote the benefits of following her instruction. In Prov. 1:20–33 she appears almost as a preacher in the streets urging the simple to heed her, but for those who refuse "I also will laugh at your calamity" (Prov. 1:26). In Prov. 9:1–6 Wisdom summons the simple to dine with her in her seven-pillared house in order to find life and insight. This is contrasted in vs. 13–18 to Folly as a foolish woman who offers the simple stolen food and leads them to death.

Most striking is the portrait in Prov. 8. In vs. 1–21 Wisdom speaks again in public promoting the benefits of her path and making known the qualities needed to pursue it (e.g., prudence and intelligence, v. 5), but her speech takes quite a different course in vs. 22–36:

> The LORD created me at the beginning of his work,
>   the first of his acts of long ago . . .
> when he marked out the foundations of the earth,
>   then I was beside him, like a master worker;
> and I was daily his delight,
>   rejoicing before him always,
> rejoicing in his inhabited world
>   and delighting in the human race.
>   (Prov. 8:22, 29b-31)

This text clearly affirms the existence of Wisdom before creation and gives her a role in God's creating work. Wisdom 7:22 also contains a reference to Wisdom as a craftsperson working with God in the creation of the cosmos. It is equally clear that she remains in the world promoting her way and delighting in humans (8:31).

Who is this figure and how are we to understand her? Most scholars do not believe that we are dealing here with a hypostasis of divine attribute but with the personification of a fundamental principle inherent in the very fabric of God's creation. One of the most appealing views is offered by Gerhard von Rad, who rejects the identification as an attribute of God, and then suggests:

> It is also . . . something separate from the works of creation. This "wisdom," this "understanding," must, therefore, signify something like the "meaning" implanted by God in creation, the divine mystery of creation.[25]

Dianne Bergant builds on von Rad's suggestion:

> This mystery always calls out to, always beckons to women and men, cajoling, enticing, challenging them to search out the secrets of creation and of life. And yet, as the wisdom poem in Job so accurately states, only "God understands the way to it," only God "knows its place" (28:23).[26]

In the later book of Sirach, Dame Wisdom takes up residence in Jerusalem and is identified with Torah (24:23). This is part of the later joining of wisdom tradition with other Israelite theological traditions.

Wisdom as the personified agent through whom God communicates in the midst of creation seems clearly reflected in the development of Christology in the New Testament. Christ is called the "wisdom of God" in 1 Cor. 1:24, and Dame Wisdom seems reflected in the *logos* Christology of John 1, "In the beginning was the Word."

Moral Dimensions of the Wisdom Tradition

While we have begun with the divine role in establishing the order and meaning of creation, wisdom literature and the tradition it reflects does not begin with the divine but with the human. This clear anthropocentrism and features which flow from it are among the clearest marks of Israelite wisdom.

The Centrality of Human Experience

The wisdom view of reality begins with a human orientation.[27] Its fundamental question is a moral question: How can human beings find and embody what is good for them? In wisdom we are not dealing with any effort to discern the will of God made known somehow outside of or apart from human experience.

Wisdom is intended to aid in the human search for a long and good life and operates with confidence that all that is necessary for this task is to be found in human experience. Human behavior and the world which is the human context became the objects of intense scrutiny. Collections of maxims in Proverbs make clear that no matter is too trivial for careful observation. God the Creator had ordered the world in such a way that all the clues and signs necessary for a full and harmonious life are included within the realm of human experience. It is the human task to search for the truth God implanted in reality. It is the task of wisdom to aid in that search. Since human experience is cumulative, collections like those in Proverbs seek to pass on insights gathered from experience which judge some qualities and courses of action to be better than others to ensure full and harmonious life. Since human experience is common to all of humanity there is nothing distinctive to Israel or its particular faith traditions here. This basis in human experience makes wisdom both universal and international. The lessons to be learned are available to all who will see, hear, and learn. Thus, Israel's collection of proverbs can even include borrowing from an Egyptian collection (Prov. 22:17–24:22 parallels sections of the Instruction of Amenemope, an Egyptian work from around 1200).

Wisdom is possessed of enormous confidence in the capacity of human reason to discover the truth of reality and in human abilities to embody that truth in productive patterns of personal and community life. Even though God's work as Creator lies ultimately behind all life, the authority of wisdom is based on the cumulative experience of observing what brings life and what does not. Wisdom believes that we have the capacity to choose life and live wisely, and that these choices cannot be avoided.[28] If we do not choose the path of wisdom, we are thereby fools. Because of its confidence that persons have the capacity to determine their own destiny, wisdom in its classic expressions in Proverbs is very optimistic. When even the greatest effort to live in accord with wisdom's path does not bring a harmonious and happy life, then optimism gives way to difficult wrestling with the limits to human capacities (e.g., Job, Ecclesiastes).

Although God created the world, human actions taken without wisdom and discernment can threaten its harmony and strengthen the power of chaos which creation holds back (see chapter 3). Human decisions are of great importance and are not in any way aided by divine activity in the world.

> At some moment in remote antiquity God had created the universe orderly, bestowing upon that creation the necessary clues to assure its continued existence. From then on the Creator left human survival to its own devices. Those who used their intelligence to learn the universe's secrets and to live in accord with those secrets fared well; those who refused to do so suffered grievous consequences. In such a world, grace played no role; indeed, to ask for special consideration approached blasphemy. . . . Belief in order, though pervasive and highly significant to sages, cannot qualify as distinctively sapiential. What does is a conviction that men and women possess the means of securing their own well being—that they do not need and cannot expect divine assistance.[29]

Most would now agree that wisdom literature in the Old Testament in its present shape represents a development. Early wisdom, represented in Prov. 10ff., presents wisdom as the product of human reason and discernment although God is the ultimate source of the created order. In Prov. 1–9, from a later period, wisdom is the gift of God, offered to those who, in intelligence and discernment, choose wisely. Indeed, the personified figure of Dame Wisdom actively urging the choice of wisdom's path to passersby would seem at least the agent of God's desire to influence wise choices rather than rely on self-sufficient human reason. "When Prov. 1–9 is read as an introduction to chs. 10ff., the effect is that the search for wisdom emerges as a subtle dialectic between its being a divine gift and an actively pursued acquisition."[30] In Sirach and Wisdom the erosion of wisdom's confidence in human self-sufficiency can be seen further. Wisdom tradition merges with elements of Yahwistic faith, and wisdom is itself identified with Torah.

The Good Life

Drawing upon the cumulative observations of human experience common to family and clan, and later formalized in the court and the school, Israel's sages offered specific advice and admonition on what constitutes the good life. In their collections and reflections we can discern the shape of morality as seen through the lens of the wisdom traditions.

The Righteous Person. It has long been recognized that Job 31 provides us with a rather comprehensive portrait of wisdom's understanding of the righteous person (*ṣaddiq*)—a portrait of the good life. Most scholars have also considered the passage one of the high points of biblical ethics. "It cannot be disputed that the Job who utters the oath of purity in chapter 31 stands almost alone upon an ethical summit."[31]

In the concluding segment of his final summation speech (Job 29–31) Job seeks to gain vindication before God through a recitation in the form of an oath of purity (ch. 31). Job vows that he is innocent of various transgressions. Each offense listed and denied by oath implies a positive code of conduct which Job has fulfilled. Georg Fohrer offers the following list of offenses disavowed by Job: lasciviousness, falsehood, covetousness, adultery, disregard for the rights of servants, hardheartedness against the poor, trust in riches, superstition, hatred of enemies, inhospitality, hypocrisy, and exploitation of land.[32]

What distinguishes this list of offenses and the manner in which Job speaks of them is that they are not merely a list of crimes or violations of the law. They include intentions, attitudes and dispositions as well as actions (e.g., Job avows that he has not only refrained from adultery but restrained the lust which might lead to it, Job 31:9–12). "Job's list of offenses covers external deed and inner disposition, abuse of humans and affront to deity, active misdeeds and passive acquiescence in wrongdoing."[33] Some of the virtues here reflected are also embodied in the traditions of covenant and law, but the concern of Job does not primarily reflect the fulfillment of the law. Much of his recitation goes beyond the law's requirements. It is from the wisdom ideal of the wise and righteous life that this text comes. Job's purpose is not to affirm accepted moral standards of the community and its faith so much as it is to affirm his own virtue as a righteous man.[34]

The collections of wise sayings in Proverbs represent accumulated observation of experience and the lessons learned which can enable one to live the good life. Included are attention, on the one hand, to the positive virtues that one must acquire (e.g., patience, industriousness, restraint in speech, etc.) while, on the other hand, warnings are issued to help in avoiding the vices which make for folly and hinder the acquisition of wisdom (e.g., sloth, imprudence, greed, etc.). Seemingly of special concern to the sages responsible for Proverbs was the danger of sexual enticement by strange or foreign women (e.g., Prov. 2:16–19).[35] The large number of references on this matter probably reflects both a limited view of women's sexuality (it was regarded primarily as dangerous and a threat to the family) and, in the present postexilic form of the book, a concern for intermarriage and the identity of the community.

The virtues and vices that must be recognized and espoused or avoided in order to become wise are given moral valuations. To be wise is to be righteous; to be foolish is to be wicked. Maxims on wisdom and folly are interspersed with those on righteousness and wickedness. Here morality is not based on understanding of covenant relationship to God and neighbor so much as appeal to a code of conduct which attempts to guide individuals in appropriate behavior that will make life whole and harmonious.

No subject of ordinary human life escaped the attention of the sages. They commented on what makes for wisdom and righteousness or folly and wickedness in family matters, the political arena, business dealings, common etiquette, sexual conduct, parenting, and social relations in general. The collections of Proverbs are testimony to the comprehensive interests of the wisdom tradition.

Characteristics of Wisdom Ethics. Several features common to wisdom's perspective on morality persist throughout the literature.

Wisdom literature demonstrates a persistent *pragmatism*. One acted in a certain manner because it brought harmonious results in one's life. The accumulated observations of experience did not recommend behavior as a matter of principle but as a matter of utility. Maxims frequently state virtue in terms of expected result: "The hand of the diligent will rule" (Prov. 12:24); "A generous person will be enriched" (11:25); "A slack hand causes poverty, but the hand of the diligent makes rich" (10:4). This strikes many commentators as self-centered. Von Rad objected to the description of Proverbs as ethical in character because he viewed its morality as based only upon expediency: "This instruction has little or no interest in acquiring theoretical knowledge, . . . it supplies, rather, pragmatic knowledge."[36] From wisdom's perspective it was God who ordered the world in this way. To learn from accumulated experience what brings harmony and happiness is to honor God's creation. Strangely, this form of self-interest almost becomes an act of devotion.

Moderation and restraint are predominant modes in wisdom.[37] Pragmatic self-interest usually was not served by extremes. On the one hand, this served as a check on excessive self-indulgence. Drunkenness and gluttony are condemned. Even good things taken to excess become dangerous or evil. On the other hand, the concern for moderation gives a bias to maintaining of the status quo and finding of the safe middle ground. Anger was to be avoided by all means and it was never appropriate to give offense. One cannot find here any basis for social reform or willingness to risk conflict for the sake of principle. If necessary to maintain one's position and influence, even bribes are useful (Prov. 17:8).

It is obvious in what has already been said that *individualism* prevails over any form of communitarianism. The community is served by the righteous lives of individuals. There are not community interests to be served which transcend the interest of individual well-being. The assumption is that community is best served by urging more individuals to righteous and wise living. This notion is in tension with the mainstream covenant tradition which we have discussed elsewhere in the Old Testament. This form of individualism is still very appealing to many pious folk in the modern church. Like the sages of Proverbs they see no realities in the life of communities or in the wider social order that are more than the sum of individual lives. Thus, there is no concept of social responsibility which transcends the pursuit of personal righteousness.

The wisdom collections of Proverbs were not intended as rigid, prescriptive formulae which guaranteed a result. The sages knew experience to be more ambiguous than this, so their accumulated advice is also characterized by *flexibility and concern for appropriate action*. The wise act is the appropriate act taken at the appropriate time.[38] "Wisdom is not a body of experiential knowledge to be mastered and applied in situations of life, but the flexibility of mind that assists one in discerning the right time and the fitting place for the appropriate behavior."[39] The concern for discovering the secrets of divinely created order discussed earlier cannot be read as a belief that human behavior can be made utterly predictable. The collections of Proverbs are not intended as absolute and prescriptive truths, but as available information based on experience to be learned and used with discernment in the proper times and places. One of the things to be observed about human experience is that there are few complete absolutes. Indeed, the sages sometimes left seemingly contradictory advice side by side, each presumably available as it is discerned to be appropriate.

> Do not answer fools according to their folly,
>   or you will be a fool yourself.
> Answer fools according to their folly,
>   or they will be wise in their own eyes.
>   (Prov. 26:4–5)

As Ecclesiastes' famous list of polarities in life suggests, "For everything there is a season" (Eccl. 3:1; cf. 3:1–8).

The Moral Dynamics of Wisdom. If Job 31 implies a code of conduct, it is not because the sages applied themselves to the task of some systematized set of rules for wise and righteous living. It is because Job himself internalized a diverse set of teachings and observations, developed qualities of personal wisdom and integrity, and put them to practice in his life. Indeed, some sections of Proverbs give the impression that the sages intentionally resisted any systematizing of their maxims which might give the impression of a set of rules.

The sages' concern was with qualities of the wise life not the prescribing of behavior, with formation of character rather than formal codes of conduct.[40] Their intention is to provide insight into the way things are. The hope is to shape the qualities of personal life in ways that reflect wisdom, righteousness, and discernment. Thus, Proverbs offers simple observations and thoughtful reflections as well as moral admonitions. Their collections are not intended in the same manner as the legal codes of the covenant tradition.

The predominant concern with character formation is evident in the constant concern for education and discipline, and the frequency of reference to an audience among the young. Proverbs is rightly considered to be pedagogical literature.[41]

Its opening passage makes the scope of its character-forming pedagogy clear.

> The proverbs of Solomon son of David, king of Israel:
> For learning about wisdom and instruction,
>   for understanding words of insight,
> for gaining instruction in wise dealing,
>   righteousness, justice, and equity;
> to teach shrewdness to the simple,
>   knowledge and prudence to the young—
> Let the wise also hear and gain in learning,
>   and the discerning acquire skill,
> to understand a proverb and a figure,
>   the words of the wise and their riddles.
>
> (Prov. 1:1–6)

Thomas Ogletree has rightly observed that the wisdom literature represents the emergence of a moral tradition in Israel dominated by perfectionist conceptions of ethics. These were not absent earlier in Israel's history but were subordinated to the wider concerns of covenant community and its notions of responsibility to God and neighbor. "Instead of almost exclusive attention to the deontological concern with the requisites of social existence, we now find a perfectionist interest in the accomplishment of individual human excellence as something significant in its own right."[42]

Problems of Wisdom Morality. The social context out of which wisdom arose, especially as it developed into a formal literature, necessarily affects the moral stance which it adopts. The result in some areas is unacceptable by the standards of most modern moral perspectives. This may be especially seen in wisdom's attitudes toward the poor and women.

Among the collections of Proverbs are a number of references suggesting kindness and compassion toward the poor. "Those who oppress the poor insult their Maker, but those who are kind to the needy honor him" (Prov. 14:31). A cursory glance at these texts might tempt us to see some convergence of interest in justice between the wisdom and prophetic traditions. Nothing could be further from the truth. J. David Pleins, in particular, has subjected these references to study. Most of the references to the poor and needy are instrumental in character and reflect an acceptance of economically stratified society. Unlike the prophets there is no awareness of the wealthy profiting at the expense of the poor, no desire to seek a social ordering that would lift them from poverty, no hope for a divine transformation to redeem them from their fate, no conception of friends and corporate support which transcend economic condition, and no conception that poverty is not brought by the poor upon themselves.

> The teachings of the wise support their concerns for social status, class distinction, and the proper use of wealth—concerns which are rooted in the values cultivated by the ruling elite from which the wisdom literature arises. To the wise the poor are insignificant elements in the social order from whom nothing can be taken. . . . The wisdom teacher is only concerned to make the student aware of the need to limit one's enjoyment of wealth, and for this purpose, reference to poverty was a useful teaching device.[43]

In general, Proverbs in its present canonical form reflects the interests of a more elite, educated class and their natural concern to maintain the status quo in Israel. This is in spite of those who would argue for wisdom roots in family and clan tradition. Even if some popular wisdom originates at the grassroots level, the development of *written* collections to be used in formal schools, and the obvious royal connections which develop from Solomon onward, make clear that the final shape of Proverbs in particular is influenced by the interests of the wealthy and the powerful.[44]

Wisdom literature also displays the subordinating and derogatory view of women which characterized patriarchal societies. Beyond the mere reflection of ancient social reality in Israel wisdom seems frequently to regard women as the source of potential danger and linked primarily to folly and wickedness.

> A definite bias against women permeates biblical wisdom. Women are responsible for perverting a good creation, and they "drink from any available fountain or open their quiver for every arrow," to paraphrase Sirach. At the same time, women are a gift of God and deserve praise from husbands and children, particularly because good wives enhance the reputation of a man in the community.[45]

Only in the role of wife do women receive affirmation, and even the relative independence and initiative of the good wife in Prov. 31:10–31 finds the meaning in her efforts only in the degree to which they enhance her husband's reputation and well-being.

Retributive Justice

The concept of retributive justice is most strongly associated with the wisdom literature. Wisdom and folly not only carried moral valuation (righteousness and wickedness), they carried their own consequences. The righteous prosper and the wicked perish. Although recognizing some degree of unpredictability in life, the sages taught that one could shape one's own destiny. Life lived in harmony with wisdom's revealing of the divine order led to wealth, long life, descendants, health, renown, honor, and happiness. The life of folly led to disaster.

Retribution as the consequences which result from evil deeds and the blessing which comes from righteousness is present elsewhere in the Old Testament (esp. Deuteronomy and the prophets), but most often applies to the nation as a whole rather than to the individual.[46] Retribution in the wider canon is also tempered by the activity of God in relationship to Israel and the nations. That activity can take the form of grace, mercy, and forgiveness (see Jonah's dismay in Jonah 3), and thus, retributive consequences are never inevitable.

In a famous article, Klaus Koch has argued that in the Old Testament, actions are seen to carry their own built-in consequences.[47] The consequence of an evil deed is thus inevitable rather than the direct action of God. "They [the evil] make a pit, digging it out, and fall into the hole that they have made. Their mischief returns upon their own heads, and on their own heads their violence descends" (Ps. 7:15–16). Yahweh's involvement is simply to ensure the completion of built-in consequences which result from human action, although God retains the freedom to intervene in that connection. Koch's contention is particularly pertinent to wisdom where there is no attention given to God's intervention in human experience. Even here texts like Prov. 10:3, 22 suggest a more direct relationship of God to consequences than Koch's suggestion of built-in consequences would allow.

What is generally agreed upon by all is that the friends of Job represent a hardening of the notion of retribution to which the book of Job is itself a protest. Even in Proverbs, misfortune to the righteous could be seen as temporary testing or chastisement (Prov. 3:11–12; cf. Ps. 94:12; Job 5:17). Apart from Eliphaz's brief offering of this possibility in Job 5:17, it quickly becomes clear that the friends of Job can see no possible explanation for suffering or misfortune than wrongdoing. Whether deeds carry inevitable consequences or God is seen as mechanically rewarding and punishing every act, it is clear that wisdom has reached a rigidity which cannot be accepted. The careful observance of human experience becomes the basis for wisdom's own protest in Job and Ecclesiastes to its own orthodox rigidity. The wisdom tradition comes to experience its own limits.[48]

The Moral Limits of the Wisdom Tradition

The books of Job and Ecclesiastes are rightly seen as protests to the formalized understandings of wisdom represented in Proverbs which grow out of the experience of limits to the search for human knowledge and control of one's own destiny. What is less often seen are the roots of that protest in the sages' own sense of wisdom's limits already reflected in Proverbs.[49]

Limits to Human Capacities

The sages responsible for Proverbs were already aware, as we have seen, that one of the lessons of human experience was that outcomes were not always predictable. "Experience . . . teaches that you can never be certain. You must always remain open for a completely new experience."[50]

> Do not boast about tomorrow,
>   for you do not know what a day may bring.
>   (Prov. 27:1)

These wise teachers understood that no knowledge could be complete; an element of mystery remained as a part of observable human experience. Therefore, one should be wary about claiming to be wise as if one could rest fully secure in trust of one's own knowledge.

> Those who trust in their own wits are fools;
>   but those who walk in wisdom come through safely.
>   (Prov. 28:26)

> Do you see persons wise in their own eyes?
> There is more hope for fools than for them.
> (Prov. 26:12)

It was at the limits of trust in one's own wisdom that one who was truly wise must trust Yahweh.

> Trust in the LORD with all your heart,
> and do not rely on your own insight.
> (Prov. 3:5)

It was because of the sages' careful observation of human experience that they realized there was a realm of mystery and unpredictability beyond the control of even the most wise. It was in this arena—between human intention and the reality of events themselves—that God was most clearly to be seen. Divine activity was not limited to creating and sustaining an order that operated without potential for divine surprises. Though secular in its profound trust in human capacities, wisdom was nevertheless theological in its understanding of ultimate reality.

> The human mind plans the way,
> but the LORD directs the steps.
> (Prov. 16:9)

> The human mind may devise many plans,
> but it is the purpose of the LORD that will be established.
> (Prov. 19:21)

> No wisdom, no understanding, no counsel,
> can avail against the LORD.
> The horse is made ready for the day of battle,
> but the victory belongs to the LORD.
> (Prov. 21:30–31; cf. also 16:1–2;
> 20:24; 19:14)

Ultimately there is a reality that rests in God which is beyond calculation and remains a mystery. It is perhaps the recognition of an active element of wisdom which is from God and representative of the divine that led to the appearance of the female figure of personified wisdom with her strange presence in both the divine and the human realms. It is also in recognition of a divine activity beyond what humans can calculate and control that leads Job to attack both the friends and God for insensitivity to his plight and disregard for his innocence.

Despite its shift of focus to the arena of human behavior and the world in which humans live, the wisdom tradition remains more profoundly theological than many commentators have given credit for.

Given the world in which they found themselves, the teachers considered it appropriate to speak at great length of valid rules and orders, even feeling obliged to include human activity as a factor. On the other hand, they regarded themselves equally justified in drawing attention from time to time to the hand of God intervening directly in human life. Only in this way were they able to do justice to the dialectic of all experience.[51]

The Challenge of Skepticism

The experience of human limits led to increased attention to the mystery of God beyond human discernment, but in another stream of tradition led to the development of profound skepticism. This skeptical tradition is found in Job and Ecclesiastes, but also in the sayings of Agur in Prov. 30.

Crenshaw has rightly observed that skepticism does not arise out of a lack of faith. "The matrix formed by the disparity between the actual state of affairs and a vision of what should be both sharpened critical powers and heightened religious fervor. Doubt, it follows, is grounded in profound faith."[52]

The skeptical traditions in wisdom seem to take two foci. On the one hand, a critical challenge is directed at the justice of God. Particularly in the face of human suffering that does not seem deserved the sages question the justice by which God orders and manages the cosmos. This is the predominant question in the book of Job. On the other hand, a critical challenge is directed at human capacities for knowledge and understanding. An increased awareness of human frailties leads to a loss of faith in human beings and a concomitant, though grudging acknowledgment of God's sovereignty and the ultimate hiddenness of true wisdom (see Job 28). This is the predominant focus of Ecclesiastes.

It is remarkable that the wisdom tradition itself was able to spawn its own severest critics. As wisdom understandings of retribution and human control of one's own destiny rigidify (see Job's friends) the poet of Job and the elderly teacher of Ecclesiastes challenge the wisdom tradition to look again at human experience in a more critical light. This ability for critical examination precisely at the point of dangerous and dog-

matic trust in human control of divine favor or disfavor is a
moral example worth reclaiming in any time.

Both Job and Ecclesiastes have been labeled theological wisdom as opposed to the practical wisdom of Proverbs. Such a
distinction cannot be pressed too far. As we have seen, even
in its pragmatic focus on human experience Proverbs is possessed of a profound theological foundation, albeit one different from that of Israelite covenantal theology. Job and
Ecclesiastes are more different in form than in degree of theological seriousness. The form of dialogue and narrative drama
in Job, and of reflections out of the life of a single teacher in
Ecclesiastes allow for fuller development of sustained theological reflection than the collections of Proverbs.

Job and Theodicy. Interpretation of the book of Job is notoriously complex, and the literature on Job is voluminous and
rich.[53] Here we can only make some brief observations on
Job's place in the framework of our discussion.

An opening prose prologue (Job 1–2) gives us the context
for the book. A righteous man named Job is plunged into deep
loss and personal pain in order to test whether his piety is
disinterested or not (the test put forward as a wager between
God and Satan). In the prologue Job piously accepts his fate
and expresses confidence in God. In Job 3–31 a poetic dialogue ensues between Job and three friends who have come to
visit him. The tone changes radically. Job is rebellious, angry,
blasphemous. He alternately attacks the friends and their arguments, and hurls challenges at God to show him his guilt or
declare his innocence. The friends are more interested in de-
fending their own theology than in responding to Job's plight.
It eventually comes clear that they can imagine no reason for
Job's suffering other than that he is guilty of some transgres-
sion for which this is the deserved consequence. After
speeches further stating orthodox wisdom theology by a new
speaker named Elihu (chs. 32–37), Yahweh confronts Job and
challenges him to contemplation of God's creation, the complexities of which Yahweh unfolds in revealing detail (chs.
38–41). In the face of this theophanic confrontation Job is
transformed and his response (42:1–6) is variously interpreted
as repentant, accepting, overwhelmed, or reoriented in understanding. A prose epilogue (vs. 7–17) sees Job's fortunes
restored.

We might first observe that in spite of Job's defense of his own righteousness in his life prior to affliction (Job 31), his behavior in the dialogues with the friends represents an abandonment of the wisdom ideal. He is not restrained and judicious in speech. He has abandoned pragmatism and moderation for angry challenge—to the friends and to God.

The friends present the most rigid form of wisdom theology in the canon. There are no areas of ambiguity or mystery for them. Job's suffering, and presumably that of anyone, is evidence for them that he is among the wicked and deserves his fate. "Know then that God exacts of you less than your guilt deserves" (Job 11:6b). They believe they are among the wise and possess the secrets of God's ordering of the universe, and their picture of that ordering is rigidly retributive. In Job's challenge to them he accuses them of being poor observers of human experience, replacing observation with dogma, for Job regards it as self-evident that the wicked often prosper and the innocent perish (ch. 21).

Nevertheless, Job himself is unable to escape the retributive framework of the wisdom perspective. Although he sees its limits, his wish is not to replace it but to get it to work properly. Since he is innocent he believes he deserves restoration to prosperity. In both the speeches of the friends and of Job it becomes evident that a dogmatic belief in retributive justice cannot be sustained; it is inadequate to deal with the ambiguity and complexity, ofttimes the tragedy, of human existence. We agree with those who see one of the purposes of Job to be the demolition of this retributive perspective. In scattered passages Job begins to show some openness to a new perspective, but he cannot himself construct it.

As the bankruptcy of retributive theology becomes clear, the reader realizes that it is not Job on trial here, but God. "It is not suffering, as has so often been said, which has become so utterly problematic, but God."[54] If the world is not ordered in the dogmatic way the friends assume and Job hopes, then what of the God who created it? Theodicy is the issue. How is God's justice to be understood if not in terms of rewards and punishments? Seeking resolution of these questions Job constantly calls for a confrontation with God in court (the place where disputes naturally get resolved and guilt or innocence established). At length in ch. 9 and frequently throughout subsequent speeches Job issues a legal challenge to God, culminating in his formal oath of purity in ch. 31. Such oaths, taken before judicial authority required an accuser to appear and give evidence or the party taking the oath is judged innocent.[55]

It is clearly in the Yahweh speeches (Job 38–41) that the book of Job intends to make its contribution toward resolution of these issues. Interpretation of these passages has been very diverse. It is along the lines of Norman Habel's recent commentary on Job that our own view of these passages moves.[56]

Yahweh appears to Job out of the whirlwind (Job 38:1). This in itself is a startling development—to the reader as well as the characters in the story—particularly in the context of the wisdom tradition. Theophany (the appearance of God) honors Job and places him in a most select biblical group (e.g., Moses, Elijah). Completely apart from the content of God's speeches the theophany itself represents the appearance of a revelatory element in the wisdom tradition that is not a part of earlier wisdom.

God does not address the question of Job's innocence. Indeed, God lets the oath of purity stand unchallenged and thus grants Job's innocence. The focus of God's speeches is on presenting the divine case in response to Job's lawsuit. God's justice and the ordering of God's creation is more at issue than Job's innocence. Thus, God's speeches present an elaborate and complex picture of creation—one for which God is responsible and not Job. "Will you condemn me that you may be justified?" (Job 40:8). Retributive justice does not characterize this creation. Chaos, death, and evil are not eliminated but controlled, and it is God who upholds order in the face of their reality.

> Job's efforts to make God the accuser and specify his charges against Job are completely bypassed. Yahweh's defense operates from the assumption that Job is innocent but ignorant. . . . Nor does Yahweh challenge Job's protestation of innocence, his accusation that the innocent suffer unjustly, his claim to have been afflicted unjustly, or his complaint against the hardships of mortal existence. . . . Instead Yahweh challenges Job to change his orientation and view his case in the light of the total cosmic design of his Creator. . . . In his world of paradoxes, Yahweh continues to operate with the opposites of life and death, chaos and order, freedom and control, wisdom and folly, evil and blessing. What he challenges Job to do, he himself has done or continues to do. . . . In a world where paradox and incongruity are integral to its design, there is no simplistic answer to the problem of innocent

suffering. The baby eagle survives because another young creature dies. God does not eliminate the forces of chaos, the role of Death, or the presence of the wicked. They operate within the eternal constraints of his design. . . . No mechanical law of reward and retribution operates in this design.[57]

One of the striking features of this development in the book of Job is that while dismantling a rigidified form of wisdom represented in the friends and in Job's hopes for restoration, the Yahweh speeches summon Job to a task in complete harmony with the wisdom tradition as we have discussed it earlier. Job is summoned by God to new discernment of the creation and the way in which it has been ordered by God. God does not appeal to divine prerogative or mystery, but calls Job to look at the world as it is—more complex and paradoxical than retributive dogma assumes. The evidence is laid out in example from the natural world of Job's own experience, although the speeches transcend his experience in speaking of Behemoth and Leviathan (40:15–41:34, representative of chaos, controlled within the constraints of God's cosmos).

In the face of this theophanic experience and in the light of his new understanding Job withdraws his case against God. "Therefore, I withdraw, and forsake the dust and ashes" (42:6, author's translation).[58] The outcome is one in which Job's innocence is accepted and his integrity honored, but in which God's integrity is also acknowledged by Job's withdrawal of his legal complaint.

The epilogue, perhaps a traditional ending to the old story begun in the prologue, now appears in an ironic light. Job's fortunes are restored and the friends are rebuked. The behavior regarded by the wisdom tradition of the friends as foolish and wicked (namely Job's) is rewarded rather than punished, perhaps illustrating the very complexity and paradox which Job has newly come to understand.

Ecclesiastes and Moral Relativism. Ecclesiastes further represents the crisis of skepticism in Israel's wisdom tradition.[59] Qoheleth (the "Teacher," traditionally rendered "Preacher," of Ecclesiastes) is faced with the same crisis of confidence we saw in Job. One cannot succeed in controlling and securing one's own existence. His response takes quite a different direction from that of Job.

"All is vanity" (Eccl. 1:2); "There is nothing new under the

sun" (v. 9); "For everything there is a season" (3:1), but only
God seems to know when the proper time is (v. 11).
Qoheleth—seemingly a sage himself, now in old age—reflects
on his observation of experience, and he can find no knowable
order to things. The virtuous are not rewarded and the wicked
are not punished. The Creator is not involved in the world,
except to determine the course of events and humans cannot
find that out. Efforts to give life meaning (knowledge, justice,
work) bring no ultimate gain because in the end death cancels
them all. In the end Qoheleth can find no more meaning than
to enjoy the few pleasures that life affords before old age and
death take them from one. Some see this as affirming the value
of life in the living since these things are acknowledged as
from God, but the overwhelming tone of the book is pessimis-
tic and resigned.

The result of Ecclesiastes' radical pessimism is a moral relativism which finds no norms by which to judge the good. Attention to character or to conduct brings no profit. One can only
affirm a limited taking of pleasure while viewing even that as
radically circumscribed. Although some scholars would defend
the contribution of Ecclesiastes more positively, we are inclined
to see its main value in its sharp confrontation of optimistic
wisdom perspectives with the limits of human existence. It
forces a new and critical look at reality which will not allow the
wisdom tradition to ignore its own limitations. It is not incon-
ceivable that it is to avoid the dead end of Ecclesiastes that late
wisdom (e.g., Sirach, Wisdom of Solomon) moved toward a
connection with the wider theological tradition of Israel where
alternatives to Qoheleth's pessimism are available.

Wisdom and Torah

Although starting at very different places and operating
with very different understandings of moral authority, wisdom's picture of the righteous person overlaps a good deal
with the picture given in the law of the obedient person within
the covenant.[60]

With the development of written Torah it seemed inevitable
that the reading and study of Torah would itself come to be
considered as a way to knowledge and discernment, alongside
its character as a testimony to the revealing of God in Israel's
history. The psalms usually classed as wisdom psalms reflect
this development.[61] In Ps. 19, following testimony to the evi-

dences of God in creation, the law (here surely referring to the written Torah) is celebrated as the creation of God whose secrets are to be discovered and applied to life. The language is remarkably similar to that used of wisdom in Proverbs.

> The law of the LORD is perfect,
>   reviving the soul;
> the decrees of the LORD are sure,
>   making wise the simple;
> the precepts of the LORD are right,
>   rejoicing the heart; . . .
> the fear of the LORD is pure,
>   enduring forever;
> the ordinances of the LORD are true
>   and righteous altogether.
> More to be desired are they than gold,
>   even much fine gold;
> sweeter also than honey,
>   and drippings of the honeycomb.
>   (Ps. 19:7–10; cf. Ps. 119)

With the "wisdom of Jesus ben Sira" (Sirach) law and wisdom are identified and the salvation history of Israel enters the wisdom tradition through the study of Torah (see Sir. 39). Dame Wisdom is explicitly identified with Torah in 24:23. In Sirach it is also clear that the sages have become worshipers and the cultic observances of Israel's life are a part of the appropriate life of wisdom and piety.[62] Although the eventual result lies beyond the bounds of the Hebrew canon proper, the canonical conversation of disparate traditions is finally reflected in new and creative interrelationships with one another.

With our consideration of the wisdom literature we have come to the boundary of the Hebrew canon and to the end of our journey through its testimony seeking to make its resources available to the church in ways that will inform and enrich its moral life. It is our hope that this representative sampling of the wealth of resources to be claimed in the Old Testament will encourage others in the academy and the church to engage its texts in wider and deeper conversations about the ways in which scripture continues to speak God's word through the church in its life and witness in the world.

Notes

1. See the critique of this discussion in Donn Morgan, *Wisdom in the Old Testament Traditions* (Atlanta: John Knox Press, 1981), and James L. Crenshaw, "Method for Determining Wisdom Influence Upon 'Historical' Literature," *JBL* 88 (1969): 129–142, reprinted in James L. Crenshaw, ed., *Studies in Ancient Israelite Wisdom* (New York: KTAV Publishing House, 1976), pp. 481–494.

2. See the discussion and references in James L. Crenshaw, *Old Testament Wisdom: An Introduction* (Atlanta: John Knox Press, 1981), pp. 42–65.

3. See Carol Fontaine, *Traditional Sayings in the Old Testament*, Bible and Literature Series, 5 (Sheffield: JSOT Press, 1982).

4. R. N. Whybray, *The Intellectual Tradition in the Old Testament* (Berlin and New York: Walter de Gruyter, 1974), vigorously argues against the development in Israel of a class of professional sages. He argues for a generalized intellectual tradition in Israel, but his view has not gathered wide support. See the counterarguments in Crenshaw, *Old Testament Wisdom*, pp. 27–36; and Roland E. Murphy, "Introduction to Wisdom Literature," *NJBC*, ed. R. E. Brown, J. A. Fitzmyer, and R. E. Murphy (Englewood Cliffs, N.J.: Prentice-Hall, 1990), pp. 447–452.

5. This is especially stressed by Whybray, *Intellectual Tradition in the Old Testament*, and James L. Crenshaw, "Wisdom in the OT," *IDBSup*, ed. Keith Crim (Nashville: Abingdon Press, 1976), pp. 952–956.

6. See Georg Fohrer, "Sophia," in Crenshaw, ed., *Studies in Ancient Israelite Wisdom*, pp. 63–83.

7. Crenshaw, *Old Testament Wisdom*, p. 19; elsewhere Crenshaw offers a more compact definition: "the quest for self-understanding in terms of relationships with things, people and the Creator" ("Method for Determining Wisdom Influence Upon 'Historical' Literature," p. 484).

8. See the comments of Brevard S. Childs on these older approaches as too narrow a construal of the proverbs in *Old Testament Theology in a Canonical Context* (Philadelphia: Fortress Press, 1985), p. 211.

9. This shift in assessment of Israelite wisdom can be seen by comparing the place and scope of its discussion in Gerhard von Rad, *Old Testament Theology*, vol. 1 (New York: Harper & Row, 1962; original German ed. 1957), pp. 418–440, with von Rad's later major reassessment of Israelite wisdom in *Wisdom in Israel* (Nashville: Abingdon Press, 1972).

10. Joseph Blenkinsopp, *Wisdom and Law in the Old Testament: The Ordering of Life in Israel and Early Judaism* (Oxford: Oxford University Press, 1983), pp. 26, 27.

11. Crenshaw, "Wisdom in the OT," p. 952.

12. See Crenshaw, *Old Testament Wisdom*, pp. 19–20; Crenshaw, "Wisdom in the OT," p. 954; von Rad, *Wisdom in Israel*, pp. 74–96; Walter Brueggemann, *In Man We Trust: The Neglected Side of Biblical Faith* (Richmond: John Knox Press, 1972), pp. 22–23.

13. See especially the discussion in von Rad, *Wisdom in Israel*, pp. 53–73, a section entitled "Knowledge and the Fear of God."

14. Brueggemann, *In Man We Trust*, p. 23.

15. Roland E. Murphy, "Wisdom—Theses and Hypotheses," in *Israelite Wisdom: Theological and Literary Essays in Honor of Samuel Terrien*, ed. J. G. Gammie, W. A. Brueggemann, W. L. Humphreys, J. M. Ward (Missoula, Mont.: Scholars Press, 1978), pp. 35–42.

16. Von Rad, *Wisdom in Israel*, pp. 106–107, also identifies this tension but concludes that wisdom is willing to erode the principle of divine freedom (but not to totally abrogate it) for the sake of its persistent belief in a divinely established order to be discovered.

17. Roland E. Murphy, "Wisdom Theses," in *Wisdom and Knowledge: Papin Festschrift*, ed. J. Armenti (Philadelphia: Villanova Press, 1976), p. 197. Dianne Bergant, commenting on this suggestion, wryly and correctly asks, "Would not this make chaos the basic construct?" *What Are They Saying About Wisdom Literature?* (Ramsey, N.J.: Paulist Press, 1984), p. 15.

18. Roland E. Murphy, "The Kerygma of the Book of Proverbs," *Int* 20 (1966): 3–14. He identifies the kerygma of Proverbs as "life." See also Murphy, "Introduction to Wisdom Literature," *NJBC*, p. 447, and Brueggemann, *In Man We Trust*, pp. 14–16.

19. Walther Zimmerli, "The Place and Limit of the Wisdom in the Framework of the Old Testament Theology," *SJT* 17 (1964): 158; reprinted in Crenshaw, ed., *Studies in Ancient Israelite Wisdom*, pp. 314–328.

20. On these issues see Roland E. Murphy, "Wisdom and Creation," *JBL* 103 (1985): 3–11; James L. Crenshaw, "Prolegomenon," in idem, ed., *Studies in Ancient Israelite Wisdom*, pp. 26ff.

21. Von Rad, *Wisdom in Israel*, p. 62.

22. Crenshaw, "Prolegomenon," pp. 26–34; "Wisdom in the OT," p. 956; *Old Testament Wisdom*, pp. 19–25.

23. Bergant, characterizing Crenshaw's position in *What Are They Saying About Wisdom Literature?*, p. 13.

24. See Claudia Camp, *Wisdom and the Feminine in the Book of Proverbs*, Bible and Literature Series 11 (Sheffield: JSOT Press, 1986); Murphy, "Introduction to Wisdom Literature," *NJBC*, p. 450.

25. Von Rad, *Wisdom in Israel*, p. 148.

26. Bergant, *What Are They Saying About Wisdom Literature?*, p. 5.

27. See Walther Zimmerli, "Concerning the Structure of Old Testament Wisdom," in Crenshaw, ed., *Studies in Ancient Israelite Wisdom*, pp. 175–207.

28. Brueggemann, *In Man We Trust*, pp. 17–24, elaborates these elements of wisdom and their pertinence to modern culture.

29. Crenshaw, *Old Testament Wisdom*, pp. 19, 24.

30. Childs, *Old Testament Theology in a Canonical Context*, p. 211.

31. Georg Fohrer, "The Righteous Man in Job 31," in *Essays in Old Testament Ethics*, ed. James L. Crenshaw and John T. Willis (New York: KTAV Publishing House, 1974), p. 19. See also for Job 31, E. Osswald, "Hiob 31 im Rahmen der alttestamentlichen Ethik," *Theologische Versuche* 2 (1970): 9–26; Crenshaw, *Old Testament Wisdom*, pp. 14–16; Norman C. Habel, *The Book of Job, A Commentary*, OTL (Philadelphia: Westminster Press, 1985), pp. 423–440.

32. Fohrer, "The Righteous Man in Job 31," p. 7.

33. Crenshaw, *Old Testament Wisdom*, p. 15.

34. A similar point is made by Thomas W. Ogletree, *The Use of the Bible in Christian Ethics* (Philadelphia: Fortress Press, 1983), p. 77.

35. See Crenshaw, *Old Testament Wisdom*, p. 23.

36. Von Rad, *Wisdom in Israel*, p. 74.

37. See Crenshaw, *Old Testament Wisdom*, p. 20.

38. See the section in von Rad, *Wisdom in Israel*, pp. 138–143, entitled "The Doctrine of the Proper Time."

39. Bergant, *What Are They Saying About Wisdom Literature?*, p. 17.

40. Murphy, "Introduction to Wisdom Literature," *NJBC*, p. 448.

41. James L. Crenshaw, "Education in Wisdom," *JBL* 104 (1985): 601–615.

42. Ogletree, *Use of the Bible in Christian Ethics*, p. 76; cf. pp. 76–79.

43. J. David Pleins, "Poverty in the Social World of the Wise," *JSOT* 37 (1987): 61–78, quotation from p. 72; see also J. David Pleins, "Biblical Ethics and the Poor: The Language and Structures of Poverty in the Writings of the Hebrew Prophets" (unpublished doctoral diss., University of Michigan, 1986), pp. 258–296, where he compares the prophetic and wisdom perspective on the poor. He finds the attitude reflected in Job to move more toward that of the prophetic literature than is the case with Proverbs.

44. See Brian W. Kovacs, "Is There a Class-Ethic in Proverbs?" in Crenshaw and Willis, eds., *Essays in Old Testament Ethics*, pp. 171–187.

45. Crenshaw, *Old Testament Wisdom*, p. 23. See also Camp, *Wisdom and the Feminine in the Book of Proverbs*.

46. See W. Sibley Towner, "Retribution," *IDBSup*, pp. 742–744; and Murphy, "Introduction to Wisdom Literature," *NJBC*, p. 449.

47. Klaus Koch, "Is There a Doctrine of Retribution in the Old Testament?" in *Theodicy in the Old Testament*, ed. James L. Crenshaw (Philadelphia: Fortress Press, 1983), pp. 57–87. The longer German text of this article was first published in *ZTK* 52 (1955): 1–42.

48. It is remarkable how tenaciously a rigid doctrine of retribution is maintained by many in the modern church. Televangelist bashing of those with AIDS could have taken their script from Job's friends. The popularity of Rabbi Har-

old S. Kushner's book *When Bad Things Happen to Good People* (New York: Avon Books, 1983) is largely attributable to its helpful release of people burdened with a retributive understanding of their own experiences of pain and loss.

49. Von Rad's discussion of these matters in his section "Limits of Wisdom," *Wisdom in Israel*, pp. 97–110, is still the most important treatment of this subject and our discussion is deeply indebted to his insights.

50. Von Rad, *Wisdom in Israel*, p. 106.

51. Ibid., p. 105.

52. Crenshaw, *Old Testament Wisdom*, p. 191. In this chapter on "Wisdom's Legacy" Crenshaw helpfully focuses on the contribution of the skeptical literature to the wider theological traditions of Israel.

53. My own understanding and appreciation of Job has been especially helped by Norman C. Habel, *The Book of Job, A Commentary*, OTL (Philadelphia: Westminster Press, 1985); Matitiahu Tsevat, "The Meaning of the Book of Job," *HUCA* 37 (1966): 73–106; J. Gerald Janzen, *Job*, IBC (Atlanta: John Knox Press, 1985); Gustavo Gutiérrez, *On Job: God-Talk and the Suffering of the Innocent* (Maryknoll, N.Y.: Orbis Books, 1987). All of these represent a recent trend to treat the book of Job as a literary unity, which we find convincing over against the fragmenting interpretation of earlier treatments of Job.

54. Von Rad, *Wisdom in Israel*, p. 221.

55. See Habel, *Book of Job*, pp. 423–440.

56. Ibid., pp. 517–586.

57. Ibid., pp. 528, 534, 535.

58. Numerous recent studies have suggested that the verb usually translated as "despise myself" (*m's*) in Job 42:6a cannot be treated as a reflexive but must be translated as "recant" or "retract" with an object in view. Since the same verb appears in Job 31:13 in Job's own usage as the retracting of a legal complaint it seems very likely, as several recent commentators have suggested, that Job is here withdrawing or recanting his legal suit against Yahweh. To "forsake the dust and ashes" is a reference to Job's abandonment of his position of complaint on the ash heap. See Habel's discussion of the evidence, *Book of Job*, p. 576; Marvin Pope, *Job*, AB, 3rd ed. (Garden City, N.Y.: Doubleday & Co., 1973); S. H. Scholnick, "Lawsuit Drama in the Book of Job" (doctoral diss., Brandeis University, 1975), p. 303.

59. See Crenshaw, *Old Testament Wisdom*, pp. 126–148; James L. Crenshaw, "Ecclesiastes," *HBC*, ed. James L. Mays (San Francisco: Harper & Row, 1988), pp. 518–524; von Rad, *Wisdom in Israel*, pp. 226–236.

60. Childs, *Old Testament Theology in a Canonical Context*, pp. 211–212, observes this and comments on the ability of the canon to hold these approaches in conversation for the truth of their perspective without needing to resolve the tension.

61. See Roland E. Murphy, "A Consideration of the Classification 'Wisdom Psalms,' " in Crenshaw, ed., *Studies in Ancient Israelite Wisdom*, pp. 456–467; Kenneth Kuntz, "The Canonical Wisdom Psalms of Ancient Israel: Their Rhetorical, Thematic, and Formal Dimensions," in *Rhetorical Criticism*, ed. J. J. Jackson and M. Kessler (Pittsburgh: Pickwick Press, 1974), pp. 186–222.

62. See Crenshaw, *Old Testament Wisdom*, pp. 149–173.

Epilogue:
Canon and Continuity

The Hebrew canon (the Old Testament) ends somewhat abruptly. The collection of the Writings which make up its final segment is a miscellaneous gathering of books. No one book takes us systematically to the final historical moment and then offers a concluding comment. The reader is left in the middle of something which has been abruptly interrupted.

For Christians it is common to move from this point to the reading of the New Testament. Protestants do not even recognize the canonicity of those intertestamental books commonly referred to as the Apocrypha. Although Roman Catholics acknowledge their canonicity, they are not widely read or studied. The result is a great sense of discontinuity between the Old Testament and the New. It is a discontinuity not only in a historical sense, but often it is considered a discontinuity in a theological sense as well. The result has been distorted understandings of the relationship between the Testaments, such as the common caricature of the Old Testament as law and the New Testament as gospel.

If we are truly to claim the Old Testament as a resource for Christian ethics, then we must understand that the text of these ancient Israelite witnesses are in continuity with later religious tradition, Jewish and Christian, and not in discontinuity. The end of this volume and of the Hebrew canon itself is misleading because God and God's people, Israel, continue their journey beyond the ending of the canon.

As Christians we must abandon the language of discontinuity if the Old Testament is to play its full role as scriptural foundation for the life and work of the church. We must embrace a new language of continuity in its place.

There is a *continuity of God's grace*. Grace does not wait until the New Testament for its appearance. God's graceful activity is already manifest in full measure in creation, promise, deliverance, steadfast love, forgiveness, redemption, and renewal in the pages of the Old Testament witness. It is our knowledge of God's grace from creation onward that allows us to fully understand the divine grace we see in Jesus Christ. The God of Israel is the same God made incarnate in Jesus Christ.

There is a *continuity of God's people*. The community of God's people did not cease to exist at the end of the Hebrew canon, only to be resumed or reconstituted in the early church. Christians are largely ignorant of the history, literature, and religious traditions of Second Temple Judaism which bridge the period between the Testaments. Without increased awareness of this middle segment of tradition and history it is difficult to see how deeply and unalterably the early church is in continuity with the Israelite and Jewish traditions that precede them, including the moral and ethical dimensions of those traditions. Recognition of our continuity as the church with the Judaism that links us to the community of Israel would also serve to link us more closely to modern Judaism as a sister religion with whom we share deep common roots.

There is a *continuity of God's Word*. Recognizing that God and the people of God are continuously connected in the two Testaments of the Christian canon, we can more truly do theology and ethics in a canonical context. Too much of modern exegesis in scholarship and church focuses on texts as isolated witnesses, or limits their conversation only to immediate literary context. In the church it is the whole of the Bible that is received as scripture by church people, and they read it as a wide-ranging conversation with all of its parts. Scholars and church leaders must address themselves more seriously to the continuities as well as the discontinuities in God's Word and discover what new Word may address us out of conversations across the boundaries of books and canons. A serious regret in the writing of this volume was that it could not be more fully in conversation with the New Testament trajectories of its themes. Perhaps this is an encouragement to further investigation.

There is a *continuity of God's work*. One of the great hopes in undertaking this volume was that the reader might emerge not only with knowledge of God's character and activity in the time of the biblical communities but with a sense that God's work is made more visible in the midst of our own world. Likewise, our hope is that in the study of the ancient community of God's people and its moral witness we might find renewed commitment as the church to life as God's people in courageous and creative moral witness to the needs of our broken world.

Index of Subjects

Index of Authors

Index of Hebrew Words

373

Index
of
Scripture References

375